CONSCRIPTION

CONSCRIPTION
A SELECT AND ANNOTATED BIBLIOGRAPHY

Edited by
MARTIN ANDERSON

Compiled by
Martin Anderson and Valerie Bloom

THE HOOVER INSTITUTION PRESS
STANFORD UNIVERSITY • STANFORD, CALIFORNIA

1976

Hoover Bibliographical Series 57

International Standard Book Number 0–8179–2571–6
Library of Congress Catalog Card Number 75–41906

To the memory of
DANIEL WEBSTER
statesman, lawyer, and orator—
the first American to state,
eloquently and persuasively,
the case against conscription.

Contents

Contents

Preface

This is the first volume of a projected three-volume work on the problems involved in raising an armed force in a free society. It is intended to be a comprehensive, current guide to the literature on conscription, with special emphasis on the United States.

The second volume of the series will be a collection of selected reading on various important aspects of conscription. It will present a number of writings that have been scattered and hitherto virtually unobtainable to all but the most persistent and diligent scholar. Culled from the vast mass of writing on conscription, the pieces selected will exemplify the clearest and most rigorous analyses and views—both pro and con—on particular issues concerning the raising of military manpower.

The third volume will be an essay on the basic principles and issues involved in the question of how best to raise an armed force in a free society. Special emphasis will be placed on the application of these principles to U.S. military manpower policy.

The Hoover Institution on War, Revolution and Peace at Stanford University has sponsored this work as part of a more general study on the raising of an armed force in a free society, and I should like to express my appreciation to the Director, Dr. W. Glenn Campbell, for his encouragement and his patience. Generous support for the project has been provided by funds from the Smith Richardson Foundation, Inc.

Special thanks and acknowledgment go to my research assistant, Valerie Bloom. Much of the searching, annotating, and compiling was done by her, and without this diligent, accurate work the first volume could not have been completed. Toward the end of the project she left to become a senior financial analyst with the Bank of America, and was replaced by Judy Gans, who did an excellent job in assisting with the completion of the manuscript. I, of course, take responsibility for the organizational structure, selection of entries, and final editing.

I should also like to acknowledge the helpful suggestions and comments that were given by Peter Duignan, Senior Fellow at the Hoover Institution and editor of a truly monumental bibliography on Africa, *Guide to Research and Reference Works on Sub-Saharan Africa*; I'm especially grateful to him for not telling me all that would be involved when I started. Special thanks go to Barbara Campbell for her copy-editing assistance during the summer of 1975 and to Agnes Peterson, curator of the Western European collection at Hoover, who cheerfully answered the innumerable questions Valerie Bloom and I asked her.

The final copy editing was done by Liselotte Hofmann, and her skillful and meticulous work can be appreciated only by someone familiar with the original manuscript. The book was designed and set in type by Ted Ligda with great care and warm enthusiasm. Throughout the entire process both Dennis Bark and Mickey Hamilton of the Hoover Institution Press were helpful and generous with their time and advice.

It is reasonably certain that conscription will be an important issue in the United States, as well as in other countries, in the years to come. To those who try to cope with conscription in the future when it does become a major issue once again, I hope that this volume will be a helpful guide.

Introduction

The act of conscription is one of the most controversial public policy issues that can confront a society. It involves some of the most fundamental questions of individual rights, especially the relationship between the individual and the state. Generally arising at a time when the basic security of a country is threatened by the armed might of a foreign power, the idea of conscription flows from deep fears and passionate feelings.

Whenever military conscription does become a clear issue, proponents and opponents alike step forward quickly and the public policy debate is usually prolonged and heated. The public's interest in conscription is, as might be expected, cyclical; it seems to be closely correlated, especially in the United States, with the degree of, or propensity to, the country's involvement in armed conflict. The flaring of intellectual interest during times of impending or actual hostilities and its rapid decline during peace seem to have led to a curious, though not unusual, situation: the participants in each new round of debate often have little more than a cursory knowledge of the conscription debates that preceded them, although there is a striking similarity to the arguments and specific issues that do arise in the course of the debate.

One likely reason for this failure to make better use of the rich and varied work of the past has been the absence of any reasonably comprehensive guide to the literature of conscription. Books, articles, and other studies dealing with conscription are catalogued under a variety of subject headings. Many relevant writings, especially Master's theses and Ph.D. dissertations, chapters in books dealing with broader subjects, articles, pamphlets, and certain government documents are listed only sporadically in small bibliographies appended to some of the studies. The basic standard history textbooks barely touch the issue of conscription. And, of course, there are those studies that fail to make anyone's list—sometimes because they were forgotten, sometimes because they are too new.

The idea for this bibliography grew out of the frustration I encountered while doing research on the problem of raising an armed force in a free society and, in particular, the problem of raising an armed force in the United States. Most of the entries in this bibliography grew out of this research, although some were gathered as the bibliography took on a life of its own.

At the outset it was decided that the purpose of the bibliography was not to try to be exhaustive, but rather to identify, select, and annotate those studies and documents that would be most important and useful to any scholar, government official, or otherwise interested party pursuing the study of conscription, particularly from the viewpoint of public policy recommendations. As a result the primary emphasis is on major works; no attempt has been made to provide a listing of newspapers, periodicals, or archival material.

The purpose of this bibliographic project has been to create a guide to the literature that focuses on the major issues of conscription, is reasonably comprehensive, has extensive, useful annotations, is clearly categorized by subject area, and is up-to-date. The bibliography as it now stands has some 1,385 entries—over ten times the number of the next largest annotated bibliography known.

While the purpose may have been achieved to some degree, relatively speaking, the bibliography is certainly not complete (and perhaps no bibliography of a living public policy issue ever is). Virtually every week continues to produce one or two previously undiscovered entries, and at the same time new writings continue to proliferate. If you know of, or should discover, any noteworthy works that have been omitted in the pages that follow, it would be greatly appreciated if you could take the time to forward the information so that it (or they) might be included in a future edition— revised, updated, and expanded.

Classification

This bibliography is divided into 17 chapters, each chapter representing a major subject area. Within most of the chapters the writings are further classified into five groups:

(1) Books
(2) Unpublished Manuscripts
(3) Articles
(4) Pamphlets, Reprints, and Speeches
(5) Government Documents

Introduction

All entries under books, unpublished manuscripts, articles, and pamphlets, reprints, and speeches are listed alphabetically by author. Entries under government documents are divided into two parts: (1) publications of departments, agencies, and commissions of the federal government, listed alphabetically by the issuer or author, and (2) hearings of the U.S. Congress, listed chronologically by the year of the hearings.

Most of the entries follow normal bibliographical practice; however, there are a few exceptions. Because the works cited are classified in five main areas—books, articles, etc.—it was not necessary to use the typical methods of differentiation to distinguish, say, books from articles. Thus, all titles of works cited in the bibliographic data are printed in *italics*; all authors are printed in SMALL CAPITALS; and the remaining material is set in regular type. This should simplify and accelerate the search process for anyone perusing the bibliography for special references: whenever *italics* are used they represent titles, whereas SMALL CAPITALS always represent authors.

A large part of the material cited can be found in the archives and library of the Hoover Institution on War, Revolution and Peace. In instances where the material listed is unique to the Hoover Institution a special note has been made in the entry.

Chapter 1, *United States History*, is concerned with the historical development of conscription in the United States, covering works dealing with various aspects of conscription from the time of the earliest settlers in the 1600s. Most of the works focus on the periods encompassing the Revolutionary War, the Civil War, World Wars I and II, the Korean War, and the Vietnam War.

Chapter 2, *General History*, contains works that refer primarily to past uses of conscription in parts of the world outside the United States.

Chapter 3, *General Works*, contains those writings that consider conscription in a more comprehensive, more systematic manner. They typically deal with a number of specific aspects of conscription, often examining the interrelationships among these issues. The studies are generally policy-oriented and frequently contain specific recommendations for government action.

Chapter 4, *All-Volunteer Armed Force*, is concerned primarily with recent studies in the United States that focus on the question of the desirability and feasibility of ending the draft and moving to an all-volunteer force. For example, it is in this section that one finds the 1970 report of the President's Commission on an All-Volunteer Armed Force, a report considered by many to be the most comprehensive work on the question of raising military manpower in the United States.

Chapter 5, *Selective Service*, contains works that focus specifically on the operations of the Selective Service System in the United States. About half of the entries cited are government documents.

Chapter 6, *Universal Military Training*, includes books and articles dealing with the question whether every able-bodied male citizen of the United States should be required to perform military service. The universality of the military obligation is the key focus of most of the works in this section.

Chapter 7, *National Guard and Reserves*, consists primarily of books, articles, and government documents that examine the role of the National Guard and the reserves in the armed forces and, in some cases, their relation to the historical development of the militia in the United States.

Chapter 8, *Universal National Service*, comprises those works that consider conscription on a broader basis; military conscription becomes simply one aspect of a diversified form of conscription that would force both men and women to perform a wide variety of public service jobs, including social work, teaching, and rebuilding cities.

Chapter 9, *Economics*, essentially contains those references and studies wherein the traditional methods of economic analysis are applied to the issue of conscription. These works, many of them articles in economic journals, typically are more analytically oriented than those in other chapters.

Chapter 10, *Law and the Constitution*, is composed primarily of law journal articles analyzing the validity of conscription laws under the U.S. Constitution.

Chapter 11, *Philosophy*, contains works that, while few in number, focus on what many consider to be the heart of the conscription issue— whether it is a moral or immoral procedure.

Chapter 12, *Conscientious Objection*, covers those writings primarily concerned with the religious and moral issues posed by those who refuse to serve when conscripted. A number of the works contain the narratives of individual conscientious objectors.

Chapter 13, *Race*, includes works that examine the development of government policy and legislation pertaining to the conscription of blacks in the United States. Other works trace the history of the role of blacks in the U.S. armed forces.

Chapter 14, *England*, is devoted solely to the English experience with conscription. A large part of the English-language literature on conscription has been written by Englishmen about England. Much of the analysis and many of the ideas and principles developed in these writings offer a key to an understanding of the ideological underpinnings of the development of military manpower procurement policies in the United States. However, most of the material in the studies included here primarily concerns British institutions and people, and for this reason it was decided not to intersperse them with works more directly applicable to the United States.

Chapter 15, *Other Foreign Countries*, comprises English-language references that may be helpful for those scholars who wish to investigate how the institution of conscription has been implemented in other parts of the world.

Chapter 16, *Miscellanea*, turned out to be very necessary. The original intent was to classify every entry into a reasonably precise category, but at the end there were some 75 entries that, while important enough to include, did not fit neatly into any of the classifications established.

Chapter 17, *Bibliographies*, lists all the separately published bibliographies that were discovered. There are, of course, a large number of smaller bibliographies that are included as part of the individual works cited in the preceding sections.

The *Index of Authors* lists all authors cited in the bibliography, including those mentioned in the annotations. The *Index of Titles* is divided into five sections: books; unpublished manuscripts; articles (in periodicals and in composite works); pamphlets, reprints, and speeches; and government documents. All titles cited, including those in the annotations, are indexed within these sections, which conform essentially to those in the bibliography itself.

CHAPTER 1

United States History

> History offers the best training for those who are to take part in public affairs.
> —Polybius, *Histories*, I, circa 125 B.C.

Books

ALLEN, H. C., and C. P. HILL (editors). *British Essays in American History.* 1957. St. Martin's Press. New York. 348 pages.

Of particular interest is the essay by Marcus Cunliffe, "The American Military Tradition" (pages 207–224). It reviews the "American heritage of anti-militarism: a deep prejudice against standing armies, a milder sentiment with regard to naval forces, and a positive feeling that the 'palladium of liberty' must be safeguarded by militiamen." Noting the gradual decay of the old militia, as defined by the statute of 1792, the author holds that the early militia system's principle of compulsion "was objectionable, not merely to Quakers and others who had conscientious scruples, but perhaps to a majority of the population." Proposals for universal military training have been unsuccessful, just as more modest proposals to enforce compulsory military training have been rejected at frequent intervals; and, while European nations have been accustomed to conscription, America still has only a selective draft. Cunliffe concludes that Americans are "neither anti-military nor pro-military, but a-military."

AMBROSE, STEPHEN E. *Upton and the Army.* 1964. Louisiana State University Press. Baton Rouge, Louisiana. Index. Illustrations. Bibliographical note: pages 177–183. 190 pages.

Describes Emory Upton's attempt to strengthen the position of the Regular Army by first convincing the American people "that the militia and volunteer systems had never provided an adequate defense." Upton's model for army reform was the Prussian army, and his "inability to understand the interrelationship between politics and war in a democratic state prevented him from fashioning an acceptable system." Ambrose notes that later army leaders did espouse Upton's program and that his contributions to American military policy were "essential to the development of a modern armed force."

ANDREWS, CHARLES MCLEAN (editor). *Essays in Colonial History Presented to Charles McLean Andrews by His Students.* 1931. Yale University Press. New Haven, Connecticut. 345 pages.

Of particular interest is the essay by Dora Mae Clark, "The Impressment of Seamen in the American Colonies" (pages 198–224). It describes the British press gang imposed by the Admiralty in the late 17th century when voluntary enlistments consistently fell short of quota requirements. The opposition to impressment "had little or no effect upon the policy of the government before the institution died a natural death at the close of the Napoleonic wars." In the American colonies, opposition to impressment was even more vehement than in England, and became more intense "as the colonists grew more independent in spirit, objecting to every means of force or compulsion used by the British government."

ASBURY, HERBERT. *The Gangs of New York: An Informal History of the Underworld.* 1928. Alfred A. Knopf. New York. Index. Illustrations. Bibliography: pages 381–382. 400 pages.

Chapters 7 and 8 describe the July 1863 draft riots in New York. It is the author's view that the riots "began as a protest against the Conscription Act which had been passed by Congress in March, but that phase of the struggle was soon forgotten, and thereafter the riots were an insurrection of the criminal element against the established order."

BACON, CORINNE (compiler). *Selected Articles on National Defense.* 1915. Debaters' Handbook Series. H. W. Wilson Co. White Plains, New York. Bibliography: pages xixx–xxix. 243 pages.

General, affirmative, and negative discussions on national defense, focusing on the question of preparedness prior to the entry of the United States into World War I.

BALES, WILLIAM A. *Tiger in the Streets.* 1962. Dodd, Mead & Co. New York. Illustrations. Bibliography: pages 209–212. 212 pages.

Chapter 6 recounts the events of the 1865 draft riots in New York, based on contemporary sources.

BARNES, DAVID M. *The Draft Riots in New York July 1863.* 1863. Baker & Godwin. New York. Index. 117 pages.

A contemporary record of the riots, based on articles appearing in the *New York Times.* It is noted that the riots commenced "ostensibly in opposition to . . . the Draft," but that they "early took the character of an outbreak for the purposes of pillage, and also of outrage upon the colored population."

BERNARDO, C. JOSEPH, and EUGENE H. BACON. *American Military Policy: Its Development Since 1775.* 1957. Military Service Publishing Co. Harrisburg, Pennsylvania. Index. Bibliography: pages 494–500. 512 pages.

Traces the development of military policy at the political level since the birth of the nation, attempting to demonstrate that results on the battlefield are largely determined by what prior governmental policy has provided in manpower and weapons. The discussion considers manpower procurement from the days of the American Revolution and the traditional fear of standing armies to the 1950s and the attempts to prepare for war in time of peace.

BLUM, ALBERT A. *Drafted or Deferred: Practices Past and Present.* 1967. Bureau of Industrial Relations, Graduate School of Business, University of Michigan. Ann Arbor, Michigan. Tables. Bibliographical notes at end of each chapter. 249 pages.

Examining the draft from 1940 to the present, Blum describes the various legislative developments in this period. A number of recommendations are presented for reform of military manpower procurement policy. One alternative considered is the abolition of the Selective Service System and the draft itself; by raising the salaries and benefits given to soldiers, "more men would enlist and thus make the draft unnecessary." It is concluded, however, that only "when war disappears as an instrument of national policy" will the draft "disappear as an instrument of national manpower policy."

BOLTON, CHARLES KNOWLES. *The Private Soldier Under Washington.* 1902. Charles Scribner's Sons. New York. Index. Illustrations. 258 pages.

A reconstruction from contemporary literature of the origin, operations, and conditions of George Washington's Continental army. Describes efforts to combat the local prejudices of both Northerner and Southerner; the operation of the wage and bounty systems; the deprivations accompanying a depreciating currency; the fear of militarism; and incidences of resistance to discipline. Bolton notes Washington's convictions that paying men only a small wage prevented their becoming mercenaries, but that bounties were an appropriate means of securing enlistments.

BOORSTIN, DANIEL J. *The Americans: The Colonial Experience.* 1958. Random House. New York. Index. Bibliographical notes: pages 375–421. 434 pages.

Part 13, "A Nation of Minute Men," describes the early militia of the American colonies. The armed citizenry is seen as an "American 'regression,' . . . a revival of the medieval Assize of Arms (1181), from which the English had developed a militia consisting of every able-bodied freeman, each required to provide himself with arms, to train periodically under a local officer, and to be ready on sudden call." The American militia, however, was unprofessional, poorly trained, and unprepared for warfare, and the "long-standing myth of a constantly prepared citizenry helps explain why Americans have always been so ready to demobilize their forces."

BOWMAN, ALLEN. *The Morale of the American Revolutionary Army.* Revised edition. 1964. Kennikat Press. Port Washington, New York. Index. Bibliographic references: pages 105–151. 160 pages.

Introduction by Arthur Pope. Originally published in 1943, this book discusses the following factors as contributing to the morale of the American Revolutionary Army: (1) physical factors—the quality of troops, supplies, sickness, and wages; (2) psychological factors—provincialism, discipline, behavior in action, fluctuation in morale, and devotion to the cause; (3) absenteeism and desertion—the extent and prevention of desertion, and leniency toward it; and (4) the maintenance of morale—rewards, recreation and regalia, and propaganda. Bowman points up some of the difficulties of maintaining morale among mixed (conscripted and volunteer) troops in light of the alleged inequities and inefficiencies of the militia drafts, the enlistment of convicts and other "undesirables," and the failure of the bounty system.

CARTER, WILLIAM HARDING. *The American Army*. 1915. Bobbs-Merrill Co. Indianapolis, Indiana. 294 pages.

This book addresses itself to "the urgent need of nationalizing and organizing our military resources while there is no war-cloud on our horizon." The author, an army officer, states that "all our military students down to the present time exhibit a consensus of opinion that the correct principle on which our nation should predicate its defense has as its basis a federal army of regulars and volunteers, under the direct command and control of the President, and that the militia of the states should be comprised of men whose enlistments should be made with the distinct agreement that their services should not be demanded otherwise than as provided in the Constitution." Carter asserts that "the failure of the execution of the conscription or draft act, during the Civil War, makes it most unlikely that the principle of compulsory service will ever be acceptable to our people, unless the very existence of republican institutions shall be at stake." Individual chapters deal with colonial troops, reserves, federal volunteers, expeditionary forces, and the organized militia.

CATTON, BRUCE. *America Goes to War*. 1958. Wesleyan University Press. Middletown, Connecticut. Illustrations. 126 pages.

This book discusses the implications of and lessons to be learned from the Civil War. Explored is the impact of the war on future events as well as the eras it ended. The author's purpose is to examine how we as a nation approached the war, how we fought it, and what we did with the baffling combination of triumph and defeat with which it left us. Significant aspects of the war considered are its status as the first modern war, the fact it was a political rather than a military war, specific problems in the command structure of the armed forces, and postwar problems between the North and the South.

COOK, ADRIAN. *The Armies of the Streets: The New York City Draft Riots of 1863*. 1974. University of Kentucky Press. Lexington, Kentucky. 323 pages.

Examines the 1863 draft riots and related developments. The author notes that between 1834 and 1874 there were 16 major civil disturbances and numerous minor disorders in New York, owing to a number of factors. He concludes that the draft riots were "fundamentally an insurrection of anarchy" and were not the result of "white workers' fears of competition from cheap black labor."

COULTER, E. MERTON. *A History of the South,* Volume VII: *The Confederate States of America 1861–1865.* 1950. Louisiana State University Press. Baton Rouge, Louisiana. Index. Illustrations. Critical essay on authorities: pages 569–612. 644 pages.

Chapter 15, "Raising Troops," describes the manner in which conscription was instituted in the South, as well as developments and difficulties in its implementation. Included are contemporary reactions to the conscription law. Coulter concludes that "conscription in the South was a failure" and that it "destroyed the strongest weapon the Confederacy had, the co-operation of the state governments and their people."

CRONAU, RUDOLF. *The Army of the American Revolution and Its Organizer: A Thrilling Story of the Times That Tried Men's Souls.* 1923. Rudolf Cronau. New York. Illustrations. 150 pages.

Lamenting the perceived trends to undermine the significance of the American War for Independence, the author discusses the life and work of Baron Frederick William von Steuben, a figure in that war and one whose importance, according to the author, has been persistently ignored. Cronou credits him with being the organizer of the Revolutionary Army, the man "who infused the unorganized bands of defeated and discouraged volunteers and the militia men assembled at Valley Forge with a sense of discipline as well as of confidence, the man who converted them into an excellent fighting machine in many respects superior to that of the enemy and able to win victories at Monmouth, Stony Point, Yorktown and other places." The book discusses specific battles and Steuben's role in them, chronicles Steuben's life, and concludes with a discussion of the Steuben Society of America.

CUNLIFFE, MARCUS. *Soldiers and Civilians: The Martial Spirit in America 1775–1865.* 1969. Eyre & Spottiswoode. London. Index. Illustrations. Chapter notes: pages 439–478. 499 pages.

Describes the nation's "confused heritage" that gave Americans an an aversion to a standing army on the one hand and a strong spirit of self-defense on the other. Reviews the British influence and lessons from the colonial and revolutionary periods, seeing the U.S. Constitution as summing up "some of the lessons America had learned from long and from recent experience." Cunliffe discusses popular attitudes toward the military—Regulars, militia, and volunteers—at various periods, and the influence that these attitudes had upon military manpower procurement policy and practice.

CURTIS, EDWARD E. *The Organization of the British Army in the American Revolution.* 1926. Yale University Press. New Haven, Connecticut. Index. Tables. Bibliography: pages 191–212. 223 pages.

Chapter 3 describes the recruiting of the army, noting the difficulties that led to the hiring of the Hessians and of many Germans into British regiments and to attempts to procure mercenaries from Russia. It is suggested that widespread British sympathy with the colonial policy of the government checked recruiting. Other factors that hampered recruiting included the inadequacy of pay for both officers and men, and the prevailing lack of national recognition for military service. The two methods employed by the crown to obtain men were voluntary enlistments with bounties and the pardoning of criminals upon condition of their enlistment. The appendix includes pay scales for all ranks and a number of documents pertaining to recruiting.

EBY, CECIL D. *Between the Bullet and the Lie: American Volunteers in the Spanish Civil War.* 1969. Holt, Rinehart & Winston, Inc. New York. 342 pages.

This book tells the story of the more than 3,000 American volunteers who fought against the forces of General Francisco Franco during the Spanish civil war of 1936–1939. It describes recruiting in the United States for service in the Comintern-organized International Brigades. Eby notes that recruits comprised not only communists but also noncommunist sympathizers, that recruitment was "always low-key, even surreptitious," and that U.S. federal, state, and municipal agencies sought to destroy pockets of "Red Army" recruitment and support.

EKIRCH, ARTHUR A., JR. *The Civilian and the Military.* 1956. Oxford University Press. New York. Index. Bibliographical comment and notes: pages 291–327. 340 pages.

Examines the phenomenon of militarism in the United States, tracing its passage from colonial times and the tradition of civil supremacy to the present when, the author asserts, militarism has penetrated all phases of civilization and imperiled a proper balance in civil–military relations. In this view, post-World War II military policy and legislation have remained attuned to the wartime belief in the maintenance of a strong military force as the best means to secure peace. Chapter 17 describes and analyzes the events that led to the introduction of conscription during World War I.

FERBER, MICHAEL, and STAUGHTON LYND. *The Resistance.* 1971. Beacon Press. Boston. Index. Illustrations. 300 pages.

Charts the activities of The Resistance, a loose federation of draft-resistance and antiwar movements that came into being in response to the Vietnam War. Following a brief discussion of draft resistance and its precedents, the book deals with the years 1964–1970, from the first "We Won't Go" statement published by the May Second Movement to the founding conference of the Union for National Draft Opposition. It covers mass protests, burning and returning of draft cards, sit-ins, teach-ins, conferences, and interference with the Pentagon and with corporations engaged in the war effort.

FITZPATRICK, EDWARD A. *Conscription and America: A Study of Conscription in a Democracy.* 1940. Richard Publishing Co. Milwaukee, Wisconsin. Index. 153 pages.

Reviews the draft system during the Civil War and the Selective Service System in World War I. The author holds that conscription is the appropriate means to meet military manpower needs in the future, claiming that conscription is more democratic and efficient than volunteering and that the voluntary system has failed in the United States.

FONER, JACK D. *The United States Soldier Between Two Wars: Army Life and Reforms 1865–1898.* 1970. Humanities Press. New York. Index. Tables. Bibliography. 229 pages.

Includes a chapter on the enlisted soldier and the army's legal system, describing the system's alleged inequities and inhumanities that eventually instigated reform. Two tables showing enlistments and desertions in relation to the strength of the army reveal that the desertion rate was high in times of relative prosperity, and much lower in times of recession.

FORRESTAL, JAMES V. *The Forrestal Diaries.* Edited by Walter Millis. 1951. Viking Press. New York. Index. 581 pages.

Notes, letters, reports, and recorded conversations, beginning in 1944, shortly after James Forrestal became secretary of the navy, and ending with his resignation in March 1949 as America's first secretary of defense. Interspersed throughout is Forrestal's account of developments regarding draft, universal military training, and selective service proposals—much of it reflecting his belief that a strong permanent military force would be necessary in the face of a burgeoning challenge from the Soviet Union.

FRENCH, ALLEN. *The First Year of the American Revolution.* 1934. Houghton Mifflin Co. Boston. Index. Maps. Bibliography: pages 771–784. 795 pages.

The growth of the American army is treated in some detail, mostly from contemporary documents. The author describes the organization of the Massachusetts Militia and Minute-Men in 1775, the composition of the Interim Army, and the enlistment of the Massachusetts Eight Months Army and other New England armies. Comparisons are drawn between the British and American armies of the time, noting their difficulties in recruiting, problems arising from pay rates, questions of discipline, and service conditions. A chapter is devoted to Washington's remodeling and reenlistment of the army. The appendix includes notes on rates of pay, terms of service, recruitment, and the size of the army.

FROTHINGHAM, THOMAS G. *The American Reinforcement in the World War.* 1927. Doubleday, Page & Co. Garden City, New York. Index. Diagrams, maps. 388 pages.

Introduction by Newton D. Baker. Of special interest are Chapters 6, 7, and 10, which describe military manpower procurement in World War I, starting with the National Defense Act of 1916 and the creation of the Council of National Defense, and dealing with finance and manpower, the institution and operation of Selective Service in "the most efficient use of conscription in history," and increments to the Regular Army and National Guard.

FRY, JAMES B. *New York and the Conscription of 1863.* 1885. G. P. Putnam's Sons. New York. 85 pages.

A report by the then-Provost Marshal General on events surrounding the implementation of conscription in New York in 1863, including the texts of letters between various authorities. The appendix includes a report on the draft riots in New York in July 1863.

GALVIN, JOHN R. *The Minute Men: A Compact History of the Defenders of the American Colonies 1645–1775.* 1967. Hawthorn Books. New York. Index. Notes and bibliography: pages 259–271. 286 pages.

A military officer's attempt to dispel the popular myth of the spontaneous rise of the Minute Men. Traces the development of the minutemen concept as an outgrowth of the militia, yet as a departure from the old English militia system. The New England colonies coordinated their defense by combining alarm and muster with the system of levying soldiers for expeditions, providing for a permanent levy in a continual state of readiness. The new regulation, established in 1645, ordered company commanders to appoint 30 percent of their companies to be "ready at half an hour's warning upon any service they shall be put upon by their chief military officers." From this minute-men concept grew a number of adaptations, including not only the snowshoe men, the picket guards, and the April 19 minute men, but during the Revolutionary War several other variations. In the author's view, the Minute Men were not the exception to the rule of preparedness, but were "one of the best examples the country has provided."

GANOE, WILLIAM ADDLEMAN. *The History of the United States Army.* Revised edition. 1942. D. Appleton–Century Co., Inc. New York. Index. Illustrations. Selected bibliography: pages 557–593. 640 pages.

In this history of the U.S. Army from its inception to 1942, the author provides information throughout concerning manpower procurement policies and practices, pay, and other conditions in the service.

GREENE, FRANCIS VINTON. *The Revolutionary War and the Military Policy of the United States.* 1911. Charles Scribner's Sons. New York. Index. Maps. 350 pages.

Part 2, on the military policy of the United States, presents an overview of the history of military recruitment from the formation of the Continental army in 1775 to the Militia Act of 1903. Upholding the concept of a moderate-sized standing army, Green concludes: "Our military policy still remains, and is likely to remain, somewhat different from that of the nations of Europe. Enormous armies, conscription and universal military service seem not to be necessary with us. We still rely upon voluntary service; but universal liability to service is the law of the land, and conscription is in the background if volunteers are not sufficient."

GUTHMAN, WILLIAM H. *March to Massacre: A History of the First Seven Years of the United States Army 1784–1791.* 1974. McGraw-Hill. New York. Illustrations. Bibliography: pages 249–259. 275 pages.

Chapter 3 describes recruiting practices in the early American army, noting that the quota of 700 men for the 1st American Regiment was never fulfilled. Some of the reasons for this failure, not least the trying conditions in the service, are discussed.

HAGEDORN, HERMANN. *Leonard Wood: A Biography.* Volume II. 1931. Harper & Bros. New York. Index. Illustrations. 524 pages.

Of particular interest are Chapters 5 and 8, describing Wood's campaign for a shortening of the term of enlistment and for the organization of trained retired men into a powerful national reserve. The author charts Wood's efforts to influence public opinion and government leaders toward preparedness and the concept of the citizen soldier as the key to national defense.

HATCH, LOUIS C. *The Administration of the American Revolutionary Army.* 1904. Harvard Historical Studies, Volume 10. Longmans, Green & Co. New York. Index. List of authorities: pages 210–215. 229 pages.

This study devotes considerable attention to the demands for better pay and better conditions during the army's early years. The causes and grievances involved in the mutinies of the time revolved largely around the question of whether Congress had the power to tax to pay the army. Pay and conditions improved somewhat after March 1783 when the anonymous Newburg Addresses exhorted officers to "compel Congress to do them justice." The appendix contains the text of the Newburg Addresses and related papers.

HAUSER, WILLIAM L. *America's Army in Crisis: A Study in Civil-Military Relations.* 1973. Johns Hopkins University Press. Baltimore, Maryland. Index. Bibliography: pages 227–237. 242 pages.

A critical analysis of the U.S. Army as an institution in transition, examining the internal social and political roots of the army's problems. Part 1 presents three case studies—the German army since World War II, the French army after Algeria, and the British army at the end of the Empire—and the conclusion is drawn that there are three broad areas of similarity that the current American experience shares: recruitment, isolation, and increased specialization within the profession. Part 2 is concerned exclusively with the U.S. Army, Chapters 9, 11, and 12 dealing with recruitment.

HUIDEKOPER, FREDERIC LOUIS. *The Military Unpreparedness of the United States: A History of American Land Forces from Colonial Times Until June 1, 1915.* 1915. Macmillan Co. New York. Index. Notes: pages 557–719. 735 pages.

Introduction by Leonard Wood. The author contends that the history of the United States demonstrates that the nation has never prepared in time of peace for war, and that it has been its fortune through other circumstances to have fared as well as it has in the various wars in which it has engaged. The Regular Army has invariably been too small, never properly organized or so constituted that it could be automatically expanded to the requisite strength when war was recognized to be inevitable; no proper reserves have ever existed from which could be drawn the trained men necessary to raise the Regular Army to war strength; in consequence of a lack of such reserves, the army has almost invariably been compelled to accept recruits deficient in training; and enlistments have been too short. Huidekoper addresses himself to "the persistent failure of Congress to realize that, in a military system combining the use of Regulars and volunteers or militia, men, in the absence of compulsion or strong inducement, will invariably enlist in the organization most lax in discipline." He sees the need for a general staff, responsible to the central government for utilization of military resources, and believes "any delegation of that power to the States must obviously weaken the national military strength and correspondingly increase the national expenditures beyond all justification."

HULL, WILLIAM I. *Preparedness: The American Versus the Military Programme.* 1916. Fleming H. Revell Co. New York. 271 pages.

Reviewing the World War I preparedness movement, the author opposes either a large standing army or a system of universal military training and service, contending that preparedness breeds militarism and war.

JACOBS, JAMES RIPLEY. *The Beginning of the U.S. Army 1783–1812.* 1947. Princeton University Press. Princeton, New Jersey. Index. Bibliography: pages 387–397. 419 pages.

Examines the new nation's failure to prepare itself for war. The book describes the weaknesses in the early militia system, the inadequacies of the first federal troops, and the reluctance of many, both within government and across the new nation, to establish a standing army. It follows the attempts of such men as Josiah Harmar, Arthur St. Clair, and Anthony Wayne to form viable armies, and the influences on military policy of such men as George Washington, James Wilkinson, Thomas Jefferson, Henry Dearborn, and Henry Knox.

LEACH, JACK FRANKLIN. *Conscription in the United States: Historical Background.* 1952. Charles E. Tuttle Publishing Co. Rutland,Vermont. Index. Bibliography: pages 470–494. 501 pages.

An in-depth examination of public policy and military practice in regard to conscription in the United States, beginning with a view of conscription during the formative period of American history and ending with a postwar appraisal of the Civil War draft. Includes a detailed discussion of the first definite proposals for national conscription, during the War of 1812, showing that the public reaction to, the congressional debates on, and the fate of those plans formed an important segment of American constitutional evolution. The initiation and adoption of national conscription in the Lincoln Administration, as well as the public reaction to it, are documented, and some opinions and decisions concerning its constitutionality are reviewed. The author notes, in conclusion, that the United States has entered each war with its militia organizations unprepared, but suggests that the 1951 proposal for universal selective service represents an advance toward the institution of a well-regulated militia that would be ready for national emergencies.

LOGAN, JOHN A. *The Volunteer Soldier of America.* 1887. T. S. Peale & Co. Chicago. Index. Illustrations. 706 pages.

This history of the volunteer soldier is authored by a U.S. congressman who served as a volunteer general in the Civil War. The introductory chapter deals with the birth and origins of the American volunteer soldier, his peculiar characteristics and motivations. Part 1, on the history of military education in the United States, describes Washington's attempts to diffuse military knowledge among the people and to "make soldiers without resorting to the dangers of a standing army," and includes the text and a discussion of Knox's paper on the organization of the militia (see also page 40 below). Part 2 considers the present military system of the United States, with its alleged tendency to class distinction. Part 3, "A Demand for Justice," describes the "usurpation by the West Point influence of the military affairs of the country" and proposes a military system independent of "European models" in which military knowledge and power of the government would not repose in a select circle. Logan advocates educating "the whole youth of the country to the preliminary knowledge and training of the soldier" so as to create "a vast army of citizen-soldiers."

LONN, ELLA. *Desertion During the Civil War.* 1928. Century Co. New York. Index. Bibliography: pages 237–242. 251 pages.

This heavily documented study of desertion and its causes in the Civil War notes the effects that conscription and its attendant substitute and exemption practices had on the caliber of recruits, on morale and efficiency, and on the overall cost of manpower recruitment. It is shown that, in both the North and the South, men conscripted for service or hired as substitutes were "potential material for desertion." Second only to conscription in the list of causes of desertion cited is "lack of the most ordinary necessities for the soldier—food, clothing, pay, and equipment."

LONN, ELLA. *Foreigners in the Confederacy.* 1940. University of North Carolina Press. Chapel Hill, North Carolina. Index. Bibliography: pages 505–536. 566 pages.

Chapter 13, "The Attitude of the Confederacy Toward Foreigners," discusses the effect of the Confederate conscription laws on aliens, noting alleged injustices and hardships imposed by the laws, not least the coercion of many into the Confederate army.

LONN, ELLA. *Foreigners in the Union Army and Navy.* 1951. Louisiana State University Press. Baton Rouge, Louisiana. Index. Bibliography: pages 688–710. 725 pages.

Of particular interest are Chapter 14, "Eager Volunteers and War Immigrants," and Chapter 15, "The Draft and Abuses in Recruitment." The author finds that the "spontaneous plan of nationality units" in the Civil War stimulated enlistments by producing "rivalry among the groups of adopted sons to show their gratitude and devotion."

MAHON, JOHN K. *The American Militia: Decade of Decision 1789–1800.* 1960. University of Florida Press. Gainesville, Florida. Bibliographical footnotes. 69 pages.

The ten-year period from the start of government under the Constitution to the election of Jefferson is examined as the time when "American leaders chose between a national militia system and a congeries of state militias," the result of their choice setting the basic tone of U.S. military policy for a century thereafter. A sketch of the English and the colonial antecedents of the system provides the background for a treatment of the militia clauses of the Constitution, followed by an analysis of the operation of the militia system at the state and local levels, and of the volunteer and standing (conscripted) militias—the first the precursor of the National Guard, the second soon to decline.

MARSHALL, GEORGE C. *Selected Speeches and Statements of General of the Army George C. Marshall.* Edited by H. A. DeWeerd. Revised edition. 1973. De Capo Press. New York. Index. Bibliographical references. 263 pages.

Originally published in 1945, this volume presents Marshall's positions on various aspects of military manpower procurement policy, including selective service, pay and conditions of service, and universal military training. A firm advocate of preparedness, Marshall upholds conscription in 1940 on the basis that volunteer enlistments may not meet military needs in time of peace, much less in the event of war. In this view, there is no "better, more democratic method" of securing the necessary men than by "some form of selective service." Included are the texts of legislative hearings concerned with manpower needs in World War II.

MARTIN, BESSIE. *Desertion of Alabama Troops from the Confederate Army: A Study in Sectionalism.* 1932. Columbia University Press. New York. Index. Bibliography: pages 259–274. 281 pages.

Examines the military and political causes of desertion in Alabama, noting that evasion of military service by those liable to conscription was interpreted as desertion according to law, military orders, and executive proclamation. The Conscription Act of 1862 stimulated volunteering and, while many "so-called volunteers were not in the army from choice," some conscripts would have been "real volunteers if they had been free from private obligations to enter the Confederate States' service. The method of enlistment, therefore, did not always determine the spirit of the soldier" and compulsory service was a cause of desertion of both conscripts and volunteers. Martin notes also that "features of the maintenance of the army which tended to lower its morale and cause desertion were inadequate supply of clothing and food, arrears in pay, and infrequency of furloughs."

MILTON, GEORGE F. *Abraham Lincoln and the Fifth Column*. 1942. Vanguard Press. New York. Index. Illustrations. Bibliography: pages 335–344. 364 pages.

Chapter 7 discusses the consequences of the Civil War draft in the North, contending that "one of the chief purposes of the Copperhead fifth column, from its organization in the summer of 1861 until the final crash of the conspiracies in November, 1864, was to induce desertions from the Union soldiery." According to Milton, however, the Copperhead fifth column "aided and abetted," but did not cause, resistance to the draft. As for the 1863 New York draft riots, he states that though Confederate agents were charged with the chief responsibility for the riots, the available evidence does not indicate complicity.

MINOT, GEORGE RICHARDS. *History of the Insurrection in Massachusetts in the Year Seventeen Hundred and Eighty Six and the Rebellion Consequent Thereon*. 1810. James W. Burdett & Co. Boston. 192 pages.

Seeks to investigate the causes and trace the progress of the Massachusetts insurrection and to mark the means by which a resolution was reached in 1786 to provide the understanding necessary for "preserving the future transquility of the commonwealth." Chronicles issues and events of the insurrection, and concludes that the conflict was resolved through the "spirited use of constitutional power," the end result being government without repression.

MITCHELL, BROADUS. *The Price of Independence: A Realistic View of the American Revolution*. 1974. Oxford University Press. New York. Index. Selected bibliography: pages 349–357. 374 pages.

This book describes recruiting in the American Revolutionary Army, dealing with enlistment problems, draft resistance, desertion, and mutinying. Mitchell discusses congressional disabilities in relation to recruiting, financial problems, pay and other conditions in the service, and the recruitment of foreign troops. He notes that "the most eager enlistment for war service" seems to have been that of "privateers," among whom "recruiting was intensive, with the promise of adventure and booty."

MONTROSS, LYNN. *Rag, Tag and Bobtail: The Story of the Continental Army 1775–1783*. 1952. Harper & Bros. New York. Index. Bibliography: pages 475–490. 519 pages.

Told in story form, this work chronicles the events of the War for Independence, discussing the soldiers, conditions, problems, and limitations faced by the army. Specific battles from 1776 to 1783 are described in anecdotal detail. The problems posed by the undisciplined, individualistic nature of the revolutionary soldier are also discussed in the context of General Washington's leadership.

MOORE, ALBERT BURTON. *Conscription and Conflict in the Confederacy*. 1924. Macmillan Co. New York. Index. 367 pages.

A historical study of the conscription system in the Confederacy and the conflicts it produced between Confederate and state authorities. Basing his work largely on the Official Records, newspapers, and personal interviews, the author discusses the inherent weaknesses of conscription in the Confederacy—the use of substitution, exemption, and bounties—in light of the larger problem of enforcement as the new government, set up as the agent of the sovereign states, attempted to build and maintain an effective centralized force.

MURDOCK, EUGENE C. *One Million Men: The Civil War Draft in the North*. 1971. State Historical Society of Wisconsin. Madison, Wisconsin. Index. Illustrations, tables. Bibliographic note: pages 357–359. 366 pages.

The Civil War draft in the North is seen as "only a semidraft, a device to raise a one-million-man army by encouraging volunteering." Based largely on contemporary official sources, the book documents the many abuses that "almost defeated the law"—commutation, "which brought in money, but not men"; substitution, which "brought in men, but of such poor quality that large numbers deserted very shortly"; and bounties, which "gave rise to bounty jumping and a vast middleman business."

MURDOCK, EUGENE CONVERSE. *Patriotism Limited 1862–1865: The Civil War Draft and the Bounty System.* 1967. Kent State University Press. Kent, Ohio. Index. Illustrations, tables. 270 pages.

An examination of the Civil War bounty system, focusing chiefly on New York State, "center of the most elaborate broker and jumper operations," yet representative of all Northern states. The author finds that patriotism was at a low ebb during the war, and that the bounty alone was the spur to much recruitment. He provides a chronological survey of the bounty system, explains how it was instituted by Lincoln when the call for volunteers was not met, and describes the activities of the bounty jumpers and bounty brokers, the systems of exemption, substitution, and commutation, abuses, and attitudes in the community—all against the background of related political developments. The appendix includes factual and statistical materials on bounty expenditures, enrollment board personnel, and draft figures, and comments on the widespread belief that the Civil War was a "poor man's fight" and on the Conkling and Blaine–Fry Controversy that erupted in 1866 as a result of the Haddock recruiting fraud court-martial.

O'CONNOR, RAYMOND G. (editor). *American Defense Policy in Perspective: From Colonial Times to the Present.* 1965. John Wiley & Sons. New York. 377 pages.

Selections of individual writings on various aspects of the role of military power in American national development and the fundamentals of defense policy. Of interest in regard to military manpower procurement policy are extracts from the writings of Louis Morton, Emory Upton, Howard White, Frederic Huidekoper, Frederic Paxson, Mark Watson, and Samuel Huntington.

OPPENHEIMER, MARTIN (editor). *The American Military.* 1971. Distributed by Aldine Publishing Co. Chicago. Transaction Books, TA 19. 180 pages.

A compilation of essays on American military life, originally appearing in the May 1966–March 1970 issues of *Transaction* magazine. The essay by John Cooney and Dana Spitzer, "Hell No, We Won't Go!" (pages 117–137), deals with American draft dodgers and deserters in the Vietnam War. The book also includes case studies illustrating the attitudes of those refusing to enter military service or refusing to stay in once they have joined.

O'SULLIVAN, JOHN, and ALAN M. MECKLER (editors). *The Draft and Its Enemies: A Documentary History.* 1974. University of Illinois Press. Urbana, Illinois. Index. Bibliography: pages 281–285. 289 pages.

Foreword by Senator Mark Hatfield and introduction by Russell Weigley. This is an examination and analysis of opposition to military conscription in America since colonial times. Individual chapters on six distinguishable eras of the nation's history present a summary of issues involved in military manpower procurement. In addition, documentation from each period illustrates the varied opinions of each era relative to the draft and the environment in which the issue was debated. These eras are: (1) 1607–1783: The Birth of the Citizen Soldier; (2) 1783–1861: Reliance on the Militia; (3) 1861–1900: The Beginning of Federal Conscription; (4) 1900–1940: Conscription Comes of Age; (5) 1940–1965: Conscription in War and Cold War; and (6) 1965–the Present: The Draft, Institution in Crisis.

OWSLEY, FRANK L. *State Rights in the Confederacy.* 1925. University of Chicago Press. Chicago. Index. 290 pages.

In this study of the consequences of state autonomy upon the military fortunes of the Confederacy, it is suggested that from a military point of view the local-defense policy of the Southern states and the attempts of the Confederacy to obtain control of local troops undermined the Confederate military position. In this view, "the policy of conscription would have resulted in getting many more able-bodied but reluctant gentlemen into the army if it had not been opposed so bitterly by the state-rights leaders."

PALMER, FREDERICK. *Newton D. Baker: America at War.* Volume 1. 1931. Dodd, Mead & Co. New York. 421 pages.

Based largely on the personal papers of Newton D. Baker, secretary of war during World War I, this book describes the operations of the War Department and the various problems with which it had to contend both before and after America's entry into the war. Chapter 9 deals with the draft—noting Baker's shift from an anti- to a pro-conscription orientation —while Chapter 15 discusses draft exemptions.

PALMER, JOHN MCAULEY. *America in Arms: The Experience of the United States with Military Organization.* 1941. Yale University Press. New Haven, Connecticut. 207 pages.

The author, a retired army general, contends that the implementation of George Washington's 1790 plan for universal military training and service would have prepared the nation at minimum expense for "all of our subsequent wars." He offers a version of how Washington arrived at his military philosophy, "how and why he was unable to persuade his countrymen to accept it; how their rejection of his advice affected their subsequent history; and finally how, after a century and a half, their descendants have at last been impelled to return to his guidance." With the passage of the Selective Training and Service Act of 1940, the War Department is considered able to make its defense plans with scientific precision "although it still remains to complete the Washingtonian structure by the adoption of universal military training."

PALMER, JOHN MCAULEY. *Washington, Lincoln, Wilson: Three War Statesmen.* 1930. Doubleday, Doran & Co. Garden City, New York. Index. Illustrations. 417 pages.

Introduction by John J. Pershing. George Washington's treatise on the future defense of the United States, "Sentiments on a Peace Establishment," previously overlooked by historians, forms the basis of this book. In this account of the evolution of American military institutions and the influence of that evolution upon the nation's military history, Palmer describes how "this highly constructive measure became involved in the political struggle between the followers of Hamilton and Jefferson"; and how it was "emasculated by legislative amendment and finally passed as the notorious Militia Act of 1792." In critique of Emory Upton's *The Military Policy of the United States* (see page 46, below), Palmer suggests that, lacking "the essential key to Washington's published writings," Upton was led to misconstrue U.S. military history. In this view, too, both Abraham Lincoln and Woodrow Wilson were "doomed to bear the burden of unprepared warfare." The appendix includes the text of Washington's treatise.

PARGELLIS, STANLEY McCRORY. *Lord Loudoun in North America.* 1933. Yale University Press. New Haven, Connecticut. Index. Illustrations. Bibliography: pages 366–378. 399 pages.

Deals with the period during which Lord Loudoun held command of British defense forces in the North American colonies. The author discusses colonial defense prior to and during Loudoun's command, noting his attempt to inaugurate a military union of the colonies, and detailing administrative policies and practices with regard to pay and conditions of service. In examining Americans' objection to assuming a share in British wars "under conditions and according to the formula which Great Britain imposed," he maintains that this antagonism was "based on the fear that a standing army threatened the free working of their colonial institutions."

RAYMOND, JACK. *Power at the Pentagon.* 1964. Harper & Row. New York. Index. 363 pages.

An examination of the growth of military power in the United States, with particular emphasis on the period since World War II. It is the author's thesis that, in the process of securing that military power to secure the nation, "we altered some of our traditions in the military, in diplomacy, in industry, science, education, politics and other aspects of our society," placing "tremendous peacetime authority in the hands of our defenders, military and civilian." Considerable attention is focused on military manpower mobilization policies, from Grenville Clark's "one-man campaign for the draft," which is said to have resulted in the Selective Service Act of 1940, to a consideration of whether a permanent draft policy should be adopted in the United States.

ROOT, ELIHU. *The Military and Colonial Policy of the United States: Addresses and Reports.* Edited by Robert Bacon and James Brown Scott. 1916. Harvard University Press. Cambridge, Massachusetts. Index. 502 pages.

This collection covers the period of Root's service as secretary of war, secretary of state, and senator. Of particular interest are the sections dealing with military manpower systems and the organization and disposition of the army. Root views universal military training as imperative to national defense.

SHANNON, FRED ALBERT. *The Organization and Administration of the Union Army 1861–1865.* 2 volumes. 1928. Arthur H. Clark Co. Cleveland, Ohio. Volume I: Illustrations. 323 pages. Volume II: Index. Bibliography: pages 287–294. 348 pages.

Volume I concerns itself primarily with the problems of recruiting, equipping, and training the Union army in the Civil War. Much of the text is descriptive and colorful. It concludes with a discussion of the collapse of state recruiting and the enactment of the Enrollment Act of 1863. Volume II discusses the operation of the Civil War draft, particularly in regard to the hiring of substitutes, the payment of enlistment bounties, and the general problem of draft evasion.

SPAULDING, OLIVER LYMAN. *The United States Army in War and Peace.* 1937. G. P. Putnam's Sons. New York. Index. Bibliography: pages 501–513. 541 pages.

Examines the organization of the nation's armies from the Revolutionary War through World War I. The opening chapter covers the military background of the American colonists. The final chapter, on the reorganization of the army, contends that compulsory service was so successful during World War I "that there was a strong sentiment both within and without the Army, if not for actual compulsory service, at least for some amount of compulsory training," but that "this idea was dropped after some discussion, and the volunteer basis was retained for times of peace," although it was "taken for granted" that conscription would "probably be adopted again in case of a great war."

STERN, PHILIP VAN DOREN (editor). *Soldier Life in the Union and Confederate Armies.* 1961. Fawcett Publications, Inc. Greenwich, Connecticut. Index. Illustrations. 400 pages.

Designed to describe the day-to-day life of the common soldier, this book focuses on the "lighter side of army life." Discussed are enlistment and recruitment, housing conditions, supplies, food, discipline, hospital conditions, fighting conditions, and general army morale. The similarities and differences between the two armies are noted.

SULLIVAN, MARK. *Our Times: The United States 1900–1925,* Volume 5: *Over Here 1914–1918.* 1933. Charles Scribner's Sons. New York. Index. Illustrations. 676 pages.

Chapter 9 discusses the movement for military preparedness and the initial opposition of President Wilson. In Chapter 15, Wilson sides with army leaders in favor of conscription and, with Secretary of War Newton Baker, works to bring about national acceptance of a wartime draft. Chapter 16 describes the operation of the Selective Service System and the government's attitude toward conscientious objectors.

USEEM, MICHAEL. *Conscription, Protest, and Social Conflict: The Life and Death of a Draft Resistance Movement.* 1973. John Wiley & Sons. New York. Index. References: pages 295–317. 329 pages.

An analysis of the American radical-left protest movement against conscription organized during American involvement in the Vietnam War. Traces the strategic justification for the formation of the movement, its political and social consolidation, and its demise. Other 20th century anti-conscription movements formed for the purpose of generating strikes of prospective draftees are drawn in comparison: the Australian Draft Resisters' Union, organized in 1970 to oppose the Vietnam War; the Jeune Résistance (Young Resistance), formed in France in 1959 in response to the Algerian conflict; and the British No-Conscription Fellowship, initiated in 1914 after England's entry into World War I.

UTLEY, ROBERT M. *Frontier Regulars: The United States Army and the Indian 1866–1891.* 1973. Macmillan Publishing Co., Inc. New York. Index. Illustrations, maps. Bibliographic footnotes. 462 pages.

A history of the Regular Army that "contended" with Indian tribes of the western frontier from 1866 to 1891. The author attempts to chronicle events objectively, balancing the polar stereotypes of the Frontier Regulars as being either "the advance guard of civilization, sweeping aside the savage to make way for the stockman, the miner, the farmer, the merchant," or "butchers, rampaging around the West gleefully slaughtering peaceable Indians and taking special delight in shooting down women and children." Topics covered include the return to the frontier after the Civil War, the postwar army, weapons, uniforms and equipment, army life on the border, and specific battles.

WARD, HARRY M. *The Department of War 1781–1795.* 1962. University of Pittsburgh Press. Pittsburgh, Pennsylvania. Index. Bibliography: pages 244–271. 287 pages.

A history of the Department of War from its establishment in 1781 to the quelling of the Indian and Whiskey uprisings in 1794. Contains much information on recruitment of the early American armies and on problems held to be attributable to the absence of an adequate system of compensation for the troops.

WEIGLEY, RUSSELL F. *History of the United States Army.* 1967. Macmillan Co. New York. Index. Illustrations. Bibliographic notes: pages 570–653. 688 pages.

Beginning with the colonial militias, this study traces the development of the American army up to the present, noting its ideological inheritance from England and the various forces that have since shaped it. Viewing the American military tradition as "a duality between professional and citizen soldiers, whose partnership was sealed in 1917–18 and 1941–45," the author sees a "historic tension between the two American armies, professional and citizen." It is suggested that "the effort to balance and harmonize their rival claims, in order best to assure both military security and a democratic polity, has dominated the history of American military institutions, apart from the Navy." Military manpower procurement policies and practices are dealt with in depth throughout.

WEIGLEY, RUSSELL F. *Towards an American Army: Military Thought from Washington to Marshall.* 1962. Greenwood Press. Westport, Connecticut. Index. Bibliography: pages 277–285. 297 pages.

Examines the development of military policy from the American Revolution to the present. The author discusses the military legacy of the Revolution; George Washington's army; John C. Calhoun and the expansible army plan; William T. Sherman and Ulysses S. Grant and the rise of total war; Emory Upton, his disciples and his foes; Leonard Wood and the citizen army; and John McAuley Palmer and George C. Marshall and universal military training. Weigley concludes that "the conflicting elements in the military legacy of the American Revolution are no more reconciled than in Washington's day. Americans still seek the proper path towards an American army."

WILLIAMS, T. HARRY. *Americans at War: The Development of the American Military System.* 1960. Louisiana State University Press. Baton Rouge, Louisiana. Index. Bibliography: pages 127–134. 138 pages.

This volume consists of three essays: (1) The American Military System: From the Revolution to 1860; (2) The Military Systems of North and South; and (3) The American Military System: From Civil War to Global Conflict. While the main emphasis is on "the attempts of the government of the United States to achieve a workable command system," manpower procurement policies during the various periods are discussed.

WOOD, LEONARD. *Our Military History: Its Facts and Fallacies.* 1916. Reilly & Britton Co. Chicago. 240 pages.

A brief review of U.S. military policy and a recommendation for adequate national preparedness in a system that would "rest upon equality of service for all who are physically fit and of proper age." The nation should no longer "place reliance upon plans based upon the development of volunteers or the use of the militia." Citizen soldiers should form a purely federal force "trained under some system which will permit the instruction to be given in part during the school period or age, thereby greatly reducing the time required for the final intensive period of training, which should be under regular officers and in conjunction with regular troops." Wood advocates a system on the general lines of the Australian or Swiss (both described in the appendix) with modifications to meet U.S. conditions.

Unpublished Manuscripts

ALDRIDGE, FREDERICK STOKES. *Organization and Administration of the Militia System of Colonial Virginia.* 1964. Ph.D. dissertation. American University. Washington, D.C. 271 pages.

Examines the composition of the Virginia militia and its changing role in the defense of the colony. Notes that the militia had as its immediate forebear the British militia and in turn was the prototype of the militia of many other states.

BITTLE, GEORGE CASSEL. *In the Defense of Florida: The Organized Florida Militia from 1821 to 1920.* 1965. Ph.D. dissertation. Florida State University. Tallahassee, Florida. 457 pages.

A study of the role of the militia in the history of Florida, attempting to determine the effectiveness of Florida's militia in meeting the demands of both state and national emergencies during the period 1821 to 1920. The larger problem considered is the relation of the state militia to the nation's central military power.

BROOKS, EDWARD H. *The National Defense Policy of the Wilson Administration 1913–1917.* 1950. Ph. D. dissertation. Stanford University. Stanford, California. Bibliography: pages 275–282. 282 pages.

This study deals with the pre-World War I preparedness movement, the several bills introduced in Congress in 1913 and 1914 "to increase the efficiency of the militia," and the efforts of President Wilson to maintain neutrality when war came. It notes the calls from heads of the armed services for increased naval and military strength as European mobilizations and the calling of reservists underscored the U.S. Army's "very obvious lack." According to the author, it was largely because of Wilson's inexperience and distinterest in military matters, as well as the absence of competent advisers, that he was not, until July 1915, persuaded by events to throw the weight of his administration behind the drive for military military and naval preparedness. The theory that the President endorsed was the "expansible" standing army with units filled up to war strength when an emergency appeared and followed by whatever militia and volunteer organizations were raised, "the success of the filling-up process [being] predicated on the existence of a trained reserve." This position was examined in the congressional debates leading up to the National Defense Act of 1916.

BRUNDAGE, LYLE D. *The Organization, Administration, and Training of the United States Ordinary and Volunteer Militia 1792–1861.* 1959. Ed.D. dissertation. University of Michigan. Ann Arbor, Michigan. 466 pages.

An examination of the militia system of the United States and the effort to diffuse among the people a knowledge of military matters during the first half of the 19th century, with particular reference to two kinds of militia—volunteer and regular. Includes discussion of the first militia law of 1792, the general organization of the militia from 1792 to 1840, the volunteer or uniformed militia organizations from 1792 to 1860, methods for calling the militia into service of the United States or one of the several states, and the provisions for exemptions and substitutes during peacetime and wartime. A number of weaknesses are indicated in the militia system in regard to manpower procurement and retention, and pay and other conditions of service.

CAINE, PHILIP DAVID. *The American Periodical Press and Military Preparedness During the Hoover Administration.* 1966. Ph.D. dissertation. Stanford University. Stanford, California. 285 pages.

Investigates the amount of public concern about preparedness, the viewpoints that were presented to the public by selected periodicals, and the degree to which Herbert Hoover's military policies were in harmony with the desires of the people, as reflected in contemporary periodicals. Caine finds that the periodicals of the time failed to exercise any significant voice in shaping public opinion, and that there seems to have been no serious effort by the Hoover Administration to use them as a vehicle to convey to the public its plans regarding military matters.

CHAMBERS, JOHN WHITECLAY, II. *Conscripting for Colossus: The Adoption of the Draft in the United States in World War I.* 1973. Ph.D. dissertation. Columbia University. New York. Bibliography: pages 356–394. 397 pages.

The thesis of this dissertation is that the adoption of a national draft in 1917 represented a radical departure from traditional methods of raising wartime armies in the United States and that this unprecedented change resulted not only from American entry into World War I but also from the emergence of a national economy and a more powerful national government during the preceding decades. "The wartime draft of 1917–18, while representing a major modification of past practice, conformed to the general movement towards greater efficiency, predictability, and equity through increased national control which especially characterized the Progressive period." The author contends that the deviation of 1917–1918 set a precedent for raising armies in future wars: "The country might not be ready to accept peacetime conscription, but it agreed to primary reliance upon a national wartime draft for use at home or abroad for the first time in its history."

COLE, DAVID W. *The Organization and Administration of the South Carolina Militia System 1670–1783.* 1953. Ph. D. dissertation. University of South Carolina. Columbia, South Carolina. Bibliography: pages 141–145. 145 pages.

Deals with English and colonial precedents for the South Carolina militia system and with its organization and administration during the Proprietary, Royal, and Revolutionary periods. The author finds that the South Carolina militia system, which called upon every able-bodied male between 16 and 60 years of age to aid in the defense of the colony, "obviously worked well as the colony brushed aside every effort of its enemies to upset the new unit of English colonial government." There was one "striking difference" between the South Carolina militia system and that of England, however, in the use made of the militia: "In South Carolina the militia was called out rarely by entire companies or regiments; instead, the use of the militia was that of the commissioners of array system of medieval England [so that] in almost every campaign against Indians or Spaniards volunteers were called from the militia units and the volunteers were paid."

CUTLER, FREDERICK MORSE. *The History of Military Conscription with Especial Reference to the United States.* 1922. Ph.D. dissertation. Clark University. Worcester, Massachusetts. Bibliographical footnotes. 106 pages.

A survey of conscription from its militia origins up to modern selective service. It is contended that the nation's progress from militia, through professional soldiers, volunteers, the draft, to selective service, represented not a cyclical, but a spiral movment. In this view, selective service as introduced by the United States in World War I was "the final coming of age of the western republic" and "a precedent for possible future emergencies."

DAYTON, ARETAS ARNOLD. *Recruitment and Conscription in Illinois During the Civil War.* 1940. Ph.D. dissertation. University of Illinois. Urbana, Illinois. Bibliography: pages 225–244. 244 pages.

This detailed account of recruitment and conscription in Illinois during the Civil War examines the procedures used and the problems involved in raising troops. Dayton discusses various difficulties encountered by the state in connection with conscription, such as the problem of evasion and the effects of the bounty system.

DAYTON, DELLO GRIMMETT. *The California Militia 1850–1866.* 1951. Ph.D. dissertation. University of California. Berkeley, California. Illustrations. 460 pages.

The characteristic organization of the California militia during the formative period 1850–1866 was the volunteer militia company, some three hundred units having been formed by 1866. The companies participated actively in community social affairs, acted as auxiliary law and order agencies, furnished protection against Indian depredations, provided a security force in the absence of adequate regular troops, and supplied a training agency and a reservoir for troops who served in the Civil War. Although the organized militia during the period of this study never consisted of more than 9,000 men, the initial and necessary foundations were laid for the development of California's present National Guard.

FABIANO, GERALD JAMES. *The Analysis and Interpretation of the Use of Presidential Authority to Order United States Armed Forces into Military Action to Quell Domestic Disturbances.* 1962. Ph.D. dissertation. New York University. New York. 422 pages.

Fifty-five selected incidents in which presidents ordered U.S. armed forces into military action to quell domestic disturbances between 1790 and 1960 are examined with regard to possible trends in the stated bases of authority upon which the actions were undertaken. Fabiano finds that "the use of presidential authority to order the armed forces of the United States into military action to quell domestic disturbances is an historically established practice regardless of doubts or debates [about] its precise constitutionality."

FINNEGAN, JOHN P. *Military Preparedness in the Progressive Era 1911– 1917.* 1969. Ph.D. dissertation. University of Wisconsin. Madison, Wisconsin. Bibliographical essay: pages 329–344. 344 pages.

In this study, the propaganda of the preparedness movement for universal military training is seen as gradually conditioning the public to accept conscription. The plans drawn up by the General Staff to train men under universal service were readily adapted to fit the needs of a national army raised by the draft, while the Plattsburg movement provided the necessary framework to recruit and train the vast number of reserve officers the huge wartime force needed. In contrast with the more lasting effect that 'the preparedness movement before World War II would have, the fate of the preparedness movement at the close of World War I reflects the reluctance of the nation at that time to "arm itself in time of peace to await an indefinite enemy."

HANNA, ARCHIBALD, JR. *New England Military Institutions 1693–1750.* 1950. Ph.D. dissertation. Yale University. New Haven, Connecticut. Bibliography: pages 309–316. 316 pages.

Describes the New England colonies' adaptation of the traditional English system of trainbands to American conditions, and the supplementing of the trainbands by men drawn by conscription and volunteering from the organized militia. Hanna finds that while pay and other conditions in the service were poor, "the New England military institutions performed with reasonable success the functions for which they were created."

LEACH, JACK FRANKLIN. *The Law, Theory, and Politics of National Conscription in the United States to the End of the Civil War.* 1943. Ph.D. dissertation. University of California. Berkeley, California. Bibliography. 775 pages.

A detailed and critical analysis of the development of the national government's power to conscript and to control the manpower resources of the United States. Leach concludes that "the framers of the Constitution and those who ratified it thought they were conferring upon Congress the rather limited power to raise and support a small military force by voluntary means, and the right to call upon the state militia organizations when that force proved inadequate. There was no indication that final and direct authority over the whole of the manpower resources was being granted in the military clauses." He suggests that "the Constitution would have failed of ratification if suspicions had been aroused that so extensive a power was being entrusted to the central government. Nevertheless, Congress has taken a very broad view of its military competency and has assumed authority to conscript directly. Acquiesence by the states, the courts, and the people has resulted in imparting a new and enlarged meaning to the military clauses and in greatly expanding the power of the central government."

LORD, FRANCIS ALFRED. *The Federal Volunteer Soldier in the American Civil War 1861–1865.* 1949. Ph.D. dissertation. University of Michigan. Ann Arbor, Michigan. 570 pages.

Includes a discussion of motivations for enlistment and reactions to the draft in the Civil War. Treats in depth the contributions of foreigners and blacks.

MALONE, PATRICK MITCHELL. *Indian and English Military Systems in New England in the Seventeenth Century.* 1971. Ph.D. dissertation. Brown University. Providence, Rhode Island. 343 pages.

Compares the military system of the American Indians with that of the colonists and examines the ways in which each affected the other before 1677. Describes the military service obligations of the colonists.

MARCUS, RICHARD HENRY. *The Militia of Colonial Connecticut 1639–1775: An Institutional Study.* 1965. Ph.D. dissertation. University of Colorado. Boulder, Colorado. 389 pages.

This study draws largely from manuscript collections of the Connecticut Archives relating to the militia and colonial wars, and from the published papers of the governors of colonial Connecticut. It examines the militia of the colony both as an institution and as a component of the defense system of the northern British American colonies. Marcus discusses the obligations and the rights of militiamen, and concludes that colonial conditions, economic factors, and tradition made a militia format the only practical answer to Connecticut's military problems.

MENEELY, A. HOWARD. *The War Department 1861: A Study in Mobilization and Administration.* 1928. Ph.D. dissertation. Columbia University. New York. Index. Bibliography: pages 378–386. 400 pages.

Examines the military conditions, held to be "the direct outgrowth of a short-sighted military policy," as the Lincoln Administration found them, in an attempt to show how they "complicated its task" and to describe "the obstacles it had to face in putting the department and the army on an adequate war footing." Traces the way in which the federal government by January 1862, and with the departure of discredited Secretary of War Simon Cameron, had "finally succeeded, clumsily and at an excessive cost, in placing more than half a million men in the field and had built up an establishment to sustain them." Assailing the nation's consistent resistance to military preparedness, Meneely finds that "jealousy and distrust of a standing army, confidence in the ultimate success of the raw recruit and remoteness from powerful nations have been significant factors in determining our military program and our national history."

MONAGHAN, JAY. *Opposition to Involuntary Military Service in the United States.* 1918. Master's thesis. University of Pennsylvania. Philadelphia.

All known copies of this work are lost or missing.

RADABAUGH, JACK SHELDON. *The Military System of Colonial Massachusetts 1690–1740.* 1965. Ph.D. dissertation. University of Southern California. Los Angeles. 609 pages.

Discusses the "enormous strains" that confronted the Massachusetts colonial military system "in terms of personnel, volunteers, impressment, and draft dodging." Notes the rewards that existed in the forms of "scalp money, plunder, and land grants."

RUTMAN, DARRELL BRUCE. *A Militant New World 1607–1640: America's First Generation, Its Martial Spirit, Its Tradition of Arms, Its Militia Organization, Its Wars.* 1959. Ph.D. dissertation. University of Virginia. Charlottesville, Virginia. 838 pages.

It is the author's thesis that "even today, more than a hundred years after the use of the discredited formal militia organization was abandoned, the idea that the protection of the American states rests on the citizen himself is a part of the American psychology and the foundation of America's real strength. It is cemented into the national fabric by the existence of the National Guard, the military reserves and conscription." Rutman finds that the military activity and the militant spirit in the colonies were closely intertwined with the social, religious, and economic life of the citizen and with the politics of the earliest colonial governments. Thus, "the existence of militia as the foundation-stone of colonial defense was insured at the very time that England herself was moving toward reliance on a standing army. And the colonial citizen-soldier assumed a militancy and aggressiveness almost unknown in the average Englishman."

SPERRY, JAMES RUSSELL. *Organized Labor and Its Fight Against Military and Industrial Conscription 1917–1945.* 1969. Ph.D. dissertation. University of Arizona. Tucson, Arizona. 308 pages.

Describes how "organized labor feared military and industrial conscription because it believed the draft could be used to destroy trade unionism in America." After Selective Service was enacted in 1917, organized labor accepted this as a necessary evil, but attempted to assure labor rights by fighting for labor representation on local and district draft boards and preventing the extension of the draft to include "the manipulation of America's workers by National Service." In the decades between the wars, the major catalyst for labor's increased isolationism was the fear of conscription. The effectiveness of organized labor's opposition to the 1940 Burke–Wadsworth selective service bill, the first peacetime conscription bill in American history, was hindered by the break between the American Federation of Labor and the Congress of Industrial Organizations.

STERLING, ROBERT E. *Civil War Draft Resistance in the Middle West.* 1974. Ph.D. dissertation. Northern Illinois University. De Kalb, Illinois. Bibliography: pages 685–693. 693 pages.

A narrative account that examines the motives and attitudes of the Midwestern draft resisters and how these were affected by specific events of the Civil War. Concludes that Midwesterners resisted the draft for many reasons, including an aversion to compulsory military service, objection to the centralizing effects of national conscription, and partisan opposition to the Lincoln Administration.

TINSLEY, WILLIAM W. *The American Preparedness Movement 1913–1916.* 1939. Ph.D. dissertation. Stanford University. Stanford, California. Bibliography: pages 356–361. 361 pages.

Based largely upon contemporary newspaper and congressional sources, this study traces the interplay of forces that "foisted upon the public through a campaign of propaganda" a policy of military preparedness "which was to prove as futile as it was costly." It notes the efforts of Leonard Wood to secure the adoption of universal military training, as well as his role in persuading the National Education Association to accept military training as a part of the public school program. A large share of the responsibility for successfully propagandizing the public, and for exerting pressure upon Congress for appropriations and increased defense measures, however, is attributed to the National Security League, the Navy League, the Army League, and the Military Training Camps Association.

CONSCRIPTION

ZIMMERMAN, JAMES F. *Impressment of American Seamen.* 1925. Ph.D. dissertation. Columbia University. New York. Index. 279 pages.

An account of British impressment, with a review of its legislative and displomatic history. Notes that the system of impressment was not only unpopular but inefficient, and that once Britain had established an adequate system for enlisting seamen the practice was never again seriously considered. Correspondingly, the loss of British seamen by desertion to U.S. vessels became less prevalent as British terms of service were liberalized. Zimmerman suggests that without the stimulus of American sentiment against British impressment, war with Britain might not have been declared.

Articles

ALEXANDER, J. ARTHUR. *How Maryland Tried to Raise Her Continental Quotas.* Maryland Historical Magazine. September 1947. Volume XLII, Number 3. Pages 184–196.

Discusses the various expedients that were adopted in Maryland during the Revolutionary War to fill the depleted ranks of the Continental army. Shows that "it was only after these expedients had been tried and found wanting that Maryland actually resorted to compulsory service."

ALEXANDER, J. ARTHUR. *Service by Substitute in the Militia of Northampton and Lancaster Counties (Pennsylvania) During the War of the Revolution.* Military Affairs. Fall 1945. Volume I, Number 3. Pages 278–282.

A study based on an examination of the counties' militia records for age, country of origin, occupation, and remuneration of the various substitutes. The author notes, among other things, a high incidence of "professional substitutes," those who substituted for more than one militiaman.

ALGER, JOHN. *The Objective Was a Volunteer Army.* United States Naval Institute Proceedings. February 1970. Volume 96, Number 2. Pages 62–68.

United States History

Critically reviews the consequences of the Doolittle Board's recommendations for liberalized regulations and procedures designed to make the armed forces more attractive to potential recruits. The implementation of the board's recommendations in 1947, it is alleged, resulted in a decline in performance and disciplinary standards that was underscored by the nation's entry into the Korean War.

AMBROSE, STEPHEN E. *Emory Upton and the Armies of Asia and Europe.* Military Affairs. Spring 1964. Volume XXVIII, Number 1. Pages 27–32.

Commentary on Emory Upton's *The Armies of Asia and Europe*, attempting to show that Upton was responsible for many changes in American military policy and that eventually most of Upton's proposals, including "universal conscription," were adopted.

BAKER, NEWTON D. *Newton D. Baker on Executive Influence in Military Legislation.* American Political Science Review. September 1956. Volume 50, Number 3. Pages 700–701.

Text of a letter from the former secretary of war to historian Howard White. In it Baker describes the developments that led President Wilson to ask Congress to enact draft legislation in 1917.

BILLINGS, ELDEN E. *The Civil War and Conscription.* Current History. June 1968. Volume 54, Number 322. Pages 333–338, 366.

Describes the respective methods used to conscript men by the Union and the Confederacy during the Civil War. The author notes that of the more than two and a half million men raised for service in the Union army, only about 6 percent were raised directly by the draft: "The Act clearly was more of a whip in the hands of the government to spur state activity than a source of manpower." In the South, "whether conscription was worth the trouble and effort it involved is doubtful. . . . Undoubtedly, it was a failure, except in that it propelled people into volunteering."

BLUM, ALBERT A. *Sailor or Worker: A Manpower Dilemma During the Second World War.* Labor History. Fall 1965. Volume 6, Number 3. Pages 232–243.

Describes how "the dream of a volunteer Navy during wartime" was ruled out as the navy "slowly, perhaps unwillingly, but nonetheless inexorably [became] involved in the workings of the Selective Service System."

BRIGGS, JOHN E. *The Enlistment of Iowa Troops During the Civil War.* The Iowa Journal of History and Politics. July 1917. Volume 15, Number 3. Pages 323–392.

Examines the military unpreparedness of Iowa at the outset of the Civil War, the formation of independent military companies, the calls for volunteers and the bounties offered as inducements, and the introduction and operation of the draft.

BROOKS, R. P. *Conscription in the Confederate States of America 1862–1865.* The Military Historian and Economist. October 1916. Volume 1, Number 4. Pages 419–443.

The author doubts whether conscription in the Confederate States, especially in regard to numbers conscripted, was "worth the exertion, internal dissension, and opposition it aroused." He considers that compulsory service was "a weakening force in that it brought conflicts with the states" and that 'the very lax laws of exemption provided an easy and more or less honorable avenue of evasion, thereby keeping out of the army thousands who might otherwise have been forced by public opinion to volunteer." The most important service that conscription rendered, in this view, was to keep in the armies the men of conscript age already there.

BURDETT, THOMAS F. *Mobilizations of 1911 and 1913: Their Role in the Development of the Modern Army.* Military Review. July 1974. Volume LIV, Number 7. Pages 65–74.

The author attributes in large measure the U.S. Army's transition from "an archaic assemblage of regiments" to a "modern, homogeneous force" to the tenure of Leonard Wood as Chief of Staff. Wood, in this view, "perceived that war in the future would involve the total capabilities of nations" and advocated "unremittingly the creation of a large, expansible cadre army with ample reserves." Thus the mobilizations of 1911 and 1913, with their "single-minded emphasis on combat-readiness and efficiency," are seen as "the forerunners of the austere mass armies that would fight the wars of the future."

CARLETON, WILLIAM G. *Raising Armies Before the Civil War.* Current History. June 1968. Volume 54, Number 322. Pages 327–332, 363–364.

Contends that despite "the weaknesses of a repeatedly improvised volunteer system," Americans clung to it because it expressed basic American conditions and values. It is noted in particular that the practice of recruiting wartime volunteers for short terms "played havoc with military operations."

CLARK, J. MURRAY. *Lincoln and Conscription.* Canadian Law Times. September 1917. Voulme 37, Number 9. Pages 737–739.

The author suggests that, based on the American experience in the Civil War, Canada should enforce conscription without delay. He further contends that conscription has "always been part of the fundamental law of Canada," and the voluntary system "a modern makeshift which has been tried and found wanting."

COMMITTEE ON CIVIL LIBERTIES. DISTRICT OF COLUMBIA CHAPTER. *Civil Liberties and Conscription.* Lawyers Guild Review. December 1940. Volume 1, Number 2. Pages 6–13.

An analysis of "problems and dangers to civil liberties and organized labor inherent in the Burke–Wadsworth and Smith Acts," as viewed against the background of the administration of similar legislation in World War I. The major problems and dangers concern deferments, job protection, and free speech.

COSMAS, GRAHAM A. *From Order to Chaos: The War Department, the National Guard, and Military Policy, 1898.* Military Affairs. Fall 1965. Volume XXIX, Number 3. Pages 105–122.

Discusses the "mismanagement and confusion" of the U.S. Army's mobilization for the Spanish–American War, and traces the political developments alleged to have created this situation.

COTTRELL, ALVIN J. *The Changing Roles of Land Armies in the 20th Century.* Current History. June 1968. Volume 54, Number 322. Pages 321–326, 367.

An evaluation of the changing manpower needs of American defense.

Discusses the decline in the use of large land armies as "the principal instrument of ultimate decision."

DAVIS, HENRY C. *The System of Military Conscription Proposed by George Washington and General Henry Knox.* Journal of the Military Service Institution. January–February 1916. Volume 58, Number 199. Pages 1–13.

Examines the proposals made by President George Washington and Secretary of War Henry Knox for a national system of defense. Quotes heavily from Volume 1 of the American State Papers on the question of the role of the militia.

DEWEERD, H. A. *The Federalization of Our Army.* Military Affairs. Fall 1942. Volume VI, Number 3. Pages 143–152.

Examines the process of federalization of U.S. military policy. Traces military manpower procurement policy through American history, showing its "slow evolutionary steps from the time when the main reliance was placed on the militias of the several states, through a process of using long-term volunteers to augment the small Regular Army, to a point where the nature of war no longer allowed the profitable employment of partially-trained state troops."

FISH, CARL RUSSELL. *Conscription in the Civil War.* American Historical Review. October 1915. Volume 21, Number 1. Pages 100–103.

Contends that the Union army under the draft law drew, on the whole, the same men who would have served without the high pay or bounties offered, and that the army did not lose its characteristic as a volunteer force: "The draft may have been a necessary lash to apply to volunteering, or it may not, but in any study of the fighting effectiveness of armies or the economic effectiveness of war-time industry, the North must be classed among the regions employing the voluntary rather than the compulsory system of selection for military service."

FISH, CARL RUSSELL. *The Raising of the Wisconsin Volunteers 1861.* The Military Historian and Economist. July 1916. Volume 1, Number 3. Pages 258–273.

Argues that the acknowledged superiority of the Wisconsin recruiting effort in the first year of the Civil War must be attributed, not to any special superiority of system, but to the fact that Governor Randall "knew how to use the best talent of the state for emergency service."

FLIEGEL, DORIAN J. *The Façade of Equity: Forgotten History of the Draft.* The Nation. April 10, 1967. Volume 204, Number 15. Pages 454–456.

Reviews the shifts in recent years in civilian, government, and military attitudes toward military manpower procurement policy. Contends that "the one major alternative to the current procurement system, which could have recaptured democratic control of the new politico–military policy, would have been the establishment of a professional army. A highly trained and technically skilled professional army restricted in size and budget would place obvious limitations on the ability of the Executive and the Military to involve this country in wars of intervention and occupation without Congressional and popular approval."

FRENCH, ALLEN. *The Arms and Military Training of Our Colonizing Ancestors.* Massachusetts Historical Society Proceedings. November 1941. Volume 67. Pages 3–21.

Discusses the precolonial military obligations and training of those who migrated to Massachusetts in the 1629–1642 period.

HERSHEY, LEWIS B. *Procurement of Manpower in American Wars.* The Annals of the American Academy of Political and Social Science. September 1945. Volume 241. Pages 15–25.

Holds that conscription in World War I was "the first conscription ever to meet the general approval of the American people." The Selective Training and Service Act of 1940, in the author's view, further improved the operation of the Selective Service System by adding the obligation of the government to protect the citizen's interests "during the period he is bearing arms and to make provisions which will enable him to return to the civilian job he left to fulfill his obligation, without suffering any penalty in regard to rank, seniority, prestige, or pay."

HIGGINSON, THOMAS W. *Regular and Volunteer Officers.* The Atlantic Monthly. September 1864. Volume XIV, Number 83. Pages 348–357.

Discusses the relationships between the regular and volunteer officers and their respective attitudes toward the requirements and demands of military service.

HUZAR, ELIAS. *Prewar Conscription.* Southwestern Social Science Quarterly. September 1942. Volume 23, Number 2. Pages 112–119.

A review of public and legislative reactions in the United States to military recommendations for conscription during World War II.

KIMMONS, NEIL C. *Federal Draft Exemptions 1863–1865.* Military Affairs. Spring 1951. Volume XV, Number 1. Pages 25–33.

Documents legislative actions concerning exemption from military conscription during the Civil War, noting the efforts of the Union government to "convince the public at once of the justice and wisdom of conscription."

KNOX, HENRY. *A Plan for the General Arrangement of the Militia of the United States.* Proceedings of the Massachusetts Historical Society 1862–1863. 1863. Volume 6. Pages 364–403.

This paper presents a brief history of the origins and characteristics of the colonial militia, followed by a proposal for a national militia in order to "place the national defense on a firm foundation." The author seeks the most efficient system compatible with the interests of a free society, drawing a distinction between national service and a standing army. The plan includes proposals for terms of service, classes and numbers of soldiers, and ranking within military units.

KOHN, RICHARD H. *The Coup d'Etat That Failed.* Society. May–June 1975. Volume 12, Number 4. Pages 30–36.

Examines the conspiracy of 1783 in which officers of the Continental army's Newburgh cantonment petitioned to Congress for redress of their pay and other grievances. "Officers and men had not received their salaries in months. More important, the officers were concerned about receiving the half-pay pensions promised by Congress in 1780. To the officers, half-pay was 'an honorable and just recompense for several years [of] hard service' during which their 'health and fortunes' had been 'worn down and exhausted.' But they feared, and with good reason, that its general unpopularity might induce Congress to repudiate the promise."

LONDON, LENA. *The Militia Fine 1830–1860*. Military Affairs. Fall 1951. Volume XV, Number 3. Pages 133–144.

Deals with the question of imprisonment for failure to pay the "militia fine" imposed upon American males during the pre-Civil War period for absence from a militia muster or for appearing without the specified arms and equipment. Shows that the compulsory military system with its militia fine was closely allied in the minds of the people with "the evil of imprisonment for debt."

MAHON, JOHN K. *A Board of Officers Considers the Condition of the Militia in 1826*. Military Affairs. Summer 1951. Volume XV, Number 2. Pages 85–94.

Discusses the work of an eight-man board of military officers appointed by Secretary of War James Barbour in 1826 to examine the condition of the U.S. Militia. Considers the effect of volunteering on the standing militia, as well as public attitudes toward the different methods of recruiting.

MEAD, SPENCER P. *The First American Soldiers*. The Journal of American History. 1907. Volume 1. Pages 120–128.

Describes the military organizations formed by the early colonial settlers in America. From these "trained bands" were recruited the soldiers that the colonies were called upon to furnish from time to time in the various wars in which the home government was engaged.

PAONE, ROCCO M. *The Last Volunteer Army 1946–48*. Military Review. December 1969. Volume XLIX, Number 12. Pages 9–17.

Examines the War Department's efforts to create an all-volunteer army during 1946–1948. Notes the army's failure, despite "a valiant and expensive" recruiting campaign, to secure an adequate supply of volunteers. By April 1948, "there was little else to do except to alert the Secretary of the Army that the effort to enlist an all-volunteer Regular Army had failed, and that, in view of the aggressive nature of Soviet policy in Europe, Selective Service was necessary." This failure is attributed by the author to the "mood of the Nation": the people "desired a return to normal peacetime living at the same time that U.S. security policy was involved in a turbulent international struggle to restore and maintain economic and political stability."

RADABAUGH, JACK S. *The Militia of Colonial Massachusetts*. Military Affairs. Spring 1954. Volume XVIII, Number 1. Pages 1–18.

Describes the recruitment, pay, and conditions of militia service in colonial Massachusetts in the 17th century. Notes the problem of procuring men and supplies and paying for them: "The volunteer method, at one time or another, was tried in Massachusetts, but was a failure financially, and from a disciplinary point of view. The General Court then turned to the draft as a means of obtaining militia personnel." The author discusses exemptions under the draft system, including the practice of substitution and other "special contributions," such as personal ownership of firearms, that "tended to reduce a man's liability for service."

RAPPAPORT, ARMIN. *The Replacement System During the Civil War*. Military Affairs. Summer 1951. Volume XV, Number 2. Pages 95–106.

Deals with the question of how the Union armies, when depleted by deaths, injuries, sickness, desertions, and expired enlistments, were maintained at effective strengtth. Examines the relative positions of state and federal authorities, as well as the political exigencies that were taken into consideration in recruiting men for the war.

RICKEY, DON, JR. *The Enlisted Men of the Indian Wars*. Military Affairs. Summer 1959. Volume XXIII, Number 2. Pages 91–96.

Describes the recruitment of men in the U.S. Army from 1875 to 1890, with information on pay and conditions in the service. Notes the "temptation to desert and earn high wages in the labor-hungry frontier economy."

SANDBURG, CARL. *Lincoln and Conscription*. Illinois State Historical Society Journal. March 1939. Volume 32, Number 1. Pages 5–19.

Examines the political evolution of the 1864 draft law, noting Abraham Lincoln's difficulty in reaching a settlement with Congress on such questions as compensation and terms of service.

SMITH, JONATHAN. *How Massachusetts Raised Her Troops in the*

Revolution. Massachusetts Historical Society Proceedings. June 1922. Volume 55. Pages 345–370.

A critical examination of the militia and volunteer systems of recruitment in the Revolutionary War. The author maintains that the superiority of conscription as "the most equitable and most democratic method to fill the armies of a republic" in time of war was demonstrated by the U.S. conscription in World War I.

SMITH, PAUL TINCHER. *Militia of the United States from 1846 to 1860.* Indiana Magazine of History. March 1919. Volume 15. Pages 20–47.

Describes the administration of the militia in individual states. The legal basis for militia service during the period 1846 to 1860 was the Militia Act of 1792, whose purpose was to establish a uniform militia throughout the United States.

TRYON, WARREN S. *The Draft in World War I.* Current History. June 1968. Volume 54, Number 322. Pages 339–344, 367– 368.

Contends that the feeling of patriotism ran so high in the United States during World War I that a "holiday spirit was evident" notwithstanding the "iron hand of coercion" that stood behind the "joyous pilgrimage" to military service.

WEINERT, RICHARD P. *The Confederate Regular Army.* Military Affairs. Fall 1962. Volume XXVI, Number 3. Pages 97–108.

Describes recruiting practices and problems in the Confederate Regular Army during the Civil War. Three factors are identified as having hampered recruiting as compared with ordinary volunteer units: (1) enlistment in the Regulars was for the duration of the war, no matter how long it lasted, whereas volunteers served for specific terms; (2) the Confederates did not offer bounties for enlistment in the Regulars, whereas this was increasingly the practice with volunteer units; and (3) discipline and training were more demanding in the Regular Army than in the volunteer units.

WHITRIDGE, ARNOLD. *Washington's French Volunteers.* History Today. September 1974. Volume XXIV, Number 9. Pages 593–603.

Discusses the motivations and ideologies of key Frenchmen who fought for General Washington: Lafayettte, Charles François Braglie, and Baron de Kalb. The article is set in the context of the French government's desire to undermine British military power through aid to the colonies.

WILLIAMS, WESLEY R. *Call to Arms: Notes from the Pages of Army Recruiting History.* Army Digest. July 1970. Volume XXV, Number 7. Pages 41–44.

Briefly traces the history of army recruiting in the United States, from General Washington's efforts during the American Revolution to the work of the U.S. Army Recruiting Command, which in five and a half years was able to bring more than one million volunteers into army ranks. Trends in recruiting problems, citizen attitudes, and overall conditions are contrasted in each of the following periods: the time of John C. Calhoun, secretary of war from 1817 to 1825; the Mexican War; the Civil War; and the turn of the century.

YLVISAKER, HEDVIG. *Public Opinion Toward Compulsory Peacetime Military Training.* The Annals of the American Academy of Political and Social Science. September 1945. Volume 241. Pages 86–94.

A review of contemporary public opinion polls. Asserts that at the time that Congress began to discuss the measure, "the American people apparently commended the principle of compulsory peacetime military training with as much vigor as the educators condemned it. Somewhat less enthusiastic than their elders, but tending to agree with them rather than with their teachers, stood the group most immediately concerned—American youth."

Pamphlets, Reprints, and Speeches

BOND, P. S. *Our Military Policy.* 3rd edition. 1928. Society of American Military Engineers. Washington, D.C. Reprint from the July–August and September–October 1922 issues of The Military Engineer. 63 pages.

A study presenting the main features of U.S. military policy from 1774 to 1922. This policy, from the earliest colonial days to the nation's entry into World War I, is said to have been characterized by: (1) entrance into every war without an army with which to fight it; (2) development of an army during the course of the war; and (3) complete disbandment of the war army immediately after the close of hostilities. While the National Defense Act of 1916 and the amendments to it in 1920 sought to correct these shortcomings in military policy, the War Department had been constrained by the refusal of Congress to provide sufficient funds to carry out the letter of these acts. The author maintains that ultimately only a policy of universal military training in peacetime would "insure an adequate defense and render us largely immune from the threat of war, and quite immune from the danger of defeat."

HESSELTINE, WILLIAM B. *Conscripting History.* Circa 1945. Post War World Council. New York. 3 pages.

This leaflet counters the argument that there is a historical basis for conscription. It cites positions taken by the Framers of the Constitution and later leaders, all of whom are said to have been opposed to conscription, a large standing army, and peacetime military training.

Government Documents: Publications

BAUER, WILLIAM E., and JOHN P. JUDGE, JR. (compilers). *Baltimore and the Draft: An Historical Record.* 1919. Draft Board, Maryland 1st District. Illustrations. 256 pages.

A photographic and statistical history of the operation of the Selective Service Law in the City of Baltimore in World War I. Includes a compilation of state and national statistics, official documents, and presidential proclamations relating to the enforcement of the Selective Service Law throughout the United States.

U.S. DEPARTMENT OF THE ARMY. *American Military History.* By Maurice Matloff (general editor). 1969. Department of the Army. Washington, D.C. Index. Illustrations. 701 pages.

This book is part of the Army Historical Series prepared by the Office of the Chief of Military History and is intended to be used primarily as a text in the Reserve Officers' Training Corps. It includes a discussion of military manpower procurement policy in the United States from pre-colonial times to the present.

U.S. DEPARTMENT OF THE ARMY. *History of Military Mobilization in the United States Army 1775–1945*. By Marvin A. Kreidberg and Merton G. Henry. 1955. Department of the Army. Washington, D.C. Charts, tables. Bibliography: pages 698–705. 721 pages.

A comprehensive account of the manpower aspects of military mobilizations in the United States from the Revolutionary War to World War II. It concludes that, despite the lessons of the various wars in which the United States has been engaged, we have "never adequately and fully planned for a mobilization before it occurred" because of the "reluctance of the nation's leaders· to confide in Congress and the people in time to permit certain defense measures to be taken." The authors contend that there is historical support for the adoption of war mobilization plans, including a system of selective service and prohibition of voluntary enlistments, as well as the planned utilization of women, limited service personnel, indigenous personnel and prisoners of war, and, if necessary, children.

U.S. DEPARTMENT OF THE ARMY. *The Personnel Replacement System in the United States Army*. By Leonard L. Lerwill. 1954. Department of the Army. Washington, D.C. Bibliography: pages 480–485. 492 pages.

An extensive review of the military recruitment policy of the U.S. Army and its results during various periods of American military history. The chapters on the earlier periods show the foundation for the recruitment system laid during the Revolution, the War of 1812, the Mexican conflict, and the Civil War.

U.S. MILITARY ACADEMY. *Military Policy of the United States 1775–1944*. 1944. U.S. Military Academy. West Point, New York. 51 pages.

A brief history of U.S. military policy, with the conclusion that enactment of the War Department's proposed legislation for inauguration of the first peacetime universal compulsory military service system would constitute "the one dependable assurance that peace will be preserved."

UPTON, EMORY. *The Military Policy of the United States*. 1912. Government Printing Office. Washington, D.C. Maps, tables. 495 pages.

Preface by Elihu Root. Upton's death in 1881 left the manuscript for this work nearly completed; it was published for the first time by the War Department in 1904. It discusses the policies followed in each war from 1775 through the Civil War, including those of the Confederate States. Recommending reorganization of most aspects of U.S. military policy, Upton maintains that the nation's wars have been prolonged for want of judicious and economic preparation. He attributes this unpreparedness to opposition to a standing army, to the persistent use of raw troops, to the want of an expansive organization, to short and voluntary enlistments carrying with them large bounties, and to reliance upon the states to provide troops in time of war. It is noted that many of the measures recommended by Upton subsequently were implemented.

CHAPTER 2

General History

History can be well written only in a free country.
—Voltaire, *Letter to Frederick the Great*, 1737

Books

ADCOCK, FRANK E. *The Greek and Macedonian Art of War.* 1957. University of California Press. Berkeley, California. Index. 109 pages.

Of particular interest are Chapter 1, "The City-State at War," and Chapter 2, "The Development of Infantry." Adcock describes the hoplite army of the city-states, "the army of the upper and middle classes," and the increasing use of mercenaries who, unlike citizen troops, could be continuously employed. Mercenaries are said to have lacked the local patriotism of the citizen troops, but were "loyal to their paymasters and had no republican principles which could make a tyrant distrust them." And, while the lives of citizens were valued by their cities, mercenaries were "expendable."

ADCOCK, FRANK E. *The Roman Art of War Under the Republic.* 1940. Martin Classical Lectures, Volume 8. Harvard University Press. Cambridge, Massachusetts. Index. Bibliographical notes: pages 127–131. 140 pages.

Describes the social composition of the Roman armies, recruiting practices, terms of enlistments, and conditions of service. Notes that Roman armies were comparatively small, and that "the usual Roman practice was to concentrate on quality and avoid the friction that is produced by the movement of unwieldy forces."

AMERICAN FRIENDS SERVICE COMMITTEE. *Sourcebook on Conscience and Conscription and Disarmament.* 1943. Pendle Hill, Pennsylvania. 164 pages.

A collection of materials for the Seminar on Conscription, Coercion and Disarmament. This debater's handbook includes summaries of the historical development of conscription in a number of countries, as well as diverse views abstracted from books, journals, public records, and speeches.

ANDERSON, J. K. *Military Theory and Practice in the Age of Xenophon.* 1970. University of California Press. Berkeley, California. Index. Illustrations. Select bibliography: pages 339–343. 419 pages.

Describes conditions in the ancient Greek armies and the influence of political events on military developments. The introduction notes the wide opposition of ancient Greeks to a tax-supported standing army, notwithstanding the willingness on the part of richer citizens to serve with person and fortune. The appendix includes a description of the organization of the Spartan army in the classical period.

ANDRESKI, STANISLAV. *Military Organization and Society.* Revised edition. 1968. University of California Press. Berkeley, California. Index. Bibliography: pages 225–231. 238 pages.

Foreword by A. R. Radcliffe-Brown. In this sociological study of military organization through the ages, the author examines demographic and cultural variables as determinants of the types of military institutions in various countries.

BEAUMONT, ROGER. *Military Elites.* 1974. Bobbs-Merrill Co., Inc. New York. Index. Illustrations. Bibliography: pages 209–240. 251 pages.

A study of units of military elites formed in the 20th century. The author examines forces in their formation, and uses cases to illustrate the problems that corps d'élites pose for military and civilian policymakers, analysts, and citizens. Three questions are asked: (1) Why did these units thrive in the face of collectivization? (2) How did they reflect or contradict the values of their parent systems? and (3) How much did corps d'élites match their creators' hopes and justify immunity from orthodox control? The author concludes that the symbol of elite forces has been used for positive results in spite of potentially dangerous and unpredictable side effects, that the proliferation of corps d'élites in the 20th century is a symptom of stress in social institutions, and that the prospect for the future of elites is good.

BROWN, ALVIN. *The Armor of Organization: A Rational Plan of Organization for the Armed Forces and, as a Preliminary Thereto, an Inquiry into the Origins of Existing Military Organization.* 1953. Hibgert Printing Co. New York. Index. 597 pages.

A historical review and critique of military organization, tracing its evolution in the United States and its origins in Europe. Includes a proposal for a new, "rational" alternative. Brown discusses the procurement of military personnel during both peacetime and wartime.

BURGH, JAMES. *Political Disquisitions.* Volume III. 1971. Da Capo Press. New York. Index. 500 pages.

The "Disquisitions," written by a radical Whig and originally published in England (1774–1775), were widely read by Revolutionary leaders in America and helped to reinforce their conviction that the English government was corrupt and that all ties with England must be severed. The conclusion of Volume III touches on issues of the militia throughout the text in the context of other affairs of state. Specific topics indexed include: a militia as a replacement for a standing army, Fletcher's plan for a militia, the militia in Holland and Portugal, the militia under the command of the crown, and the militia against insurrections and invasions.

CAIRNES, JOHN ELLIOT. *Essays in Political Economy, Theoretical and Applied.* 1873. Macmillan & Co. London. 371 pages.

Of special interest is the chapter "Our Defenses: A National or a Standing Army?" (pages 199–255). Cairnes reviews the three leading types of military organization—standing, national, and conscripted armies—as exemplified by England, Prussia, and France, respectively. In order to attract a sufficient supply of men to the ranks, the standing army must constantly "raise its bid, not merely to keep pace with the progress of the labor market, but to compensate for the unpopularity of the service," while "the recruits thus attracted come more and more from the lowest and least reputable classes of the community." Under the Prussian system, in contrast, the state obtains recruits "on its own terms," drawing, "with strict impartiality, from all classes of the community." The French system, calling men to service through conscription by lot, accords to those who have the means the privilege of purchasing exemption from service, "throwing the burden of service exclusively on the poorer classes of the population." Thus the points in which the French system differs from the Prussian are the same as those in which the British differs from the Prussian, the British system "exaggerating in every instance those features of organization which were peculiar to the French," and to which "the collapse of that system has been mainly due." Cairnes concludes, therefore, that the British military system should be reorganized along Prussian lines, whereby each man would "know his place and fall into line with the certainty of disciplined habit."

ELLACOTT, S. E. *Conscripts on the March: The Story of the Soldier from Napoleon to the Nuclear Age.* 1965. Abelard-Schuman. New York. Index. Illustrations. 160 pages.

A descriptive history dealing with conditions of service under various voluntary and compulsory systems. The author notes that the most significant change during the past 200 years is that "the professional, volunteer soldier of the standing army has ceased to hold pride of place in wartime. He has been superseded as the basis of his nation's armed strength by the conscripted citizen soldier, serving, at some periods and in some countries, for many years even in peacetime."

FOOT, M. R. D. *Men in Uniform: Military Manpower in Modern Industrial Societies.* 1961. Frederick A. Praeger. New York. Tables. 163 pages.

A comparative analysis of the ways in which different countries raise and maintain military manpower, written as a guide to and basis for public debate. The military recruitment systems of 13 major Western countries, as well as one theoretical system, are discussed in sections on conscription, citizen arms, and mixed and voluntary systems. The author concludes that for industrially advanced societies, mixed systems—a substantial element of volunteer, career personnel, combined with either universal basic military training or selective service conscription—would appear to be the most efficacious. The appendix includes a chart of comparative strengths and systems in 31 countries.

FREYTAG-LORINGHOVEN, BARON VON. *A Nation Trained in Arms or a Militia? Lessons in War from the Past and the Present.* 1918. Constable & Co. London. 171 pages.

Introduction by C. E. Callwell. The author contends that a short-term, decentralized militia possesses neither the requisite firmness nor the flexibility to meet national emergencies, and, in any event, cannot dispense with the services of trained professional officers. He gives an account of the German military machine of World War I, attributing German successes to training, organization, and morale. Three chapters are devoted to an analysis of the development of Prussia's military forces from the French Revolution to 1859, the difficulties in obtaining funding for the army, and the public's aversion to the principle of standing armies or any system requiring a considerable proportion of the country's young men to serve more than a few months. The author opposes the concept of a hired professional army—whose "dark side" is said to be evident from a study of French history between 1815 and 1870—in favor of universal military service and the "high moral value which attaches to the personal fulfilment of the military obligation."

FULLER, J. F. C. *The Conduct of War 1789–1961: A Study of the Impact of the French, Industrial, and Russian Revolutions on War and Its Conduct.* 1961. Rutgers University Press. New Brunswick, New Jersey. Index. 352 pages.

Reviews various forms of war, from the limited wars of the absolute kings to the unlimited and cold wars of more recent times. In each case, policies governing the composition of armies are discussed, as well as the writings and intellectual legacies of men who influenced those policies and the lessons to be drawn from the conduct of war to date.

FULLER, J. F. C. *The Reformation of War.* 1923. Hutchinson & Co. London. 287 pages.

In Chapter 12, "The Reformation of the Army," Fuller argues that World War I "proved" the defects of large conscript armies, indicating that mobility, carrying with it enhanced offensive and defensive power, and not numbers, is the line of economic direction along which any remodeling of the army should proceed. He proposes, however, a national registration of the entire civilian population, with all registrants going on war pay at the outbreak of hostilities.

GRANT, MICHAEL. *The Army of the Caesars.* 1974. Charles Scribner's Sons. New York. Index. Illustrations, maps, tables. Bibliography: pages 337–341. 365 pages.

Noting the significance of the Roman Imperial Army as the world's first standing army in which soldiers were regularly recruited, cared for, and pensioned by the state, the author looks at the history of the army and its impact on Rome's contributions to civilization. The book's main theme is the army's influence on internal affairs of the empire and the role it played in the policies and political decisions of successive emperors. The army's place as conqueror of and peace-keeper within the borders of the Roman Empire is also examined. The author concludes that, while the army was the cohesive force within the empire, it also presented a constant threat of overthrow to each of the emperors it served, and that this dual nature is characteristic of strong military organizations throughout the world today.

HASWELL, JOCK. *Citizen Armies.* 1973. Peter Davies. London. Index. Illustrations, maps. Bibliography: pages 247–248. 255 pages.

A citizen army is defined here as a force that (1) results from a supreme national crisis such as defense of territorial boundaries, (2) has the support of local recognized government, (3) has been developed into a properly constituted field force, and (4) consists largely of soldiers and officers who are volunteers and whose life and interests are not normally associated with soldiering. The author discusses various examples of citizen armies through history in different parts of the world, contrasting their characteristics and historical environments. He concludes that few citizen armies have fought for political power; rather, their rallying point has been freedom. And while few have achieved their aims, they have had a definite impact on history through their alteration of social and political institutions.

HEWITT, H. J. *The Organization of War Under Edward III, 1338–62.* 1966. Barnes & Noble. New York. Index. Illustrations, plates, maps. Sources and bibliography: pages 187–192. 206 pages.

Chapter 2, "Men Going to the War," describes recruiting procedures of the period, noting the practice of granting charters of pardon to criminals for military service, the incentives offered for voluntary enlistment, and the prevailing wages.

LEIGH, RANDOLPH. *Conscript Europe.* 1938. G. P. Putnam's Sons. New York. Index. 308 pages.

The author contends that the European concept of conscription is "utterly alien" to the "American ideal." In this view, "Europe itself is conscript" and "in practically every European nation the conscription, material, spiritual and personal, is based not on a desire to maintain the present boundaries and liberties of the State, but on a plan to enable it to keep its illegal and violent dominion over distant races, or to take that power of domination away from some more fortunate rival." Leigh attempts to build a case to show that "Europe's rampant and impoverished nationalism" has been "reduced to absurdity by the infinite regress of the idea of self-determinism."

MOCKLER, ANTHONY. *The Mercenaries.* 1970. Macmillan Co. New York. Index. Illustrations, maps, table. 303 pages.

A history of the mercenary soldier in various countries, culminating with the modern example of the mercenary in the Congo. Discusses the strengths and weaknesses of the mercenaries, mercenary life, and the future of such soldiering. The appendix contains a contemporary contract for service as a mercenary in the Congo, and a 1776 treaty in which the British monarch contracts to receive mercenary troops from the Landgrave of Hesse-Cassel.

NEF, JOHN U. *War and Human Progress: An Essay on the Rise of Industrial Civilization.* 1950. Harvard University Press. Cambridge, Massachusetts. Index. Bibliographic notes: pages 419–449. 464 pages.

In Chapter 16, "The Enlightenment and the Progress of War," the author discusses French and Prussian influences in 18th century warfare. He notes, in particular, the harshness of early conscription systems; while the Prussians sought to conscript "the choicest men," the French believed that "the army should represent the dregs rather than the cream of the national man power."

NICOLAI, G. F. *The Biology of War.* 1918. Century Co. New York. 553 pages.

Translated by Constance A. Grande and Julian Grande. Chapter 6, "How the Army Has Been Transformed," discusses national and professional armies, the defensive militia versus the aggressive army, the Prussian militia, and militarism in the 19th century. The author asserts that the distinctions between compulsory and voluntary armies, between professional and national armies, and between standing armies and militias have faded. "Universal *liability to serve*," he states, "is merely a great historical misconception of the universal *duty of bearing arms*."

NORMAN, A. V. B. *The Medieval Soldier*. 1971. Thomas Y. Crowell Co. New York. Index. Illustrations. Bibliography: pages 159–163. 278 pages.

Discusses the military system of most of Western Europe during the 12th and 13th centuries. The first section of the book describes the elements from which feudalism and chivalry evolved, namely the organization, ideals, and technology of Teutonic tribes. The second section deals with the organization, arming, training, equipment, and ideals of the knight and of the troops who supported him in action during the period before the decline of feudalism.

POOLE, AUSTIN L. *Obligations of Society in the XII and XIII Centuries*. 1946. Clarendon Press. Oxford, England. Index. 115 pages.

In this study society is divided into three categories: (1) peasants, (2) knights, and (3) sargeants. The military and other obligations of each category are examined, as well as the various ways by which these obligations could be fulfilled.

PRESTON, RICHARD A., and others. *Men in Arms: A History of Warfare and Its Interrelationships with Western Society*. 1956. Frederick A. Praeger. New York. Index. Illustrations, maps. Bibliography: pages 341–357. 376 pages.

A study of the role that warfare has played in the history of Western society. Examines the rise of the feudal array, the development of modern armies, the nation in arms, and manpower policies of 20th century warfare.

SPAULDING, OLIVER LYMAN, and others. *Warfare: A Study of Military Methods from the Earliest Times*. 1937. The Infantry Journal, Inc. Washington, D.C. Index. Plates. Bibliography: pages 573–587. 601 pages.

Preface by General Tasker H. Bliss. An examination of warfare from the early Oriental monarchies to the 18th century armies of Marlborough and Frederick. While the main emphasis of this book is on tactics and strategy in warfare, information is provided throughout relating recruitment policies and practices to the shifting methods of war.

TURNER, GORDON B. *A History of Military Affairs in Western Society Since the Eighteenth Century.* 2 volumes. 1952. Advisory Committee of the Princeton University Military History Project. Princeton, New Jersey. Volume 1: 348 pages. Volume 2: 345 pages.

Political and administrative problems incidental to the raising and maintenance of large military establishments in democratic society are discussed in this survey, and comparisons are drawn between European and American policies and practices. Volume 1 covers the period to 1914. Volume 2 reviews reforms in the British and American military systems in the early 20th century, with reprints of Elihu Root's reports and addresses and an article on Haldane's reorganization of the British army.

VAGTS, ALFRED. *A History of Militarism, Civilian and Military.* 1959. Meridian Books, Inc. Elnora, New York. Index. Illustrations. Bibliography: pages 525–531. 542 pages.

Defines militarism as "rejecting the scientific character of the military way and displaying the qualities of caste and cult, authority and belief" and "presenting a vast array of customs, interests, prestige, actions and thought associated with armies and wars yet transcending true military purposes." Vagts traces the history of militarism in Western civilization, discussing the transition from the feudal warrior to the mass army, the development of militarization of mass armies, the military and politics, and post-1918 militarization of society.

VIETH VON GOLSSENAU, ARNOLD FRIEDRICH [Ludwig Renn, pseudonym]. *Warfare: The Relation of War to Society.* 1939. Faber & Faber. London. Index. 278 pages.

Translated by Edward Fitzgerald. Part 1 contains a comparative discussion of traditional forms of recruiting in various countries and at various times. It is suggested that British troops who fought in the Crimean War were "unfree" because, although they were not formally slaves, "they were men who had engaged themselves as mercenaries for a

settled term to go anywhere and do anything . . . a very great abandonment of personal liberty." In this view, "military service at any time, and
still more so in time of war, so limits the freedom of the individual that it
is often difficult to draw the line between freedom and slavery."

WATSON, G. R. *The Roman Soldier.* 1969. Cornell University Press.
Ithaca, New York. Index. Illustrations. 256 pages.

A descriptive study of the recruitment and conditions of service of the
Roman soldier. Life in the Roman army is described from the point of
view of the soldier, in which the main emphasis is laid on the ranks below
the centurionate, the ranks in which the majority of the men would continue to serve for the whole of their careers. The study seeks to reconstruct
the life and training of the Roman soldier from enlistment to discharge,
and focuses upon issues that were "of profound concern to the individual
soldier," such as prospects of promotion, the adequacy of pay, the nature
and frequency of rewards and punishments, the problems of religion and
marriage, and, particularly toward the end of his service, the question of
discharge and resettlement.

Unpublished Manuscripts

FORAND, PAUL GLIDDEN. *The Development of Military Slavery Under
the Abbasid Caliphs of the Ninth Century A.D. (Third Century A.H.),
with Special Reference to the Reigns of Mu'tasim and Mu'tadid.* 1962.
Ph.D. dissertation. Princeton University. Princeton, New Jersey. 146
pages.

Examines the operation of the institution of military slavery at the time
of its introduction into the Abbasid system of government, and sketches
its development through the period when the caliphate was centered in
Samarra. Reviews the history of two slave militias, the Buxâriyyah and
the Shâkiriyyah, which existed in pre-Abbasid, Islamic times, being primitive forms of the later caliphal slave army. The beginning of this army
under the Abbasids is discussed with particular emphasis upon the methods of recruitment of the Turkish slaves who were used almost exclusively,
although the simultaneous recruitment of nonservile Transoxianian elements for military purposes is investigated. Forand also considers the
relative positions of slaves and freedmen in the military establishment.

Articles

BEELER, JOHN. *The Composition of Anglo-Norman Armies.* Speculum. July 1965. Volume 40, Number 3. Pages 398–414.

Finds that, contrary to the long-held theory of the "knightly monopoly of military service," the military forces put into the field by the Anglo-Norman kings were recruited from a variety of sources, including not only feudal units but also mercenary contingents from time to time.

BLUM, ALBERT A. *Comparative Recruiting Systems.* Military Review. March 1971. Volume LI, Number 3. Pages 10–29.

Examines the experience of Great Britain, Canada, Australia, Germany, France, and the Soviet Union in regard to military recruitment.

BOHIGAS, NURIA SALES DE. *Some Opinion on Exemption from Military Service in Nineteenth-Century Europe.* Comparative Studies in Society and History. April 1968. Volume 10, Number 3. Pages 261–289.

A comparative review of the practices of substitution, purchase, and commutation in a number of European states. Examines the mid-century controversy over commutation in the press and in European parliaments, and the developments that led to the eventual abolition of commutation.

COULTON, G. G. *Continental Democracies and Compulsory Military Service.* Fortnightly Review. July 1916. Volume 106. Pages 55–65.

Contends that "universal service is one natural and inevitable direction of true democratic development," claiming that "in past history a compulsory military system has nearly always been the note of a democracy, while despots have generally preferred a voluntary or semi-voluntary system." Citing the cases of the French Revolutionary Government in 1793 and Abraham Lincoln's Civil War draft bill, Coulton suggests that "where such a national compulsory system has been seriously resisted in its execution, the main resistance has come from [elements in the community] with whom the majority of our working classes could have no real sympathy."

GWYNN, STEPHEN. *Conscription: Servitude or Service.* Fortnightly Review. December 1936. Volume 140. Pages 740–741.

Compares British and French attitudes toward military conscription, urging that the question be "lifted out of party politics" and treated as "a national necessity," as is said to be the case in France.

HACKETT, JOHN WINTHROP. *The Profession of Arms* (two parts). Military Review. (1) October 1963. Volume XLIII, Number 10. Pages 34–44. (2) November 1963. Volume XLIII, Number 11. Pages 50–59.

Examines the practice of the bearing of arms in world history, including the feudal array, mercenaries, militia, and conscript, standing, and national armies. Finds that (1) universal national service inhibits professionalism; (2) conscription produces good soldier material, but only for a short time; and (3) conscription reduces volunteer potential in the general community.

MEARS, JOHN A. *The Emergence of the Standing Professional Army in Seventeenth-Century Europe.* Social Science Quarterly. June 1969. Volume 50, Number 1. Pages 106–115.

The examples of France, England, and Brandenburg-Prussia are drawn on to demonstrate that the military and political developments associated with the emergence of the standing army varied from state to state. "The tradition of standing armies went back to the late Middle Ages, but they did not appear on a wide scale prior to the Thirty Years' War because until that time neither the political nor the economic structure of Europe could support extensive military establishments. By 1650 the larger states possessed sufficient wealth and manpower to create standing armies and the capacity to mobilize their resources on a scale adequate to meet the needs of the new military system."

MILLAR, GILBERT. *The Landsknecht: His Recruitment and Organization, with Some Reference to the Reign of Henry VIII.* Military Affairs. October 1971. Volume XXXV, Number 3. Pages 95–99.

Examines the origins of the German *landsknechte mercenaries* and their role during the time of Henry VIII.

MURPHY, ORVILLE T. *The American Revolutionary Army and the Concept of Levee en Masse.* Military Affairs. Spring 1959. Volume XXIII, Number 1. Pages 13–20.

Finds a striking similarity "between the French popular image of the American colonists arming themselves against England and the later French idea of the levee en masse." Contends that "while the parallel does not indicate that the French concept came from America, it does mean that this idea of a nation in arms to preserve its liberties had already become an integral part of the paraphernalia of late eighteenth century thought. It represented the corollary of force, or the military consequence, of ideals which characterized this period of intellectual history. The American Revolutionary Army appeared to give substance to a set of abstractions already prevalent."

Pamphlets, Reprints, and Speeches

TANSILL, CHARLES C. *Militarism.* 1935. Digest Press, American University. Washington, D.C. Tables. 31 pages.

A compilation of views on the development of standing armies in Europe, the beginnings of the conscription system and the evolution of universal military service, preparedness, militarism, armaments, and war profits. The author suggests that "one of the most significant arguments in favor of universal military training is that such a system definitely promotes social efficiency."

CHAPTER 3

General Works

The introduction of compulsory military service is, to my
mind, the prime cause for the moral decay of the white race
and seriously threatens not merely the survival of our civilization but our very existence. This curse originated, together
with great social blessings, with the French Revolution and
soon swept over all other nations.
> —Albert Einstein, 1931

Books

ABSHIRE, DAVID M., and RICHARD V. ALLEN (editors). *National Security:
Political, Military, and Economic Strategies in the Decade Ahead.*
1963. Frederick A. Praeger, Publisher. New York. Index. 1039 pages.

Published for the Hoover Institution on War, Revolution and Peace.
Introduction by Admiral Arleigh Burke. This is a compilation of papers
presented at the conference "National Security: The Demands of Strategy
and Economics in the Decade Ahead," held in Washington, D.C., in
January 1963. Of particular interest is Murray L. Weidenbaum's "Costs
of Alternative Military Strategies" (pages 785–802), which examines
three alternative military environments for the 1962–1972 period: (1) the
current approximate level of military preparedness resulting from continued tensions, (2) continued tensions punctuated by a limited war, and
(3) step-by-step disarmament. Weidenbaum indicates the general range
of costs these environments are likely to require. The volume also includes
papers by Henry A. Kissinger, Edward Teller, James R. Schlesinger, and
W. Glenn Campbell.

AMBROSE, STEPHEN E., and JAMES A. BARBER, JR. (editors). *The Military and American Society: Essays and Readings.* 1972. Free Press.
New York. Index. Bibliographical references. 322 pages.

Includes 23 studies dealing with the relationships between the military and American society. Of special relevance to the question of military manpower procurement policy are the essays by James Alden Barber, Jr., Morris Janowitz, and Vincent Davis.

AMERICAN FRIENDS SERVICE COMMITTEE. *The Draft?* 1968. Hill & Wang. New York. Bibliography: pages 103–111. 112 pages.

A discussion of the influence and effects of military conscription on American life. Eight co-authors, all actively opposed to compulsory conscription, view with skepticism the continued reliance on military solutions to problems that they contend are basically social, political, and economic. Included are a brief history of conscription in the United States and an examination of a volunteer army as an alternative to military conscription.

BALDWIN, HANSON W. *The Price of Power.* 1947. Harper & Bros. New York. Index. Bibliographic notes at end of each chapter. 361 pages.

Chapters 13 and 14 deal with military manpower procurement policy and costs. Baldwin recommends that the peacetime army be maintained only at the level necessary for occupation duties in ex-enemy countries, for garrisoning overseas bases, for national defense, and to provide a strategic reserve. Peacetime training in the National Guard or reserves of the armed forces, if efficiently conducted, would materially lessen the time required for combat-readiness and these groups, together with the Regulars, would provide the framework for expansion in case of emergency. Baldwin advocates that contingency legislation be enacted in peacetime for a wartime draft.

BEAUMONT, ROGER, and MARTIN EDMONDS (editors). *War in the Next Decade.* 1975. Macmillan Press. New York. 217 pages.

A collection of articles dealing with issues and problems of modern warfare. Topics include "Reserve Forces: Mobilization Demand in Modern War," "The Future of ROTC," "Science, Technology and the Future of Warfare," and "The Military Bureaucracy: A Case Study of a Civilian Contribution."

CALLAN, JOHN F. *The Military Laws of the United States, Relating to the Army, Volunteers, Militia, and to Bounty Lands and Pensions from the Foundation of the Government to the Year 1863.* 2nd edition. 1863. George W. Childs. Philadelphia. Index. 607 pages.

Embraces all congressional legislation in regard to the army, volunteers and militia, bounties and pensions, chronologically arranged. Includes those laws that have been repealed or are obsolete, with notes and references, and the legal decisions in cases where they have been given.

CARMICHAEL, LEONARD, and LEONARD C. MEAD (editors). *The Selection of Military Manpower: A Symposium.* 1951. National Academy of Sciences and National Research Council. Washington, D.C. Figures, tables. 269 pages.

Report of a symposium on the selection and classification of military manpower held under the auspices of the National Academy of Sciences in April 1951, with participants from the armed forces, the Research and Development Board, the National Academy of Sciences, the National Research Council, and national scientific societies. Aspects of selection and classification of military manpower considered include: human resources, medical factors, administration, manpower utilization, morale and endurance, and anthropological factors.

CHORLEY, KATHARINE. *Armies and the Art of Revolution.* 1973. Beacon Press. Boston. Index. 274 pages.

Foreword by B. H. Liddell Hart. Discussion and comparative analysis of the military and political roles of the army in eight different national revolutions. The author maintains that if a modern democratic society is to avert excessive power by the military as well as external threats from political extremes, then the army must be "a microcosm of society, representing the will of the people as a whole." It is reasoned, therefore, that military service should be compulsory although, in the case of new post-revolutionary armies, voluntary recruitment of the rank and file might better suit the conditions than conscription until the new regime has become the settled social system of the country.

CLARKSON, JESSE D., and THOMAS C. COCHRAN (editors). *War as a Social Institution: The Historian's Perspective.* 1941. Columbia University Press. New York. 333 pages.

Of particular interest is the essay by Herman Beukema, "The Social and Political Aspects of Conscription: Europe's Experience" (pages 113–129). Viewing conscription as a function of social and political conditions, he discusses three major types of conscription: (1) democratic conscription, universally applied, as in the mass levies, (2) despotic conscription, corrupted by exemptions, and (3) autocratic conscription. Beukema gives examples of each type and relates them to modern practice.

COCHRAN, CHARLES L. (editor). *Civil-Military Relations: Changing Concepts in the Seventies.* 1974. Free Press. New York. Index. Tables. Bibliographical references. 366 pages.

A compilation of 12 addresses, essays, and lectures on the question of civil supremacy over the military in the United States. Of particular interest are: "Civil Rights Versus Military Necessity," by Elmer J. Mahoney, and "The Reserves and National Guard: Civil-Military Nexus of the United States Armed Forces," by John R. Probert.

COULTON, G. G. *The Case for Compulsory Military Service.* 1917. Macmillan & Co. London. Index. 378 pages.

A pro-conscriptionist discussion of compulsion and voluntarism in various nations from the time of the Roman Empire. The author considers compulsory service a question of "military expediency" and "one of the most essential functions" of a civilized state. He contends that no law can be combated in the name of civilized liberty so long as that law tends toward the well-being of the state and mankind; that, historically, compulsory service has been the usual note of democracies while despots have preferred a paid army; that the quest for liberty of action for the community at large validates the imposition of certain restrictions upon individuals; and that "compulsion freely accepted is no longer compulsion." Coulton quotes widely from such British authorities as John Stuart Mill, Lord Asquith, Lord Haldane, J. R. Seely, Ian Hamilton, Lord Roberts, F. N. Maude, and Bertrand Russell.

EINSTEIN, ALBERT. *Einstein on Peace.* Edited by Otto Nathan and Heinz Norden. 1960. Simon & Schuster. New York. Index. 704 pages.

Preface by Bertrand Russell. In this collection of Einstein's writings on peace, Chapters 4 and 5 are of particular interest as they reflect Einstein's opposition to military conscription during the period 1928–1932.

ELIOT, GEORGE FIELDING. *The Ramparts We Watch: A Study of the Problems of American National Defense.* 1938. Reynal & Hitchcock. New York. Index. Maps. Bibliography: pages 361–362. 370 pages.

A study of the military principles upon which U.S. security rests, and of the military instruments by which that security may be conserved. Eliot supports those military measures, "in harmony with our national characteristics," that would for the first time assure the nation of being prepared for war. The military institutions of various modern democracies are examined as a preliminary to the discussion of appropriate military policy for the United States. Chapter 13, "The Army and the Citizen Soldier," discusses the place of the National Guard in defense policy; Chapter 16, "The Defense of Freedom," takes the position that Selective Service should be enacted at the outset of any war in order to reaffirm the constitutional "obligation of every citizen to defend his country in war," but its actual operation withheld until required, "in the meantime making full use of the moral value of volunteer service in war."

FLYNN, JOHN T. *As We Go Marching.* 1944. Doubleday, Doran & Co. Garden City, New York. Index. Bibliography: pages 259–263. 272 pages.

Examines the question whether the essential ingredients of fascism exist in the United States. Militarism is defined as an ingredient of fascism and as "that institution in which the nation maintains large national armies and navies in time of peace, usually raised on the principle of conscription." Militarism, in this view, does not exist "until you have the principle of universal military service or some form of conscription in time of peace as a permanent institution of national policy." A chapter on democratic militarism predicts that the end of World War II will witness a powerful movement for a continuance of the principle of universal service during peace, and examines some of the social, political, and economic aspects of peacetime conscription.

FRIEDMAN, ROBERT P., and CHARLEY LEISTNER (editors). *Compulsory Service Systems: A Critical Discussion and Debate Source Book.* 1968. Artcraft Press, Publishers. Columbia, Missouri. Index. Annotated bibliography: 44–62. 509 pages.

Issued also as Volume 42, Numbers 1–3, of *The Forensic Quarterly.*

Position papers, arguments, and comments provide a debate format. Topics covered are: alternative compulsory military systems, all-volunteer and national service alternatives to selective service, programs in other countries, opinions on the draft, views of veterans' organizations, students and the draft, conscience and military procurement, and principles of voluntarism. Included are critiques of and proposals regarding compulsory service systems by Lewis Hershey and Burke Marshall, and the views of some 30 U.S. senators.

GAULLE, CHARLES DE. *The Army of the Future.* 1941. J. B. Lippincott Co. Philadelphia. 179 pages.

Foreword by Walter Millis. An American edition of the 1934 book *Toward the Career Army,* setting out de Gaulle's assessment of future military needs based on rapid mechanization. He foresees a return to the idea of the long-service, fully equipped, expertly trained professional army as the first line and basic element in national defense. The civilian mass army introduced in Napoleonic times would remain as a second line, both in defense and in following up and occupying ground taken in an offensive.

GERHARDT, JAMES M. *The Draft and Public Policy: Issues in Military Manpower Procurement 1945–1970.* 1971. Ohio State University Press. Columbus, Ohio. Index. Tables. Bibliographical notes: pages 383–408. 425 pages.

This study traces the evolution of American military manpower procurement policy over the past 25 years, and examines current pressures for changes in Selective Service and related programs. Gerhardt analyzes explicit and implicit issues debated by major participants in this area of policy-making: the presidency, the defense establishment, the Selective Service System, and other executive agencies; Congress and its armed service committees; and various organized pressure groups. The study follows a chronological structure, relying almost entirely on publicly available documents and contemporary journalistic accounts for its construction of events. Its major sections are: "Frustration of Postwar Policy (1945–47)"; "Return of Selective Service (1948–50)"; "Korean Rearmament and Cold War Policy (1950–52)"; "The Quiet Triumph of Selective Service (1953–60)"; "New Challenges to Selective Service (1961–70)"; and "Military Manpower Policy, Past and Future."

General Works

GINZBERG, ELI. *Human Resources: The Wealth of a Nation.* 1958. Simon & Schuster. New York. Index. Bibliography: pages 174–176. 183 pages.

The departure point for this study is the fact that "during World War II almost two million young Americans of draft age were rejected for military service because of a mental or emotional defect, and another three-quarters of a million were discharged from the Armed Forces for these same reasons while the war was still under way." In evaluating the factors responsible for the inadequate performance of large numbers of young Americans and specifically those who were called up for military service, Ginsberg cites four major conditions underlying the current "squandering of our human-resource capital: unemployment, under-employment, inadequate training, and arbitrary barriers to employment." Charging social and educational discrimination against certain sectors of American society, he concludes that "a wise society will invest liberally in its people in order to accelerate its economic expansion and strengthen its national security."

GINZBERG, ELI, and others. *The Ineffective Soldier: Lessons for Management and the Nation.* 3 volumes. 1959. Columbia University Press. New York. Volume 1: Index. Figures, tables, maps. Bibliography: pages 213–220. 225 pages. Volume 2: Index. Bibliography: pages 277–279. 284 pages. Volume 3: Index. Bibliography: pages 329–334. 340 pages.

Volume 1, *The Lost Divisions*, seeks to determine the reasons for in-service breakdown and the impact of army personnel policies and procedures on the performance of soldiers. The deficiency of nearly two and a half million men in World War II, it is concluded, stemmed from the failure of military and government leaders to develop the nation's human resources to their optimum. Volume 2, *Breakdown and Recovery*, analyzes case records of ineffective soldiers to illuminate crucial aspects of personal performance, as a contribution not only to the improvement of military manpower policy, but to the advancement of basic understanding about the development and utilization of human resources. Volume 3, *Patterns of Performance*, studies individual performance after return to civilian life, and presents policy recommendations.

HABER, WILLIAM, and others. *Manpower in the United States: Problems and Policies.* 1954. Harper & Bros. New York. Tables. 225 pages.

Of particular interest is the study by Eli Ginzberg and James K. Anderson, "The Shape of Military Manpower Policy" (pages 169–189). The authors review military manpower procurement policy, summarizing selected manpower data "to indicate the limits within which policy solutions must be developed." Urging that the relation between the size of the manpower pool and military manpower policies be made explicit, they note two objectives: to have sufficient men to meet emergency needs and occupational or defense commitments, and to maintain an adequately trained reserve force. Recommendations include a review of pay and emoluments.

HAGOOD, JOHNSON. *We Can Defend America.* 1937. Doubleday, Doran & Co. Garden City, New York. 321 pages.

The stated purpose of this book is "to devise some simple, practical, commonsense plan of national defense that is based upon the genius of the American people and that is well within the price range of the taxpayer." The author advocates a policy of containment, a return "to the old idea that national defense is for defense only" under which "men drafted or called out for fighting in time of war shall be used solely for the purpose of repelling invasion and shall not be used for fighting upon a foreign shore." There would then be no question of "running into the difficulties of the old militia laws or inflicting upon our people any of the European ideas of compulsory military training and service." The author presents detailed proposals for the composition, size, and disposition of this "essentially defensive army."

HAHNEL, ROBERT. *Man-power, U.S.A.: A Draftable Man's Balance Sheet of Conscription.* 1941. The League of Draftable Men. St. Louis, Missouri. 95 pages.

An eclectic, uneven collection of commentaries on conscription. The author states his purpose is to "clarify issues and bring major facts into focus," asserting that "conscription is here regarded as neither good nor bad in itself."

HALLGREEN, MAURITZ A. *The Tragic Fallacy: A Study of America's War Policies.* 1937. Alfred A. Knopf. New York. Index. Bibliography: pages 445–452. 474 pages.

A review and critique of U.S. military manpower procurement policy, and a discussion of the positions of statesmen and military leaders who have influenced the development of that policy at various periods. The author charges that military leaders have been permitted to promote armed preparedness not for national self-defense but in order to further aggressive imperialism.

HAMMOND, PAUL Y. *Organizing for Defense: The American Military Establishment in the Twentieth Century.* 1961. Princeton University Press. Princeton, New Jersey. Index. 403 pages.

This study examines "the operation of the armed service departments in the context of the American government as a whole, attempting to reinterpret the formal administrative structure in the light of the public or political environment of its operation." Of particular interest are the author's discussions concerning the army reorganization of 1903 and the reforms of Elihu Root, Newton Baker and the National Defense Act of 1916, and the Truman Administration and the National Security Act of 1947.

HART, ALBERT BUSHNELL (editor). *America at War: A Handbook of Patriotic Education References.* 1918. George H. Doran Co. New York. Index. 425 pages.

Preface by James M. Beck. Published for the National Security League's Committee on Patriotism Through Education. Articles of particular interest are Peter Clark Macfarlane's "Weakness of the Volunteer System" (pages 204–207), Charles W. Eliot's "Shall We Adopt Universal Military Service?" (pages 209–215), The *Indianapolis Star*'s "Now Let Us Have Universal Military Training" (page 215), and Theodore Roosevelt's "Military Training and Policy" (pages 284–287).

HERRING, PENDLETON. *The Impact of War: Our American Democracy Under Arms.* 1941. Farrar & Rinehart. New York. Index. Bibliography: pages 285–294. 306 pages.

Chapter headings include "The Politics of Military Policy"; "The Place of the Army in National Life"; "How Congress Treats Military Affairs"; "The Decades of Divided Purposes, 1919–1939"; and "The Influence of War on Society." Herring finds that American military policy "has been much affected by traditional attitudes" toward a standing army, and that these attitudes, coupled with the country's geographical isolation from any threatening nation, have served to perpetuate an army "militarily inadequate for any real crisis." It is suggested that "democratic thought has failed to reconcile in adequate theoretical terms the need for professional trained soldiers with the general pattern of civilian life," and, in consequence, various mistakes have been made in managing military affairs through democratic institutions.

HOWE, LUCIEN. *Universal Military Education and Service: The Swiss System for the United States.* 2nd edition. 1917. G. P. Putnam's Sons, Knickerbocker Press. New York. Index. Bibliographic sources: pages 141–143. 147 pages.

First published in 1916, this book seeks to determine "whether the two problems of education and national defense are so related to each other that to solve one means also to solve the other." Howe discusses the "supposed disadvantages of universal military education" and holds that universal military education not only would be "the best guarantee of peace" but would provide advantages to the individual in health, knowledge, character, and efficiency. He concludes that the solution of both education and defense problems depends largely upon the adoption of universal military education.

HUNTINGTON, SAMUEL P. *The Common Defense: Strategic Programs in National Politics.* 1961. Columbia University Press. New York. Index. Bibliographic footnotes: pages 449–487. 500 pages.

Deals with the political process by which military policy is made. Focuses on changes in patterns of decision-making in American military policy between 1945 and 1960. Specific reference is made to strategic decisions on overall military size, force levels, and weapons, from the perspective of the "interaction between the desire for a stable military effort and the need to shift from a strategy of mobilization to a strategy of deterrence."

HUNTINGTON, SAMUEL P. *The Soldier and the State: The Theory and Politics of Civil–Military Relations.* 1957. Belknap Press of Harvard University Press. Cambridge, Massachusetts. Index. Bibliographical notes: pages 469–517. 534 pages.

A theory of civil-military relations in which the author defines as the principal components of a system of interdependent elements "the formal, structural position of military institutions in the government, the informal role and influence of military groups in politics and society at large, and the nature of the ideologies of military and nonmilitary groups." According to this theoretical framework, it should be possible to "analyze the extent to which the system of civil-military relations in any society tends to enhance or detract from the military security of that society" and to "suggest changes in the component elements of the system which would be necessary if the system were to approximate closer an equilibrium of 'objective civilian control.' " Chapter 7 discusses "the conservative Constitution versus civilian control."

JANOWITZ, MORRIS. *The Professional Soldier: A Social and Political Portrait.* Free Press of Glencoe, Illinois. Glencoe, Illinois. Index. Tables. 464 pages.

A social inquiry into the professional life, organizational setting, and leadership of the American military as they have evolved during the first half of the 20th century.

JAURÈS, JEAN. *Democracy and Military Service.* Edited by G. G. Coulton. 1916. Simpkin, Marshall, Hamilton, Kent & Co. London. 148 pages.

Preface by Pierre Renaudel. In this abbreviated translation of *L'Armée nouvelle* (1910), the French Socialist statesman sets forth his proposal for the "nation in arms" as the only just and efficient system so long as international disarmament continues to be elusive. Such a "national" army, being universally applied, would not only "democratize" the military but would be conducive to a defensive rather than offensive policy and strategy. Jaurès believes that a nation that desires peace must interest as many citizens as possible in the risks of war, and he urges the expeditious and large-scale training of reserves.

JESSOP, W. N. (editor). *Manpower Planning: Operational Research and Personnel Research.* 1966. American Elsevier Publishing Co., Inc. New York. Figures, charts. 291 pages.

Papers delivered at a conference on operational and personnel research in the management of manpower systems, held in Brussels in 1965 under the aegis of the NATO Science Committee. Of particular interest is Session III, on human resources and manpower planning (pages 155–228), which includes "U.S. Draft Study," by William Gorham; "Formal and On-the-Job Training in Military Occupations," by C. W. Bateman; "Occupational Pay Differentials for Military Technicians," by Gorham C. Smith; and "Major Manpower Planning Problems," by W. V. Combs.

JOHANNSEN, ROBERT W. (editor). *The Union in Crisis 1850–1877.* 1965. Sources in American History, 5. Free Press. New York. Bibliographical footnotes. 294 pages.

Includes the text of an address by Alexander H. Stephens as vice-president of the Confederate Government to the Georgia legislature on March 16, 1864 (pages 204–226). Stephens opposes the action of Congress in extending conscription to include all men between the ages of 17 and 50 and continuing the suspension of the writ of habeas corpus—measures recommended by President Davis as necessary to the war administration. Representing the conservative states'-rights opposition, Stephens charges the Davis Administration with pursuing an unconstitutional policy.

JOHNSEN, JULIA E. (compiler). *Peacetime Conscription.* 1945. The Reference Shelf, Volume 18, Number 4. H. W. Wilson Co. New York. Bibliography: pages 297–327. 327 pages.

A compilation of materials on military training as a postwar problem, classified and arranged for debaters. The major opposing viewpoints on the question of peacetime conscription are documented in affirmative and negative discussions.

JOHNSEN, JULIA E. (compiler). *Selected Articles on National Defense.* 1928. The Handbook Series, Series II, Volume 6. H. W. Wilson Co. New York. Bibliography: pages xxxix–lxxxiii. 469 pages.

Includes several articles on military manpower procurement and training. The discussion falls roughly into two divisions: (1) general, affirmative or favoring defense, and (2) negative or opposed to a defensive policy and advocating disarmament. The bibliography is grouped by subject.

JOMINI, BARON DE. *The Art of War.* 1862 (1971 edition). Greenwood Press. Westport, Connecticut. 410 pages.

In Chapter 2, on military policy, the author contends: "Experience has constantly proved that a mere multitude of brave men armed to the teeth make neither a good army nor a national defense." Twelve "essential conditions" that "concur in making a perfect army" include a good recruiting system, a well-organized system of national reserves, a "well-digested system of rewards, suitable to excite emulation," and a capacity for "exciting and keeping alive the military spirit of the people." The permanent army of a nation "should be capable of being doubled, if necessary, by reserves, which should always be prepared."

JORDAN, DAVID STARR. *War and the Breed: The Relation of War to the Downfall of Nations.* 1915. Beacon Press. Boston. 265 pages.

Chapter 6 discusses military conscription, focusing on the nation in arms, compulsory service, military drill as physical training, the Australian plan, and the eugenics of conscription. The appendix includes extracts on eugenics, military training in the schools, and military service in Germany and France.

KIRK, GRAYSON, and RICHARD P. STEBBINS. *War and National Policy: A Syllabus.* 1942. Farrar & Rinehart. New York. Bibliography: pages 107–131. 131 pages.

Foreword by Lindsay Rogers, Carlton J. Hayes, and Edward Mead Earle. Chapters 9 and 10 deal with U.S. military manpower recruitment and personnel policies and include syllabus references.

LANG, KURT. *Military Institutions and the Sociology of War.* 1972. Sage Publications. Beverly Hills, California. Index. Annotated bibliography: pages 159–280. 337 pages.

Part 1 is a review of the literature on the profession of arms, military organizations, the military system, civil-military relations, and war and warfare. Part 2 is an annotated bibliography.

LITTLE, ROGER W. (editor). *Handbook of Military Institutions.* 1971. Sage Publications. Beverly Hills, California. Index. 607 pages.

Comprises fifteen individually authored articles from the disciplines of political science, sociology, economics, social psychology, history, and social work. Of particular interest to the question of military manpower procurement policy are articles by Morris Janowitz, Harold Wool, Paul D. Nelson, Amos A. Jordan, Jr., Roger W. Little, and Charles C. Moskos, Jr. The appendix includes selected manpower statistics on recruitment policies and practices.

LITTLE, ROGER W. (editor). *Selective Service and American Society.* 1969. Russell Sage Foundation. New York. Index. Tables. Bibliography: pages 197–214. 220 pages.

Within the framework of the assumption that "some system of conscription is still necessary to maintain effective military manpower levels," seven essays analyze the recruiting services within the Selective Service System, the makeup and attitudes of those who serve on local draft boards, the criteria for deferment or rejection from service, and the application of the principle of universality in current draft laws. The essays are: "Procurement of Manpower: An Institutional Analysis," by Roger W. Little; "Historical Background of Selective Service in the United States," by Harry A. Marmion; "A Social Profile of Local Draft Board Members: The Case of Wisconsin," by James W. Davis, Jr., and Kenneth M. Dolbeare; "Decision-Making in Local Boards: A Case Study," by Gary L. Wamsley; "Juvenile Delinquency and Military Service," by Merrill Roff; "The Negro and the Draft," by Charles C. Moskos, Jr.; and "Military Service and Occupational Mobility," by Irving G. Katenbrink, Jr.

LOVELL, JOHN P., and PHILIP S. KRONENBERG (editors). *New Civil-Military Relations: The Agonies of Adjustment to Post-Vietnam Realities.* 1974. E. P. Dutton & Co. New York. 352 pages.

Essays on the role of the military in the social, economic, and political affairs of contemporary America. A number of the studies concern the willingness to serve in the armed services.

McCLAIN, THOMAS B., and others. *Manpower for National Security.* 1969. National Textbook Co. Skokie, Illinois. Selected bibliography: pages 307–311. 311 pages.

Debate manual in four sections: "Research in Manpower for National Security"; "Manpower Resources and Demand"; "The Selective Service System"; and "Alternatives to the Draft." Each section contains a brief discussion of the problem, an outline of the issues, and supporting evidence in the form of quotations. A "Who's Who in Manpower for National Security" identifies individuals in diverse fields who are actively concerned with the question.

MACHIAVELLI, NICCOLÒ. *The Prince.* 1916. E. P. Dutton & Co. New York. 290 pages.

Translated by W. K. Marriott. In this treatise on military affairs written in 1513, the Italian statesman opposes the use of: (1) paid foreign mercenaries, who "have no tie or motive to keep them in the field beyond their paltry pay" and who "are ready enough . . . to be your soldiers while you are at peace, but when war is declared they make off and disappear," and (2) foreign auxiliaries paid for as a unit, who are "united, and wholly under the control of their own officers," and who "are always hurtful to him who calls them in; for if they are defeated, he is undone, if victorious, he becomes their prisoner." With mercenaries, therefore, "the greatest danger is from their inertness and cowardice, with auxiliaries from their valour." Machiavelli draws on historical examples as evidence that national armies "composed of subjects, citizens, and dependants," if maintained in a constant state of preparedness, are superior to mercenary, auxiliary, or mixed armies.

MASLAND, JOHN, and LAURENCE I. RADWAY. *Soldiers and Scholars: Military Education and National Policy.* 1957. Princeton University Press. Princeton, New Jersey. Index. Charts. 530 pages.

A study of higher education in the armed forces, analyzing the quality of preparation of career officers for positions of national policy formation. Discusses military responsibilities in modern times, growth of military education for policy roles, and aspects of the existing education system. The authors conclude that while military education does make substantial contributions to preparation of officers, it is limited by its tendency toward conformity, parochialism, and equating education with training.

MAUDE, F. N. *War and the World's Life.* 1907. Smith, Elder & Co. London. Diagrams, map. 424 pages.

In this analysis of war, a military strategist discusses the sociological, military, and political implications of manpower procurement policies in several countries, and the lessons to be drawn from the great wars. At a time when proposals for compulsory military service are being introduced in Britain, the author argues that the "existing British system of voluntary service has never yet received a fair trial." Chapter 14 considers voluntary versus compulsory service.

MAXIM, HUDSON. *Defenseless America.* 1915. Hearst's International Library Co. New York. Index. 318 pages.

Of particular interest is Chapter 5, "The Needs of Our Army." The author holds that "conscription, like that enforced in Germany, makes good citizens. It implants in them a sense of duty and obligation to the government, and creates a greater respect for ruling power and for law and order." In the United States, where "the ideas of the average individual concerning his obligations to the government and the government's obligations to him are vague and crude," conscription would "largely remedy this by teaching duty to the government." Maxim endorses Leonard Wood's advocacy of the Swiss system of compulsory universal military training and service, and includes a letter he received from Wood, in which it is stated: "It is not enough that a man should be willing to be a soldier. He should also be so prepared as to be an efficient one."

MAXIM, HUDSON (editor). *Leading Opinions Both For and Against National Defense*. 1916. Hearst's International Library Co. New York. 121 pages.

A compilation of views issued as a handbook and guide for debaters and public speakers. Includes arguments pro and con conscription.

MILLIS, WALTER. *Arms and Men: A Study in American Military History*. 1956. G. P. Putnam's Sons. New York. Index. Bibliography: pages 369–371. 382 pages.

A historian's attempt to put the social and political implications of military history into a single perspective. In a chronological review of military history the author builds a case to show that war and its preparations, tactics, and strategy, military economics, and manpower questions all are continuous components of the fabric of society, and that military institutions (and their consequences) vie with religious, economic, legal, or partisan political institutions as essential elements of social and political history. A chapter on the future of war concludes the book.

MILLIS, WALTER (editor). *American Military Thought*. 1966. Bobbs-Merrill Co. Indianapolis, Indiana. Index. Tables. 554 pages.

Basic documents indicative of the ways in which American military thought has been shaped and has developed from colonial times. The collection delineates the positions on military policy of statesmen and military men, starting with Benjamin Franklin's call for a volunteer militia in 1747 and concluding with Robert S. McNamara's proposed

"Defense Policy of the 1960s." Included are John Calhoun's views on conscription, William Tecumseh Sherman's stated belief in the superiority of volunteer over conscripted troops or bounty men, the 1792 Militia Act, Emory Upton's critical analysis of military policy, the 1912 General Staff outline of "A Well-Organized and Sufficient Army," the 1915 General Staff recommendations on "A Proper Military Policy," and War Department Chief of Staff Hugh Scott's 1916 call for compulsory military service.

MOSCA, GAETANO. *The Ruling Class.* Edited by Arthur Livingston. 1939. McGraw-Hill Book Co. New York. Index. 514 pages.

Translated by Hannah D. Kahn from Mosca's original work, *Elementi di scienza politica*, published in 1896; revised, with an introduction, by the editor. Chapter 9, "Standing Armies," discusses military power in primitive societies, mercenaries and feudal societies, the rise of standing armies, and citizen militias. Mosca notes that "the modern organization of armies . . . runs counter to the economic principle of the division of labor and to the physiological law of the adaptability of the various bodily organs to given purposes." This has implications for the application of "certain economic laws when they are applied in the field of politics."

NATIONAL SECURITY LEAGUE. *National Security Congress.* 1916. New York. Index. 407 pages.

Addresses, communications, and resolutions of the 1916 congress. Convened to consider the nation's defense needs with respect to "the individual's obligation to the State and the State's ability to avail itself thereof" and "the industrial resources of the country," the congress advocates a system of universal obligatory military training and service, wholly under the discipline and control of national authorities.

NATIONAL SECURITY LEAGUE. *Proceedings of the Congress of Constructive Patriotism.* 1917. Washington, D.C. Index. 448 pages.

Advocates the enactment of federal legislation obligating all physically fit young men to undergo "intensive, continuous field or sea training for the period necessary to produce an efficient soldier or sailor" and "to serve in war as well as to train in time of peace." Of particular interest are: "Some Reflections upon Our Military Experiments of 1916," by Henry Stimson; a letter from Theodore Roosevelt, urging "the acceptance by the nation of the principle of universal, obligatory military training in time of peace as a basis of universal, obligatory service in time of war"; and an address by Frederic Huidekoper on preparedness and compulsory military training and service. The appendix includes reports of the subcommittees on the army and on universal military training and service.

NEBLETT, WILLIAM H. *Pentagon Politics*. 1953. Pageant Press. New York. 131 pages.

A critique of Department of Defense policies, in which the military is seen as seeking to perpetuate its power by thwarting efforts to move from a costly, large professional army to a citizen army under greater civilian control. The author charges that "history shows us that large professional armies have at one time or another, on some pretext or other, always taken away the liberties of the countries they were raised and maintained to defend." He urges that Congress "set up a unified citizen force of Army, Navy and Air," and that "service in this force should be compulsory and its members recruited by a system of universal training applicable in some of its phases to all of our people—men, women and children."

NICHOLS, EGBERT RAY (editor). *Intercollegiate Debates*. Volume VI. 1916. Hinds, Hayden & Eldredge. New York. Index. Bibliography at end of each chapter. 569 pages.

Chapter 7 (pages 319–377) consists of two intercollegiate debates on the pros and cons of compulsory military service.

NICKERSON, HOFFMAN. *The Armed Horde 1793–1939: A Study of the Rise, Survival and Decline of the Mass Army*. 1940. G. P. Putnam's Sons. New York. Index. Illustrations, tables, maps. Bibliography: pages 401–407. 427 pages.

The author sees a descending curve of war; with the modern advent of limited warfare and the comparative bloodlessness of new military methods, mass armies no longer answer military needs. He believes that compulsory measures remain an essential part of any efficient land force, however, to supplement the smaller bodies of more highly trained troops.

RANSOM, WILLIAM L. (editor). *Military Training: Compulsory or Volunteer?* July 1916. Proceedings of the Academy of Political Science. Volume 6, Number 4. 262 pages.

A compilation of 29 addresses and papers on aspects of compulsory and voluntary military systems. See below: Henry B. Breckinridge, "Universal Service as the Basis of National Unity and National Defense"; Walter L. Fisher, "Fundamental Considerations Affecting the Military Policy of the United States"; C. E. Knoeppel, "Compulsory Training and Industrial Preparedness"; Oswald Garrison Villard, "The Cure-all of Universal Military Service"; George E. Chamberlain, "Universal Training and an Adequate Army Reserve"; Frederick A. Kuenzli, "The Swiss System and What It Suggests as to an American System of Universal Training for the Common Defense"; E. N. Johnston, "The Australian System of Universal Training for Purposes of Military Defense"; Matthew Woll, "Trades-Unionism and Military Training"; George Creel, "Universal Training and the Democratic Ideal"; Munroe Smith, "Democratic Aspects of Universal Military Service"; Theodore A. Christen, "The Swiss Military System and Its Adaptability to the United States"; Louis W. Stotesbury, "Compulsory Training Under State Auspices and the Place of State Militia in National Defense"; Samuel J. Rosensohn, "Legal Aspects of Federal Compulsory Service of State Militia"; and Herbert Quick, "A New Volunteer System."

ROOSEVELT, THEODORE. *America and the World War.* 1916. Charles Scribner's Sons. New York. 277 pages.

In this treatise on the need for military preparedness, Roosevelt urges the introduction in the United States of universal military training "of the kind practiced by the free democracy of Switzerland." While opposing a large standing army, he considers that "no man is really fit to be the free citizen of a free republic unless he is able to bear arms and at need to serve with efficiency in the efficient army of the republic."

ROOSEVELT, THEODORE. *Fear God and Take Your Own Part.* 1916. George H. Doran Co. New York. 414 pages.

Urging armed preparedness in the United States, Roosevelt contends: "A democracy should not be willing to hire somebody else to do its fighting. The man who claims the right to vote should be a man able and willing to fight at need for the country which gives him the vote." Universal service is advocated as "the true democratic ideal," while the volunteer system is characterized as "nothing but encouraging brave men to do double duty and incur double risk in order that cowards and shirks and mere money-getters may sit at home in a safety bought by the lives of better men."

ROPP, THEODORE. *War in the Modern World.* 1959. Duke University Press. Durham, North Carolina. Index. Bibliographical footnotes. 400 pages.

Study of the development of the modern military profession against the backdrop of political, social, and economic influences. Reviews warfare from the Renaissance to World War II, discussing the historical course of the different methods of recruitment, both compulsory and voluntary, employed at various times and under various circumstances.

SCHELLING, THOMAS C. *Arms and Influence.* 1966. Yale University Press. New Haven, Connecticut. Index. 293 pages.

A study of the "diplomacy of violence"—the threat of physical harm that nations use in diplomacy. Schelling attempts to identify a few of the principles that underlie the workings of this diplomacy by examining how countries use their capacity for violence as a bargaining tool. He contends that, when violence is involved, the interests even of adversaries overlap, making bargaining possible, rather than just a tug-of-war. Discussed are risk-manipulation, the diplomacy of ultimate survival, the dynamics of mutual alarm, and the dialogue of competitive armament. Historical examples are given.

SCHWOERER, LOIS G. *"No Standing Armies!" The Antiarmy Ideology in Seventeenth-Century England.* 1974. Johns Hopkins University Press. Baltimore, Maryland. Index. Illustrations. Bibliographical footnotes. 210 pages.

Traces the opposition to standing armies in England, from its pre-Stuart origins to the climax of the standing-army issue in Parliament and in the press during the years 1697–1699. It is suggested that the arguments against standing armies, and the political decisions they accompanied, "seeded an intellectual tradition that remained vital for at least another one hundred years not only in England but in the American colonies, where it was carried," and that "much that is said today in the United States about military organization and citizen responsibility echoes the passionate arguments of three hundred years ago."

STERN, FREDERICK MARTIN. *The Citizen Army: Key to Defense in the Atomic Age.* 1957. St. Martin's Press. New York. Index. Bibliographical notes: pages 337–348. 373 pages.

This book warns that the United States can no longer rely either upon a military policy that solves defense problems only on the national or continental level, or upon a professional army reinforced by volunteers or long-term draftees. The "globalization" of defense demands a corresponding globalization of the principles of military preparedness in the creation of a "reservoir" of U.S. and allied citizen armies based on short training periods and universal obligation. The most crucial element in the need for a new departure in military planning is the danger of nuclear warfare. Though the Soviet Union, in its own interests, might stop short of launching a nuclear attack, it might well decide upon nonnuclear, large-scale aggression, in which case the weakness in the present systems of the United States and most of its allies "may leave the free world no choice but to answer with nuclear weapons," resulting, in turn, in Soviet nuclear retaliation. The advantages and weaknesses of the various systems and of their possible combinations are explored in historical perspective, and a new military policy is formulated to "meet the requirements of the nuclear age."

STIMSON, HENRY L., and McGEORGE BUNDY. *On Active Service in Peace and War.* 1947. Harper & Bros. New York. Index. 698 pages.

The personal record of Henry Stimson during his terms as secretary of war and secretary of state. Chapters 14, 15, and 16 deal with questions of compulsory service raised during World War II, noting Stimson's conviction that selective service was "the only fair, efficient, and democratic way to raise an army"; the difficulties encountered in organizing and extending the draft; Stimson's advocacy of a national service act for directing the country's labor force; the increasing difficulties in administering the military draft; and his efforts to persuade President Roosevelt to relinquish his defense of the navy's traditional system of volunteering and to press for a single selective process.

TAX, SOL (editor). *The Draft: A Handbook of Facts and Alternatives.* 1967. University of Chicago Press. Chicago. Index. Figures, tables. 497 pages.

A collection of 25 papers delivered at a conference held at the University of Chicago in December 1966. Authors include Kenneth Boulding, Milton Friedman, Lewis Hershey, Morris Janowitz, Edward Kennedy, S. L. A. Marshall, Margaret Mead, and Walter Oi. Part 1, the papers, is organized in four sections: (1) "Problems of the Draft" describes the Selective Service System and the problems it faces; (2) "Broadening the Draft" points to the need for a system of selective service for military manpower procurement and offers proposals for its extension to non-military service; (3) "Perspectives on the Draft" views the problem in perspectives aside from immediate technical and policy questions; and (4) "Alternatives to the Draft" considers the validity of or need for conscription and includes proposals for broad programs of voluntary national service. Part 2 contains a transcript of each discussion session. Part 3 presents postconference documents relating to legislative action and proposals.

TONE, WILLIAM THEOBALD WOLFE. *Essay on the Necessity of Improving Our National Forces.* 1819. Kirk & Mercein. New York. 112 pages.

This essay attempts to show the necessity of maintaining a small standing army in the United States, expansible in wartime by the militia. The author believes that while the payment of high premiums for voluntary enlistment is a method "not calculated to procure a chosen quality of men," this method, if properly administered, "will suffice to make a good army, even out of bad elements."

TREITSCHKE, HEINRICH VON. *Politics.* Volume 2. 1916. Macmillan Co. New York. Index. 643 pages.

Translated by Blanche Dugdale and Torben de Bille. Introduction by Arthur J. Balfour; foreword by A. Lawrence Lowell. In Chapter 23, "The Constitution of the Army," Treitschke discusses the rights and obligations to serve, as interpreted under various military systems.

WEBSTER, DANIEL. *The Letters of Daniel Webster.* Edited by C. H. Van Tyne. 1902. McClure, Phillips & Co. New York. 769 pages.

The famous speech that Daniel Webster delivered in the House of Representatives on December 9, 1814, is often quoted by the foes of conscription, though few have ever read the entire speech. The manuscript was missing until the turn of the century, when it was discovered

in the archives of the New Hampshire Historical Society and published
by Van Tyne, then a Senior Fellow at the University of Pennsylvania.
This book contains the complete speech (pages 56–68), an eloquent,
powerful attack on the idea of conscription.

WHEELER-NICHOLSON, MALCOLM. *Battle Shield of the Republic.* 1940.
Macmillan Co. New York. 212 pages.

A critical analysis of the U.S. Army and a call for comprehensive
reform. The author recommends that universal military training be
retained as a permanent element of national defense, noting that "it is
based upon the fact that a citizen owes a duty to his state to defend it,"
that "it is more democratic than our peacetime habit of seeking recruits
solely among the economically least capable elements of the population,"
and that "a system of voluntary recruiting is unable to fill up the ranks of
our now larger army either in peace or in war."

WHITE, HOWARD. *Executive Influence in Determining Military Policy in
the United States.* 1925. University of Illinois Press. Urbana, Illinois.
Index. Bibliography: pages 279–286. 292 pages.

The influence of the executive branch of government is seen as running
in cycles with four distinct phases: (1) peace, when extensive reorganizations of the Regular Army or substantial increases in its size are practically
impossible to obtain, even though such periods would seem logically to be
the time for planning national defense; (2) impending war, when Congress is more inclined to heed executive requests; (3) war, when executive influence reaches its maximum; and (4) return to peace conditions,
typically marked by a weakening of the prestige of the executive and a
vigorous effort by Congress to reassume the exercise of its constitutional
powers, aided by general revolution against war and by taxpayers'
demands for retrenchment in governmental expenditures.

WILLENZ, JUNE A. (editor). *Dialogue on the Draft.* 1967. American
Veterans Committee. Washington, D.C. Bibliography: pages 102–114.
141 pages.

Report of the National Conference on the Draft, November 11–12,
1966, Washington, D.C. The conference brought together over 200 representatives of government agencies and delegates from some 100 national

private organizations. The proceedings included expositions of the activities and reasoning of the two government agencies most concerned with military manpower procurement—the Selective Service System and the Department of Defense. At the same time, serious critiques of the present draft system were made by some of the speakers, while remedies or alternative proposals were presented by others. Included are summaries of workshop sessions on the draft in relation to the individual, the group, society, education, and human resources.

WILSON, N. A. B. (editor). *Manpower Research.* 1969. American Elsevier Publishing Co. New York. 463 pages.

A compilation of papers presented at the August 1967 conference in London of the North Atlantic Treaty Organization Scientific Affairs Committee. Includes studies dealing with the development of noncommissioned officers, the effective utilization of marginal manpower, and the problems of manpower retention.

WOOD, LEONARD. *The Military Obligation of Citizenship.* 1915. Princeton University Press. Princeton, New Jersey. 76 pages.

Contains the texts of three addresses delivered by Leonard Wood in 1915: "The Policy of the United States in Raising and Maintaining Armies," "The Military Obligation of Citizenship," and "The Civil Obligation of the Army." It is held that the voluntary system "is uncertain in operation, prevents organized preparation, tends to destroy that individual sense of obligation for military service which should be found in every citizen, costs excessively in life and treasure, and does not permit that condition of preparedness which must exist if we are to wage war successfully with any great power prepared for war." The militia, in Wood's view, can be considered a dependable force only if it is under "a large measure of federal control." He advocates a system of compulsory military training and service based upon the military systems of Australia and Switzerland.

WOOL, HAROLD. *The Military Specialist: Skilled Manpower for the Armed Forces.* 1968. Johns Hopkins Press. Baltimore, Maryland. Index. Charts, tables. Bibliography: pages 201–206. 216 pages.

A study of the economic and social aspects of military service in relation to the determination of military manpower requirements and of policies affecting procurement and utilization of military personnel. Part

1 traces the institutional evolution of occupational specialization in the armed services and analyzes trends in military occupational structure and their relationship to qualitative manpower requirements, as measured by mental-aptitude test scores or educational achievement. Part 2 examines the factors influencing the supply of manpower for military service in the post-World War II era, as measured by both initial enlistment flows and reenlistment rates. The role of various economic and noneconomic factors in the propensity to enlist or continue in service is assessed, based on time-series analysis, cross-sectional data, and results of attitude surveys. The concluding chapter reviews some of the more recent developments of military manpower policy in the context of some of the findings in the body of the study.

YARMOLINSKY, ADAM. *The Military Establishment: Its Impacts on American Society.* 1971. Harper & Row. New York. Index. Charts, tables. 434 pages.

This book is concerned with the extent to which, and the ways in which, the society of the United States is affected and shaped by military purposes. Of particular interest are: Chapter 7, on the military, the budget, and national priorities; Chapters 11 and 12, on the use of troops in domestic disorders; Chapter 20, on military service and social structure; Chapter 21, on military service and race; Chapter 22, on military justice and individual liberty; and Chapter 24, on the military establishment and social values.

Unpublished Manuscripts

BRAYTON, ABBOTT ALLEN. *Military Mobilization and International Politics.* 1971. Ph.D. dissertation. University of Arizona. Tucson, Arizona. 202 pages.

An analysis of the relationship between the political system, the reserve military system, mobilization, and international politics. The purpose of the study is twofold: (1) to explore the relationship between military mobilization and international politics, and (2) to evaluate American reserve and mobilization policies with respect to political-military requirements for 1971–1985. Included are several proposals for modifying the

American reserve and mobilization system in order to meet future national security requirements.

DUGGAN, JOSEPH C. *The Legislative and Statutory Development of the Federal Concept of Conscription for Military Service.* 1946. J.D. dissertation. Catholic University of America. Washington, D.C. Index. Table of authorities: pages 163–173. 178 pages.

A legal-historical study showing how the U.S. concept of conscription has been developed through legal processes, how historical experience has guided and influenced the development of federal laws relating to the military (as distinguished from both military and martial law), and how, based primarily on English patterns, the United States has, in its martial character, relied mainly on four types of organizations to provide a means for the common defense: the standing army (Regular Army), the volunteer army, the federalized state militia (National Guard), and the conscript army, with a fifth component, the reserve corps, serving as an adjunct of the Regular Army. Duggan traces the inception, construction, and process of enactment of successive draft laws, exploring both the reasons for America's adoption of conscription and the positions of elected representatives in the formulation of legislation.

GIEBEL, HOWARD A. *Procurement of Manpower for Armed Defense in a Bipolar World.* 1953. M.A. thesis. Columbia University. New York. Bibliography: pages 162–166. 179 pages.

Assesses military manpower procurement policy in the United States, investigating the legislative background, organization and administration, and operation of the Selective Service System, the proposed Universal Military Training plan, and the Swiss military manpower procurement system. Giebel concludes that the U.S. military and national security policy should be based upon: (1) a citizen reserve under compulsory universal military training; and (2) a standing armed force responsible for manning coastal defenses, garrisoning outposts, and holding off an aggressor until mobilization of the citizen reserve can be effected. The procurement of manpower for the standing force, in this view, should be based either upon a selective service system or upon voluntary enlistment, but not a combination of the two.

PHILIPPS, DENIS S. *The American People and Compulsory Military*

Service. 1955. Ph.D. dissertation. New York University. New York. Bibliography: pages 504–522. 522 pages.

Examines America's experience with compulsory military service in light of the various political, ideological, and international forces that have influenced its development. Philipps attempts to explain "how such an attitude developed that the American people, in contrast to the people of other nations, might consider themselves exempt, or immune," from the burdens of conscription, "this most ancient of man's institutions." He suggests that the "undue importance ascribed to volunteering during the Revolutionary War . . . became an integral part of the Legend of America," serving to explain "the emotional fervor with which Americans have resisted compulsory military service; even to an extent that at times the national interest has been endangered."

Articles

ANGELL, NORMAN. *The Real Implications of Conscription.* The New Republic. April 8, 1916. Volume 6, Number 75. Pages 266–268.

The author suggests that in considering the possible adoption of military conscription, the United States must "face squarely" what conscription involves: "Not bemusing ourselves with the irrelevant consideration that it is in itself desirable, but recognizing its dangers and to that extent having the greater chance of escaping them, resorting to it for a specific and limited purpose, just as we might administer a dangerous drug to an invalid, something necessary it may be for his very life, but something also which may cost him his life if we have to go on increasing the dose."

BALDWIN, HANSON W. *Conscription for Peacetime?* Harper's Magazine. March 1945. Volume 190, Number 1138. Pages 289–300.

The author states: "Whether or not [peacetime conscription] is adopted, upon two things we should insist. First, that peacetime conscription is not a separate issue; it should be treated as part of a far broader problem—the whole problem of postwar defense. Second, that it must stand or fall on its military merits. If it is adjudged essential to implement our postwar military policy we must have it, but we must remember that the harm it may do to our political and economic and social institutions may well outweigh its incidental political, economic, and social benefits."

BALDWIN, HANSON W. *The Draft Is Here to Stay but It Should Be Changed*. New York Times Magazine. November 20, 1966. Pages 48–49, 89–96, 102–104, 107–112.

A consideration of several means of military manpower procurement. Alternatives include (1) the existing Selective Service System, either as is, or with some degree of modification, (2) abolition of the draft, (3) universal military training, and (4) national service. The pros and cons of each of these are examined, with the conclusion that the present Selective Service System be retained and modified. Baldwin contends that it would be unthinkable to shift the entire manpower procurement process into new and untried channels, especially in the midst of a war.

BARNETT, CORELLI. *On the Raising of Armies*. Horizon. Summer 1968. Volume 10, Number 3. Pages 40–47.

Argues that "militias are fine for defending the homeland, and conscript armies can be raised for wars of survival. But no world power has ever found it practical to depend on drafted soldiers for fighting distant border-wars." Referring to the U.S. military role in Vietnam, the author contends that "compulsory military service to make possible a general foreign or imperial policy has never, anywhere, been otherwise than extremely unpopular." He suggests that the United States address itself to its "global commitments" by considering the expansion of its Regular Army "to a size where it would be capable by itself of fighting a war like Vietnam."

BLACK, FORREST R. *Conscription for Foreign Service*. American Law Review. January–February 1926. Volume 60. Pages 206–231.

Advocates a constitutional amendment giving Congress, in the event of invasion of U.S. territory by a foreign power, the authority to conscript wealth and men for purposes of defense, but otherwise prohibiting such conscription by the federal government.

BOGARDUS, EMORY S. *Peacetime Conscription*. Sociology and Social Research. July–August 1945. Volume 29, Number 6. Pages 472–478.

Presents a summary of frequently advanced arguments for and against peacetime conscription. Suggests that some method is needed for weighing each of the positive and negative contentions in regard to (1) social value, (2) social control and social change, and (3) democratization both of persons and of the nation.

BROWN, FRANCIS J. *The Issue Should Be Decided Later.* The Annals of the American Academy of Political and Social Science. September 1945. Volume 241. Pages 77–85.

"Whether deliberately or not," writes Brown, "the military, by pressing the issue of conscription now, is forcing the American people to express a vote of confidence." He calls for an open, reasoned debate, with all the facts made known, such as the material and human cost of military training. Various other arguments against a hasty passage of legislation are raised, and the opposition of a number of diverse groups is noted.

COBB, JOE MICHAEL. *Emigration as an Alternative to the Draft.* New Individualist Review. Spring 1967. Volume 4, Number 4. Pages 26–36.

Examines the "obstacles placed in the path of that minority who would rather emigrate than perform military service, by a government determined to shore up an anti-liberal institution with illiberal restrictions on a basic freedom." Charges that, although the United States maintains no general barriers to emigration, the Selective Service System has in the past operated to deny the right of emigration, and currently maintains regulations that cast doubt upon the legal status of draft-liable emigrants.

COLBY, ELBRIDGE. *Compulsory Military Training.* Current History. April 1929. Volume 30, Number 1. Pages 61–62.

Notes that "among the principal nations of the world, the United States and Great Britain are the only ones which do not have compulsory military service in time of peace." Suggests that support for standing armies is on the decline, "so universal is acceptance of the practice of compulsory service."

CONGRESSIONAL DIGEST. *Roosevelt's National Defense Program.* March 1938. Volume 17, Number 3. Pages 67–96.

Contains diverse views on the national defense program submitted to Congress by President Roosevelt. Includes discussion of military and industrial conscription proposals.

DAWSON, DAVID J. *The Draft* (seven parts). Persuasion. (1) April 1966. Volume 3, Number 4. Pages 43–52. (2) May 1966. Volume 3, Number 5. Pages 63–79. (3) October 1966. Volume 3, Number 10. Pages 139–151. (4) November 1966. Volume 3, Number 11. Pages 153–163. (5) January 1967. Volume 4, Number 1. Pages 1–11. (6) March 1967. Volume 4, Number 3. Pages 1–12. (7) May 1967. Volume 4, Number 5. Pages 1–19.

Part 1, "Posse Comitatus," reviews the historical background of the practice of military conscription and points to injustices and inequities inherent in it. Part 2, "Posse Praesedentis," discusses military conscription in relation to the U.S. Constitution and presidential authority. Part 3, "Labor as Property vs. Labor as Natural Resource," examines conscription as a slave system. Part 4—"What Price Liberty?"—examines the proposal for an all-volunteer armed force. Part 5—"Who Shall Serve?"—suggests ways in which a voluntary system could attract sufficient recruits. Part 6, "Privileges and Obligations," examines the practice of deferment under the Selective Service System. Part 7, "General Hershey's Carrot," compares the positions of two different schools of thought both upholding compulsory military service.

DICKINSON, WILLIAM B., JR. *Military Manpower Policies.* Editorial Research Reports. February 14, 1962. Volume 1. Pages 101–120.

Deals with the mobilization of reserves in peacetime, past and future reserve-forces policy, and the pros and cons of reliance on conscription for manpower.

FISHER, WALTER L. *Fundamental Considerations Affecting the Military Policy of the United States.* Proceedings of the Academy of Political Science. July 1916. Volume 6, Number 4. Pages 18–39.

Advocates a "defensive" army, one that would be developed by confining the standing army "to the number of soldiers appropriate in times of peace, and by training, through that army, an adequate reserve of officers and men for our first line of defense in the event of war." In this view, men should not be enlisted for long terms of active service, and the militia should be standardized under general federal control and maintained as the second line of reserves. Fisher opposes as unnecessary any form of conscription, and rejects "the theory that military training is essential for the inculcation of civic virtue."

General Works

GARBER, ALEX, and others. *Military Service in a Free Society.* War/Peace Report. May 1967. Volume 7, Number 5. Pages 15–16.

This Harvard Study Group focuses on underlying problems of military service in a democratic society in light of two questions: What sort of military service is best? and What are the ramifications of any sort of military service? Three main views are presented: (1) the draft is coercive and in basic contradiction with principles of liberty although justifiable in the face of national emergency; (2) taxes and the draft have long been recognized as legitimate and defense of state should not be left to free enterprise; and (3) the specifics of military organization and recruitment are incidental to the fundamental problem of war and its origins.

GARD, ROBERT G., JR. *The Military and American Society.* Foreign Affairs. July 1971. Volume 49, Number 4. Pages 698–710.

Discusses "the search to adapt traditional concepts and practices of military professionalism to changing requirements and radically new demands." The author believes that to obtain sufficient numbers of adequately qualified personnel, it is essential to continue the Selective Service Act. He acknowledges, however, that "while reliance on the draft will ensure closer contact of the military establishment with society, it will also increase the difficulty of preserving the traditional values necessary to an effective military force."

GILLAM, RICHARD. *The Peacetime Draft: Voluntarism to Coercion.* Yale Review. June 1968. Volume 57, Number 4. Pages 495–517.

Calls attention to the "ethical and intellectual" dimensions of the peacetime draft "in the hope of providing information and perspectives which may lift discourse to a more sophisticated level and perhaps free debate from the seeming impasse at which it now stands." Reviews recent political debate on peacetime conscription, including interpretations of the concepts of equality and universality of obligation to military service. Gillam claims that, with the 1967 conscription legislation modifying the Selective Service System, "coercion was perfunctorily accepted and the argument for equality laid quietly to rest with the ghost of American voluntarism."

HAYS, SAMUEL H. *Military Training in the U.S. Today.* Current History. July 1968. Volume 55, Number 323. Pages 7–12, 50–51.

The author links military training with social benefits, both for the individual and for the community. Thus: "Military training engenders a feeling of identification with and responsibility for service to the nation"; "History tells us that no nation can long survive if its citizens are either unwilling or unable to bear arms in its defense or in the defense of its liberties and ideas"; and "Training a substantial number of our citizens in the military skills remains today, as in the past, our most positive insurance that we will be able to pass on to our descendants the democratic freedoms and economic advantages we inherited from our fathers."

JOHNSON, KEITH R. *Who Should Serve?* The Atlantic Monthly. February 1966. Volume 217, Number 2. Pages 63–69.

Reviews the draft and analyzes possible improvements in or alternatives to it. Considers universal military training, the lottery, deferments, local boards, and induction standards. Included is a chart assessing the various programs open to young men who prefer to volunteer for military service rather than be drafted.

MORTON, LOUIS. *The Origins of American Military Policy.* Military Affairs. Summer 1968. Volume XXII, Number 2. Pages 75–82.

Reviews the origins of the national defense establishment, showing that the seeds of U.S. military policy go back to the experience of the English people. Concludes that the militia is based upon "the obligation of universal service" and that, "though often ignored," it "has never been abandoned" and "constitutes yet today the basis of our military organization."

REDMOND, D. G. *Conscription After the War.* Current History. October 1944. Volume 7, Number 38. Pages 291–296.

Discusses current proposals for post-World War II military manpower procurement policies. Suggests that until the nature of the military necessity is known, serious consideration of a peacetime draft should be postponed.

SCHELLING, THOMAS CROMBLE, and others. *On the Draft.* The Public Interest. Fall 1967. Number 9. Pages 93–99.

An examination of how government should obtain military manpower in times of war and peace in light of various practical and ethical criteria.

Among the authors' recommendations are revision of salary scales and levels; use of nondiscriminatory lottery in selective service; and more incentives (increased training and nonpay benefits) to keep people in the army.

SMITH, LYNN D. *The Unsolved Problem.* Military Review. June 1964. Volume XLIV, Number 6. Pages 3–12.

Deals with problems posed by the military manpower recruitment and retention needed to maintain an armed force of deterrent strength. Traces the evolution of manpower procurement policy and notes the problems of the current system. In discussing alternatives, Smith proposes offering lifetime career opportunities in the military, incorporating active and civilian duty. He cites as advantages the lowered cost of military manpower procurement and increased efficiency through reduced turnover of military personnel.

STRAUSZ-HUPE, ROBERT. *Mobilizing U.S. Man Power.* Current History. August 1940. Volume 51, Number 12. Pages 32–36.

The author comments: "Compulsory service in peacetime is a measure to be applied cautiously and with due regard to cushioning its impact upon the civilian scheme of things. To introduce it in times of domestic prosperity and international quiet would still require care; to graft it on the body politic in times of economic stress at home and political chaos abroad requires a cool head and a sure hand. Drafting the nation's youth for war must not serve as an expedient for curing surreptitiously such economic ills as unemployment."

SWOMLEY, JOHN M., JR. *The Army Gets Its Way.* The Progressive. April 1959. Volume 23, Number 4. Pages 29–32.

Commenting upon the extension of the peacetime draft in the United States for another four years, Swomley charges that the record "produces inescapable evidence that the inception and perpetuation of the peacetime draft can be laid at the feet of Army officers who are adamant advocates of conscription." The army, in this view, "has prevailed upon Congress to renew a draft law that nobody else seems to want, and nobody, including the Army, needs."

SWOMLEY, JOHN M., JR. *Twenty-five Years of Conscription.* The Christian Century. April 12, 1967. Volume LXXXIV, Number 15. Pages 465–468.

Notes that the present Selective Service System has been in continuous operation since June 1948, and looks at ways in which the draft has made inroads in individual liberty in various facets of society. Concludes that for Americans to have accepted the peacetime draft for 25 years must mean that "Americans have accepted the idea that subordination of the individual to the state not only is necessary but is preferable to a voluntary society."

THOMAS, NORMAN. *Arming Against Russia.* The Annals of the American Academy of Political and Social Science. September 1945. Volume 241. Pages 67–71.

Enumerates objections to peacetime military conscription: "(1) If conscription is passed, suspicion and fear of Russia will be the dominant reason; (2) Conscription will inevitably increase that suspicion and fear, be the signal for an armament race, and make war more likely; (3) To the degree that peacetime conscription and mass armies are an aid to the war of the future, the U.S.S.R. will be the gainer rather than the United States because of its greater population and birth rate, its geographic and strategic position, and its totalitarian government to which conscription is a more appropriate weapon than to our democracy."

WALLER, WILLARD. *A Sociologist Looks at Conscription.* The Annals of the American Academy of Political and Social Science. September 1945. Volume 241. Pages 95–101.

Attempts to present a logical analysis of conscription by examining individually such aspects as: the prospect of future war, whether conscription would increase or decrease the probability of war, conscription as a measure of preparedness, social costs and incidental benefits, and timing of a decision for or against peacetime conscription. Concludes that "some form of preparedness is necessitated by the present state of our international relations and conscription is a necessary element in any program of preparedness." Thus the currently proposed conscription measure should be adopted but with an attempt made to "cut its costs and avoid its hazards as best we can."

WOLL, MATTHEW. *Trades-Unionism and Military Training.* Proceedings of the Academy of Political Science. July 1916. Volume 6, Number 4. Pages 134–145.

"While there may have been for centuries a vague acquiesence in more or less compulsion in military service," Woll contends, "compulsory military service is now neither legal, constitutional, nor justified. The finding of men for military service has rightfully become and should remain nothing more than an ordinary contract of service, which one may accept or refuse at discretion." He asserts that "organized labor favors voluntary military service maintained by means of enlistment and is unalterably opposed to a revival of a compusory system. That many nations, especially ancient and medieval, have in desperate time of fortune resorted to compulsory military service should scarcely be deemed a lawful or meritorious origin for an American rule of law."

WOOLSEY, THEODORE S. *Freedom of the Land and Freedom of the Seas.* Yale Law Journal. December 1918. Volume 28, Number 2. Pages 151–157.

Asserts that "the one factor above all others which dominates the nation possessed by militarism . . . is the principle of conscription." In this view, once any single powerful state institutes conscription, it is inevitable that other nations adopt the practice "in the name of national defense." Accordingly, the only way to abolish the "military caste" is to surrender the universal-service principle that gave rise to it.

Pamphlets, Reprints, and Speeches

AMERICAN FRIENDS SERVICE COMMITTEE. *America Questions Peacetime Conscription.* 1945. Philadelphia. 47 pages.

Selections from the testimony before the House Select Committee on Military Affairs, June 4–19, 1945. This booklet presents extracts from the testimony offered by those speaking in opposition to conscription, together with a summary of the arguments pro and con, and a list of the organizations and individuals who testified.

AMERICAN FRIENDS SERVICE COMMITTEE. *Peace Time Conscription ... A Problem.* 1944. Philadelphia. 14 pages.

This pamphlet discusses briefly the origin of modern military conscription, current and former proposals for peacetime conscription, universal military training, and the implications of conscription for democracy, education, morality, and national security.

BOSS, CHARLES FREDERICK, JR. *Goose-Step Legislation: Shall the United States Adopt Peacetime Compulsory Military Training?* 1946. Commission on World Peace of the Methodist Church. Chicago. 30 pages.

Presents various argument against proposed legislation for compulsory military training; advocates instead efforts to establish security by international agreement, including the universal abolition of compulsory military training.

BULLITT, WILLIAM C. *Report to the American People.* 1940. Houghton Mifflin Co. Boston. 29 pages.

Text of a speech on August 18, 1940, to the American Philosophical Society. In this plea for public support for the introduction of conscription, the U.S. ambassador to France calls upon Americans to "tell our Government that we want to defend our homes and our children and our liberties, whatever the cost in money or blood." He notes that, "in the name of the preservation of individual liberty, the national liberty of France was condemned in advance to destruction" by the Germans in 1939 because of the failure of the French to mobilize for national defense by compulsory national service.

CALHOUN, DONALD W. *Conscription and the Four Freedoms.* Circa 1946. Plowshare Press. New York. 10 pages.

This booklet presents a concise set of arguments against conscription, based on the "four basic freedoms" inherent in the American system. Freedom of religion implies the right of an individual to choose the principle and allegiance toward which his or her ultimate loyalty will be directed; freedom of speech and criticism presupposes the right to think for oneself, which is contrary to the military principle that one thinks as one's superior thinks; freedom from fear is impossible in a society where the state is primary and the individual secondary; and freedom from want would be undermined by conscription in that it presupposes a chain from military preparedness to military expenditure to production reorientation from consumer goods into noneconomic channels.

COMMITTEE FOR ECONOMIC DEVELOPMENT. *Military Manpower and National Security: A Statement of National Policy.* 1972. New York. 41 pages.

The statement addresses itself on the one hand to the question of manpower policies, including the draft and long-term procedures for the recruitment and management of military personnel, and on the other hand to the question of accountability, focusing on ways in which Congress might assume greater responsibility for the commitment of military manpower. The statement proposes an annual military manpower review to provide a framework for informed public discussion and debate.

COMMITTEE TO OPPOSE THE CONSCRIPTION OF WOMEN. *Before It Is Too Late.* Circa 1942. Distributed by the Post War World Council. New York. 3 pages.

In this Statement of Purpose, the National Committee to Oppose the Conscription of Women announces its "campaign to arouse the general public, organizations and legislatures to the dangers inherent in a move to widen the draft to include women." Popular support is sought for a stand "against both compulsory registration and conscription of women for war work, whether by law or by executive order."

DOLE, CHARLES F. *Will Conscription Destroy War?* The Association to Abolish War. Brookline, Massachusetts. 16 pages. Reprint from The Libertarian, June 1925.

Suggests that it is futile to argue the constitutionality of conscription so long as war itself is "licensed by 'civilized' nations." In this view, both war and conscription are "survivals of barbarism" to which we in the modern world have not yet applied the same degree of reason that we have applied to such outdated practices as gladitorial games and slavery. Dole predicts that conscientious objection will eventually rise to a point where the unity necessary for prosecuting a war would be rendered impossible.

EISENHOWER, DWIGHT D. *Statement on Demobilization.* January 15, 1946. Army Times. Washington, D.C. 16 pages.

Statement by U.S. Army Chief of Staff Dwight D. Eisenhower to supplement his remarks on demobilization made to members of Congress on January 15, 1946. The statement is concerned with the postwar army and the need to assure an adequate number of volunteers.

ETTER, ORVAL. *The Compulsion of Conscription.* 1949. Fellowship of Reconciliation. Berkeley, California. 11 pages.

Compares compulsion in conscription with compulsion in the jury system, the tax system, the schools, and other compulsory systems such as compulsory fire-fighting, compulsory assistance to police officers making arrests, and traffic regulations. The compulsion of conscription, it is contended, is even more extreme than that of the prison system, inasmuch as the latter, while imposing restrictions on freedom of movement and denying choice of occupation, does not entail compulsory homicide.

FARRER, JAMES ANSON. *The Moral Cant About Conscription.* 1912. International Arbitration and Peace Association. London. 48 pages.

This booklet, issued during the debate on conscription that preceded World War I, attempts to counter public arguments of the pro-conscriptionist National Service League and its chief protagonists, Lord Roberts and George Shee, who advocate various systems of compulsory military training and service. Arguing from an antimilitarist base, the author denies that evidence exists to support the league's assertion that a causal relationship obtains between universal compulsory military training and service, on the one hand, and the moral, physical, or industrial betterment of the nation or of individuals, on the other.

FELLOWSHIP OF RECONCILIATION. *Why America Should Not Adopt Conscription.* 1940. New York. 3 pages.

Contends that the enactment of conscription in the United States would "undermine by our own hand foundations on which our democratic liberties have rested for 167 years." It is argued that "any legislation embodying military conscription—such as the Burke–Wadsworth Bill—is a Trojan horse which, under the guise of defending our country and equalizing the burdens of defense, would in fact introduce the very disease which has proved so deadly to Europe and against which our democracy would be no more proof than were the democracies of France and England."

FOSDICK, HARRY EMERSON. *The Crisis Confronting the Nation.* Vital Speeches of the Day. September 1, 1940. Volume 6, Number 22. Pages 686–687.

"In a time when we are not at war, and when an overwhelming majority of the American people are determined not to go to war," states Fosdick, "we are being rushed pell-mell into military conscription as a settled national policy." By opening the door, instead, to one-year voluntary enlistment, it might be possible to secure adequate manpower, increase the length of training (from the eight-month training period proposed by the current conscription bill), and at the same time "avoid the whole radical dislocation of American life involved in conscription."

FREEMAN, HARROP A., and RUTH S. FREEMAN. *Conscription After the War?* 1945. Fellowship Publications. New York. Illustrations, tables. 63 pages.

This booklet is oriented to the high school student facing the possible prospect of conscription for military training after World War II. It presents and evaluates arguments for and against peacetime conscription in regard to questions of health, law, religion, education, and military necessity. Questions for discussion and research follow individual chapters.

FREEMAN, HARROP A., and RUTH S. FREEMAN. *Now Is the Time for International Abolition of Conscription.* 1945. No Conscription Council. London. 7 pages.

Brief discussion of proposals for international abolition of conscription during and since World War I. Focuses on Britain, the United States, and the Soviet Union.

GRAHAM, JOHN. *The Universal Military Obligation.* 1958. Fund for the Republic. New York. 16 pages.

A short study of "the role of the government in its capacity as an organization for the common defense, and, in particular, the relation of this function to individual freedom." It is possible, Graham maintains, to achieve a more equitable, more stable system that fulfills the basic manpower requirements of the defense establishment without discrimination and injustice. He advocates enactment of the Cordiner proposals for a revised military pay structure; reliance on civilian organization for support functions; and raising initial pay rates, to convert the military to a long-service, highly trained professional force with a reserve system designed to meet only actual requirements.

HUIDEKOPER, FREDERIC L. *Is the United States Prepared for War?* 1907. North American Review Publishing Co. New York. 47 pages. Reprint from North American Review. February and March 1906.

Introduction by William H. Taft. Huidekoper contends that, "thanks to the parsimony and short-sightedness of Congress, our Regular Army has invariably been much too small to meet our requirements in time of war—and, indeed, often in time of peace—so that it has always been necessary to depend largely upon the Militia and Volunteers." Examining the cost of wars, in men and money, in which the United States has been engaged, he urges the application of "sound business foresight and judgment and progressive business methods" to military manpower policy. An adequate standing army would number one soldier to each 1,000 of population in peacetime; the militia should be relegated to the third line of defense, and "nothing more should be expected of it"; while the creation of a "First Reserve similar to that which exists in every European army" should be considered imperative.

LIBBY, FREDERICK J. *Military Training in the Making of Men.* Circa 1944. American Union Against Militarism. Washington, D.C. 15 pages.

Opposing a permanent policy of conscription after the war, Libby argues that military training may inculcate patriotism in time of war, but is not likely to do so in peacetime. He discusses various arguments used in support of a permanent system of universal military training.

LITTEL, J. McGREGOR. *The Draft (Compulsory Training).* 1940. Mount Arlington, New Jersey. 30 pages.

A businessman's attempt to rally support against postwar conscription. Includes statements of Secretary of War Henry L. Stimson, Senator B. K. Wheeler, the American Federation of Labor, the Congress of Industrial Organizations, and the Chamber of Commerce of the United States.

LUCEY, WILLIAM L. *Get the Record Straight on Permanent Conscription.* Reprint from America: A Catholic Review of the Week. May 13, 1944. 2 pages.

A critique of current legislative proposals for permanent peacetime conscription by Representatives Andrew J. May and James W. Wadsworth. Argues that proposals for conscription must be considered on their own merits and must be divorced from the postwar need for military manpower and the physical, moral, and spiritual training of youth, and that conscription is not the solution to either of these problems.

MALLERY, LAWRENCE R., JR. (compiler). *Sourcebook: Peacetime Compulsory Military Training.* 1948. American Friends Service Committee. Philadelphia. 55 pages.

A compilation of quotations from U.S. military and government leaders, scientists, educators, and journalists, as reported in the daily press. Intended as a worker's manual on the question of militarism in the United States in general and peacetime compulsory military training in particular.

MARLIN, JEFF. *Conscription and War.* 1940. American Peace Mobilization. Washington, D.C. 15 pages.

Handbook soliciting support for repeal of the draft law. Discusses conscription and national defense, the mechanism of the draft, the shift to military law, conscription and organized labor, conscientious objectors, war protestors, and conscription and foreign wars.

NATIONAL COUNCIL AGAINST CONSCRIPTION. *Conscription Factfolder 1–12.* Circa 1954. Washington, D.C.

A series of 12 four-page folders on various aspects of proposed programs for conscription, universal military training, and reserve forces.

NATIONAL COUNCIL AGAINST CONSCRIPTION. *Conscription News.* November 21, 1944, to October 23, 1959. Numbers 1–262. Washington, D.C.

A newsletter issued irregularly by the council, presenting reports and analyses of legislative and political developments in regard to military manpower procurement policy in the United States.

NATIONAL COUNCIL AGAINST CONSCRIPTION. *The Facts About Compulsory Military Service and . . .* Circa 1951. Washington, D.C.

A series of 10 folders issued by the council in opposition to proposals for permanent peacetime conscription. The respective folders deal with conscription in relation to army life (i.e., *The Facts About Compulsory Military Service and Army Life*), casualties, crime, democracy, health, indoctrination, lawlessness, peace, security, and compulsory military service in other countries.

NATIONAL COUNCIL AGAINST CONSCRIPTION. *The Facts About the Pentagon's New Conscription Plans.* 1955. Washington, D.C. 34 pages.

Presents 45 questions and answers concerning the peacetime conscription plan before Congress, to follow expiration of the 1950 law that was used to raise troops for the Korean War. Taking an anticonscriptionist, antiwar posture, this sourcebook deals with such questions as manpower and cost; conscription and war; science and technology; higher education; administration; volunteering; and reserve systems. It draws heavily on congressional testimony and other contemporary analyses and reports.

NATIONAL COUNCIL AGAINST CONSCRIPTION. [Miscellaneous pamphlets] (Hoover Institution Collection). 1946 to 1958. Washington, D.C.

This collection includes about 30 pamphlets taking various positions, all in opposition to conscription. Most of the pamphlets were issued in response to specific proposals for legislation, in particular the proposal to introduce peacetime conscription and subsequent proposals for universal military training.

NATIONAL FEDERATION FOR CONSTITUTIONAL LIBERTIES. *Conscription and Civil Liberties.* Reprint from the International Juridical Association Monthly Bulletin. August 1940. 30 pages.

A critical analysis of the Burke–Wadsworth conscription bill and subsequent amendments, which would introduce the first peacetime conscription in the United States.

NEW YORK PEACE ASSOCIATION. *The Truth About Conscription.* Circa 1940. New York. 16 pages.

Pamphlet urging popular resistance to proposed military conscription legislation.

NORTHERN CALIFORNIA COMMITTEE TO OPPOSE PEACETIME CONSCRIP-
TION NOW. *Peacetime Conscription.* Circa 1947. San Francisco. 5 pages.

Illustrated pamphlet questioning whether peacetime conscription can
provide security, democracy, or peace, and whether military service is the
proper avenue for tackling national problems such as health, vocational
training, and employment.

POGUE, FORREST CARLISLE. *The Revolutionary Transformation of the
Art of War.* 1974. American Enterprise Institute for Public Policy
Research. Washington, D.C. 21 pages.

Address delivered at the U.S. Military Academy, West Point, New
York, on May 9, 1974. Reviews the development of the American military
system and the manpower policies at different periods. Upholding the
concept of the obligation of the citizen to the nation, Pogue states that
"the basic military lesson of the American Revolution lay in the importance to a democracy of a well-trained army, representative of the whole
people."

POST WAR WORLD COUNCIL. [Unlisted material] (Hoover Institution
Collection). 1942–1948. New York.

A collection of some 50 circular letters sent to members, prospective
members, and supporters of the council. Each letter documents at least
one area in which the council is actively involved; many of them concern
conscription. There are attachments to many of the letters, including
petitions and position papers. The letters provide a record of the council's
activities and positions during and after World War II and of the individuals most active in the council, notably Norman Thomas and Oswald
Garrison Villard.

REEVE, JULIET, and others (compilers). *Sourcebook on Peacetime Conscription.* 1944. American Friends Service Committee. Philadelphia.
Index. Tables. Bibliography: pages 48–49. 52 pages.

Containing extracts from books, articles, and statements, this booklet
presents opposing viewpoints on conscription and its military, psychological, economic, political, and social impact upon society.

SCHUHLE, BILL. *Illustrated Arguments for Peacetime Conscription.* Circa
1945. Fellowship of Reconciliation. New York. 8 pages.

Eight arguments used by proponents of peacetime conscription in the United States are illustrated, with counterarguments. The eight arguments contend that conscription: (1) imposes discipline, (2) provides defense, (3) maintains peace, (4) eases unemployment, (5) decreases crime, (6) builds health, (7) develops citizenship, and (8) stops aggression.

STIMSON, HENRY L. *Our Duty Is Clear.* Vital Speeches of the Day. August 15, 1940. Volume 6, Number 21. Pages 647–648.

Address of the secretary of war before the House Military Affairs Committee in support of the Burke–Wadsworth bill, urging the adoption of compulsory military service. Stimson maintains that "the Selective Compulsory System is the closest approximation to both efficiency and justice which the experience of this country has yet evolved."

SWOMLEY, JOHN M., JR. *The Cost of Conscription: A Critical Review of the Universal Military Training and Service Act.* 1959. National Council Against Conscription. Washington, D.C. 12 pages.

Appealing for support against extension of the power to induct, this pamphlet describes the present law as discriminatory and inequitable, and maintains that conscription is not only inefficient, but cannot accomplish the end for which it was adopted. Swomley discusses a voluntary military establishment as the alternative to conscription.

THOMAS, NORMAN. *Conscription: The Test of the Peace.* 1944. Post War World Council. New York. 14 pages.

Foreword by Broadus Mitchell. In this pamphlet Thomas contends that the only enduring peace is one that "requires the end of competitive aggressive armaments and the abolition of universal military conscription." He argues that the acceptance of military conscription has proved itself "the cornerstone of totalitarianism" in both Germany and the Soviet Union. While armies to some extent temporarily equalize civilian inequalities, they introduce their own inequalities. Conscription works against the interests of labor and cannot be considered an economic "cure" for unemployment; and, far from being a builder of health and character, the military system "is undemocratic when it is not anti-democratic."

THOMAS, T. H. *What the Draft Means: Selective Service Neither Militaristic nor Disruptive.* 1940. American Defense, Harvard Group. Cambridge, Massachusetts. 22 pages.

A supportive analysis and comparison of the Burke–Wadsworth conscription bill and the 1917 Selective Service Act. Argues that enactment of the bill would neither commit the nation permanently nor transform regular forces into "a conscript army of the European type."

VILLARD, OSWALD GARRISON. *Universal Military Service.* 1916. Branch of the Woman's Peace Party. Boston. 7 pages.

Presents arguments against conscription, discussing conscription in Germany and elsewhere and its relationship with democracy, conscience, personal liberty, and militarism.

WASHBURN, H. C. *The American Blind Spot: The Failure of the Volunteer System as Shown in Our Military History.* Doubleday, Page & Co. Garden City, New York. 42 pages. Reprint from the United States Naval Institute Proceedings.

This essay contends that only when Americans are educated in "their true military history" and their "ignorance and prejudice" eradicated will the nation be ready to adopt universal compulsory military training as the solution to American problems of preparedness. Washburn argues that the duty of military service is inherent in citizenship, that universal service is the only scientific method since it distributes the loss of men among all classes or grades of human value to the nation, and that compulsion in military service should be as acceptable to Americans as compulsion in taxation, police regulation, sanitation and pure food laws, and education.

WEBSTER, DANIEL. *Daniel Webster on the Draft.* 1917. Reprint by the American Union Against Militarism. Washington, D.C. 9 pages.

Text of a speech delivered by Webster in the House of Representatives on December 9, 1814. The speech was not published at the time Webster gave it, and early editions of Webster's works did not mention it. Finally published in 1902 (see *The Letters of Daniel Webster*, above, page 84), it is an eloquent, powerful attack on the idea of conscription, and was instrumental in defeating the 1814 legislation that proposed to draft all males in the United States between the ages of 18 and 45.

WHEELER, BURTON K. *Marching down the Road to War.* Vital Speeches of the Day. September 1, 1940. Volume 6, Number 22. Pages 689–692.

Contends that peacetime conscription is not militarily necessary in the United States, that is would violate individual liberty, and that its enactment would represent an unwarranted departure from traditional national policy.

WOOD, LEONARD. *National Defense.* Circa 1916. N.p. 42 pages.

Contains the text of Major-General Wood's speech to St. Paul's School, Concord, New Hampshire. He argues against a large standing army, but in favor of an army sufficient for an expeditionary force or to deal with internal disorders that neither police nor militia may be adequate to control. The army and the navy must be supported by adequate reserves, with a militia and reserves under federal control, backed by volunteers trained in peacetime. Universal military training is seen as beneficial to the morals, physique, and character of youth. The booklet includes an article by Henry Ferguson contending that the Swiss system can with convenience and economy be adapted to the needs of the United States, and another, by Anton T. McCook, advocating compulsory military training in the schools.

WRIGHT, FRANK LEE. *The Case Against Conscription.* Reprint from the Christian Century. March 7, 1945. 7 pages.

Enumerates 10 reasons why current congressional bills proposing peacetime conscription should be rejected.

Government Documents: Publications

BORAH, WILLIAM E. *Conscription.* 1917. Government Printing Office. Washington, D.C. 16 pages.

Speech by the Idaho senator on April 28, 1917, opposing conscription "because it does not provide the best army" and "because it is fundamentally at war with the essential principles of free institutions."

U.S. CONGRESS. HOUSE. COMMITTEE ON ARMED SERVICES. *Civilian Advisory Panel on Military Manpower Procurement.* 1967. Government Printing Office. Washington, D.C. 30 pages.

Report to the House Committee on Armed Services by the Civilian Advisory Panel on Military Manpower Procurement headed by Mark Clark and charged with analyzing and evaluating the equity and effectiveness of existing laws and policies relating to military personnel procurement. Dated February 28, 1967.

U.S. CONGRESS. SENATE. COMMITTEE ON ARMED SERVICES. *Report of Citizens' Advisory Commission on Manpower Utilization in the Armed Services.* 1953. Government Printing Office. Washington, D.C. 85 pages.

Final report of the Sarnoff Commssion, which studied manpower utilization in the armed forces.

U.S. DEFENSE MANPOWER COMMISSION. *Defense Manpower: The Keystone of National Security.* April 1976. Government Printing Office. Washington, D.C. Charts, tables, graphs. 518 pages.

Chartered to "conduct a broad and comprehensive study and investigation of the overall manpower requirements of the Department of Defense (DoD) on both a short-term and long-term basis" the Commission addressed itself to these major subject areas: (1) National Defense in Perspective, (2) Leadership and Human Relations Within the DoD, (3) Managing Defense Manpower, (4) The Total Force and Its Manpower Requirements, (5) Recruiting the Military for the Total Force, (6) Developing and Utilizing the Total Force, (7) Shaping the Military Career Force of the Future, (8) Compensation and Retirement, and (9) The All Volunteer Force and Its Future. One of the most thorough studies ever undertaken of the defense manpower needs of the United States, the report concludes that U.S. manpower needs can be met with the All Volunteer Force over the next 10 years and contains many recommendations for improving the recruitment, training, compensation, and utilization of defense manpower.

U.S. DEPARTMENT OF DEFENSE. CENTRAL ALL-VOLUNTEER TASK FORCE. *Utilization of Military Women (A Report of Increased Utilization of Military Women—FY 1973–1977).* 1972. National Technical Information Service, U.S. Department of Commerce. Springfield, Virginia. 173 pages.

This study examines the utilization of military women and prepares contingency plans for increasing the use of women to offset possible shortages of male recruits after the end of the draft. It focuses on the critical transition period of fiscal years 1973–1977 when male accessions may not meet requirements or the cost of attracting males of the requisite quality may be increased. The report concentrates on six main areas: (1) history of women in the armed forces; (2) potential supply of women for the armed forces; (3) assignment policies; (4) attrition rates; (5) costs of military women versus men; and (6) service plans for increasing use of military women.

U.S. DEPARTMENT OF THE ARMY. *The Army and Industrial Manpower.* By Byron Fairchild and Jonathan Grossman. 1959. Office of the Chief of Military History, Department of the Army. Washington, D.C. Index. Charts, tables. Bibliographical note: page 261–268. 291 pages.

This volume, one of the series United States Army in World War II, is the seventh published in the subseries The War Department. It examines the War Department's role in industrial mobilization, and the problems into which the army was drawn in dealing with organized labor. Of particular interest are Chapters 10 and 11 (pages 197–245), which discuss such subjects as selective service as a sanction, and the War Department and national service.

U.S. DEPARTMENT OF THE ARMY. *Chief of Staff: Prewar Plans and Preparations.* By Mark Skinner Watson. 1950. Historical Division, Department of the Army. Washington, D.C. Index. Illustrations, charts, tables. Bibliographical note: pages 521–526. 551 pages.

This volume is the sixth published in the series United States Army in World War II and the first in the subseries The War Department. Chapters 6, 7, and 8 deal with the army's activities in mobilizing, organizing, and employing its forces in World War II. Included is a discussion of military manpower procurement policy development and the implementation of the draft.

U.S. DEPARTMENT OF THE ARMY. *The Procurement and Training of Ground Combat Troops.* By Robert R. Palmer, Bell I. Wiley, and

General Works

William R. Keast. 1948. Department of the Army. Washington, D.C. Index. Tables. Bibliographical note: pages 657–663. 696 pages.

This volume is the second published in the series United States Army in World War II, and the second in the subseries The Army Ground Forces. It deals with the procurement and training of enlisted men and officers, looking at such questions as the problems of quality in the period of mobilization, and the provision of replacements.

U.S. DEPARTMENT OF THE ARMY. *The Women's Army Corps.* By Mattie E. Treadwell. 1954. Department of the Army. Washington, D.C. Index. Illustrations, charts, tables. Bibliographical notes. 841 pages.

Prepared in the office of the Chief of Military History, this volume in the series The United States Army in World War II deals with the integration of women into the army. Chapters 13 and 14 are of special interest, discussing recruitment policies and practices as well as public attitudes.

U.S. LIBRARY OF CONGRESS. *The Military Selective Service Act of 1967: A Survey of Proposals and Studies Concerning Its Revision or Replacement.* By Albert C. Stillson. 1968. Library of Congress. Washington, D.C. 39 pages.

Part 1 surveys proposals for selective service reform that were made prior to the enactment of the Military Selective Service Act of 1967, the Selective Service System as it exists subsequent to the act, and some of the editorial opinion expressed with respect to the act. Part 2 considers proposals for a lottery induction system, administration of the Selective Service System, and proposals for selective service reform currently before Congress. Part 3 discusses replacement of selective service, including proposals for a volunteer military establishment, universal military training, and national service.

U.S. LIBRARY OF CONGRESS. *Selected Views on Conscription in the United States.* 1941. Bulletin No. 2, Topics of Interest to Congress. Library of Congress. Washington, D.C. 18 pages.

Consists primarily of extracts from the *Congressional Record*, including statements of members of Congress and others favorably or unfavorably disposed to the reintroduction of conscription in World War II.

U.S. MILITARY ACADEMY. *Economics of National Security.* Edited by G. A. Lincoln and T. H. Harvey. 1950. Prentice-Hall. New York. Index. Diagrams, tables. 601 pages.

Chapter 3, on manpower, discusses universal military training, current manpower mobilization planning, national service, and "work or fight."

U.S. MILITARY ACADEMY. *Essays on American Military Institutions.* Volume 1. By Samuel H. Hays. 1969. West Point, New York. Bibliography: pages 184–211. 211 pages.

This collection of essays considers the military organization as a social system, military institutions and national objectives, the social impact of military support systems, and organization and control. Of particular interest are: "American Military Institutions in Perspective," "Changing Roles Within American Military Systems," "Military Roles in Peace and Crisis," and "National Control in a Federal System."

U.S. NATIONAL ADVISORY COMMISSION ON SELECTIVE SERVICE. *In Pursuit of Equity: Who Serves When Not All Serve?* 1967. Government Printing Office. Washington, D.C. Charts, tables. 219 pages.

Report of the commission established under Burke Marshall by President Lyndon B. Johnson. Rejects propositions for: (1) elimination of the draft and reliance on an all-volunteer military force; (2) a system of universal training; (3) a system of compulsory national service; and (4) volunteer national service as an alternative to military service. Recommended is a modified Selective Service System "consolidated and operated under a more centralized administration, with its controlling concept the rule of law, to assure equal treatment for those in like circumstances."

U.S. OFFICE OF DEFENSE MOBILIZATION. *Manpower Resources for National Security.* 1954. Government Printing Office. Washington, D.C. Illustration. 70 pages.

Report of the Appley Committee, which studied manpower needs for national security. Includes recommendations on manpower utilization by the director of the Office of Defense Mobilization.

U.S. PRESIDENT'S TASK FORCE ON MANPOWER CONSERVATION. *One-Third of a Nation: A Report on Young Men Found Unqualified for*

Military Service. 1964. Government Printing Office. Washington, D.C.
Charts, tables. 86 pages.

The report notes that one of every two selective service registrants
called for preinduction examination is found unqualified, and it finds
that if all the 1,400,000 young men turning 18 in 1964 were to be
examined, about one-third would be found disqualified, half for medical
reasons, the remainder through inability to qualify on the mental test.
The majority of those disqualified appeared to be victims of inadequate
education and health services. The task force recommends a nationwide
manpower conservation program to provide military rejectees with education, training, health rehabilitation, and related services.

U.S. SELECTIVE SERVICE SYSTEM. *Manning the U.S. Armed Forces in a
Post All-Volunteer Force Era: The Historic Lessons of Conscription
and All-Volunteer Force Successes and Failures in the U.S. and Eight
Other Countries*. By Kenneth J. Coffey. 3 volumes. [1975] Selective
Service System. Washington, D.C. 1437 pages.

A study prepared for the Selective Service System by Kenneth J. Coffey
(submitted under the name of Research and Evaluation Services, Inc.,
formerly P.S.C. Company). The body of the study, contained in Volumes
1 and 2, has nine chapters dealing respectively with: (1) military conscription systems and policies from pre-World War II through 1973;
(2) armed forces policies and activities from pre-World War II through
1973; (3) conscription of women; (4) conscientious objection policies
and procedures; (5) a comparative study of recent all-volunteer force
programs; (6) military manpower procurement policies from post-World
War II through 1973; (7) a comparative evaluation of the systems of
military manpower procurement; (8) the possible alternatives in military
manpower procurement systems; and (9) the procurement of military
manpower in the post all-volunteer force era. Volume 3, the appendix,
contains 514 pages of documents related to the text and organized by
country, comparative summaries of key data, and selected bibliographies
on each country. The countries covered in the study are the United States,
Australia, Canada, France, Germany, Israel, Switzerland, the U.S.S.R.,
and the United Kingdom.

U.S. WAR DEPARTMENT. *Epitome of Upton's Military Policy of the
United States*. 1916. Government Printing Office. Washington, D.C.
23 pages.

Extracts from Emory Upton's *Military Policy of the United States*, reproduced by the War Department "in order to bring to the attention of our citizens the facts of our military history as bearing upon the present problem of national preparedness for defense." (See also page 46, above.)

U.S. WAR DEPARTMENT. *Measures to Provide for the Common Defense.* 1916. Government Printing Office. Washington, D.C. 20 pages.

Statement by the secretary of war to the House Committee on Military Affairs on January 6, 1916. Recommends a highly trained, expansible Regular Army, together with federal volunteers raised, officered, and trained in time of peace, and the National Guard for state uses.

U.S. WAR DEPARTMENT. *Proposed Military Policy.* 1915. Government Printing Office. Washington, D.C. 8 pages.

Outline of a military policy for the United States proposed by Secretary of War Lindley Garrison. Proposes a voluntary system based on "existing conditions of a legal and constitutional nature" and recognition of "existing institutions and the feeling of the people."

U.S. WAR DEPARTMENT. *Three-Year Enlistment for the Army.* 1912. Government Printing Office. Washington, D.C. 71 pages.

Contains the views of the President, the secretary of war, the Army Chief of Staff, and various military institution leaders on the question of enlistments in the U.S. Army.

WEEKS, JOHN W. *Increase of Military Establishment.* 1917. Government Printing Office. Washington, D.C. 27 pages.

Speech of the senator from Massachusetts on April 23, 1917, urging the introduction of conscription. It is contended that in each of the wars fought by the United States, volunteering has entailed greater costs, both in money and in lives, than would have been the case under a system of conscription.

Government Documents: Congressional Hearings

1916. U.S. CONGRESS. HOUSE. COMMITTEE ON MILITARY AFFAIRS. *Efficiency of the United States Military Establishment.* Government Printing Office. Washington, D.C. 1294 pages.

Hearings between January 8 and February 11, 1916, before the House Committee on Military Affairs to consider ways to increase the efficiency of the U.S. military establishment.

1926. U.S. CONGRESS. HOUSE. COMMITTEE ON MILITARY AFFAIRS. *Council of National Defense.* Government Printing Office. Washington, D.C. 77 pages..

Hearings between April 6 and 20, 1926, before the House Committee on Military Affairs on House bills 10243, 10982, and 10985, considering the establishment of a council of national defense. Includes testimony on military manpower procurement policy.

1927. U.S. CONGRESS. HOUSE. COMMITTEE ON MILITARY AFFAIRS. *The National Defense.* Government Printing Office. Washington, D.C. Index. Tables. 659 pages.

Hearing on March 3, 1927, before the House Committee on Military Affairs. Contains historical documents relating to the reorganization plans of the War Department and to the National Defense Act.

1928. U.S. CONGRESS. HOUSE. COMMITTEE ON MILITARY AFFAIRS. *Universal Draft.* Government Printing Office. Washington, D.C. 55 pages.

Hearings on May 21, 1928, before the House Committee on Military Affairs on House bills 455, 8313, and 8329 on the conscription of manpower, wealth, and industrial resources in time of war.

1933. U.S. CONGRESS. HOUSE. COMMITTEE ON MILITARY AFFAIRS. *Gen. Johnson Hagood on National Defense and the Reorganization of the Army.* Government Printing Office. Washington, D.C. 87 pages.

Hearing on April 12, 1933, before the House Committee on Military Affairs. Contains General Johnson Hagood's testimony on national defense and the reorganization of the army.

1943. U.S. CONGRESS. HOUSE. COMMITTEE ON MILITARY AFFAIRS. *To Make the Women's Army Auxiliary Corps a Part of the Regular Army.* Government Printing Office. Washington, D.C. 40 pages.

Hearing on March 9, 1943, before the House Committee on Military Affairs on Senate bill 495 to establish a women's army auxiliary corps for service in the U.S. Army for the duration of World War II.

1943. U.S. CONGRESS. HOUSE. COMMITTEE ON MILITARY AFFAIRS. *Full Utilization of Manpower.* Government Printing Office. Washington, D.C. 1068 pages.

Hearings between March 25 and May 7, 1943, before the House Committee on Military Affairs on House bills 2239, 1742, 1728, and 992 to amend the Selective Service and Training Act of 1940 and to provide further for the successful prosecution of the war by prohibiting acts interfering with the full utilization of manpower.

1945. U.S. CONGRESS. HOUSE. COMMITTEE ON MILITARY AFFAIRS. *Demobilization of the Army of the United States.* Government Printing Office. Washington, D.C. 94 pages.

Hearings on August 28 and 31, 1945, before the House Committee on Military Affairs considering legislation to remove legal impediments to the maximum procurement of volunteers and to furnish inducements so as to stimulate voluntary enlistments and reduce inductions.

1946. U.S. CONGRESS. HOUSE. COMMITTEE ON MILITARY AFFAIRS. *Demobilization of Army.* Government Printing Office. Washington, D.C. 32 pages.

Hearing on January 22, 1946, before the House Committee on Military Affairs on the demobilization of the army. Includes a 16-page statement by Dwight D. Eisenhower on the problem of effecting expedient demobilization of World War II conscripts while continuing to maintain an adequate and effective overseas force. Eisenhower upholds the superiority of an all-volunteer army.

1946. U.S. CONGRESS. HOUSE. COMMITTEE ON MILITARY AFFAIRS. *International Abolition of Conscription.* Government Printing Office. Washington, D.C. 83 pages.

Hearings on February 27 and 28, 1946, before the House Committee on Military Affairs on House Resolution 325, urging "that before the United States adopts compulsory military service, the President of the United States, the Secretary of State, and the personal representative of the President of the United States in the United Nations Organization, Edward R. Stettinius, Junior, be, and hereby are, urged to work unceasingly for an immediate international agreement whereby compulsory military service shall be wholly eliminated from the policies and practices of all nations." Giving testimony in favor of the international abolition of conscription are: Congressman Joseph W. Martin, Jr.; Harrop A. Freeman, Cornell University; Edward V. Stanford, National Catholic Educational Association; Senator Arthur Capper; and William G. Carr, National Education Association.

1947. U.S. CONGRESS. SENATE. COMMITTEE ON ARMED SERVICES. *Women's Armed Services Integration Act of 1947.* Government Printing Office. Washington, D.C. 109 pages.

Hearings between July 2 and 15, 1947, before the Senate Committee on Armed Services on (1) Senate bill 1103 to establish the Women's Army Corps in the Regular Army; (2) Senate bill 1527 to authorize the enlistment and appointment of women in the Regular Navy and Marine Corps and the Naval and Marine Corps Reserve; and (3) Senate bill 1641 to establish the Women's Army Corps in the Regular Army and to authorize the enlistment and appointment of women in the Regular Navy and Marine Corps and the Naval and Marine Corps Reserve.

1948. U.S. CONGRESS. HOUSE. COMMITTEE ON ARMED SERVICES. *Women's Army Corps.* Government Printing Office. Washington, D.C. 184 pages.

Hearings between February 18 and March 3, 1948, before Subcommittee No. 3, Organization and Mobilization, of the House Committee on Armed Services, on Senate bill 1641 to establish the Women's Army Corps in the Regular Army and to authorize the enlistment and appointment of women in the Regular Navy and Marine Corps and the Naval and Marine Corps Reserve.

1960. U.S. CONGRESS. HOUSE. COMMITTEE ON ARMED SERVICES. *Utilization of Military Manpower.* Government Printing Office. Washington, D.C. 804 pages.

Hearings between May 12, 1959, and February 4, 1960, before the Special Subcommittee on Utilization of Military Manpower of the House Committee on Armed Services. Includes testimony on enlisted manpower procurement.

1966. U.S. CONGRESS. HOUSE. COMMITTEE ON ARMED SERVICES. *United States Army Combat Readiness.* Government Printing Office. Washington, D.C. 68 pages.

Hearings on May 3 and 4, 1966, before the Preparedness Investigating Subcommittee of the House Committee on Armed Services, considering the army's ability to meet current manpower needs and to maintain an adequate reserve at the same time.

1967. U.S. CONGRESS. HOUSE. COMMITTEE ON ARMED SERVICES. *Female Officers in the Armed Forces.* Government Printing Office. Washington, D.C. 13 pages.

Hearing on April 20, 1967, before Subcommittee No. 1 of the House Committee on Armed Services on House bill 5894 to amend Titles 10, 32, and 37, U.S. Code, in order to remove restrictions on the careers of female officers in the U.S. Army, Navy, Air Force, and Marine Corps.

CHAPTER 4

All-Volunteer Armed Force

Where is it written in the Constitution, in what article or
section is it contained, that you may take children from
their parents, & parents from their children, & compel them
to fight the battles of any war, in which the folly or the
wickedness of Government may engage it?
—Daniel Webster, 1814

Books

BARNES, PETER. *Pawns: The Plight of the Citizen-Soldier.* 1972. Alfred
A. Knopf. New York. Index. Bibliography: pages 279–284. 284 pages.

Criticizes various aspects of the current military organization in the
United States, including the recruiting process, the court-martial system,
and the treatment of conscientious objectors, and offers an interpretation
of the intentions of the framers of the Constitution with regard to a standing army. Alternative systems are considered, including an all-volunteer
force, but the author concludes that reform of the current system must
come first, through public pressure, before any major reorganization, such
as the replacement of the draft by an all-volunteer force, should be considered.

BAYNES, J. C. M. *The Soldier in Modern Society.* 1972. Barnes & Noble,
Inc. New York. 227 pages.

Written by a British army officer, this book is directed largely to that
service. The main portion of the book is devoted to an examination of
current public attitudes toward the army on such questions as recruitment, training, and career development. A four-point program is recommended: (1) promoting the "science of recruiting," (2) emphasizing the

welfare of the individual soldier, (3) establishing a system of national voluntary service to include organizations other than the armed forces, and (4) assuring credible public relations.

BINKIN, MARTIN. *The Military Pay Muddle.* 1975. The Brookings Institution. Washington, D.C. 66 pages.

The author argues that the United States is not getting the best value for its recently increased expenditure in military pay. He criticizes the current armed forces pay structure, asserting that the nation is paying more than is necessary to its present military forces as a whole, and that more effective forces could be obtained without increasing current levels of defense spending. To overhaul what is viewed as a paternalistic system and to make it more responsive to market forces, the author recommends: (1) paying salaries to military personnel according to the principle of equal pay for equal work; (2) making the military retirement system more nearly parallel with the federal civilian retirement system; and (3) revising the dependent health-care program.

BRADFORD, ZEB B., and FREDERIC J. BROWN. *The United States Army in Transition.* 1973. Sage Publications. Beverly Hills, California. Index. Tables, figures. 256 pages.

Foreword by Sam C. Sarkesian. Part 1 examines the changing context of national security policy, from cold war to coalition security, and its implications for armed forces policy. Part 2 deals with the development of volunteer forces, reserve force policies, and cost factors. Part 3 discusses the army and its response to social change—its social responsibilities and its need to move toward a pluralistic army "which will attract and retain quality manpower in competition with the American economy, while adjusting to pressure for diversity."

CANBY, STEVEN L. *Military Manpower Procurement: A Policy Analysis.* 1972. Lexington Books. Lexington, Massachusetts. Index. Figures, tables. Bibliography: pages 273–283. 291 pages.

This study first establishes criteria for assessing the relative merits of alternative recruitment systems. It then examines six ways of procuring manpower for the military: selective service, voluntarism, lottery, universal service, sequential system, and mixed systems. Each of these six alternatives is considered in the contexts of peace, limited war, and full mobilization. Canby finds that: (1) no single procurement system is appropriate in all contexts; (2) military manpower policy remains geared to a mobilization strategy rather than to current strategies of nuclear deterrence and less-than-general war; (3) many of the military's manpower difficulties stem from its inefficient compensation system; (4) the additional budget cost of a peacetime volunteer force would be much less than the estimates formerly cited in the public debate; and (5) except under special conditions, deferments are militarily unnecessary, economically undesirable, and possibly unfair.

CHAPMAN, BRUCE K. *The Wrong Man in Uniform: Our Unfair and Obsolete Draft—and How We Can Replace It.* 1967. Trident Press. New York. 143 pages.

Introduction by Congressman Thomas B. Curtis. This book analyzes the inefficiencies and inequities that have developed in the draft due to the rapid increase in population and the changing technological needs of the military. The author advocates replacing the draft with a volunteer, career military force and a strong citizen-reserve, arguing that the overall cost of a volunteer army could be significantly below that estimated by the Department of Defense. Large savings could be made in training costs through expanded use of civilians in support positions and through increased use of the civilian vocational educational system in the training of noncombat military personnel.

CHU, DAVID S. C., and others. *Physical Standards in an All-Volunteer Force.* 1974. The Rand Corporation. Santa Monica, California. Tables. 136 pages.

A comparison of U.S. military enlistment standards with (1) those of the armed forces of other advanced nations and (2) those for entry-level jobs in the U.S. civilian sector suggests that they may be higher than necessary, especially for support positions. The conclusion that American enlistment standards may be higher than necesasry is reinforced by a comparison of enlistment standards with the standards used for retention and mobilization. Suggested for review are several areas where certain changes might reduce the current rate of physical disqualification by as much as 40 percent; and the costs implied in lowering physical standards are analyzed.

COLBY, ELBRIDGE. *The Profession of Arms.* 1924. D. Appleton & Co. New York. 183 pages.

Describes career officer opportunities in the U.S. Army of the 1920s, stressing the army's need for quality recruits. The professional soldier, in the author's view, enters the army "in the spirit of public service," and is prepared both to accept pay "small by comparison with what he might earn elsewhere" and to "lay aside all worries as to promotion, leaving that to the accidents of the lineal list."

ELIOT, GEORGE FIELDING. *The Strength We Need: A Military Program for America Pending Peace.* 1946. Viking Press. New York. Index. 261 pages.

Chapters 6 through 10 analyze "the framework of the military policy and the character and strength of the armed forces which the United States will require to meet these conditions in the immediate future." It is suggested that two categories of trained manpower will be required: the professional soldier and the citizen soldier. The former will be competitively recruited on the labor market, while, to fill the need for citizen soldiers, "the training of every young American for one year in the fundamentals of some form of military duty must be the foundation on which we build." The author believes that, with adequate incentives, "the nation can have voluntarily enlisted armed forces of the size which the national security demands." Thus, conscription for service, as distinguished from compulsory training, "will prove politically out of the question as a permanent policy," and the "real choice lies between making the [professional] services sufficiently attractive to get and keep enough good men, or returning to our former and customary state of military weakness."

GRIFFIN, THOMAS L., JR. *U.S. Marine Corps Officer Procurement for the 70's: Problems and Solutions.* 1972. U.S. Army War College. Carlisle Barracks, Pennsylvania. Bibliography: pages 62–68. 68 pages.

Finds that the implementation of an all-volunteer armed force and zero draft will cause some officer procurement problems for the U.S. Marine Corps—problems of quality more than of quantity.

HAENNI, A. L. *Draftees or Volunteers? An Analysis of Contemporary Military Personnel Policies, Suggested Alternatives and Proposals for a*

New Kind of Military. 1969. Vantage Press. New York. Tables. Biblio-graphical footnotes. 134 pages.

Presents the case for a volunteer military after considering the present draft system, universal military training, and national service. Discusses recent proposals for reforming the military manpower procurement system and delineates the positions of government officials, legislators, and military leaders on the respective merits of the various proposals. The author rebuts the major arguments posed by opponents of a voluntary system as to racial composition, efficiency, democracy, and cost, and offers "a new career pattern for a new kind of army" involving revised pay, incentive, and promotion systems.

HUMAN RESOURCES RESEARCH ORGANIZATION. *Attitudinal Studies of the VOLAR Experiment: Men in Training 1971.* By S. James Goffard, James S. DeGracie, and Robert Vineberg. 1972. Presidio of Monterey, California. Tables. 147 pages.

Prepared for the Office of the Chief of Research and Development, Department of the Army; issued in connection with Project VOLAR, a field experiment conducted in 1971 as part of the Modern Volunteer Army (MVA) program, to evaluate the effects of innovations under the program. In this report, data are discussed from the three questionnaires —VOLAR I, II, and III—that were administered to men during Basic Combat Training and Advanced Individual Training at two posts (Fort Ord and Fort Jackson). Included are substudies of attitudes and absentee-ism, attitudes of a Midwestern sample, and attitudinal effects of accelera-tion in the Basic Combat Training cycle at Fort Jackson.

HUMAN RESOURCES RESEARCH ORGANIZATION. *Attitudinal Studies of the VOLAR Experiment: Permanent Party Personnel 1971.* By S. James Goffard, James S. DeGracie, and Robert Vineberg. 1972. Alexandria, Virginia. Figures, tables. 208 pages.

Prepared for the Office of the Chief of Research and Development, Department of the Army; issued in connection with Project VOLAR, a field experiment conducted in 1971 as part of the Modern Volunteer Army (MVA) program, to evaluate the effects of VOLAR innovations on attitudes toward the army and army career intentions of officers and enlisted men. In this report, data are discussed from questionnaires administered to random samples of permanent party officers and enlisted men (1) at Forts Ord, Jackson, Benning, Carson, and Knox; (2) at Fort Bragg and three posts in USAREUR; and (3) in an army-wide (except Southeast Asia) sample. The questionnaires covered backgrounds, attitudes, plans for the future, and evaluations of possible VOLAR innovations. The analyses of the data are examined.

HUMAN RESOURCES RESEARCH ORGANIZATION. *The Concepts of Performance-Oriented Instruction Used in Developing the Experimental Volunteer Army Training Program.* By John E. Taylor, Eugene R. Michaels, and Mark F. Brennan. 1972. Alexandria, Virginia. Figures, tables. 54 pages.

Prepared for the Office of the Chief of Research and Development, Department of the Army. This report describes the planning and implementing of the Experimental Volunteer Army Training Program (EVATP) at Fort Ord early in 1971. This was the army's first effort to effect major training innovations in the conversion toward an all-volunteer army. By the fall of 1971, the program was being used as a model for implementing the EVATP at other Army Training Centers. In developing the EVATP system, six established learning principles were applied to Basic Combat Training and Advanced Individual Training to modify the conventional training system. Course objectives and performance tests used were developed jointly by Fort Ord and the Human Resources Research Organization. In a comparison with a conventionally trained group, independently conducted by the Infantry School at Fort Benning, EVATP graduates performed significantly better on five out of seven Basic Combat Training subjects, and seven out of nine Advanced Individual Training subjects. In general, these gains were shown by men at all levels of aptitude.

HUMAN RESOURCES RESEARCH ORGANIZATION. *Summary and Review of the VOLAR Experiment 1971: Installation Reports for Forts Benning, Bragg, Carson, and Ord, and HumRRO Permanent Party Studies.* By Robert Vineberg and Elaine N. Taylor. 1972. Alexandria, Virginia. Figures, tables. Sources: page 91. 91 pages.

Prepared for the Office of the Chief of Research and Development, Department of the Army; issued in connection with Project VOLAR, a field experiment conducted in 1971 as part of the Modern Volunteer Army (MVA) program, to evaluate the effects of VOLAR innovations on attitudes toward the army and the army career intentions of officers and enlisted men. The report provides an evaluative summary and consolidation of findings in several studies that focused upon permanent party officer and enlisted personnel. It encompasses (1) evaluations conducted by each VOLAR installation—Forts Benning, Bragg, Carson, and Ord—and described in their post reports, and (2) the HumRRO studies of permanent party personnel at Forts Benning, Carson, Jackson, Knox, and Bragg and at three installations in USAREUR, and of an army-wide sample. Recommendations for future action are made, based on findings concerning conditions that appear to be important to men in making the army a more satisfactory place in which to work and live.

JOHNSTON, JEROME, and JERALD G. BACHMAN. *Young Men and Military Service.* 1972. Institute for Social Research, University of Michigan. Ann Arbor, Michigan. Index. Figures, tables. Bibliography: pages 245–248. 254 pages.

Volume 5 in the Survey Research Center's series Youth in Transition, this work is concerned with attitudes toward military service and with prospects for an all-volunteer armed force. Part 1 studies choice behavior of young men at the end of high school, exploring the reasons why some choose to enlist after high school rather than take a civilian job or continue their education. Part 2 examines issues in the debate over an all-volunteer force, and the feasibility of attracting volunteers by using various incentives. Part 3 considers the implications of the findings for military manpower policy and includes a number of specific recommendations.

KIM, K. H., SUSAN FARRELL, and EWAN CLAGUE. *The All-Volunteer Army: An Analysis of Demand and Supply.* 1971. Praeger Publishers. New York. Figures, tables. Selected bibliography: pages 207–208. 208 pages.

This volume is a revised and edited version of a study made in 1969 by Leo Kramer, Inc., under contract to the Department of the Army. Its purpose was to support and assist the department in formulating its recommendations to the President's Commission on an All-Volunteer Armed Force. The focus of the study is the feasibility of maintaining an all-volunteer army, the major concerns being (1) the personnel requirements of the army, and hence the number of young men who must be brought into the army in a given year, and (2) the budgetary cost of making compensation high enough to draw this required number from volunteers. The study concludes that increased compensation will attract enough volunteers to meet personnel needs up to a point. Beyond that point, the outlay for compensation necessary to attract enough volunteers rises so sharply that an all-volunteer force becomes virtually an impossibility.

KING, EDWARD L. *The Death of the Army: A Pre-mortem.* 1972. Saturday Review Press. New York. Index. 246 pages.

This book calls for various reforms of the army. Asserting that "an end to the draft is necessary except during times when war is declared by Congress," the author charges that military leaders are "making the required noises in support of the volunteer concept, but this is superficial rhetoric that will be accompanied by as many roadblocks as possible."

LIDDELL HART, B. H. *The Remaking of Modern Armies.* 1928. Little, Brown & Co. Boston. Index. 315 pages.

A military officer's treatise on the need for added mobility in U.S. military organization and preparedness. The author scores the deployment of unwieldy conscript armies and calls for a reversion to highly trained, volunteer professional forces. Much of the book deals with specifics of organization, strategy, and tactics.

LIDDELL HART, B. H. *Thoughts on War.* 1944. Faber & Faber. London. Index. 327 pages.

In Chapter 1, on the nature of war, the author contends that a precipitating, if not primary, cause of war in recent times has been provided by conscription; that a nation's fear of a military dictatorship may engender the belief that a conscript army is necessarily a cheap military insurance; and that a conscript army is inherently less ready for war than a professional army and therefore, paradoxically, more conducive to war.

LIDDELL HART, B. H. *Why Don't We Learn from History?* 1944. George Allen & Unwin. London. 64 pages.

A treatise against conscription, viewing the compulsory principle followed by France and Prussia as "fundamentally inefficient" and ill-fitting to the conditions of modern warfare. Argues that "every unwilling man is a germ-carrier, spreading infection to an extent altogether disproportionate to the value of the service he is forced to contribute."

LISTON, ROBERT. *Greeting: You Are Hereby Ordered for Induction ...* 1970. McGraw-Hill Book Co. New York. Index. 157 pages.

A journalist discusses the origins of the draft, the draft in war and peace, and such questions as whether the draft is archaic and discriminatory. The alternative to an all-volunteer army is considered.

MARMION, HARRY A. *The Case Against a Volunteer Army.* 1971. Quadrangle Books. Chicago. Index. 107 pages.

Four possible solutions to existing draft problems in the United States are discussed: random selection (but with educational deferments abandoned), universal military training, national service, and an all-volunteer army. The national service proposal favored by the author is said to offer registrants three choices: (1) volunteering for the armed forces; (2) volunteering for "equivalent" civilian service; or (3) taking their chances on being drafted if military needs are not met by volunteers. Marmion argues that a volunteer army would isolate the military from the rest of society, that it would be a "class" army giving rise at the enlisted level to a "significantly high proportion of blacks, poor Appalachian whites, and other working-class groups, particularly in combat units," and that the arguments against the compulsory aspects of the draft are inconsistent with existing institutions of compulsion in education and taxation.

MILLER, JAMES C., III (editor). *Why the Draft? The Case for a Volunteer Army.* 1968. Penguin Books. Baltimore, Maryland. Index. Tables. Selected references: pages 189–191. 197 pages.

Introduction by Senator Edward W. Brooke. A group of economists examines the draft and alternatives to the draft. After summarizing the cases for and against selective service, national service, the lottery, and the volunteer army, they consider these alternatives in regard to equity, feasibility, national tradition, and social balance and democratic ideals. It is concluded that conscription in any form is inequitable inasmuch as it places a tax-in-kind on those forced into service and that, while each of the alternatives is feasible, the volunteer army has the lowest real cost. The authors then examine in detail the proposition of a volunteer army, relating it to national tradition and to the volunteer armies of Britain and Canada, and answering critics of the volunteer system.

New Individualist Review. *Symposium on Conscription.* Spring 1967. Volume 4, Number 4. 64 pages.

Based largely on papers delivered at a conference on the draft at the University of Chicago in December 1966 (see Tax, Sol, page 83, above), this entire issue is devoted to conscription. It includes: "Why Not a Volunteer Army?" by Milton Friedman; "Conscription in a Democratic Society," by Richard Flacks; "The Real Costs of a Volunteer Military," by Walter Y. Oi; "The Politics of Conscription," by Bruce K. Chapman; "Emigration as an Alternative to the Draft," by Joe Michael Cobb; and "Anti-Militarism and Laissez Faire," by James Powell. Also included are the texts of speeches by Robert A. Taft, Oswald Garrison Villard, and Daniel Webster on the antimilitarist tradition in the United States. (For further data, see individual entries.)

Palmer, John McAuley. *An Army of the People: The Constitution of an Effective Force of Trained Citizens.* 1916. G. P. Putnam's Sons. New York. 158 pages.

A military officer looks ahead five years to 1921, when he hopes to witness the establishment of a national volunteer army, trained and organized in time of peace and composed principally of nonprofessional citizen soldiers. In a fictionalized forecast, the Regular Army is reorganized in 1918 and restricted to those special functions that cannot be performed by a citizen soldiery but must be met by an organized body of professional soldiers. The Regular Army maintains the peace administration and trains the volunteer army. The National Guard organized under the Dick Law is disbanded but its trained personnel is passed into the new volunteer army to become the main source of its first contingent of officers and noncommissioned officers. Palmer's system would do away with state militias and would found a centralized army of trained citizenry.

Palmer, John McAuley. *Statesmanship or War.* 1927. Doubleday & Co. Garden City, New York. 232 pages.

Introduction by James W. Wadsworth, Jr. Describes the essential features of the Swiss military system and explains how they can be adapted to American conditions on a purely voluntary basis in the interests of national economy, stable republican institutions, and better world organization, and as a step away from war-provoking militarism. The author, a retired general and military adviser to Congress, draws on America's traditional suspicions of large standing armies, and recommends that the peacetime volunteer army be supplemented by a citizen army drafted in time of national need.

REEDY, GEORGE E. *Who Will Do Our Fighting for Us?* 1969. World Publishing Co. New York. 127 pages.

Introduction by Senator Edward M. Kennedy. The author, former press secretary for President Lyndon Johnson and a draftee in World War II, presents an aggressive attack on the principle of the all-volunteer armed force. Arguing from a layman's point of view, he upholds the morality of the draft, maintaining that "there is no other safeguard of freedom."

REEVES, THOMAS, and KARL HESS. *The End of the Draft: A Proposal for Abolishing Conscription and for a Volunteer Army, for Popular Resistance to Militarism and the Restoration of Individual Freedom.* 1970. Random House. New York. Bibliographical notes at end of each chapter. 200 pages.

Prefaces by Senators Mark O. Hatfield and George McGovern. Contending that the end of the draft is central to the problems of growing militarism in America and to the restoration of individual freedom, this book discusses the abuses of the draft system—its arbitrariness, its inequity, its encouragement of a class system by which only the deprived actually serve, and the way in which it contributes to a war economy, to a "warfare" state of mind, and to increasing control over lives by the military and its allies. The authors present evidence for their arguments that an all-volunteer army need be neither mercenary nor fiscally unsound. They believe that the end of the draft is essential to the restoration of individual freedom in the United States.

SARKESIAN, SAM C. *The Professional Army Officer in a Changing Society.* 1975. Nelson-Hall Publishers. Chicago. Index. Bibliography: pages 256–259. 268 pages.

An analysis of the role of the U.S. military establishment in the post-Vietnam War era. The study focuses on the army "because its problems are visible and urgent," stemming "not only from the Army's ground role in Vietnam but from the number, size, and location of Army posts in the United States and abroad, past reliance on conscription to fill its ranks, the image as the least glamorous of all the services, and the impact of all-volunteer forces."

SARKESIAN, SAM C. (editor). *The Military–Industrial Complex: A Reassessment.* 1972. Sage Publications. Beverly Hills, California. 340 pages.

This book "seeks to reassess the military-industrial complex, not only with respect to conceptual clarity, but to the empirical and substantive issues that are at the core of the debate. In addition to a number of issues dealing with military-industrial linkages, it seeks to explore the potential role of the military in alternative strategies and arms limitations." Of particular interest is the essay by Morris Janowitz that examines "the nature of the emerging military establishment and the impact of the all-volunteer military force." Janowitz suggests that "the end of selective service will have important consequences in both domestic and international areas" and that the "Western European reaction will include a rapid move towards an all-volunteer system in NATO, thereby raising a fundamental question regarding the capability of an all-volunteer system to fulfill international commitments and perform a deterrence role."

STAFFORD, ROBERT R., and others. *How to End the Draft: The Case for an All-Volunteer Army.* Edited by Douglas L. Bailey and Stephen E. Herbits. 1967. National Press. Washington, D.C. Charts, tables. 145 pages.

Authored by five congressmen and endorsed by 17 other congressmen; researched by the editors. This book proposes the creation of an all-volunteer armed force for the United States and an end to conscription. It considers the main argument against an all-volunteer army—that it would be mercenary, predominately black, and undemocratic—and discusses manpower requirements, pay and living conditions, and recruiting. The authors recommend raising initial pay scales of military personnel to the equivalent of civilian pay scales.

SWOMLEY, JOHN M., JR. *The Military Establishment.* 1964. Beacon Press. Boston. Index. Bibliographical notes: pages 255–260. 266 pages.

Foreword by Senator George McGovern. An attempt to trace the growth of military influence over civilian American government. A major portion of the book details the repeated defeats experienced by military leaders in their efforts to establish universal military training following World War II. Swomley, a leader of the National Council Against Conscription, argues for the abolition of peacetime conscription on the basis that "there is no question whatever about the ability of the Army to raise, by volunteering, the number of men it actually needs for combat purposes" and that "it could do this more economically than is possible under conscription."

WALTON, GEORGE. *The Tarnished Shield: A Report on Today's Army.* 1973. Dodd, Mead & Co. New York. Bibliography: pages 263–274. 274 pages.

An overview of American military history and a closer look at some of the current problems facing the army—such as race, drugs, and discipline —lead to the conclusion that today's army reflects similar ills in the greater society. Walton considers the draft versus a volunteer army, presenting the arguments on each side, but does not see either system as being a total solution to the army's dilemma.

Unpublished Manuscripts

CUSICK, JOSEPH D. *Careers for Civilians in the Armed Forces.* 1974. Sloan-Stanford Program, Graduate School of Business, Stanford University. Stanford, California. Charts. Bibliography: pages 106–107. 107 pages.

This study asks: (1) What effect, if any, will the all-volunteer uniformed armed forces have on the career development opportunities of civilian employees of the armed forces? and (2) Will the roles of civilian and uniformed personnel become better defined, more specific, and/or more separate? The discussion focuses on two apparent dichotomies: the specialist-generalist dichotomy and the combat-support dichotomy. Cusick believes that the all-volunteer armed force "will result in greater specialization among the uniformed members of the armed forces," and that "this course of development will create a situation tending towards increased conflict between military and civilian members of the armed forces vying for generalist positions in the management structure."

FRITZSCH, RALPH BURRY. *The Quantity and Quality of Volunteers for Air Force Enlistment in the Absence of a Draft.* 1972. D.B.A. dissertation. George Washington University. Washington, D.C. 212 pages.

Estimates the number of individuals who would apply for Air Force enlistment under present conditions if the draft were eliminated, as well as the distribution of applicant mental aptitudes in the absence of a draft. The subject population used is a 15 percent sample of all individuals applying for Air Force enlistment in 1970. A comparison of the quantity and mental capacity of the applicant population expected in the absence of a draft with the Air Force's stated manpower quantity and quality requirements indicates that the Air Force will have difficulty meeting its requirements in the absence of a draft, especially in areas requiring higher mental aptitudes.

STODDARD, MICHAEL M. *American Conscription: A Policy Evaluation.* 1969. Ph.D. dissertation. University of California. Los Angeles. Bibliography: pages 341–348. 348 pages.

Examines the policy significance of the various systems of conscription (selective service, universal national or military service, the lottery, and the volunteer army) that "the nation could conceivably adopt." Analyzes the nature, values, and impact upon constituents of each of these military recruitment systems, noting their respective goals, methods, and consequences.

Articles

ARBOGAST, KATE A. *Women in the Armed Forces: A Rediscovered Resource.* Military Review. November 1973. Volume LIII, Number 2. Pages 9–19.

Discusses various aspects of the greater utilization of womanpower in the U.S. armed forces resulting from the change to an all-volunteer force. Suggests that women could prove to be the answer to the military's qualitative and quantitative personnel problems.

BARNES, PETER. *All-Volunteer Army?* The New Republic. May 9, 1970. Volume 162, Number 19. Pages 19–23.

Suggests that "there are a number of philosophical reasons, as well as considerations of social equity, which argue against a large all-volunteer army under present conditions." If the draft could be modified "so that limits are placed on the power of the President to conscript, then an army within which there is some freedom and ferment would be the safest, most humane, and most worthy kind of army for our young people and for a healthy democracy."

BARRON'S. *Uncertain Trumpet: The Draft Is Hardly the Best Way to Rally the Troops.* October 25, 1965. Page 1.

This editorial examines the current status of the military in the United States, naming problem areas and outlining solutions. It is contended that the "no-win" policies of the government undermine army morale and that "in rallying the troops, as in waging war, there is no substitute for victory." Draft resisters and opponents, given current law, are considered subversive, giving comfort to the enemy. Deferments and exemptions are opposed as arbitrary and as placing an undue burden on a minority of the population. For now, it is concluded, the draft should continue, all exemptions should be eliminated by executive order, and, as a long-run policy, an all-volunteer army should be considered.

BERGER, ED, and others. *ROTC, Mylai and the Volunteer Army.* Foreign Policy. Spring 1971. Number 2. Pages 135–160.

Reports on a study designed to measure the attitudes toward military service of ROTC students and their service-academy counterparts. Finds that ROTC students "appear to be less belligerent and less militaristic than either non-college or service academy officers" and that humanities majors "should be encouraged to become military officers" inasmuch as they assertedly were, for example, less willing to obey "immoral" orders or to use nuclear weapons. A large majority of those who felt that the military was "most dangerous" to the U.S. government also favored a volunteer army.

BINDER, L. JAMES. *Military Service Is Not a Commodity.* Army. April 1970. Volume 20, Number 4. Pages 14–16.

The author takes issue on a number of points with the Report of the President's Commission on an All-Volunteer Armed Force. Even though the draft law is "full of inequities," it is held that "until any new plan is thoroughly tested and found successful, the draft must not be shelved."

BLIVEN, BRUCE, JR. *A Reporter at Large: All-Volunteer Armed Forces* (two parts). The New Yorker. (1) November 24, 1975, Volume LI, Number 40. Pages 55–91. (2) December 1, 1975. Volume LI, Number 41. Pages 137–156.

Part 1 of this report on the operation of the all-volunteer armed forces discusses recruiting statistics, the sociology of military organization, and the question of "public goods" in raising an army. It focuses on the views of Morris Janowitz and Dr. Albert Biderman and on work done by Stephen Herbits in making the volunteer force a reality. Part 2 deals with the racial composition of the all-volunteer force, race relations in the military, women in the volunteer army, and intellectuals in the military. The views of Charles Moskos, Jr., Mrs. Nancy Goldman, and Major General Robert G. Gard, Jr., are presented. Bliven concludes with Janowitz's comment: "Civilian society should direct the military in redefining its professional outlook" and that "the vitality of the military profession depends on a delicate balance between a special sense of inner-group loyalty and participation in the larger society. . . . It is enormously important that military personnel take part in civic affairs and public affairs . . . both for reasons of self-respect and as an antidote to social isolation."

BOORSTIN, DAVID. *Volunteer Army*. Editorial Research Reports. June 1975. Volume 1, Number 23. Pages 445–462.

An evaluation of the all-volunteer armed force after two years' experience. Also reviews the U.S. experience with the use of volunteers and conscripts, and considers the future prospects of the volunteer army.

BROOKS, LEON PRESTON. *Vital Interests and Volunteer Forces*. United States Naval Institute Proceedings. January 1971. Volume XCVII, Number 1/815. Pages 18–23.

Expresses concern about the existing relationship between military action and foreign policy, arguing that "containment of Communism" is an unattainable goal that should be abandoned. Suggests that both foreign policy and military organization need to be better attuned to technical and political realities in order to eliminate archaic policies and institutions and successfully recruit and retain military personnel under an all-volunteer system. Brooks suggests restructuring the military to reflect the need for large numbers of highly skilled technical personnel rather than large field armies.

BROWN, FREDERIC J. *The Army and Society.* Military Review. March 1972. Volume LII, Number 3. Pages 3–17.

Includes a discussion of public attitudes toward the army, and how social involvement by the army can be a means to attract quality personnel to voluntary military service.

CAMERON, JUAN. *Our Gravest Military Problem Is Manpower.* Fortune. April 1971. Volume LXXIII, Number 4. Pages 60–140.

Reviews the problems of quality and quantity of military manpower and analyzes the sources of dissatisfaction with military life. Concludes that the problems are so pervasive that a volunteer army is probably not possible at present.

CHAPMAN, BRUCE K. *The Politics of Conscription.* New Individualist Review. Spring 1967. Volume 4, Number 4. Pages 17–25.

A critical review of the operations of the Selective Service System. Charges that pro-conscription political and military elements have permitted misleading data to be disseminated with regard to the level of legislative and popular support for the draft.

CHAPMAN, BRUCE K. *Why Not Abolish the Draft?* National Review. March 21, 1967. Volume XIX, Number 11. Pages 303–305.

Reviews diverse political views on the draft, and recommends that it be abolished on ideological and economic grounds.

CLARK, BLAIR. *What Kind of Army?* Harper's Magazine. September 1969. Volume 239, Number 1432. Pages 80–83.

Favors draft reform and opposes an all-volunteer armed force. Purely professional armies, in Clark's view, "have always attracted the disadvantaged," and he suggests that the establishment of an all-volunteer armed force in the United States would produce a disproportionate number of blacks.

CONGRESSIONAL DIGEST. *Controversy over Proposals to Revise the U.S. Military Draft System: Pro and Con.* August–September 1968. Pages 193–224.

Presents opposing views on three questions: (1) Should the present draft system be replaced by all-volunteer armed forces? (2) Should the United States adopt a lottery system for the draft? (3) Should the draft include nonmilitary "national service"?

CONGRESSIONAL DIGEST. *The Question of an All-Volunteer U.S. Armed Force.* May 1971. Volume 50, Number 5. Pages 130–160.

A pro and con discussion of whether the proposed conversion of U.S. armed forces to an all-volunteer force is a sound national policy. On the pro side are the views of the President's Commission on an All-Volunteer Armed Force, Senator Mark Hatfield, Representatives William Steiger and Shirley Chisholm, and Roger T. Kelly; on the con side, those of Senator Sam Ervin, Jr., Joseph A. Califano, Jr., the Association of the United States Army, the National Guard Association of the United States, and the Reserve Officers Association of the United States.

CONGRESSIONAL QUARTERLY WEEKLY REPORT. *Congressional Battle: Draft or All-Volunteer Army.* April 2, 1971. Volume XXIX, Number 14. Pages 752–758.

Summarizes debate on the four legislative proposals relating to the draft and volunteer army. Comparisons are made of the provisions in each proposal on key issues. Inserts include a summary of the impact of lobbying, and a brief mention of military public-relations efforts on television to recruit volunteers.

CURTIS, THOMAS B. *Conscription and Commitment.* Playboy. February 1967. Volume 14, Number 2. Pages 89–90, 167–170.

A U.S. congressman proposes a plan that would end the draft yet meet the nation's military needs. Advancing a number of reasons why the draft should be abolished and an all-volunteer manpower policy adopted, Curtis claims that "the draft has only been justifiable as a measure of necessity; now that it is no longer necessary, it is no longer justifiable." His plan calls for: (1) better pay, housing, and other benefits; (2) coordination between military and civilian sectors in training and use of manpower; (3) lower physical standards where appropriate; (4) improved capabilities of reserves; and (5) revision of the military justice code.

DEANS, RALPH C. *Rebuilding the Army.* Editorial Research Reports. November 17, 1971. Volume 2, Number 19. Pages 885–902.

Discusses morale and discipline problems in the army, public attitudes toward the army, proposals for the post-Vietnam army (including arguments for and against ending conscription), and the impact of an all-volunteer armed force on national security.

DISSENT. *Volunteer Army: Pro and Con.* September–October 1969. Volume XVI, Number 5. Pages 449–454.

Presents readers' reactions to an article (May–June 1969 issue) arguing against the volunteer army, and a rebuttal by Henry Rabasseire, author of the article (see below, page 144). Rabasseire, who favors a program of national service, defends his position by emphasizing the citizen's obligation to the nation. He regards a professional volunteer army as a body of mercenaries and a mechanism whereby the poor and the blacks would be exploited as a tool of imperialism.

DUGGAN, P. T. *The All-Volunteer Force and Its Impact on the Marine Corps.* Marine Corps Gazette. June 1970. Volume 54, Number 6. Pages 20–24.

Discusses the possible consequences of an all-volunteer military on the future number and quality of Marine Corps recruits, with a brief history of military manpower procurement in the United States. Expresses concern that in the absence of the draft, the Marine Corps may have trouble competing with larger services for recruits in view of what the corps can offer in schooling and career fields.

FLACKS, RICHARD. *Conscription in a Democratic Society.* New Individualist Review. Spring 1967. Volume 4, Number 4. Pages 10–12.

This article is concerned "not with the many inequities of the present draft system, but with discussing ways of limiting the impact of this alien system and of preventing or diluting some of its more pernicious effects." Flacks argues that the current draft system delegates undue power to the President in the mobilization of national resources, and that "conscripts ought not to be used indiscriminately in foreign wars," but used only "for the defense of the nation's most vital interests."

FREDLAND, JOHN ROGER. *Retention: The High Cost of Leaving.* United States Naval Institute Proceedings. January 1970. Volume 96, Number 1/803. Pages 44–47.

Challenges as simplistic the notion that personnel recruitment and retention problems under an all-volunteer military would be solved merely by paying wages comparable to those in nonmilitary occupations. Argues that some aspects of military life involve such a high disutility that monetary compensation alone would not be enough. Fredland suggests as a goal the rekindling of emotional payoffs such as esprit de corps and pride of uniform, as well as some basic policy reforms designed to make military life more attractive. He concludes that in military recruitment there are two alternatives—coercion or persuasion—and that "persuasion is not simply a matter of adequate wage compensation."

FRIEDMAN, MILTON. *A Volunteer Army.* Newsweek. December 19, 1966. Volume LXVIII, Number 25. Page 100.

Contends that a military draft is undesirable and unnecessary, and counters common objections to a volunteer army. Friedman concludes, "One of the greatest advantages in human freedom was the commutation of taxes in kind to taxes in money. We have reverted to a barbarous custom. It is past time that we regain our heritage."

FRIEDMAN, MILTON. *Why Not a Volunteer Army?* New Individualist Review. Spring 1967. Volume 4, Number 4. Pages 3–9.

"So long as compulsion is retained," Friedman maintains, "inequity, waste, and interference with freedom are inevitable. A lottery would only make the arbitrary element in the present system overt. Universal national service would only compound the evil—regimenting all young men, and perhaps women, to camouflage the regimentation of some." He proposes a gradual transition to a voluntary system to accompany a phasing-out of conscription.

GEERE, FRANK. *Future Recruitment.* Journal of the Military Service Institution. May–June 1916. Volume 58, Number 201. Pages 365–379.

Maintains that voluntary enlistments can be increased, noting that "since the pay and other material inducements in the Army were advanced in 1908 to a reasonable basis, the regular service has been kept fairly well recruited."

GOETZ, RONALD. *Drop the Draft?* The Christian Century. February 19, 1969. Volume LXXXVI, Number 8. Pages 245–246.

Claims that "coercion is not eliminated in voluntary recruitment; it is simply disguised." If an all-volunteer armed force were to be implemented in the United States, "the overwhelming majority of the volunteers would come from the ranks of the economically dispossessed"—serving to perpetuate "the present injustice in terms of the disproportionate number of black men and poor men facing the risks of war."

GOLDMAN, NANCY. *The Changing Role of Women in the Armed Forces.* American Journal of Sociology. January 1973. Volume 78, Number 4. Pages 892–911.

Examines the organizational resistances and role strains associated with increasing the concentration of women in the armed forces. It is hypothesized that those women who voluntarily select the military profession would be likely to accept its existing authority structure and its internal values. Goldman finds "no reason to believe that the proportion of women in the armed forces will increase or that the range of their employment and responsibility will expand rapidly or dramatically with the advent of the all-volunteer armed force."

GOLDWATER, BARRY. *End the Draft!* The New Guard. May 1967. Volume 5. Page 10.

Contrasts philosophical assumptions underlying positions on the draft. The Liberal position, Goldwater states, is "based solidly upon the notion that every form of compulsion and every sacrifice of the individual may be justified and demanded in the name of 'society,' " while the Conservative view is "based solidly upon the notion that man's most fundamental right and responsibility is to live his own life." He argues for ending the draft not only on philosophical grounds but also on the practical grounds that an all-volunteer army is more efficient.

HARGREAVES, REGINALD. *What Sort of Recruit?* Military Review. January 1972. Volume LII, Number 1. Pages 58–67.

Discusses recruiting problems and methods from the days of the Roman Legion up to the War of 1812. The author regards an all-volunteer army as "the ideal" military service, but believes that this is difficult to achieve inasmuch as an all-volunteer army "costs considerably more to maintain than most civil administrations are prepared to furnish." He maintains, however, that given a "hard-core of 'professionals,' " it is possible for a mixed force of volunteers and draftees to attain a high standard of military efficiency.

HATFIELD, MARK O. *The Draft Should Be Abolished.* Saturday Evening Post. July 1, 1967. Volume 240, Number 13. Pages 12–14.

Charges that the draft is "inherently unfair, monstrously inefficient, and pernicious in its invasion of the individual liberty that eight generations of Americans have fought to preserve." Argues that "the principle of 'universal sharing' of the national defense effort—the principle on which the system was sold to the public years ago—is a transparent falsehood today." Hatfield suggests that the only system of manpower recruitment that would provide the maximum amount of individual liberty, that would be fair, and that would supply the services with the necessary quantity and quality of men as economically as possible would be an all-volunteer military.

HOEFLING, JOHN A. *Leadership in the Modern Volunteer Army.* Army. August 1971. Volume 21, Number 8. Pages 38–42.

Suggests that while military leadership theory has begun to accommodate a more democratic style, many future recruits may not adapt to formal organization of any kind. Rather than excluding these people from the service, consideration should be given to employing them in unstructured—perhaps even un-uniformed noncombat units. A master leadership model is predicated upon assignment to groups based on basic behavior patterns established through psychological testing. In this way it may be possible to have "a modern volunteer Army of highly disciplined, elite, professional combat units supported by properly motivated support units."

HOLBROOK, JAMES R. *Volunteer Army: Military Caste?* Military Review. August 1971. Volume LI, Number 8. Pages 91–95.

Examining "the specter of a Volunteer Army creating a military caste," the author considers it "highly unlikely that a professional military force will ever again be isolated or alienated from the civilian population."

JANOWITZ, MORRIS. *The Decline of the Mass Army.* Military Review. February 1972. Volume LII, Number 2. Pages 10–16.

Suggests that the ending of the draft in the United States "will have a deep impact on military manpower systems in Western Europe," encouraging those nations to adopt an all-volunteer system or to consider new forms of militia systems. The all-volunteer armed force, in the author's view, "represents the end of the historical phase of the mass armed force, and represents not a purely military phenomenon, but the character of the larger society."

JANOWITZ, MORRIS. *Toward an All-Volunteer Military.* The Public Interest. Spring 1972. Number 27. Pages 104–117.

Discusses the transition from a selective service system to an all-volunteer armed force, noting that "major reorganizations are necessary in the areas of education, career system, deployment, and participation of the military in civilian life, if the men of the quality that is necessary are to be attracted to the service and if the military is to be compatible with the standards of a democratic society."

JANOWITZ, MORRIS. *Volunteer Armed Forces and Military Purpose.* Foreign Affairs. April 1972. Volume 50, Number 3. Pages 427–443.

Considers that, "sociologically, in the contemporary context an all-volunteer force can be made compatible with American political forms if two conditions are met. First, U.S. foreign policy must be one of flexible deterrence and the military must incorporate a 'constabulary' type of strategy. Second, new and higher levels of military professionalism must be developed which recognize that the armed forces, while distinct in many of their operating procedures, must be based more and more on contractual and public service conceptions and less on sheer traditional authority."

JEFFREY, TIMOTHY B. *Today's Army Wants to Join You.* Military Review. January 1973. Volume LIII, Number 1. Pages 62–68.

Notes that the traditionally severe initiation to army life is being eliminated, and hypothesizes that the impact of this change will be an increase in internal turmoil for the military in the future.

KRAMER, DAVID. *The Modern Volunteer Army*. The Freeman. February 1972. Pages 95–99.

Reprinted from *The Castle*, July 21, 1971 (newspaper of Ft. Belvoir, Virginia). Considers the "draft-army mentality . . . , a set of attitudes and ideas belonging to an agency which has long been using coercion to supply its manpower requirements, but ideas that are incompatible with the principles behind an all-volunteer defense force." Contends that "the whole Army philosophy" needs to be evaluated if the principle of voluntarism in the procurement of military manpower is to succeed.

LANG, KURT. *Military Career Structure: Emerging Trends and Alternatives*. Administration Science Quarterly. December 1972. Volume 17, Number 4. Pages 487–497.

Discusses alternative means of supplementing professional officer recruitment: the para-professional force, lateral recruitment, and the contracting of services from civilian organizations.

LEKACHMAN, ROBERT. *How to Raise a Small Army in a Large Country*. Challenge. May–June 1967. Pages 14–16, 37–38.

Takes the position that on the grounds of efficiency alone a volunteer army makes "a good deal of economic and military sense," but that in a democracy the dilemma of who shall serve "cannot be resolved that easily." Suggests that while higher pay and more liberal benefits would attract more minority enlistees, such improvements of themselves would do nothing to increase the percentage of minority officers. In this view, an all-volunteer force would be manned largely by black enlisted men and led almost entirely by whites.

MITRISIN, JOHN. *The Pros and Cons of a Voluntary Army*. Current History. August 1968. Volume 55, Number 324. Pages 86–92, 107.

According to the author, "Monetary gain, training and veteran's benefits are not the only reasons men join the armed forces; if they were, there would be almost no true volunteers today. Men join because of patriotism, family tradition, the military's image of manliness and the chance to travel. These attractions are strong, but they are presently nullified by low salaries."

MOORE, JOHN. *Defense Report/Draft: Volunteer Army Proposals Head for Showdown in Congress.* National Journal. March 6, 1971. Volume III, Number 10. Pages 489–498.

Specific features of pending bills are analyzed with focus on President Nixon's program for ending the draft. Reactions to the proposals by various interest groups and key congressional leaders are noted. Inserts include a rundown of the basis of Nixon's support, a graph of past levels of drafting and enlistment, a discussion of the pros and cons of a volunteer army, and a brief history of U.S. military conscription.

MOSKOS, CHARLES C., JR. *The Emergent Army.* Parameters. 1974. Volume 4, Number 1. Pages 17–30.

Discusses the social composition of an all-volunteer force, posing the question: "What lessons does the experience of the recent past offer for an understanding of the kind of Army we can expect to emerge from the institution of an all-volunteer force?" Claims that "on the assumption that social groups will generally behave in their economic self-interest, an all-volunteer force will be forced to sustain its membership largely from the less-educated and minority groups of American society." Moskos considers three alternative developmental models of the army—civilianized, traditional, and plural—and suggests that "it is the plural model of the Army—with its compartmentalized segments—which seems to offer the best promise of an armed force which will maintain organizational effectiveness while remaining consonant in the main with civilian values."

NICHOLS, ROBERT L., and others. *The Officer Corps in an All-Volunteer Force: Will College Men Serve?* Naval War College Review. January 1971. Volume XXIII, Number 5. Pages 31–50.

A study to determine whether the army raised under a system of voluntary procurement would provide adequate national defense. A survey of 2,400 ROTC students and 1,978 OCS students concludes that implementation of voluntary military manpower procurement would significantly lower the number of college recruits. The authors contend that increased pay would not attract necessary numbers of volunteers and favor a continuation of conscription with increased incentives to volunteer. They recommend increasing ROTC monthly allowances, expanding scholarship programs, and upping first-term pay.

PHILLIPSON, IRVING J. *The Infantry's Recruiting Problem.* Infantry Journal. May 1920. Volume XVI, Number 11. Pages 967–971.

Believes that with the careful selection of recruiters the infantry can obtain the men it needs, even though confronted with the competition of unprecedented industrial prosperity.

POWELL, JAMES. *Anti-Militarism and Laissez Faire.* New Individualist Review. Spring 1967. Volume 4, Number 4. Pages 37–42.

"Decisive to the continuation of conscription is the general presumption that the government is morally and technically qualified to administer the lives of citizens; only by overthrowing this presumption, and reviving libertarian ideas, can conscription be ended." In this view, "there is much support for conscription as an instrument of social reform ... as a consequence of the general presumptions for state-oriented over citizen-centered policy, which have guided social reform for many decades." Hence, militarism and conscription have thrived not so much because these particular ideas are popular, but because state-oriented ideas generally are popular.

QUICK, HERBERT. *A New Volunteer System.* Proceedings of the Academy of Political Science. July 1916. Volume 6, Number 4. Pages 257–262.

Contends that the necessary numbers of men can be recruited under a voluntary military service system by offering educational opportunities— but no pay—to economically disadvantaged youths and ethnic minorities.

RABASSEIRE, HENRY. *Do We Really Want an All-Volunteer Army?* Dissent. May–June 1969. Volume XVI. Number 3. Page 200.

The author lists arguments against an all-volunteer army, maintaining that it is a mercenary army, "pressing into service those who have no other means of making a living." Such an army, he believes, would be a will-less instrument in the hands of commanders capable of beating down insurrection, and vulnerable for use in colonial and imperialistic wars. (See also Dissent, page 137, above.)

RAYMOND, JACK. *The Draft Is Unfair.* New York Times Magazine. January 2, 1966. Pages 5, 18, 20, 21.

Noting that the Vietnam War has rekindled discussion over whether the draft is compatible with American values, the author examines specific arguments for and against the present system. The lottery and Milton Friedman's proposal for a volunteer military are discussed.

ROGERS, SELWYN P., JR. *An All-Volunteer Force*. Military Review. September 1970. Volume L, Number 9. Pages 89–95.

In discussing the problems of the draft in the United States, the author declares: "A volunteer force is feasible; it is not too expensive for the United States to adopt in order to meet the values of our society and the defense requirements of our Nation; and there need be no adverse social consequences if the concept is supported by the proper programs."

ROSSER, RICHARD F. *A 20th-Century Military Force*. Foreign Policy. Fall 1973. Number 12. Pages 156–175.

Recommends ways in which the volunteer armed forces in the United States can be brought into harmony with the larger society so as to insure the military's continued ability to attract and retain qualified manpower.

SENIOR SCHOLASTIC. *The Draft: Retain? Reform? Or Abolish?* May 2, 1969. Volume 94, Number 13. Pages 4–9.

Considers attitudes toward the military draft in the United States and proposals to retain, reform, or abolish it. Reviews the respective positions of leading proponents of these proposals.

SHERMAN, EDWARD F. *The Great Draft Debate*. The New Republic. May 18, 1968. Pages 36–38.

Reviews the proposal for an all-volunteer armed force in the United States, examining the respective positions of proponents and opponents of the move to end the draft.

SMITH, DONALD. *The Volunteer Army*. The Atlantic Monthly. July 1974. Volume 234, Number 1. Pages 6–12.

Reviews and assesses the political and social implications of the transition from the military draft to an all-volunteer armed force in the United States. Examines the political aspects of the evolution of the volunteer army during the first Nixon Administration, noting the strong initial opposition to the plan from military and congressional leaders.

SMITH, LYNN D. *An All-Volunteer Army: Real Future Possibility or Impractical Dream?* Army. April 1969. Volume 19, Number 4. Pages 22–31.

Notwithstanding the inequities of the draft and the appeal of the concept of a highly motivated volunteer army, "the heart of the problem is not what inducements should be offered to make it possible to eliminate the draft but what are the strategic objectives of the nation and under what circumstances can they be modified (as were those of Britain) to a degree that a relatively small military establishment will attain those objectives." Smith suggests that if money is to be used as an inducement to replace the draft, it should be spent to attract volunteers to the hard-to-fill jobs rather than being spread across the board to include those that are easily filled.

SORENSEN, NEAL G. *Implications of a Volunteer Force.* Air University Review. March–April 1971. Volume XXII, Number 3. Pages 47–52.

Discusses potential changes in civilian-military relations occasioned by an all-volunteer military. Areas of concern include a possible trend toward self-containment and social isolation at the officer level. The author identifies the changes needed within the military in order to maintain social responsiveness and professional viability, recommending that recruitment be from a broad social and economic base, with opportunity for lateral entry. He also advises a complete upgrading of the quality of military life and improvement of the military public image.

STROMBERG, PETER L. *MVA on the Way.* Soldiers. June 1971. Volume XXVI, Number 6. Pages 4–11.

Programs within the army to prepare for the Modern Volunteer Army (MVA), specifically Project VOLAR, are discussed. The object of the programs is to lessen dependence on the draft by improving the attractiveness of army service to the prospective volunteer while at the same time raising army efficiency. Stromberg outlines the innovations and measures adopted through the programs.

SUMMERS, HARRY G. *Another View of an All-Volunteer Army.* Military Review. June 1972. Volume LII, Number 6. Pages 75–79.

Supports the concept of the all-volunteer army, taking issue with the assertions of the opposition in regard to certain social and political implications of a voluntary system.

SWOMLEY, JOHN, JR. *End Conscription in 1959!* The Christian Century. January 7, 1959. Volume LXXVI, Number 1. Pages 14–17.

Argues in favor of ending conscription on grounds that the draft is discriminatory and inefficient. Points out specific problems of the present system such as low reenlistment rates and inappropriate training. In discussing proposed alternatives to conscription, Swomley concludes that the best alternative to a citizen army is a career (professional) army and considers the problems and advantages associated with such an army. Regardless of the method of raising troops, he contends, the presence of a professional officer group in a professional military force makes for inherent dangers.

SYRETT, DAVID, and RICHARD H. KOHN. *The Dangers of an All-Volunteer Army.* Military Review. June 1972. Volume LII, Number 6. Pages 70–74.

States that "the real danger [of an all-volunteer army], which few opponents of the plan have raised, is internal. An all-volunteer Army at this stage might pose a tremendous threat to civilian control of policy and may even make the coup—for the first time in American history—a possibility." In this view, a professional army would be in a position to play a much larger role in U.S. domestic politics than the present army, the majority of whose junior officers and privates "are civilians in uniform."

TAFT, ROBERT A. *The Anti-Militarist Tradition.* New Individualist Review. Spring 1967. Volume 4, Number 4. Pages 43–47.

Text of a statement by Taft in September 1940 in opposition to the Burke-Wadsworth bill, which proposed peacetime conscription for the first time in U.S. history. Taft contends that "in spite of inadequate pay and in spite of three-year enlistments, from which a man cannot escape if a better job is offered," the voluntary system has not broken down, but, on the contrary, "has been accomplishing everything which had been asked of it." He suggests that an adequate supply of volunteers could be assured by making the army "only reasonably attractive."

TOMLINSON, KENNETH Y. *How Good Is Our All-Volunteer Army?* Reader's Digest. October 1975. Volume 107, Number 642. Pages 189–198.

Looks at the quality of the all-volunteer army as measured by combat-readiness, physical fitness of soldiers, the extent of the drug problem, and race relations. Concludes that the volunteer army has taken significant steps to eliminate all these problems since the expiration of the draft.

TYLER, GUS. *Dangers of a Professional Army.* The New Leader. April 24, 1967. Volume L, Number 9. Pages 12–14.

Counters specific arguments favoring the establishment of an all-volunteer army. Contends that "the most ardent words spoken for the volunteer army come from opponents of our Asian involvement who, in their eagerness to halt the draft of reluctant young men, may unintentionally institutionalize a military manpower program that would do serious damage to the objectives of American liberalism for decades to come."

WALLIS, W. ALLEN. *Abolish the Draft.* Science. January 17, 1969. Volume 163, Number 3864. Page 235.

Asserts that there is no practical or moral justification for the draft, describing it as immoral, inequitable, and detrimental to our national defense. The draft, Wallis says, allows the army to be inefficient in its use of manpower and feeds the antiwar movement in the United States—a movement that weakens our bargaining position in Paris. The benefits of an all-volunteer military are discussed, and the current arguments against such a system are briefly refuted.

WESTMORELAND, WILLIAM C. *Straight Talk from the Chief on the Modern Volunteer Army.* Army. May 1971. Volume XXI, Number 5. Pages 12–17.

Interview with General Westmoreland, U.S. Army Chief of Staff, focusing on the basic issues raised by the Modern Volunteer Army (MVA). Westmoreland states that the underlying purpose of the MVA is to achieve a better army. Efforts toward this goal include decentralization of authority and responsibility, improvement and stabilization of leadership, improvements in the quality of the soldiers through higher motivation, and increased training. Specific questions deal with the effects of relaxed rules on army discipline, programs designed to increase job satisfaction and pride in service, and measures taken to attract and retain the quality and quantity of volunteers necessary to fill positions ranging from combat to high-level administration.

WILHELM, ROSS. *How to End the Draft.* The Nation. November 15, 1965. Volume CCI, Number 16. Pages 350–352.

The author postulates that a draft is unnecessary and outlines an economic rationale for his statement. He argues that the bulk of military manpower needs are already being met through voluntary means, and that, while a volunteer army would require an increase in wages and thus in the budget, this would be offset by savings in other areas of the budget. The financial impact would be in the form of an income transfer from the taxpayer to the soldier and, thanks to increased efficiency, society as a whole would be better off.

Pamphlets, Reprints, and Speeches

ASSOCIATION OF THE UNITED STATES ARMY. *The Case for a Responsive Standby Draft.* 1975. AUSA Position Paper. Washington, D.C. 10 pages.

Proposes that the United States maintain a standby Selective Service System in a peacetime all-volunteer environment, for, it is asserted, "we have no other acceptable choice in this volatile world other than being prepared to respond to military contingencies that could arise that could generate demands for rapid increases in military manpower which could not possibly be met by volunteer means alone." The current legislative proposal to dismantle the Selective Service System is critically reviewed.

COOPER, RICHARD V. L. *Defense Manpower Issues: Testimony Before the Defense Manpower Commission.* 1975. The Rand Corporation. Santa Monica, California. 25 pages.

A report on the success of all-volunteer enlistments, with reservations. According to Cooper, "The Services have met their authorized strength requirements without lowering quality, changing regional or socioeconomic composition, or excessive cost increase. However, basic changes in manpower management are needed. The 20-year career with long retirement makes little sense for the 90% in noncombat jobs. The 'up or out' philosophy, grade limitations imposed by Congress, the assumption that senior personnel should necessarily be supervisors, the use of hidden fringe benefits rather than pay increases, and the fact that service retirement costs are not paid out of service budgets all combine to create a basically inefficient system. The Commission has the opportunity to make major, long-lasting improvements."

COOPER, RICHARD V. L. *Social Representativeness of the Volunteer Force.* The Rand Corporation. Santa Monica, California. January 1974. 43 pages.

Presents preliminary results from ongoing research at the Rand Corporation under sponsorship of the Human Resources Research Office of the Defense Advanced Research Projects Agency. Focuses on "long-run prospects for and perspectives on military manpower in a volunteer environment." Cooper considers whether voluntary procurement results in an army socially unrepresentative of the broad spectrum of American society. Included are the racial implications of the statistical data used. The tentative conclusion is that the move to a volunteer force has resulted in little change in the social composition of the force.

HAECKEL, ERWIN. *Military Manpower and Political Purpose.* 1970. Adelphi Papers, Number 72. The International Institute for Strategic Studies. London. 31 pages.

Discusses types of military manpower systems, personnel recruitment and training, manpower policy, economic and political problems, and strategic purpose. The relative merits of all-volunteer, all-militia (conscripted), and mixed forces are considered from the standpoints of national policy and collective security.

HARVARD UNIVERSITY. GRADUATE SCHOOL OF BUSINESS. *The Modern Volunteer Army.* 1973. Cambridge, Massachusetts. 32 pages.

Prepared as a case study, this paper deals with the conversion of the U.S. Army to an all-volunteer army in 1975. It discusses the President's Commission on an All-Volunteer Armed Force, military personnel requirements, qualification standards for enlisted men, pay, recruiting, action on the Gates Commission Report, and the recruiting offensive of spring 1971 and reaction to it.

JANOWITZ, MORRIS. *The U.S. Forces and the Zero Draft.* 1973. Adelphi Papers, Number 94. The International Institute for Strategic Studies. London. Tables. 30 pages.

This paper examines "the underlying factors which have brought about the decline of the mass armed force based on conscription and a mobilization format," explores the consequences of an all-volunteer military in the United States on its international political and strategic position, and identifies "problems and dilemmas of recruiting and retaining manpower." Janowitz concludes that the all-volunteer force may supply minimum manpower requirements, but at very high cost; that it cannot be upheld on moral or strategic grounds; and that "the best that can be said is that the all-volunteer force can be made to work in a period of very difficult negotiations and a renewed search for a new international order."

MUSKIE, EDMUND S. *The Draft: What Are the Alternatives?* Vital Speeches. April 1, 1969. Volume XXXV, Number 12. Pages 356–358.

This address, given at Miami University in Oxford, Ohio, on February 17, 1969, outlines the basis of Senator Muskie's opposition to an all-volunteer army. His suggested alternative is a program of national service supported by a lottery draft and a reformed selective service system.

NATIONAL COUNCIL AGAINST CONSCRIPTION. *The Case Against the Draft.* 1950. Washington, D.C. 8 pages.

Contends that the three arguments presented by the army in 1948 for the enactment of peacetime conscription—(1) that war might be imminent, (2) that the draft was needed to bring the army up to authorized strength, and (3) that voluntary enlistments had fallen off and could no longer be depended upon—were not based on fact. Counters the army's current arguments that extension of the draft is necessary to build up a reserve, and that it would eliminate a waiting period for new legislation in the event of an emergency, stimulate recruiting, and be consistent with the Atlantic Pact and the Military Aid Program. The pamphlet charges that the army is attempting to circumvent the refusal of Congress to legislate universal military training by setting up through the draft what amounts to universal military training in fact.

NIXON, RICHARD M. *The All-Volunteer Armed Force.* 1968. Nixon/ Agnew Campaign Committee. New York. 10 pages.

Text of an address by President Nixon on the CBS Radio Network, October 17, 1968. The President urges an end to compulsory military service in the United States, and a transition to an all-volunteer armed force, stating: "Just as soon as our reduced manpower requirements in Vietnam will permit us to do so, we should stop the draft and put our Selective Service structure on stand-by." He calls for this change in national defense manpower policies as a means of showing "our commitment to freedom by preparing to assure our young people theirs."

RIPON SOCIETY. *Politics and Conscription: A Ripon Proposal to Replace the Draft.* 1966. Cambridge, Massachusetts. 6 pages. Reprint from the Ripon Forum. December 1966.

Urges the federal government to eliminate the draft, to improve the salary, incentives, fringe benefits, and prestige of the military, and to establish a 2.7 million-man volunteer army. The statement is critical not only of the draft in its present form but of the principle of conscription itself, and of such proposals for change as the lottery system and compulsory national service.

WESTMORELAND, W. C. *Address Before the Association of the United States Army.* 1970. Washington, D.C. 12 pages.

Address of October 13, 1970, by General Westmoreland, Chief of Staff, U.S. Army, in which he announces that "the Army is committed to an all-out effort in working toward a zero draft—a volunteer force," as proposed by President Nixon. Discussing the problems confronting the army "as we move toward a zero draft," Westmoreland stresses the need to "double or triple our enlistments and reenlistments." The reserve components would take on added importance, since "a large part of our problem is to increase the number of volunteers in the Army Reserve and National Guard at the same time we increase volunteers in the Active

Army." Westmoreland describes the measures being adopted by the army toward the goal of an all-volunteer armed force, declaring: "We are willing to part from past practices where such practices no longer serve a productive and useful end."

Government Documents: Publications

CLARK, CHAMP. *Volunteers vs. Conscripts.* 1917. Government Printing Office. Washington, D.C. 15 pages.

Speech by the Missouri congressman during the conscription debates in the House on April 25, 1917. Contends that conscription is not yet necessary and that it should be considered only as a last resort.

MONDELL, FRANK W. *The War and the Army: Volunteers Versus Conscripts.* 1917. Government Printing Office. Washington, D.C. 16 pages.

Speeches by the Wyoming congressman during Houses debates in April and May 1917. Opposed to a War Department proposal for the enrollment of men aged 19 to 25 as the basis for selective conscription, Mondell argues that all able men aged 21 to 40 should be asked to serve—as volunteers—if the need arises.

U.S. CONGRESS. HOUSE. COMMITTEE ON ARMED SERVICES. *Recruiting and Retention of Military Personnel.* 1972. Government Printing Office. Washington, D.C. 34 pages.

Report of the Special Subcommittee on Recruiting and Retention of Military Personnel of the House Committee on Armed Services. Dated May 11, 1972.

U.S. CONGRESS. HOUSE. COMMITTEE ON ARMED SERVICES. *Utilization of Manpower in the Military.* 1972. Government Printing Office. Washington, D.C. 31 pages.

Report by the Special Subcommittee on the Utilization of Manpower in the Military of the House Committee on Armed Services. Dated June 28, 1972.

U.S. CONGRESS. SENATE. COMMITTEE ON ARMED SERVICES. *All-Volunteer Armed Forces: Progress, Problems, and Prospects*. By Martin Binkin and John D. Johnston. 1973. Government Printing Office. Washington, D.C. Figures, tables. 64 pages.

An assessment of the problems, the progress, and the remaining issues involved in the attempt to obtain manpower for the U.S. armed forces solely by voluntary means, with special reference to an analysis of all available data using appropriate statistical methods, and including an examination of options to overcome the various problems. No pro or con recommendation is made as to the basic wisdom of the volunteer concept; the discussion is restricted to the various issues pertaining to supply and demand of manpower and to cost.

U.S. DEPARTMENT OF DEFENSE. *The All-Volunteer Force and the End of the Draft*. By Elliot L. Richardson. 1973. Department of Defense. Washington, D.C. Charts, tables. 30 pages.

This special report of the secretary of defense in March 1973 describes the progress made by the military services in eliminating the draft, as well as remaining problems and their solutions in the transition to an all-volunteer system and the expiration of induction authority on July 1, 1973. The report includes data on active force strength, draft calls, trends in enlistments, quality of personnel, enlisted women, officer supply, anticipated physician shortages, and shortages in the National Guard and the reserve forces. Other questions dealt with include a program for civilian substitution, special pay legislation providing for bonuses and incentive pays, and cost data on the all-volunteer force.

U.S. DEPARTMENT OF DEFENSE. *Progress in Ending the Draft and Achieving the All-Volunteer Force*. By Melvin R. Laird. 1972. Department of Defense. Washington, D.C. Charts, tables. 51 pages

Report submitted by Secretary of Defense Melvin Laird to President Nixon in July 1972. It describes major Administration initiatives and progress toward the goal of ending reliance on the draft and moving to an all-volunteer armed force. It also delineates the remaining problems in ending the draft and recommends actions to resolve them.

U.S. DEPARTMENT OF THE ARMY. *The Modern Volunteer Army Program: The Benning Experiment 1970–1972*. By Willard Latham.

1973. Department of the Army. Washington, D.C. Index. Charts, illustrations. 146 pages.

An official publication of the army, prepared by a brigadier general, this is an account of Project VOLAR, the field experiment to develop, test, evaluate, and refine new concepts and initiatives consistent with the goals of the Modern Volunteer Army. These goals are: (1) reduced reliance on the draft, (2) more professionalism, (3) enhancement of army life, and (4) development of a modern personnel accession system. The specifics of the Fort Benning Plan as well as the workings of Project VOLAR are covered.

U.S. PRESIDENT'S COMMISSION ON AN ALL-VOLUNTEER ARMED FORCE. *The Report of the President's Commission on an All-Volunteer Armed Force.* 1970. Macmillan Co. New York. Index. Tables. 218 pages.

Contains the full text of the report of the President's Commission, headed by former Secretary of Defense Thomas S. Gates. A summary of the commission's recommendations as unanimously agreed to is followed by the detailed analysis and discussion upon which commission findings were based. The commission recommends: an increase in basic pay, primarily for first-term servicemen; increases in proficiency and reserve pay; greater recruiting effort; and other improvements in the management of military personnel. A return to an all-volunteer force, the commission states, would "minimize government interference with the freedom of the individual to determine his own life in accord with his own values" while removing present inequities that affect first-term servicemen and promoting the efficiency and dignity of the armed forces. The commission recommends "an all-volunteer force, supported by an effective standby draft" as better fulfilling the nation's interests than a "mixed force of volunteers and conscripts." This is by far the most comprehensive work available on the question of raising military manpower in the United States. For even more detailed information on the issues covered in this book one should consult the two companion volumes, which contain all the staff papers prepared for the commission (see next entry).

U.S. PRESIDENT'S COMMISSION ON AN ALL-VOLUNTEER ARMED FORCE. *Studies Prepared for the President's Commission on an All-Volunteer Armed Force.* 2 volumes. 1970. Government Printing Office. Washington, D.C. Figures, tables. Bibliographical references within each section. Volume 1: 544 pages. Volume 2: 593 pages.

This massive work contains all the major staff papers prepared for the commission and makes available to the public, perhaps for the first time, the supporting material and research of a major government commission. Volume 1 includes staff papers on such issues as the manpower and budgetary implications of ending conscription; the educational attainment of military and civilian labor forces; determinants of labor turnover costs in the military; civilian substitution; the impact of pay and draft policy on army enlistment behavior; and the impact of income, the draft, and other factors on retention. Also presented are economic analyses of first-term reenlistments and of the volunteer military, and a model of officer supply under draft and no-draft conditions. Volume 2 contains historical, political, and social research material, including studies on both the U.S. and the European experience with volunteer and conscript forces; military recruitment and militarism in Latin America; conscription and constitutional law; reserve forces policy and requirements; and the productivity of U.S. military recruiting systems.

WHITE HOUSE CONFERENCE ON YOUTH. *Report of White House Conference on Youth, April 18–22, 1971, Estes Park, Colorado.* 1971. Government Printing Office. Washington, D.C. Illustrations. 310 pages.

The report endorses the concept of an all-volunteer armed force. Specific recommendations (pages 19–28) include ending the draft on June 30, 1971, alternative service for conscientious objectors, amnesty to all draft violators when the draft expires, a standby registration system, increased military pay, modernization of the recruiting system, and an increase in ROTC scholarships.

WHITE HOUSE CONFERENCE ON YOUTH. *Task Force on the Draft, National Service, and Alternatives.* 1971. Government Printing Office. Washington, D.C. 91 pages.

Recommendations of the advisory task force cover military manpower procurement policy in relation to national defense, the responsibilities of citizenship, the social desirability of an all-volunteer force, transitional planning, and national service. Individual statements of task force members are included.

Government Documents: Congressional Hearings

1971. U.S. CONGRESS. HOUSE. COMMITTEE ON ARMED SERVICES. *Extension of the Draft.* Government Printing Office. Washington, D.C. 1103 pages.

Hearings between February 23 and March 11, 1971, before the House Committee on Armed Services on extension of the draft and on bills related to the voluntary force concept and authorization of strength levels.

1972. U.S. CONGRESS. HOUSE. COMMITTEE ON ARMED SERVICES. *Recruiting and Retention of Military Personnel.* Government Printing Office. Washington, D.C. 922 pages.

Hearings between July 29, 1971, and March 6, 1972, before the Special Subcommittee on Recruiting and Retention of Military Personnel of the House Committee on Armed Services.

1972. U.S. CONGRESS. HOUSE. COMMITTEE ON ARMED SERVICES. *Utilization of Manpower in the Military.* Government Printing Office. Washington, D.C. 278 pages.

Hearings between October 13, 1971, and March 6, 1972, before the Special Subcommittee on the Utilization of Manpower in the Military of the House Committee on Armed Services.

1972. U.S. CONGRESS. HOUSE. COMMITTEE ON FOREIGN AFFAIRS. *Volunteer Armed Force and Selective Service.* Government Printing Office. Washington, D.C. 247 pages.

Hearings on March 10 and 13, 1972, before the Subcommittee on the Volunteer Armed Force and Selective Service of the House Committee on Foreign Affairs. Reviews progress toward the all-volunteer armed force and the operation of the Selective Service System.

1974. U.S. CONGRESS. SENATE. COMMITTEE ON ARMED SERVICES. *Increased Special and Bonus Pay for Military Physicians, Expansion of Enlistment Bonus and Revision of Reenlistment Bonus Authorities.* Government Printing Office. Washington, D.C. 159 pages.

Hearings on December 13 and 14, 1973, before the Senate Committee on Armed Services on (1) Senate bill 2770 to amend Chapter 5, Title 37, of the U.S. Code to revise the special pay structure relating to medical officers of the uniformed services, and (2) Senate bill 2771 to amend Chapter 5, Title 37, of the U.S. Code to revise the special pay bonus structure relating to members of the armed forces.

1974. U.S. CONGRESS. SENATE. COMMITTEE ON ARMED SERVICES. *Military Manpower Issues of the Past and Future.* Government Printing Office. Washington, D.C. 164 pages.

Hearings on August 13 and 14, 1974, before the Subcommittee on Manpower and Personnel of the Senate Committee on Armed Services, considering projected manpower needs, the use of the Reserve and National Guard, and manpower costs of the All-Volunteer Armed Force.

CHAPTER 5

Selective Service

Everyone will now be mobilized,
And all boys old enough to carry a spear
   will be sent to Addis Ababa.
Married men will take their wives to carry
   food and cook.
Those without wives will take any woman
   without a husband.
Anyone found at home after the receipt
   of this order will be hanged.

> —Emperor Haile Selassie,
> Ethiopia, 1935

Books

BRADFORD, DAVID F. *Deferment Policy in Selective Service*. 1969. Princeton University Press. Princeton, New Jersey. Tables. 64 pages.

Analyzes the role of deferments in the Selective Service System, with particular emphasis on the way the deferment rules operated prior to 1967. Three major types of deferment are considered: dependency, occupational, and student. It is argued that, although the changes made in the selection system by the 1967 act "are likely to shift the incidence of service toward the more highly educated and thus to enhance the fairness of the system, the problem of uncertainty is likely to be more severe than under the rules previously in effect." Two alternative sets of rules are explored for determining the sequence of induction: a lottery and induction by age group. These rules are designed to "eliminate the problem of draft uncertainty, to accomplish the objective of equity in another fashion, and to achieve other advantages."

CARPER, JEAN. *Bitter Greetings: The Scandal of the Military Draft.* 1967. Grossman Publishers. New York. Index. Bibliographical notes: pages 193–198. 205 pages.

The purpose of this book is to "suggest avenues of investigation and to give readers an overall understanding of the injustices of the draft to enable them to demand such an investigation." It discusses proposals for change, concluding that "'Selective Service is beyond repair," that it is "antithetical to American freedom," and that it should be abolished in favor of a voluntary system. Individual chapters consider the "mythical manpower shortage," draft testing, exemptions, the local boards, persecution of dissenters, and the military establishment as an "accomplice" in "helping Selective Service survive."

CELLER, EMANUEL. *The Draft and You.* 1940. Viking Press. New York. 81 pages.

Forewords by Edward R. Burke and James W. Wadsworth, and statement on the draft by Franklin D. Roosevelt. Issued as a "primer [attempting to] interpret in simple fashion the Selective Training and Service Act of 1940, and the regulations to be issued under it." In addition to a question-and-answer section pertaining to Selective Service Regulations, it includes a section entitled "History of Recruiting up to Date" in which it is contended that the principle of conscription has been frequently affirmed in the course of the nation's history.

CROWDER, E. H. *The Spirit of Selective Service.* 1920. Century Co. New York. 367 pages.

The author, as U.S. Provost Marshal General in World War I, directed a draft board system that registered and classified 24 million men. Part 1 presents the historical background of the case for compulsion, discussing and comparing the systems of voluntarism, universal service, and selective service, and provides an account of the operations of the Selective Service System. Part 2 appeals for the permanent application of the selective service idea to "a newer and more perfect democracy" in which the same mechanism that generated the wartime selective service system could be adapted to define and unify national policies in such vital areas as education, labor-management, and state-federal relations. Crowder believes that selective service "is the only plan that has yet succeeded in bringing classes, factions, and races together."

DAVIS, JAMES W., JR., and KENNETH M. DOLBEARE. *Little Groups of Neighbors: The Selective Service System.* 1968. Markham Publishing Co. Chicago. Index. Figures, tables. 276 pages.

A systematic examination of the structure, personnel, and operations of the Selective Service System. The book deals also with the impact of the draft and with public attitudes toward the draft and the Selective Service System. Alternative means of conscription are considered, as are the problems and opportunities inherent in the principle of citizen participation. The last chapter analyzes the place of selective service in the political system.

GINZBERG, ELI. *Manpower Agenda for America.* 1968. McGraw-Hill Book Co. New York. Index. 250 pages.

Chapter 13, "Reforming the Draft," points out defects and merits of the Selective Service System, and discusses alternatives to the system, including universal military training, reduction of required length of service, and an all-volunteer army. Ginzberg considers that "'the real challenge is to design an alternative that will result in a more universal sharing of the risk of service while providing the armed services, at a reasonable cost, with the numbers and quality of manpower they require." In this view, a lottery system, while not entirely equitable, could be an alternative to the present system.

HAYES, SAMUEL H. *Defense Manpower: The Management of Military Conscription.* 1967. Industrial College of the Armed Forces. Washington, D.C. Tables, graphs. Bibliography: pages 71–72. 72 pages.

Focusing on the equitability of the draft, the author discusses the relationships between the armed forces and democracy, problems of the Selective Service System, and military service as a tool for social rehabilitation and vocational training. He concludes that the draft generally accomplishes its objectives but should be improved in order to solve military manpower problems; that both universal military training and a volunteer force would be too costly as alternatives and incur disadvantages outweighing foreseen advantages; and that the lottery system merely substitutes chance for "a rational system of selection" without increasing equity. Appendices, which comprise the bulk of this work, include "Defense Department Report on the Draft" and Lyndon B. Johnson's "Selective Service Message from the President of the United States to the Congress, 6 March 1967."

JACOBS, CLYDE E., and JOHN F. GALLAGHER. *The Selective Service Act: A Case Study of the Governmental Process.* 1967. Dodd, Mead & Co. New York. Index. Illustrations, tables. 209 pages.

Traces selective service through its legislative, administrative, and judicial phases to illustrate the complexities and interdependencies of policymaking in American national government. Reviews attitudes from colonial times to the present, the history of proposals for universal military training, the enactment and administration of selective service, and legal and executive processes. The problem of the conscientious objector is dealt with as a specific issue arising in the application of selective service legislation.

LYNN, CONRAD J. *How to Stay Out of the Army: A Guide to Your Rights Under the Draft Law.* 1967. Monthly Review Press. New York. 130 pages.

Discusses ways in which an individual's chances for deferment or exemption may be improved, provisions for college and postgraduate study, deferment or exemption on grounds of principle such as conscientious objection or opposition to the war in Vietnam, and how to handle one's own case within the draft machinery and up to the courts without the expense of hiring a lawyer.

MARMION, HARRY A. *Selective Service: Conflict and Compromise.* 1968. John Wiley & Sons. New York. Index. 220 pages.

This book sketches the background, organization, and operation of the Selective Service System and the various problems facing it, discusses the legislative hearings and the public dialogue, and examines recent legislation. The author sees no feasible alternative to the present system of selective service, which, "with all its weaknesses," appears to be "the only logical basis on which to conscript young men." Student deferments are upheld, "particularly on the undergraduate level, if deferment does not mean exemption." Marmion recommends the establishment of a federal manpower agency that would "inherit the present duties of Selective Service as well as the manpower functions of various other government agencies." The appendix includes texts of the *Civilian Advisory Panel on Military Manpower Procurement* (Clark Report) and the "Summary of the Report of the National Advisory Commission on Selective Service (Marshall Report)" (see also pages 109 and 112, above).

NATIONAL MANPOWER COUNCIL. *Student Deferment and National Manpower Policy: A Statement of Policy by the Council.* 1952. Columbia University Press. New York. Tables. 102 pages.

In this study of deferment of college students and apprentices, topics include the student deferment program, the military manpower pool, selection of students for deferment, skilled and specialized personnel, and student deferment and democratic values. The council believes that the deferment of students is important for development of national manpower, although this raises questions of equity. It recommends that dependency be removed as grounds for deferment, that students be able to qualify for deferment on the basis of Selective Service College Qualification Tests, and that apprentices be deferred but called for induction upon completion of training.

RIVKIN, ROBERT S. *GI Rights and Army Justice: The Draftee's Guide to Military Life and Law.* 1970. Grove Press, Inc. New York. Index. Bibliographical notes at end of each chapter. 383 pages.

A step-by-step manual, in popular language, on individual rights under existing draft laws. The author contends that while Congress has passed legislation to protect the soldier and to inform him of his rights, the military has been delinquent in carrying out the letter of the law. The appendix contains resolutions of a national conference on GI rights as well as a list of informational, counseling, and legal services available to the GI.

ROTHENBERG, LESLIE S. *The Draft and You: A Handbook on the Selective Service System.* 1968. Doubleday & Co., Inc. Garden City, New York. Index. Illustrations. 332 pages.

A guide to the operation of the Selective Service System. Includes a brief history of conscription in the United States and information regarding Selective Service local boards, registration and classification procedures, deferments, conscientious objectors, physical examination, and the induction process.

SANDERS, JACQUIN. *The Draft and the Vietnam War.* 1966. Walker & Co. New York. 156 pages.

A popular guide to the mechanics of the Selective Service System. Discusses quotas, classifications, deferments, service opportunities, local draft boards, opposition to the draft, and draft reform.

SCIENCE RESEARCH ASSOCIATES, INC. *Unfit for Service: A Review of the Draft and Basic Education in the Army.* 1966. Chicago. Figures, tables. Mimeographed. 243 pages.

While this report focuses on educational rehabilitation of draft rejectees, it also offers a perspective on "how the draft works today," on "what the critics of the draft have to say," and on proposals that have been advanced to change the draft. The appendix includes a profile of public opinion on the draft drawn from polls from 1940 to 1966 and purporting to "show that the public consistently and strongly favors universal military service— a measure Congress voted down in 1952."

SHAPIRO, ANDREW O., and JOHN M. STRIKER. *Mastering the Draft: The Comprehensive Guide for Solving Draft Problems.* 1971. Avon Books. New York. Index. Illustrations. References: pages 543–599. 626 pages.

This book defines specific draft law problems and then solves them. Its main sections deal with the structure and personnel of the Selective Service System; local-board operations; the registration process; delinquency; classification and reclassification; student and occupational deferments; the conscientious objector exemption and other exemptions; rights and avenues of appeal; medical, mental, and moral qualifications; quotas, calls, and induction; and the role of the courts.

SUTTLER, DAVID. *IV-F: A Guide to Medical, Psychiatric, and Moral Unfitness Standards for Military Induction.* 1970. Grove Press, Inc. New York. Bibliography: pages 129–135. 171 pages.

This handbook, based on Selective Service and military regulations, legal and medical research, and interviews with government officials, attorneys, physicians, and psychiatrists experienced in the field, is designed to provide the necessary information both for the draft registrant and the doctor to deal with the problem of draft exemption. The appendix includes sample forms relating to the determination of IV-F status.

TATUM, ARLO, and JOSEPH S. TUCHINSKY. *Guide to the Draft.* 3rd edition, revised. 1970. Beacon Press. Boston. Index. 278 pages.

A guide to the individual's rights and obligations under the Selective Service System. Explores the alternatives open to the man faced by decisions about the draft, describing the choices open to him and explaining the details of each choice. The authors discuss the operation and procedures of the Selective Service System, military and nonmilitary service, deferment and exemption, conscientious objection, emigration, trial and prison, and sources of counseling and legal aid.

TRIBBLE, WILLIAM D. *Doctor Draft Justified? A Management Diagnosis.* 1968. National Biomedical Laboratories. San Antonio, Texas. Index. Tables. 261 pages.

A review and analysis of the military's difficulty in recruiting and retaining physicians, and of its reliance, since 1950, on the drafting of physicians. Discusses past and current physician procurement, utilization, and retention practices, including legislative history and the national supply and demand for physicians. Hypotheses are formulated as to the factors influencing the retention of physicians, and a conceptual model for a solution of the physician retention problem is developed. The author concludes that "unless new medical management philosophies are implemented in the Department of Defense, the physician retention problem will continue to exist and the 'Doctor Draft' will be required."

WAMSLEY, GARY L. *Selective Service and a Changing America: A Study of Organizational-Environmental Relationships.* 1969. Charles E. Merrill Publishing Co. Columbus, Ohio. Index. Tables. Bibliography: pages 246–254. 259 pages.

This study attempts to show "why a nation with strong anti-militarist, anti-conscription and pro-militia traditions came to accept conscription and to do so for a long period of time." It also seeks to explain "how Selective Service achieved quiet acceptance in the face of . . . hostility to its task of conscription." It is suggested that the explanation lies in the development of a system with a structure and processes that were closely related to values in American political culture. Much of the study is devoted to an exploration of the events that had a bearing upon the way selective service planners developed the system in 1917. The author concludes that because the Selective Service System has become a political issue, it is likely to undergo change, although "it seems unlikely that the grand 'alternatives' to conscription like a volunteer army and universal national service will replace some form of Selective Service."

Unpublished Manuscripts

BRADFORD, DAVID F. *The Effects of Uncertainty in Selective Service.*
1966. Ph.D. dissertation. Stanford University. Stanford, California. 109
pages.

The major part of this study is devoted to the development of a model
of the individual's behavior in the face of draft uncertainty. A model of
the determination of the optimal enlistment age is developed, and it is
demonstrated in what way draft uncertainty is costly to the individual.
Bradford refutes the notion that volunteers for service are those for whom
military service is least costly. Rather, he argues, the present selection
system tends to shift military service incidence toward those for whom the
cost of military service rises most rapidly with age.

EDWARDS, WALKER S. *The Administration of Selective Service in the
United States.* 1948. M.A. thesis. Stanford University. Stanford, California. Bibliography: pages i-iv. 118 pages.

An assessment of the effectiveness of selective service administration
during World Wars I and II. Edwards states that while selective service
in both wars was a success from the strictly military viewpoint, the organization was administratively inefficient. Criticizing the use of several thousand draft boards, he asserts that "the very elements of the organization
which seemed most in harmony with democratic principles and local self-
government were those which contributed to the ineffectiveness of selective
service in providing an adequate national manpower policy." The insistence by national leaders that local-board members serve without compensation "tended to make board membership less representative of the
various community interests." Selective Service headquarters' "frequent
lack of clarity in defining national selective service policies to the public or
to local boards" and the system of medical examinations are cited as
examples of "poor administrative planning and procedure" at the national
level.

O'SULLIVAN, JOHN JOSEPH. *From Voluntarism to Conscription: Congress
and Selective Service 1940–1945.* 1917. Ph.D. dissertation. Columbia
University. New York. 374 pages.

Deals with the question of how Congress came to adopt the Selective
Training and Service Act of 1940. The various influences that insured

passage of the act—lobbying efforts, particularly by the Military Training Camps Association; the impact of war news from Europe, especially the fall of France; and the growing acceptance of the proposal by the American public—are assessed. Also considered are the implementation of the selective service law up to the attack on Pearl Harbor, the legislative adaptation of the draft to meet the demands of wartime, and the "fundamental shift" that took place in American attitudes toward military conscription in the years 1940–1945.

WAMSLEY, GARY L. *Selective Service and American Political Culture: The Maintenance of Equilibrium Between Demands of Function and Political Culture by an Institution of Civil-Military Juncture.* 1967. Ph.D. dissertation. University of Pittsburgh. Pittsburgh, Pennsylvania. Figures, tables. Bibliography: pages 443–456. 456 pages.

Explores the thesis that "throughout American history, military conscription has run counter to certain key values of American political culture—voluntarism, civilian control of the military, local decisions are better decisions, sovereignty of the states, etc. Selective Service was an institution designed to ease the constraints posed by these values by identifying its structure and processes with them. It has thus sought to meet the functional demands arising from defense needs without violating those values. Due to changes in the values of American political culture and to institutional rigidities developed within the system, it is becoming increasingly more difficult for it to maintain an equilibrium that satisfies both defense needs and the values of American political culture."

Articles

BLUM, ALBERT A. *The Fight for a Young Army.* Military Affairs. Summer 1954. Volume XVIII, Number 2. Pages 81–85.

Notes the efforts of the War Department to maintain a relatively low age for inductees in World War II. Recommends that in any future full-scale mobilization the total available manpower supply should be divided into two groups: those under 26 and those between 26 and 38. The younger men would be slated for military service, the older for industrial service.

BLUM, ALBERT A. *Work or Fight: The Use of the Draft as a Manpower Sanction During the Second World War.* Industrial and Labor Relations Review. April 1963. Volume 16, Number 3. Pages 366–380.

Discusses issues facing policy-makers during World War II regarding the interrelationships of the Selective Service, nonessential employment, and wartime strikes (noting the strong public sentiment against such strikes). Traces the debate and shifts in government position on whether the draft should be limited to raising an army or should also be used for nonmilitary manpower control. Blum concludes that, in the main, the draft was used for military purposes, although actual or threatened cancellation of deferments was a factor in a number of important labor disputes.

BLUM, ALBERT A., and J. DOUGLAS SMYTH. *Who Should Serve: Pre-World War II Planning for Selective Service.* The Journal of Economic History. June 1970. Volume 30, Number 2. Pages 379–404.

Examines the development of industrial and occupational deferment policies under the Selective Service System. Notes the efforts of the American Legion from 1921 to 1931 to secure "'a legislative guarantee of equality of sacrifice in future wars by means of a universal draft. Although the Legion at first did not clarify its proposals with specific recommendations, it seemed to have had in mind the conscription of all capital labor in time of war."

CLIFFORD, JOHN G. *Grenville Clark and the Origins of Selective Service.* Review of Politics. January 1973. Volume 35, Number 1. Pages 17–40.

Includes a biographical sketch of Grenville Clark and details the role of his Plattsburg movement in establishing the Selective Service in 1940. Chronicles events leading up to the Selective Training and Service Act of 1940.

CONNOR, JAMES T. *"Due Process" and the Selective Service System.* Virginia Law Review. June 1944. Volume 30, Number 3. Pages 435–461.

Examines the Selective Service Act and Regulations in order to evaluate operations under them in the light of the basic requirements of "due process." Finds that, notwithstanding its position as an administrative agency with unusual powers over the individual citizen, "there are three fundamental and withal democratic concepts represented in the organization and administration of Selective Service": (1) liability for military service in periods of emergency is the common responsibility of every qualified citizen without exception; (2) the system is administered in its important and decisive phases by civilians rather than by military personnel; and (3) decisions affecting the citizen are localized.

CORNELL, JULIEN. *Exemption from the Draft: A Study in Civil Liberties.* Yale Law Journal. January 1947. Volume 56, Number 2. Pages 258–275.

Contends that a military draft "raises a basic conflict in the democratic process: the right of nonconformist individuals to go their own way against the right of the majority to apply coercion in the name of common necessity." Considers, against this background, the exemption of aliens, ministers of religion, and conscientious objectors, as well as judicial review of Selective Service findings.

CULLIGAN, ERNEST M. *Procurement of Man Power.* The Annals of the American Academy of Political and Social Science. March 1942. Volume 220. Pages 8–17.

In a context favorable to compulsory military service, the author traces the history of the Selective Service System in the United States, discussing events and specific aspects of various plans since World War I. Topics include the Selective Service System, the lottery, local draft boards, classifications, changes in classification, and amendments to the Selective Service Act.

DENNIS, LLOYD B. *Draft Revision.* Editorial Research Reports. June 22, 1966. Volume 1. Pages 441–461.

Examines the national debate over draft inequities, selection and deferment policies, and the origins of the Selective Service System. Considers two alternatives to the present military manpower procurement system: a combination of military and nonmilitary service, and a return to a lottery method of military drafting.

FIENBERG, STEPHEN E. *Randomization and Social Affairs: The 1970 Draft Lottery.* Science. January 22, 1971. Volume 171, Number 3968. Pages 255–261.

The author suggests that, when viewed in a historical perspective, "the draft lottery is only one among a great many situations in which society has institutionalized a recognized chance mechanism as the appropriate means of arriving at a decision that is to affect many people." He examines the randomization procedures employed in the 1970 draft lottery.

GINZBERG, ELI. *The Case for a Lottery.* The Public Interest. Fall 1966. Number 5. Pages 83–89.

Calls for an alternative to the present Selective Service local boards systems "that will result in a more universal sharing of the risk of service while providing the Armed Services, at a reasonable cost, with the numbers and quality of manpower they require." It is the author's opinion that a lottery "can substantially meet the test for equity."

GRAHAM, DONALD. *Taking a McNamara Fellowship.* The Atlantic Monthly. February 1966. Volume 217, Number 2. Pages 59–60.

Argues that the draft has narrowed the choice for the college student: "It is the Army or graduate school. And when he thinks about the first alternative, his thoughts are likely to turn more and more to the second." By virtue of length-of-service conditions and of the administration of the local boards, Graham states, the services "seem to punish rather than reward enlistment." He upholds the necessity of the draft, however, calling for reform to eliminate discrimination and inequities in selection.

GRAUMAN, LAWRENCE, JR. *Prospects for the Draft.* The New Leader. March 27, 1967. Volume L, Number 7. Pages 6–10.

Looks at the results of the work of two special commissions appointed to examine the current draft system—the Marshall and Clark commissions—and discusses current possibilities and limits of draft reform. Contends that the present draft system is "unjust and obsolete" and that neither the Selective Service, nor the Defense Department, nor Congress has "begun to assume the obligation of intelligent inquiry" into manpower policy reform.

GRAUMAN, LAWRENCE, JR. *The University and the Draft.* The New Leader. August 1, 1966. Volume XLIX, Number 16. Pages 15–18.

In light of pending debate on how best to reform the Selective Service System, the author looks at arguments for and against student deferment, discusses the social and military ramifications of deferment, and outlines what he considers to be the essential issues of alternative plans. He concludes that the proponents of an all-volunteer force "have the hardest case to make" and that some sort of reform within the existing system is necessary. He refutes traditional arguments against the draft, stating that, aside from needed reforms in geographic balance and personnel efficiency, the present system is adequate.

HERSHEY, LEWIS B. *Legal Aspects of the Selective Service Act.* Indiana Law Journal. April 1942. Volume 17, Number 4. Pages 271–284.

Discusses the appeal procedure under the Selective Service Act.

HERSHEY, LEWIS B. *The Operation of the Selective Service System.* Current History. July 1968. Volume 55, Number 325. Pages 1–6, 50.

Notes that the Selective Service System "has met and solved all military manpower problems of a large and complex nature for more than a quarter of a century" and at the same time "has protected the civilian economy." Defending the system, the director declares that it is "as clear an example as exists today of government of the people, by the people, and for the people."

HORTON, MILDRED MCAFEE. *Drafting Women for the Armed Forces.* Journal of the American Association of University Women. Spring 1951. Volume 44, Number 3. Pages 141–144.

Calls for the drafting of women on the grounds that, like men, they are national resources that should be utilized for their skills, aptitudes, and interests; and that, as citizens, they should have the responsibilities as well as the rights of citizenship.

HUSTON, JAMES A. *Selective Service in World War II.* Current History. June 1968. Volume 54, Number 322. Pages 345–350, 368, 384.

Notes that "in view of the final results, the Selective Service System was clearly effective in providing in an orderly way the military manpower needed in World War II. When virtually all available men were to be called, the system of complete registration, classification and a lottery to determine the order of calls worked very well."

HUZAR, ELIAS. *Selective Service Policy 1940–1942.* The Journal of Politics. May 1942. Volume 4, Number 2. Pages 201–226.

An examination of U.S. draft legislation and implementation in the 1940–1942 period. Discusses the political background of the issue, including congressional debate, Administration policy, and War Department positions.

INTERNATIONAL JURIDICAL ASSOCIATION BULLETIN. *Peacetime Conscription—Selective Training and Service Act of 1940.* October 1940. Volume 9, Number 4. Pages 33, 37–44.

Examines the provisions of the Selective Training and Service Act of 1940 in regard to exemptions and deferments, conscientious objectors, voting rights of conscripts, job protection and other economic aspects, and penalties for violation of the act. Notes "the necessity for supplementary legislation to alleviate some of the consequences which may be expected from the operation of the conscription act."

KELLY, E. LOWELL. *Manpower Utilization Under the Selective Service Act.* The American Psychologist. November 1950. Volume 5, Number 11. Pages 641–642.

Discusses current proposals for deferring college students and professional personnel under the Selective Service Act.

KENNEDY, EDWARD M. *Random Selection: An Alternative to Selective Service.* Current History. August 1968. Volume 55, Number 324. Pages 93–96, 106.

Senator Kennedy calls for a change in the conscription system, asserting that the present system is inequitable. He advocates (1) instituting a random selection system, (2) drafting the youngest males first, and (3) establishing national Selective Service standards.

KUBIE, LAWRENCE S. *Technical and Organizational Problems in the*

Selection of Troops (two parts). Military Affairs. (1) Winter 1944. Volume VIII, Number 4. Pages 243–258. (2) Spring 1945. Volume IX, Number 1. Pages 13–32.

Contending that under the present organization of the Selective Service System "selection is a specialty without a specialist," the author recommends a number of reforms in the system of selection and induction of military manpower.

MARTIN, PETER W. *Trial by Hershey: The Draft as Punishment.* The Nation. January 29, 1968. Volume 206, Number 5. Pages 139–143.

A discussion of the events surrounding General Hershey's recommendation that draft resisters and antiwar demonstrators be termed "delinquent" and reclassified 1-A. After considering the moral and legal ramifications of both the code of Methods of Enforcements of the Selective Service Acts and the practices generally followed, Martin concludes that general practices were often in violation of both constitutional rights and specific law.

MOYNIHAN, DANIEL P. *Who Gets in the Army?* The New Republic. November 5, 1966. Volume 155, Number 19. Pages 19–22.

"We have failed," asserts Moynihan, "to perceive the potential of the Selective Service System as an instrument of social analysis and change." Thus the American armed forces, "having become an immensely potent instrument for education and occupational mobility, have been systematically excluding the least educated, least mobile young men." Moynihan suggests using the armed forces "as a socializing experience for the poor—particularly the Southern poor—until somehow their environment begins turning out equal citizens."

NEWLON, DANIEL H. *A Volunteer Draft: An Alternative to the Draft Lottery.* Military Review. February 1972. Volume LII, Number 2. Pages 83–89.

Discusses the proposal for a "volunteer draft" under which 18-year-olds would be allowed to choose among three alternatives: (1) enlistment, (2) exemption by paying their share of the cost of eliminating the draft, and (3) remaining subject to the draft. This "volunteer draft" would retain the lottery draft for those "unwilling to pay their share of the cost of a Volunteer Army."

RANKIN, ROBERT H. *A History of Selective Service.* United States Naval Institute Proceedings. October 1951. Volume 77, Number 10. Pages 1073–1081.

Contends that "history shows that any nation of consequence has built its independence and prosperity, as well as insured its security, on the principle of compulsory military service." Selective service, in this view, "is the fairest, most economical, and most democratic method of raising men for military service" and "any departure from this traditional policy, as history clearly shows, can result only in calamitous disaster."

RAPPORT, VICTOR A. *Sociological Implications of Selective Service.* American Sociological Review. April 1941. Volume 6, Number 2. Pages 225–229.

Selective service, viewed sociologically, has two aspects: (1) the application of known facts which are commonly used in the field of sociology, and (2) the application of sociological theories. Reviewing this second aspect, the author finds that "the Selective Service Act, with its accompanying Regulations, constantly demonstrates the effort to carry out the principles of democracy."

SMITH, MAPHEUS. *The Differential Impact of Selective Service Inductions on Occupations in the United States.* American Sociological Review. October 1946. Volume XI, Number 5. Pages 567–572.

Hypothesizes that "those occupations which have suffered the greatest drain from inductions are those with large proportions of young workers engaged in non-essential or less essential work, or who, if doing essential or more essential work, were more easily replaced than some other workers." Survey data show that inductions varied greatly from one major occupation group to another, and it is concluded that "the inducted man, if employed at the time of induction, was a man whose combination of age, dependency status and employment was such that his local board or an Appeal Agency considered him not to deserve a deferment, and who, when physically examined, met the minimum standards for induction."

TIGAR, MICHAEL E., and ROBERT J. ZWEBEN. *Selective Service: Some Certain Problems and Some Tentative Answers.* George Washington Law Review. March 1969. Volume 37, Number 3. Pages 510–535.

A critical review of the Selective Service System, suggesting that "even thoroughgoing reform—unlikely as that is—cannot deal with the profound sense of injustice generated by the System's performance." Questions whether, on economic, constitutional, and moral grounds, there is justification for a system of conscription in the United States.

UNIVERSITY OF PENNSYLVANIA LAW REVIEW. *Fairness and Due Process Under the Selective Service System.* May 1966. Volume 114. Pages 1014–1049.

Asks whether the Selective Service System focuses on efficiency at the expense of fairness in marshaling manpower. Outlines three problem areas: (1) changes in status after original calssification of the draftee, (2) the right to advise or counsel, and (3) dealing with the uncooperative or civilly disobedient draftee. In this article, it is noted, "issues of right to judicial review will be considered as integral to an understanding of the legal problems within the Selective Service process." The article emphasizes that different problems arise in times of peace, when service is indeed "selective," and in times of war, when universal mobilization is necessary.

WALTON, GEORGE H. *Sole Source Procurement Through Selective Service.* Army. September 1963. Volume 14, Number 2. Pages 32–34.

Proposes that all men newly enlisted in the army be inducted by the Selective Service System. This change would give the army an additional period to determine whether to accept or reject an applicant for the Regular Army, and would put an end to the quota system of recruiting— "a necessary evil of the volunteer system."

WELLES, SUMNER, and H. H. WRONG. *Application of Selective Service Act to Canadian Nationals in the United States.* Supplement to the American Journal of International Law: Official Documents. July 1942. Volume 36, Number 3. Pages 158–163.

Letters between Acting Secretary of State Sumner Welles and Canadian government officials discussing the terms under which Canadian nationals residing in the United States and eligible for service in the U.S. armed forces can opt for service in the Canadian military. The reciprocal agreement for U.S. nationals resident in Canada is also covered.

WOLFLE, DAEL. *Draft, Deferment and Scientists.* The American Psychologist. August 1950. Volume 5, Number 8. Pages 432–434.

Discusses the assignment and utilization of scientists in relation to military manpower needs, pointing out the alleged failures of current policies.

ZWERLING, MATTHEW. *Notes and Comments: The Selective Service.* Yale Law Journal. November 1966. Volume 76 Number 1. Pages 160–199.

Report of a study on the structure and administration of the draft, using both public information and empirical research. Finds that the most serious flaw in the Selective Service System is the principle of local discretion basic to the present administrative structure. Originally designed to avert resistance to conscription in the Civil War, the draft system is considered obsolete, functioning now "as a hybrid in which national policy jostles with local authority, affording neither coherent standards, responsible decision-making, nor procedural essentials." Zwerling proposes specific changes in the structure of the Selective Service System that would reduce local discretion and establish national policy for rules, adjudication, and judicial review.

Pamphlets, Reprints, and Speeches

CONGRESSIONAL QUARTERLY SERVICE. *U.S. Draft Policy and Its Impact.* 1968. Washington, D.C. Charts, tables. 44 pages.

A survey of the effect of the 1967 draft law on graduate schools and various service organizations, with views on draft changes, the lottery system, nonmilitary service proposals, and resistance to military service. Includes a summary of the history and operation of the Selective Service System, as well as positions of various groups on the question of extension of the draft law.

DONOVAN, WILLIAM J. *Should Men of Fifty Fight Our Wars?* 1940. Reprint from the New York Herald Tribune. New York. 8 pages.

World War I hero "Wild Bill" Donovan urges that U.S. draft laws be amended so that men up to 60 years of age would be liable for compulsory military service.

HERSHEY, LEWIS B. *Establishing Selective Service.* 1942. University of Pennsylvania Press. Philadelphia. 19 pages.

In a November 1941 speech to university students, Hershey discusses the recruiting and deferment policies of the Selective Service System. Suggesting that "this war is, unfortunately, a young man's war," he urges students to consider enlisting before completing their studies, for "whether a man becomes a successful leader is not always settled in the last semester or the last two semesters."

NATIONAL COUNCIL AGAINST CONSCRIPTION. *We Dare Not Risk Another Army Mistake.* Circa 1948. Washington, D.C. 16 pages.

This pamphlet reviews the "repeated and unwarranted Army demands for 'essential' draft legislation—the labor draft, nurses' draft, draft extension, and the current proposal for U.M.T. [universal military training]."

NEW YORK CITY COMMITTEE ON MENTAL HYGIENE. *A Memorandum on the Selective Process in General and on the Role of Psychiatry in the Selective Process and in the Armed Forces.* 1942. New York. 25 pages.

This memorandum, submitted to the secretary of war, focuses attention on the inadequacy of present methods of selection of personnel and of provisions for psychiatric care within the armed services. It states that a substantial proportion of all discharges for disability in recent wars have been found to be due to neuropsychiatric conditions, and that no effort has been made to prevent a repetition of the same errors in selection. Obstacles that stand in the way of remedial measures include problems in human relationships between civilian and military physicians, the bias against psychiatry, and the lack of coordination of special fields of psychiatric and psychological experience. Recommendations are made for "a plan of organization for adequate application of psychiatric knowledge to the selective process and to the armed forces."

Government Documents: Publications

U.S. CONGRESS. HOUSE. COMMITTEE ON ARMED SERVICES. *Military Service Act of 1967.* 1967. Government Printing Office. Washington, D.C. 59 pages.

Text of the Military Service Act of 1967 with an analysis and a brief description of the Selective Service System. Dated December 1, 1967.

U.S. CONGRESS. HOUSE. COMMITTEE ON ARMED SERVICES. *Review of the Selective Service System.* 1966. Government Printing Office. Washington, D.C. 16 pages.

Interim Report of the House Committee on Armed Services reviewing the administration and operation of the Selective Service System. Dated August 4, 1966.

U.S. CONGRESS. HOUSE. COMMITTEE ON MILITARY AFFAIRS. *Investigations of the National War Effort.* 1943. Government Printing Office. Washington, D.C. Tables. 21 pages.

Interim Report of the House Committee on Military Affairs pursuant to House Resolution 30 authorizing the Committee on Military Affairs and the Committee on Naval Affairs to study the progress of the national war effort. Investigates selective service deferments of men of draft age in government and industry and of men commissioned into the armed forces from civilian life.

U.S. CONGRESS. HOUSE. SUPERINTENDENT OF DOCUMENT ROOM. *Selective Service Act, as Amended.* Compiled by Elmer A. Lewis. 1943. Government Printing Office. Washington, D.C. 51 pages.

A compilation of laws passed between May 18, 1917, and July 9, 1943, by the 65th, 76th, 77th, and 78th Congresses in regard to selective service.

U.S. CONGRESS. SENATE. SUPERINTENDENT OF DOCUMENT ROOM. *Selective Service Acts.* Compiled by John W. Lambert. 1943. Government Printing Office. Washington, D.C. 35 pages.

A compilation of laws passed between September 16, 1940, and July 9, 1943, by the 76th, 77th, and 78th Congresses in regard to selective service.

U.S. JOINT ARMY AND NAVY SELECTIVE SERVICE COMMITTEE. *American Selective Service: A Brief Account of Its Historical Background and Its Probable Future Form.* 1939. Government Printing Office. Washington, D.C. 33 pages.

Describes the origins and operations of the Selective Service Act of May 18, 1917, and current plans for selective service to follow "'very closely the final form of World War [I] Selective Service." A proposed plan for volunteering in wartime decentralizes the civilian effort to the governor of each state but regards the recruitment of volunteers in wartime as "only a makeshift, adopted more in the hope than in the conviction that it will meet the situation for a couple of months until Selective Service can begin producing men at the training stations."

U.S. PROVOST MARSHAL GENERAL'S BUREAU. *Report on the First Draft Under the Selective Service Act, 1917.* 1917. Government Printing Office. Washington, D.C. Charts, tables. 159 pages.

E. H. Crowder's first report as Provost Marshal General, covering the operations of the selective draft from May 18, 1917, the date of the Selective Service Act, to December 20, 1917. The appendix contains statistical data on the operation of the draft in World War I.

U.S. PROVOST MARSHAL GENERAL'S BUREAU. *Second Report on the Operations of the Selective Service System to December 20, 1918.* 1919. Government Printing Office. Washington, D.C. Index. Charts, tables. 607 pages.

E. H. Crowder's second report as Provost Marshal General, covering the operations of the selective draft from May 18, 1917, the date of the Selective Service Act, to December 20, 1918, with special reference to the operations since December 20, 1917, the date of the first report. Includes descriptions of the Civil War draft and of conscription in Britain from 1914 to 1918. The appendix contains statistical data on the operation of the draft in World War I.

U.S. PROVOST MARSHAL GENERAL'S BUREAU. *Final Report of the Operations of the Selective Service System to July 15, 1919.* 1920. Government Printing Office. Washington, D.C. Charts, tables. 288 pages.

E. H. Crowder's final report as Provost Marshal General, covering the operations of the selective draft from May 18, 1917, to July 15, 1919, with special reference to the operations since December 20, 1919, the date of the second report. Provides statistical breakdowns by age and state of registration, classification, desertion, call, induction, acceptance, and rejection, as well as agricultural, dependency, and industrial deferment, aliens, and cost data.

U.S. SELECTIVE SERVICE SYSTEM. *Backgrounds of Selective Service: Military Obligation, the American Tradition, Compilation of Enactments of Compulsion from Earliest Settlements of Original 13 Colonies in 1607 Through Articles of Confederation 1789.* Special Monograph 1, Volume 1: *A Historical Review of the Principle of Citizen Compulsion in the Raising of Armies.* By Arthur Vollmer. 1947. Government Printing Office. Washington, D.C. Index. Bibliography: pages 83–85. 288 pages.

Records "the many instances of compulsory military service in the history of the United States, the 13 Original Colonies, and certain Old World Nations prior to the passage of the Selective Training and Service Act of 1940." Chapters deal, respectively, with the compulsion principle in ancient times, the medieval age, lessons from Continental Europe, English antecedents, colonial precedents, and the U.S. experience. The principal military recruitments acts in U.S. federal history, covering the period from the passage of the first Resolution of the Continental Congress to the beginning of consideration of selective service legislation in 1940, are presented as appendices. (See also next entry.)

U.S. SELECTIVE SERVICE SYSTEM. *Backgrounds of Selective Service: Military Obligation, the American Tradition, Compilation of Enactments of Compulsion from Earliest Settlements of Original 13 Colonies in 1607 Through Articles of Confederation 1789.* Special Monograph 1, Volume 2. 14 parts. Compiled by Arthur Vollmer. 1947. Government Printing Office. Washington, D.C. Part 1: *General Information.* 135 pages. Part 2: *Connecticut Enactments.* 263 pages. Part 3: *Delaware Enactments.* 35 pages. Part 4: *Georgia Enactments.* 160 pages. Part 5: *Maryland Enactments.* 143 pages. Part 6: *Massachusetts Enactments.* 267 pages. Part 7: *New Hampshire Enactments.* 117 pages. Part 8: *New Jersey Enactments.* 86 pages. Part 9: *New York Enactments.* 328 pages. Part 10: *North Carolina Enactments.* 128 pages. Part 11: *Pennsylvania Enactmentts.* 133 pages. Part 12: *Rhode Island Enactments.* 235 pages. Part 13: *South Carolina Enactments.* 110 pages. Part 14: *Virginia Enactments.* 440 pages.

Part 1 describes the accumulation of pre-Constitution enactments contained in Parts 2 through 14 as providing evidence of "a strong American heritage for the United States in the universalness of military obligation among adult male citizens," inasmuch as any American tradition with regard to compulsory or voluntary military service "must have had its roots within the thirteen British colonies which combined to form the United States, and must have taken form by the time of the adoption of the Constitution." Therefore, "this tradition must be sought exclusively in the laws passed within the colonies by an Assembly, by a Governor and Council, or by a special Committee of Safety, or in the charters given by the British kings, and the other English laws in some way applicable to these territories." Parts 2 through 14 each contain, for the colony indicated in the title of the respective part, a compilation of enactments of compulsion from 1607 to 1789. (See also preceding entry.)

U.S. SELECTIVE SERVICE SYSTEM. *Bulletin of Information for Persons Registered.* Form 5. 1940. Selective Service System. Washington, D.C. 5 pages.

Contains information concerning local boards, advisory boards, oaths, deferments, volunteering, conscientious objectors, physical examinations, appeals, and calls for training and service.

U.S. SELECTIVE SERVICE SYSTEM. *Evaluation of Selective Service Program,* Volume 1: *Text*; Volume 2: *Appendices A–C*; Volume 3: *Appendices D–F.* Special Monograph 18. 1957. Government Printing Office. Washington, D.C. Illustrations. Volume 1: Bibliography: pages 233–241. 254 pages. Volume 2: 286 pages. Volume 3: 328 pages.

This study was prepared in 1956 but was not published until 1967. Volume 1 provides a comprehensive treatment of the Selective Service System from September 15, 1940, through March 31, 1947, covering peacetime, wartime, and postwar operations. Included are historical data in support of selective service, which is seen as "an evolutionary and logical development of the militia concept." Volumes 2 and 3 contain appendices comprised largely of public laws, executive orders, memoranda, and statistical data relating to the Selective Service System.

U.S. SELECTIVE SERVICE SYSTEM. *Manual of Law for Use by Advisory Boards for Registrants Appointed Pursuant to Selective Training and Service Act of 1940, as Amended.* Compiled by Committee on War Work, American Bar Association. 1942. Government Printing Office. Washington, D.C. Index. 218 pages.

Compiled in cooperation with Selective Service headquarters "as a practical medium of information as to the operative steps of selective service and other matters of vital concern to registrants and their families and other persons affected by its operation." Describes in detail the Soldiers' and Sailors' Civil Relief Act of 1940 as well as other examples of civil relationships affected by military service. The appendix contains the texts of related legislation.

U.S. SELECTIVE SERVICE SYSTEM. *Occupational Bulletins Nos. 1 to 44 and Activity and Occupation Bulletins Nos. 1 to 35.* 1944. Government Printing Office. Washington, D.C. Tables. 200 pages.

Compilation of official announcements concerning activities and occupations deemed "essential to war production and to support of the war effort." Covers the period April 3, 1943, to April 22, 1943.

U.S. SELECTIVE SERVICE SYSTEM. *Outline of Historical Background of Selective Service.* 1952. Government Printing Office. Washington, D.C. Tables. 51 pages.

Prepared under the direction of Selective Service Director Lewis Hershey, this booklet briefly describes selective service as it is said to have existed from Biblical days and, in America, from colonial times to the present. The United States is said to have a firm tradition of selective service, which started with the "more than 650 laws and ordinances passed by the Colonies and other political subdivisions" between 1607 and 1775 "providing for conscription in one form or another" and progressed to the Selective Service Act of 1917 and subsequent selective training and service acts and amendments. A chronology covers selective service legislation and operations and other pertinent data for the years 1940 through 1951. There are statistics on inductions in World Wars I and II.

U.S. SELECTIVE SERVICE SYSTEM. *Problems of Selective Service,* Volume 1: *Text;* Volume 2: *Appendices A–C;* Volume 3: *Appendices D–I.* 1952. Special Monograph 16. Government Printing Office. Washington, D.C. Illustrations. Volume 1: Index. Bibliography: pages 239–241. 259 pages. Volume 2: 219 pages. Volume 3: 292 pages.

Volume 1 discusses the nature and solution of difficulties in the organization, administration, and operation of the Selective Service System from 1940 to 1947. Problems encountered in World War II are compared with those encountered in the Civil War and in World War I. Volunteering, discussed at some length, is seen as having interfered with the efficient procurement and distribution of manpower in all three wars. Volume 2 contains appendices on public laws, executive orders, aliens, and appeals. Volume 3 is composed of appendices on education, induction, lotteries, the ministry, reserves, and voluntary enlistment.

U.S. SELECTIVE SERVICE SYSTEM. *Selective Service in Wartime.* 1943. Selective Service System. Washington, D.C. Charts, tables. 674 pages.

Second report of Selective Service Director Lewis Hershey, for 1941–1942. Provides a comprehensive record of the administration of the Selective Service Act during that period, with 77 tables and 21 charts presenting statistical data on the operation of the Selective Service System during the first year of U.S. activity in World War II.

U.S. SELECTIVE SERVICE SYSTEM. *Selective Service Regulations.* 1945. Government Printing Office. Washington, D.C. Index. Tables. 711 pages.

Includes an index on the Selective Training and Service Act of 1940 as amended, regulations in effect on February 1, 1943, amendments during the period from February 1, 1943, to July 31, 1945, and forms covering regulations and amendments.

U.S. TASK FORCE ON THE STRUCTURE OF THE SELECTIVE SERVICE SYSTEM. *Report of the Task Force on the Structure of the Selective Service System.* 1967. Government Printing Office. Washington, D.C. Charts, tables. 94 pages.

The task force was commissioned jointly by the secretary of defense, the director of the Selective Service System, and the director of the Bureau of the Budget to review the report of the National Advisory Commission on Selective Service (the Marshall Commission). The report of the task force, dated October 16, 1967, recommends that the present Selective Service System be retained, with some organizational improvements. Chapter 2, which reviews the background of the Selective Service System, suggests that it is the American tradition that every man owes "an obligation to his country to bear arms," that "nowhere in colonial law did there ever appear any challenge to the power of government to require military service," and that as a result of this tradition, it remained only to enforce, by a selective service system, the concept of compulsory military service.

U.S. WAR DEPARTMENT. *Draft Deserters.* 1920. Government Printing Office. Washington, D.C. 24 pages.

Statement of War Department policy in regard to draft deserters and draft delinquents under the Selective Service law.

U.S. WAR DEPARTMENT. *The Selective Service Register.* 1917. Committee on Public Information. Washington, D.C. 4 pages.

Prepared for the Provost Marshal General's office in World War I "for the purpose of giving as much information as possible relative to the coming draft registration." It was included as a broadsheet supplement in daily newspapers.

U.S. WAR DEPARTMENT. *Selective Service Regulations.* 1918. Government Printing Office. Washington, D.C. Index. Tables. 433 pages.

Foreword by Woodrow Wilson. Rules and regulations under the Selective Service Act of May 18, 1917, and the public resolutions and amendatory acts. Delineates the functions, under the Selective Service System, of the President as reviewing officer, of the Provost Marshal General, and of governors, adjutants general, disbursing officers and inspectors, and district and local boards. Included are sections on registration, classification, selection, induction and mobilization, and physical examination.

Government Documents: Congressional Hearings

1940. U.S. CONGRESS. HOUSE. COMMITTEE ON MILITARY AFFAIRS. *Selective Compulsory Military Training and Service.* Government Printing Office. Washington, D.C. Tables. 655 pages.

Hearings between July 10 and August 14, 1940, before the House Committee on Military Affairs on House Resolution 10132 to "protect the integrity and institutions of the United States through a system of selective compulsory military training and service."

1941. U.S. CONGRESS. HOUSE. COMMITTEE ON MILITARY AFFAIRS. *Amending the Selective Training and Service Act of 1940.* Government Printing Office. Washington, D.C. Table. 57 pages.

Hearings on June 10 and 16, 1941, before the House Committee on Military Affairs on House Resolutions 4949, 4527, and 4989, and Senate bill 1524 to provide for the common defense and to prevent stoppages or interruption in the production of munitions in industrial plants.

1941. U.S. CONGRESS. HOUSE. COMMITTEE ON MILITARY AFFAIRS. *Providing for the National Defense by Removing Restrictions on Numbers and Length of Service of Draftees.* Government Printing Office. Washington, D.C. 165 pages.

Hearings between July 22 and 28, 1941, before the House Committee on Military Affairs on House Joint Resolutions 217, 218, 220, and 222 declaring a national emergency, extending terms of enlistments, appointments, and commissions in the U.S. Army, suspending certain restrictions upon the employment of retired personnel of the army, and making further provisions for restoration of civil positions to members of the army on relief from military service.

1941. U.S. CONGRESS. HOUSE. COMMITTEE ON MILITARY AFFAIRS. *Amending the Selective Training and Service Act of 1940.* Government Printing Office. Washington, D.C. Tables. 64 pages.

Hearing on December 13, 1941, before the House Committee on Military Affairs on House bill 6215 to amend the Selective Training and Service Act of 1940 to "aid in insuring the defeat of all the enemies of the United States through the extension of liability for military service and through the registration of the manpower of the nation."

1942. U.S. CONGRESS. HOUSE. COMMITTEE ON MILITARY AFFAIRS. *Lowering Draft Age to 18 Years.* Government Printing Office. Washington, D.C. Illustrations. 165 pages.

Hearings on October 14 and 15, 1942, before the House Committee on Military Affairs on House Resolution 7528 to amend the Selective Training and Service Act of 1940 by providing for the extension of liability.

1943. U.S. CONGRESS. HOUSE. COMMITTEE ON MILITARY AFFAIRS. *Amendments to Selective Service Act.* Government Printing Office. Washington, D.C. 135 pages.

Hearings between February 11 and 17, 1943, before the House Committee on Military Affairs on House bill 1730 to amend paragraph (1) of section 5(E) of the Selective Training and Service Act of 1940, as amended, to authorize the deferment of those deemed necessary to the maintenance of the national health, safety, or interest.

1943. U.S. CONGRESS. HOUSE. COMMITTEE ON MILITARY AFFAIRS. *Amending the Selective Training and Service Act.* Government Printing Office. Washington, D.C. 12 pages.

Hearing on June 8, 1943, before the House Committee on Military Affairs on House bill 1991 to amend the Selective Training and Service Act of 1940 by providing for the postponement of the induction of high-school students who have completed more than half of their academic year.

1943. U.S. CONGRESS. HOUSE. COMMITTEE ON MILITARY AFFAIRS. *Amending the Selective Training and Service Act.* Government Printing Office. Washington, D.C. 43 pages.

Hearing on October 12, 1943, before the House Committee on Military Affairs on Senate bill 763 to amend the Selective Training and Service Act of 1940 in regard to deferments from compulsory military service.

1944. U.S. CONGRESS. HOUSE. COMMITTEE ON MILITARY AFFAIRS. *Amending the Selective Training and Service Act.* Government Printing Office. Washington, D.C. 135 pages.

Hearings between February 9 and 17, 1944, before the House Committee on Military Affairs on House bill 4000 to amend the Selective Training and Service Act of 1940 to defer registrants engaged in timber or pulpwood logging operations.

1944. U.S. CONGRESS. HOUSE. COMMITTEE ON MILITARY AFFAIRS. *Investigation of the National War Effort.* Government Printing Office. Washington, D.C. 191 pages.

Hearings between March 13 and 31, 1944, before the Special Committee on Draft Deferment of the House Committee on Military Affairs pursuant to House Resolution 30 authorizing the Committee on Military Affairs to study the progress of the national war effort.

1944. U.S. CONGRESS. HOUSE. COMMITTEE ON MILITARY AFFAIRS. *Statement of Col. F. V. Keesling Before Special Subcommittee to Investigate Draft Deferments Under Selective Service.* Government Printing Office. Washington, D.C. 16 pages.

Hearings on September 12, 1944, before the Special Subcommittee to

Investigate Draft Deferments under Selective Service of the House Committee on Military Affairs. Keesling, chief liaison and legislative officer for the Selective Service System, is questioned on deferments, on various other aspects of the draft, including the current volunteering of men between ages 30 and 38 not drafted, and on the future of selective service.

1945. U.S. CONGRESS. HOUSE. COMMITTEE ON MILITARY AFFAIRS. *Mobilization of Civilian Manpower.* Government Printing Office. Washington, D.C. 493 pages.

Hearings between January 10 and 18, 1945, before the House Committee on Military Affairs on House bill 1119 to amend the Selective Training and Service Act of 1940 by enacting national service legislation that would be effective in using the services of those men classified IV-F in whatever capacity is best for the war effort.

1945. U.S. CONGRESS. HOUSE. COMMITTEE ON MILITARY AFFAIRS. *Extension of the Selective Training and Service Act.* Government Printing Office. Washington, D.C. 20 pages.

Hearing on March 22, 1945, before the House Committee on Military Affairs on House bill 2625 relating to the induction and training of 18-year-olds under the Selective Training and Service Act.

1946. U.S. CONGRESS. HOUSE. COMMITTEE ON MILITARY AFFAIRS. *Extension of the Selective Training and Service Act.* Government Printing Office. Washington, D.C. Figures, graphs, tables. 167 pages.

Hearings between March 21 and April 4, 1946, before the House Committee on Military Affairs on House bill 5682 to extend the Selective Training and Service Act. Includes testimony by Dwight D. Eisenhower on the question of the necessity of the continuance of the Selective Service Act.

1948. U.S. CONGRESS. HOUSE. COMMITTEE ON ARMED SERVICES. *Selective Service.* Government Printing Office. Washington, D.C. 592 pages.

Hearings between April 12 and May 3, 1948, before the House Committee on Armed Services on House bills 6274 and 6401 to provide for the common defense by increasing the strength of the armed forces.

1950. U.S. CONGRESS. HOUSE. COMMITTEE ON ARMED SERVICES. *Selective Service Act Extension.* Government Printing Office. Washington, D.C. 213 pages.

Hearings between January 20 and February 1, 1950, before the House Committee on Armed Services on House bill 6826 to extend the Selective Service Act for three years.

1950. U.S. CONGRESS. HOUSE. COMMITTEE ON ARMED SERVICES. *Selective Service Act Extension.* Government Printing Office. Washington, D.C. 33 pages.

Hearing on May 2, 1950, before the House Committee on Armed Services on House bill 6826 to extend the Selective Service Act for three years. Offers additional testimony following hearings January 20—February 1, 1950.

1950. U.S. CONGRESS. SENATE. COMMITTEE ON ARMED SERVICES. *Selective Service Extension Act of 1950 and Manpower Registration and Classification Act.* Government Printing Office. Washington, D.C. 98 pages.

Hearings between June 1 and 8, 1950, before the Senate Committee on Armed Services on (1) Senate bill 2861 to extend the Selective Service Act for three years, and (2) House bill 6826 to provide for the common defense through the registration and classification of certain males.

1950. U.S. CONGRESS. HOUSE. COMMITTEE ON ARMED SERVICES. *Amendments to Selective Service Act.* Government Printing Office. Washington, D.C. 90 pages.

Hearings on August 28 and 29, 1950, before the House Committee on Armed Services on House bill 9554 to amend the Selective Service Act to provide for special registration, classification, and induction of certain medical, dental, and allied specialist categories.

1952. U.S. CONGRESS. SENATE. COMMITTEE ON ARMED SERVICES. *Manpower Utilization (with Special Reference to IV-F's).* Government Printing Office. Washington, D.C. 30 pages.

Hearing on January 24, 1952, before the Task Force of the Preparedness Subcommittee of the Senate Committee on Armed Services, considering manpower utilization with special reference to IV-F's.

1955. U.S. CONGRESS. HOUSE. COMMITTEE ON ARMED SERVICES. *Extension of Doctor-Dentist Draft Act.* Government Printing Office. Washington, D.C. 158 pages.

Hearings on April 28 and 29, 1955, before the House Committee on Armed Services on House bill 5946 to facilitate the procurement of physicians and dentists for the armed forces by establishing scholarships to provide for the continuation of special pay for these categories.

1956. U.S. CONGRESS. HOUSE. COMMITTEE ON ARMED SERVICES. *Procurement of Medical and Dental Officers.* Government Printing Office. Washington, D.C. 92 pages.

Hearings between February 15 and 17, 1956, before Subcommittee No. 2 of the House Committee on Armed Services on House bill 8500 to provide procurement of medical and dental officers of the army, navy, and air force.

1956. U.S. CONGRESS. SENATE. COMMITTEE ON ARMED SERVICES. *Medical and Dental Officer Career Incentive Act.* Government Printing Office. Washington, D.C. 95 pages.

Hearing on April 11, 1956, before the Senate Committee on Armed Services on House bill 9428 to provide procurement of medical and dental officers of the army, navy, air force, and Public Health Service.

1957. U.S. CONGRESS. SENATE. COMMITTEE ON ARMED SERVICES. *Nurses and Medical Specialists Career Incentive Act.* Government Printing Office. Washington, D.C. 75 pages.

Hearing on July 1, 1957, before the Senate Committee on Armed Services on House bill 2460 to improve the career opportunities of nurses and medical specialists in the army, navy, and air force.

1959. U.S. CONGRESS. SENATE. COMMITTEE ON ARMED SERVICES. *Extension of the Draft and Related Authorities.* Government Printing Office. Washington, D.C. 270 pages.

Hearings between March 3 and 5, 1959, before the Senate Committee on Armed Services on House bill 2260 to extend until July 1, 1963, the induction provisions of the Selective Service Extension Act of 1950.

1966. U.S. CONGRESS. HOUSE. COMMITTEE ON ARMED SERVICES. *Review of the Selective Service System.* Government Printing Office. Washington, D.C. Index. Figures, tables. 559 pages.

Hearings between June 22 and 30, 1966, before the House Committee on Armed Services, considering possible changes in the administration and operation of the Selective Service System.

1969. U.S. CONGRESS. HOUSE. COMMITTEE ON ARMED SERVICES. *Procurement and Retention of Judge Advocates.* Government Printing Office. Washington, D.C. 72 pages.

Hearing on September 11, 1969, before Subcommittee No. 1 of the House Committee on Armed Services on House bill 4296 to amend Title 37 of the U.S. Code to provide for the procurement and retention of judge advocates and law specialist officers for the armed forces.

1969. U.S. CONGRESS. HOUSE. COMMITTEE ON ARMED SERVICES. *Military Service Act of 1967.* Government Printing Office. Washington, D.C. 271 pages.

Hearings between September 30 and October 14, 1969, before the Subcommittee on the Draft of the House Committee on Armed Services on House bills 14001 and 14015 to amend the Military Service Act of 1967 to authorize modifications of the system of selecting persons for induction into the armed forces under this act.

1969. U.S. CONGRESS. SENATE. COMMITTEE ON ARMED SERVICES. *Random Selection System for Induction into Armed Forces.* Government Printing Office. Washington, D.C. 25 pages.

Hearing on November 14, 1969, before the Senate Committee on Armed Services on House bill 14001 amending the Military Selective Service Act of 1967 to authorize modifications of the system of selecting persons for induction into the armed forces under this act.

1970. U.S. CONGRESS. HOUSE. COMMITTEE ON ARMED SERVICES. *Review of the Draft Law.* Government Printing Office. Washington, D.C. 421 pages.

Hearings between July 23 and November 18, 1970, before the Special Subcommittee on the Draft of the House Committee on Armed Services, reviewing the administration and operation of the draft law.

1971. U.S. CONGRESS. SENATE. COMMITTEE ON ARMED SERVICES. *Selective Service and Military Compensation.* Government Printing Office. Washington, D.C. 846 pages.

Hearings between February 2 and 22, 1971, before the Senate Committee on Armed Services on Senate bills 392, 427, and 483, Senate Joint Resolution 20, and Senate bills 494, 495, and 496, all related to selective service and military compensation.

1971. U.S. CONGRESS. HOUSE. COMMITTEE ON ARMED SERVICES. *Procurement and Retention of Judge Advocates.* Government Printing Office. Washington, D.C. 73 pages.

Hearing on June 8, 1971, before Subcommittee No. 2 of the House Committee on Armed Services on House bill 4606 to amend Title 37 of the U.S. Code to provide for the procurement and retention of judge advocates and law specialist officers for the armed forces.

1972. U.S. CONGRESS. SENATE. COMMITTEE ON THE JUDICIARY. *Selective Service and Amnesty.* Government Printing Office. Washington, D.C. 671 pages.

Hearings between February 28 and March 1, 1972, before the Subcommittee on Administrative Practice and Procedure of the Senate Committee on the Judiciary, considering Selective Service System procedures and possibilities for amnesty.

1972. U.S. CONGRESS. SENATE. COMMITTEE ON ARMED SERVICES. *Authorization for Additional Compensation for Members of the Services Who Function as Judge Advocates and Law Specialists.* Government Printing Office. Washington, D.C. 91 pages.

Hearing on September 19, 1972, before the Subcommittee on General Legislation of the Senate Committee on Armed Services on House bill 4606 to amend Title 37 of the U.S. Code to provide for the procurement and retention of judge advocates and law specialist officers for the armed forces.

1974. U.S. CONGRESS. HOUSE. COMMITTEE ON ARMED SERVICES. *Doctor-Bonus Law.* Government Printing Office. Washington, D.C. 429 pages.

CONSCRIPTION

Hearings between September 25 and October 8, 1974, before Subcommittee No. 4 of the House Committee on Armed Services, investigating the failure of the Department of Defense to properly implement the Doctor-Bonus Law.

CHAPTER 6

Universal Military Training

The Way to secure Peace is to be prepared for War. They
that are on their Guard, and appear ready to receive their
Adversaries, are in much less Danger of being attack'd, than
the supine, secure and negligent.
                    —Benjamin Franklin, *Plain Truth*, 1747

Books

ALY, BOWER (editor). *Military Training: The Fifteenth Annual Debate
  Handbook 1941–1942.* 2 volumes. 1941. Lucas Bros. Columbia,
  Missouri. Volume 1: Bibliography: pages 203–220. 220 pages. Volume
  2: 220 pages.

Debate materials on the resolution that every able-bodied citizen in the
United States should be required to have one year of full-time military
training before attaining draft age. Volume 2 presents the diverse positions
of 25 military, civilian, and government experts—most of them favoring
conscription.

ANDERSON, PAUL RUSSELL (editor). *Universal Military Training and
  National Security.* 1945. The Annals of the American Academy of
  Political and Social Science. Philadelphia. Index. Tables. 204 pages.

Presents 20 individually authored articles on the background of universal military training and manpower procurement policies, military
considerations for and against peacetime training, sociological, economic,
and educational viewpoints, alternatives to universal military training, and
a survey of national security plans in Britain, the Soviet Union, and
France. The appendix contains the text of a bill introduced in the House
on January 3, 1945, to provide military or naval training for all male
citizens 18 years of age.

CONSCRIPTION

CLIFFORD, JOHN GARRY. *The Citizen Soldiers: The Plattsburg Training Camp Movement 1913–1920*. 1972. University Press of Kentucky. Lexington, Kentucky. Index. Bibliographical essay: pages 305–315. 326 pages.

A study of the Plattsburg movement, with its voluntary training camps and its belief that universal military training could come to the United States through a process of education and demonstration. Describes how the National Defense Act of 1920, with its provisions for voluntary training, gave the Plattsburgers a laboratory to test their ideas, and follows the Plattsburg effort through the interwar years, showing that while the larger objective proved futile, voluntary military training thrived. The coming of World War II brought about a full-scale revival of the Plattsburg movement, eventually culminating, with national acceptance of the Plattsburg philosophy, in the Selective Training and Service Act of 1940. The author's thesis is that "by emphasizing the principle of universal military obligation, the Plattsburgers tried to link modern requirements with America's historic tradition of a citizen army. If civilians trained and served under an equal obligation, there would be no need for a large professional army and little danger of militarism."

FITZPATRICK, EDWARD A. *Universal Military Training*. 1945. McGraw-Hill Book Co. New York. Index. Tables. 374 pages.

Advocating adoption of a program of compulsory universal military training, the author believes that justification of such a program must be based, not on any educational or sociological considerations, but solely on considerations of "national security and preparedness for any contingency requiring armed force for the national defense." The question of universal military training is examined against the historical background of U.S. military personnel policy, the citizen army and the militia, volunteering and conscription, and the power of Congress to compel peacetime military training.

FRIENDS COMMITTEE ON NATIONAL LEGISLATION. *Resolutions Against Universal Military Training 1945–1947*. 1948. Washington, D.C. 236 pages.

A compilation of 236 statements opposing universal military training issued by national, state, and regional church, farm, labor, and educational groups and by veterans' and other organizations.

Howes, Raymond F. (editor). *Conference on Military Manpower*. 1955. American Council on Education. Washington, D.C. 79 pages.

Proceedings of a conference held January 21–22, 1955, in Washington, D.C., with participants from the American Council on Education and various government agencies. Speaking on behalf of the Department of Defense's proposed National Reserve Plan are Carter Burgess, Willard Paul, Lewis Hershey, Edgar Shelton, and Arthur Fleming, while Representative Olin Teague urges the adoption of universal military training according to the "Texas Plan." The appendix contains the text of the National Reserve Plan, approval or disapproval of which is withheld by the conference "since complete details are not available."

Johnsen, Julia E. (compiler). *Compulsory Military Training*. 1941. The Reference Shelf, Volume 14, Number 6. H. W. Wilson Co. New York. Bibliography: pages 245–265. 265 pages.

Contains a general discussion of the concept of compulsory military training, as well as diverse viewpoints in affirmative and negative discussion. Includes a summary of arguments.

Mabie, Edward Charles. *University Debaters' Annual: Constructive and Rebuttal Speeches Delivered in Debates of American Colleges and Universities During the College Year 1915–1916*. 1916. H. W. Wilson Co. New York. Index. Bibliography at end of each chapter. 294 pages.

Chapter 2 (pages 79–96) gives the text of a collegiate debate on compulsory military service.

Nichols, Egbert Ray (editor). *Intercollegiate Debates*. Volume XXII. 1941. Noble & Noble, Publishers, Inc. New York. Bibliography at end of each chapter. 439 pages.

Includes the text of an intercollegiate debate (pages 1–48) on universal military training before the age of 21.

Parker, John H. *Trained Citizen Soldiery: A Solution of General Upton's Problem*. 1916. George Banta Publishing Co. Menasha, Wisconsin. 207 pages.

Recommendations for implementation of proposals by Emory Upton in his 1880 book *The Military Policy of the United States* (see page 46, above). Parker suggests that any military system "financed on the theory of hiring military service in open competition with other bidders for labor ... is bound to fail," and that "no country ever yet maintained itself for any great length of time by hired, or mercenary military service." He contends that while "the officer or man who permanently gives up civil occupations is fairly entitled to such compensation as will enable him to live decently," military service in time of war and the necessary preparation for that service in time of peace "are an obligation of citizenship, due to the nation from every able-bodied citizen, and for the discharge of which duty he is not entitled to one cent of pay." Parker upholds the "principle that the man who is exempted by the law from rendering this personal service in time of war, or taking the necessary training in time of peace to be effective in time of war, should contribute an equivalent in cash for the benefit of the man who takes his place," thereby enabling the exempt citizen "to exercise his free choice in the matter." For drafted men, there should be no bounty, no promotion, and no pension.

PERRY, RALPH B. *The Plattsburg Movement: A Chapter of America's Participation in the World War.* 1921. E. P. Dutton & Co. New York. Index. 275 pages.

Advocating military preparedness as "the economical method of insurance against war," Perry opposes the "excessive cost of a large regular army" and recommends instead combining military training with education in civilian institutions such as the Reserve Officers' Training Corps. The merits of universal military training are said to have been "proved" by the experience of World War I, and the author urges the establishment of "voluntary citizens' training camps" directed toward educating public opinion to "a permanent change in the characteristic irresponsibility of American citizenship."

PHELPS, EDITH M. (editor). *University Debaters' Annual: Constructive and Rebuttal Speeches Delivered in Debates of American Colleges and Universities During the College Year 1916–1917.* 1917. H. W. Wilson Co. New York. Index. Bibliography at end of each chapter. 272 pages.

Chapter 2 (pages 53–98) gives the text of a collegiate debate on universal military service.

PHELPS, EDITH M. (editor). *University Debaters' Annual: Constructive and Rebuttal Speeches Delivered in Debates of American Colleges and*

Universities During the College Year 1940–1941. 1941. H. W. Wilson Co. New York. Index. Bibliography at end of each chapter. 517 pages.

Chapter 8 (pages 345–388) gives the text of an intercollegiate debate on compulsory military training.

PHELPS, EDITH M. (editor). *University Debaters' Annual: Constructive and Rebuttal Speeches Delivered in Debates of American Colleges and Universities During the College Year 1941–1942.* 1942. H. W. Wilson Co. New York. Index. Bibliography at end of each chapter. 459 pages.

Chapter 3 (pages 101–148) gives the text of an intercollegiate debate on military training.

PHELPS, EDITH M. (editor). *University Debaters' Annual: Constructive and Rebuttal Speeches Delivered in Debates of American Colleges and Universities During the College Year 1942–1943.* 1943. H. W. Wilson Co. New York. Index. Bibliography at end of each chapter. 368 pages.

Chapter 3 (pages 117–157) gives the text of an intercollegiate debate on "A Universal Draft of Man- and Woman-Power."

PHELPS, EDITH M. (editor). *University Debaters' Annual: Constructive and Rebuttal Speeches Delivered in Debates of American Colleges and Universities During the College Year 1944–1945.* 1945. H. W. Wilson Co. New York. Index. Bibliography at end of each chapter. 324 pages.

Chapter 5 (pages 165–202) gives the text of an intercollegiate debate on compulsory military training.

RANKIN, E. R. *Universal Military Training.* 1940. University of North Carolina Press. Chapel Hill, North Carolina. Bibliography: pages 96–102. 102 pages.

Debate handbook on the resolution that the United States should adopt a policy requiring one year of military training for all able-bodied men before they reach the age of 23. Contemporary views are presented in general, affirmative, and negative references.

SHURTER, E. D. (editor). *Universal Military Training: Bibliography and Selected Arguments.* 1916. University of Texas. Austin, Texas. Bibliography: pages 4–8. 50 pages.

Debate handbook on the resolution that "universal military training similar to the Swiss system should be adopted in the United States." Includes a brief of arguments pro and con, as well as other diverse views on the issue.

SUMMERS, ROBERT E., and HARRISON B. SUMMERS (compilers). *Universal Military Service.* 1941. The Reference Shelf, Volume 15, Number 2. H.W. Wilson Co. New York. Bibliography: pages 261–280. 280 pages.

Contains diverse positions on various aspects of conscription, including its historical and legislative background. The major issue is whether the Selective Service Act, enacted as an emergency measure in 1940, should be retained to provide for the compulsory training of young men as a part of America's permanent peacetime military policy.

ULMAN, RUTH (editor). *University Debaters' Annual: Reports of Debates and Other Forensic Activities of American Colleges and Universities During the Academic Year 1947–1948.* 1948. H. W. Wilson Co. New York. Index. Bibliography at end of each chapter. 325 pages.

Chapter 5 (pages 183–218) gives the text of an intercollegiate debate on universal military training.

VAN VALKENBURGH, AGNES (compiler). *Selected Articles on Military Training in Schools and Colleges, Including Military Camps.* 1917. Debaters' Handbook Series. H. W. Wilson Co. White Plains, New York. Bibliography: pages xix–xlix. 208 pages.

Contains general, affirmative, and negative discussions on the pros and cons of military training in American schools and colleges, as well as a section on military camps such as the Plattsburg Military Training Camps.

WOOD, ERIC FISHER. *The Writing on the Wall: The Nation on Trial.* 1916. Century Co. New York. 211 pages.

A case for universal compulsory military training patterned on the Swiss and Australian systems. The author holds that modern warfare is waged "in a manner so intricate and so scientific that it is impossible for untrained individuals to help defend their country," and that it is appropriate that the military system "should be planned out by those of our countrymen who have devoted their lives to the study and practice of military matters, and not by party politicians."

Unpublished Manuscripts

DRURY, JOHN WILLIAM. *Universal Military Service: A Study of Its Role in Supporting the Requirements of National Security.* 1951. M.S. thesis. Ohio State University. Columbus, Ohio. Bibliography: pages 124–126. 126 pages.

Proposes a program of universal military service that would assertedly result in nine specific benefits to the nation: It would (1) impart to each trainee a psychological understanding of his obligation as a citizen, (2) permit rapid expansion of the professional military establishment, (3) improve the efficiency and quality of regular forces, (4) assist in meeting the officer requirements of regular and reserve components, (5) establish a continuously replenished pool of young, physically fit, and trained reserves for rapid mobilization, (6) provide a large, trained group in every community capable of withstanding and dealing with the problems of civil defense, (7) provide a continuous inventory of military skills, (8) channel talented men into programs of scientific and vocational training in fields important to national defense, and (9) bring together young men from all parts of the country "to share a common experience and to fulfill a common obligation to their country."

SWOMLEY, JOHN M., JR. *A Study on the Universal Military Training Campaign 1944–1952.* 1959. Ph.D. dissertation. University of Colorado. Boulder, Colorado. 481 pages.

This study is the work of a leading figure in the campaign against universal military training. It deals with the organization and operation of the campaign, including the strategy and tactics employed. Congressional attitudes are examined, showing the role that political leadership, parties, and committees played in the consideration of the proposal for universal military training.

WARD, ROBERT DAVID. *The Movement for Universal Military Training in the United States 1942–1952.* 1957. Ph.D. dissertation. University of North Carolina. Chapel Hill, North Carolina. Bibliography: pages 464–478. 478 pages.

Surveys the third major attempt to gain enactmnet of universal military training in the United States (the first two periods of agitation were 1900–1916 and 1918–1920). Examines the reaction of the American public and its Congress to the proposal for universal training advanced by military officials "in the name of 'national security.'"

Articles

ANDERSON, PAUL RUSSELL. *National Security in the Postwar World.* The Annals of the American Academy of Political and Social Science. September 1945. Volume 241. Pages 1–7.

"The possibility of universal military training must be viewed in the light of the existence of a permanent military force of determined size and in relation to other factors in an adequate program for national security." In this view, consideration of the permanent military establishment is related to the discussion of universal military training on two bases: (1) the larger the permanent force, the less the necessity or desirability for universal military training, and (2) the more highly specialized the services, the more carefully planned any program of temporary civilian training must be if it is to be effective at all in relating this training to real military needs.

AXTELL, GEORGE C., JR., and ROBERT S. STUBBS II. *UMT: A Study.* George Washington Law Review. March 1952. Volume 20, Number 4. Pages 450–488.

Examines the concept of universal military training from the standpoint of its being "a pre-existing obligation of the citizen which is to be fulfilled [as a matter] of course" as distinct from a compulsory system involving "a superficial obligation which exists or is released at the will of the legislature." Reviews, from this standpoint, historical precedents of the current proposal for a universal military training program.

BANCROFT, WILLIAM A. *A Word for Military Training.* New England Magazine. November 1908. Volume 39. Pages 365–367.

The author urges "recognition among young men of the duty and privilege of belonging to the militia." While upholding the voluntary concept of military service in the United States, he praises German achievements under conscription.

Universal Military Training

BELLOC, HILAIRE. *The Demand for Universal Service.* Fortnightly Review. December 1913. Volume 100. Pages 1047–1056.

Considers political, military, and social arguments for and against compulsory military service. Discusses the possible resistance to such a plan from various sectors of the community.

BRUMBAUGH, A. J. *Education—by Whom, for What?* The Annals of the American Academy of Political and Social Science. September 1945. Volume 241. Pages 113–122.

Suggests that civilian organizations that support military training on educational grounds attribute benefits to military training that the representatives of the armed forces do not themselves claim for it. Examines the facilities already existing for the achievement of educational benefits that are attributed to universal military training, and considers the kind of training that would be provided under military auspices to achieve these same benefits. Brumbaugh concludes that the educational needs of society cannot be met by adopting peacetime universal military training.

CHAMBERLAIN, GEORGE E. *Universal Training and an Adequate Army Reserve.* Proceedings of the Academy of Political Science. July 1916. Volume 6, Number 4. Pages 88–93.

Recommends that a universal training program be introduced in which "every young man in the country between the ages of fourteen and twenty-one can be instructed fully in the duties of a soldier." The author sees no alternative to universal military training "if we would have a reserve which can be called upon to volunteer, or if need be compelled, to serve when danger is threatened from without."

CHRISTEN, THEODORE A. *The Swiss Military System and Its Adaptability to the United States.* Proceedings of the Academy of Political Science. July 1916. Volume 6, Number 4. Pages 179–200.

Proposes a plan for adaptation in the United States of the Swiss military system of universal compulsory military training. Once an adequate national defense force were attained, the term of liability could be reduced, induction qualifications raised, and a proportion of those eligible mobilized for industrial preparedness.

CONSCRIPTION

CHRISTIAN CENTURY, THE. *Universal Military Training.* December 19, 1951. Volume LXVIII, Number 51. Pages 1461–1484.

A special section devoted to the report of the U.M.T. Commission to Congress and the legislation that it recommends. Presents a critical analysis of the report as well as views on the question: "Do the people of the United States want the coming session of Congress to enact into law the system of permanent peacetime conscription proposed by the UMT National Security Training Commission?" Included is a short interview with Albert Einstein, who elaborates on his opposition to military conscription.

COLBY, ELBRIDGE. *Military Training in Land Grant Colleges.* Georgetown Law Journal. November 1934. Volume 23, Number 1. Pages 1–36.

Argues that the 1862 Morrill Act implied compulsion, since it was "universally accepted by the states and the colleges as *requiring* all students to take military training." Owing largely to the abolition of the compulsory feature by the Wisconsin state legislature in 1923, the federal government held that such training need not be compulsory upon all students in order to fulfill the requirements of federal laws offering aid. Colby notes, however, that state institutions generally maintained the compulsory feature.

COLLIER, CHARLES SAGER. *Shall the United States Adopt a Plan for General Compulsory Military Training for Men as a Permanent Postwar Policy?* Social Science. April 1945. Volume 20, Number 2. Pages 73–77.

Considers current proposals for universal military training in the light of military necessity and educational policies. In the event universal military training should be adopted, the author would favor integrating military instruction with the existing educational system.

CONGRESSIONAL DIGEST. *Should the United States Adopt Compulsory Military Training as a Permanent Policy?* August–September 1941. Volume 24, Numbers 8 and 9. Pages 193–224.

Examines the traditional military policy of the United States, reviewing the history of the military policies of England and the United States, the provisions of the U.S. Constitution relating to the armed forces, and the decisions of the Supreme Court in cases growing out of the Draft Act of

1917. Includes arguments for and against compulsory military service as a permanent national policy.

Cox, ALBERT L. *Military Training.* Social Science. April 1945. Volume 20, Number 2. Pages 93–96.

Argues, from a military viewpoint, in favor of compulsory military training for all able-bodied men between the ages of 18 and 21.

CREEL, GEORGE. *Universal Training and the Democratic Ideal.* Proceedings of the Academy of Political Science. July 1916. Volume 6, Number 4. Pages 146–151.

Advances several arguments in favor of compulsory military training, conceiving such a system, in sum, as "not only an adequate preparation for the defense of the nation against armed invasion or unbearable aggression, but an even finer preparation for the daily demands of citizenship."

CURRENT OPINION. *Growing Momentum of the Movement for Universal Military Training.* August 1916. Volume 61, Number 2. Pages 77–78.

Suggests that the concept of universal military training is gaining in popularity and that the advocates of such training, who initially proposed it solely as a means of national defense, "have been more and more emphasizing its educational values."

DAVIS, DWIGHT FILLEY. *Universal Service.* The Forum. March 1926. Volume 75, Number 3. Pages 375–377.

Secretary of War Davis maintains that the currently proposed law for universal compulsory military service is not, as its opponents charge, either militaristic, undemocratic, or un-American. He upholds the system as a democratic one to which the nation has twice resorted under pressure of events and which should become a permanent part of U.S. mobilization plans.

DAVIS, VINCENT. *Universal Service: An Alternative to the All-Volunteer Armed Services.* Naval War College Review. October 1970. Volume XXIII, Number 2. Pages 19–33.

States the need for appropriate military manpower procurement in the face of the political demands of the 20th century. Assumes that the existing system of conscription is unacceptable and discusses the pros and cons of and specific suggestions for a system of universal military service. Davis proposes that such a system be combined with a comprehensive national manpower policy and program to direct national energies toward the solution of social, economic, educational, and environmental problems. He concludes that a system of universal service would be desirable because it would "help once again to instill the idea of service to the American society within the broader context of service to humanity."

DAWKINS, C. E. *Compulsory Military Training: A Pan-Britannic Militia.* The Nineteenth Century and After. March 1902. Volume 51. Pages 349–359.

Asserts that "there is no more interference with liberty in making a citizen serve the State for a term than is involved in making him pay rates and taxes." Proposes general compulsory service in the militia for a period not exceeding a year between the ages of 18 and 23, with liability to short periods of training thereafter. This obligation would be preceded by compulsory drilling in the schools.

EARHART, MARY. *The Value of Universal Military Training in Maintaining Peace.* The Annals of the American Academy of Political and Social Science. September 1945. Volume 241. Pages 46–57.

Appeals for preparedness, arguing against a reduction of armed forces to the 1940 basis, for this assertedly would "awaken suspicion regarding the sincerity of the American commitments and thereby contribute to the weakening of international confidence and security." The maintenance of an adequate army and reserve force would require a system of compulsory military service: "In the modern world, universal conscription is the only democratic method of raising large armies, navies, and air fleets."

EISENHOWER, DWIGHT D. *The Country Needs Universal Military Training.* Reader's Digest. September 1966. Pages 49–55.

Argues in favor of universal military training as the fairest approach to the "thorny problem of manpower procurement" from the standpoint of military preparedness and of fitness and discipline among youth. Eisenhower discusses the problems and inequities of the Selective Service System, outlines proposals for a revised method of manpower procurement, and offers his proposal for universal military training.

ELIOT, CHARLES W. *Shall We Adopt Universal Military Service?* The World's Work. November 1916. Volume 32. Pages 16–24.

"The United States must abandon its traditional policy of isolation and build an effective democratic army and a powerful navy to insure itself against invasion and to do its duty in the world." A democratic army, in this view, would be one in which "all able-bodied young Americans should serve for several short periods, and then be held in reserve for a long period, its officers being selected from the ranks by their instructors and commanders during the prescribed periods of service, and educated as now at the Military Academy to serve for life as leaders of the successive levies of raw recruits, or held in reserve with liberty to follow civil occupations."

ELLWOOD, CHARLES A. *The Case Against Compulsory Military Training in Peacetime.* Social Science. April 1945. Volume 20, Number 2. Pages 69–72.

States that where policies of universal military training have been in effect, they have not brought peace to the nations in question, nor served well as a means of defense. Universal military training is seen as an inducement to militarism and as a menace to the civil arm of the government: "Individual freedom cannot be reconciled with the supremacy of a military program to which the whole of society is subordinated even in peacetime."

FOOTE, STEPHEN M. *Outline of a Plan for Effecting Universal Military Training in the United States.* Journal of the Military Service Institution. July–August 1917. Volume 61, Number 208. Pages 3–16.

Examines practical aspects of the proposal for universal military training, and presents an outline for implementation of the system. The objective of universal military training, Foote suggests, is "to provide a large trained reserve from which any desired military forces may be drawn whenever needed."

FORMAN, SIDNEY. *Thomas Jefferson on Universal Military Training.* Military Affairs. Fall 1947. Volume XI, Number 3. Pages 177–178.

Cites letters of Thomas Jefferson indicating support of a system of universal military training and service. Jefferson tells of having repeatedly recommended to Congress to have "the whole territory of the United States organized by such a classification of its male force, as would give to the benefit of all its young population for active service, and that of a middle and advanced age for stationary defence."

FUCHS, RALPH F. *Conference Comment*. Social Science. April 1945. Volume 20, Number 2. Pages 80–81.

Opposes the proposal of Congressman James Wadsworth for universal compulsory military training, questioning "whether we as a people wish to erect military service as the one form of national service which the federal government demands of every youth." Supports, instead, a program embracing "an undivided year of national service" on the part of "not young men alone and not military service alone."

GIDDINGS, FRANKLIN H. *The Democracy of Universal Military Service*. The Annals of the American Academy of Political and Social Science. July 1916. Volume 66. Pages 173–180.

Contends that a hired or professional army, second only to monarchy and hereditary rank, "is the most undemocratic thing that man has so far invented," and that the predication of military service upon volunteering alone engenders irritation and distrust, and intensifies the class struggle. Advocates following the examples of Switzerland and France, which recognize "the responsibility of every able bodied citizen for the defense of his country" and give every man "a good, but not too exacting military training."

GRAHAM, ROBERT A. *Universal Military Training in Modern History*. The Annals of the American Academy of Political and Social Science. September 1945. Volume 241. Pages 8–14.

"The precedent set in two world wars and the steady though slow trend of our national military practice through a century and a half scarcely leave doubt that another world conflict . . . will see universal and equal liability to military service." Advocating a wartime draft only, the author believes that a selective service system would be the most efficient and the most equitable. He foresees no danger of a wartime draft breeding militarism or militant nationalism although there would be "no guarantee that maladies will not develop under a permanent peacetime policy."

HALL, SIDNEY B. *National Service and Compulsory Military Training*. Social Science. April 1945. Volume 20, Number 2. Pages 83–92.

Reviews current arguments for and against compulsory military service.

HOLBORN, HAJO. *Professional Army Versus Military Training.* The Annals of the American Academy of Political and Social Science. September 1945. Volume 241. Pages 123–130.

Maintains that a universal military training law is needed "but its scope and character cannot be defined without fuller discussion of our entire peacetime establishment, which should be judged in the light of military experience and American democratic traditions." Considers that the present world situation demands a combination of universal peacetime military training with provisions for standing forces and organized reserves, but that additional investigation and new public discussion must precede the formulation of general principles of future defense organization.

JACOBS, RANDALL. *The Issue Should Be Decided Now.* The Annals of the American Academy of Political and Social Science. September 1945. Volume 241. Pages 72–76.

Urges early congressional passage of proposed legislation for the introduction of universal military training. Claims that to enact universal military training would not be an irrevocable step and that "it can be abolished the day we feel safe without it." A reservoir of pretrained citizens would be an essential of recast defense plans to "meet new possibilities and new dangers."

KUENZLI, FREDERICK A. *The Swiss System and What It Suggests as to an American System of Universal Training for the Common Defense.* Proceedings of the Academy of Political Science. July 1916. Volume 6, Number 4. Pages 98–112.

Advocates a modified form of the Swiss military training system that would involve the obligatory physical training and military training without arms of schoolboys from age 8, cadet corps training provided free of charge for boys who volunteer for it from age 12, and free preparatory courses for boys volunteering from ages 16 to 20. In this view, the efficiency of the Swiss system is attributable not to the short periods of compulsory service in the army but to the "foundation that every Swiss boy receives in the physical training courses in the public schools."

LUCEY, FRANCIS E. *Compulsory Military Training.* Social Science. April 1945. Volume 20, Number 2. Pages 97–100.

Presents several arguments in opposition to the introduction of peace-time compulsory military training, on military, constitutional, and moral grounds.

MacArthur, Douglas. *The Citizen Soldier.* American Legion Magazine. January 1952. Volume 52, Number 1. Pages 14–15, 52.

Calls for extension and intensification of civilian control over the citizen army, noting that the principle of universal military training, while intended and designed to strengthen freedom's defense, "carries within itself the very germs to freedom's destruction."

McCloy, John J. *The Plan of the Armed Services for Universal Military Training.* The Annals of the American Academy of Political and Social Science. September 1945. Volume 241. Pages 26–34.

Endorses the recommendations by the War and Navy Departments for a postwar system of universal military training "whereby the youth of the nation will constitute a reservoir of trained military manpower from which a balanced force can be speedily mobilized in the event of an emergency to meet any threat to our national security." Discusses the types of military organization through which the manpower of a nation may be developed and "why the proposed reservoir of trained military manpower is best suited to meet the defense needs of the nation and conforms at the same time with its ideals and traditions."

Mooney, Chase C., and Martha E. Layman. *Some Phases of the Compulsory Military Training Movement 1914–1920.* The Mississippi Valley Historical Review. March 1952. Volume 38, Number 4. Pages 633–656.

Traces the progress of the universal military training movement, principally from the viewpoint of Congress and the War Department, with some indication of public opinion on the subject as well as the activities of special organizations and individuals. The authors conclude: "The people could not be convinced, during the war or after, of the military necessity of such a program, and they must have considered that a vast training program was a very costly way to gain the alleged concomitant benefits."

Murray, Merrill G. *Civilian Aspects of Military Manpower Policy.* Proceedings of the Academy of Political Science. May 1951. Volume 24, Number 3. Pages 85–96.

Examines possible programs in administering occupational and student deferments under a universal military training and service system. Poses the question of whether these problems should be in military hands or in civilian hands exclusively, or in both.

NATIONAL ECONOMIC LEAGUE QUARTERLY. *Universal Military Training.* May 1917. Volume 3, Number 1. Pages 5–34.

A compilation of views of 24 prominent individuals on the question of universal military training.

RILLING, ALEXANDER W. *The Question of Universal Military Training.* United States Naval Institute Proceedings. August 1967. Volume 93, Number 8. Pages 65–75.

A consideration of universal military training as a solution to the problem of meeting military manpower requirements. Rilling avers that universal military training is the true and original American tradition, citing the military training laws of the colonial United States. He then traces the history of efforts to establish universal military training in the United States, outlines possible alternatives to universal military training, discusses the mechanics and ramifications of a universal program, and concludes with a call for further discussion of universal military training as a solution to the procurement of military manpower.

SHELTON, THOMAS W. *Compulsory Universal Military Training.* Virginia Law Review. March 1918. Volume 5, Number 6. Pages 476–488.

Argues, on military, psychological, economic, and legal grounds, in favor of the permanent establishment of a system of compulsory universal military training. Urges that there be conformity and uniformity between state and federal legislation, suggesting that an official commission be created to arbitrate all disputes and conflicts in regard to state and federal legislation.

SMITH, MONROE. *Democratic Aspects of Universal Military Service.* Proceedings of the Academy of Political Science. July 1916. Volume 6. Number 4. Pages 152–156.

Reviews the concept of compulsory military service in relation to historical precedent and political theory. Concludes that "the defense of the country must, on democratic principles, be secured through universal military service; and if universal military service is to be enforced, we must have universal—that is to say, compulsory—military training."

TOMPKINS, WILLIAM F. *Future Manpower Needs of the Armed Forces.* The Annals of the American Academy of Political and Social Science. March 1945. Volume 238. Pages 56–62.

Points to the "consistent practical failure" of the voluntary system and its alleged violation of the "very principle of democracy." Advocates the permanent establishment of a system of universal military training in which "a mass of trained manpower will feed the military reservoir of the country in the future in steady replacement of the age-stricken armies of the present war."

TRESIDDER, DONALD BERTRAND. *My Hands to War.* The Journal of Higher Education. October 1945. Volume XVI, Number 7. Pages 343–350.

This article, written by the president of Stanford University shortly before the end of World War II, opposes current proposals for compulsory military training, and recommends the appointment of a nonpartisan commission to examine defense needs.

TRICOCHE, GEORGE N. *Compulsory Service in the United States.* Yale Review. October 1915. Volume 5. Pages 90–104.

Suggests that compulsory military service is the one factor that would build the character of the "typically undisciplined" American male youth. Claiming that "the value of military discipline and training for young men has been recognized by American educators, psychologists and philosophers," the author asserts that "it would be much easier than many people believe to establish in the United States a compulsory service without interfering to any serious extent with the economic life of the nation."

TRYON, RUTH W. *Some Questions About Compulsory Military Training.* Social Science. April 1945. Volume 20, Number 2. Pages 78–79.

Enumerates seven questions that "American parents should be asking" before committing themselves on the issue of compulsory military training.

VILLARD, OSWALD GARRISON. *The Cure-all of Universal Military Service.* Proceedings of the Academy of Political Science. July 1916. Volume 6, Number 4. Pages 50–58.

Asserts that "the price of universal military servitude is far too great a price to pay for insuring peace by any free peoples" and far offsets "the alleged advantages which are physical betterment, greater practical efficiency and energy, and a sense of responsibility to the nation."

VILLARD, OSWALD GARRISON. *Universal Military Training and Military Preparedness.* The Annals of the American Academy of Political and Social Science. September 1945. Volume 241. Pages 35–45.

Notes that the term "universal military training" is a misnomer in that the armed services would not have need of all eligible youth. A universal military training system, in this view, would "split our military establishment into two parts"—the regular, professional army and the annual levy of youths—with little coordination between the two. Villard concludes that peacetime conscription not only is unnecessary for national security but would be a potentially dangerous departure in national policy.

WADSWORTH, JAMES W. *The Proposal for Compulsory Military Training in Peacetime.* Social Science. April 1945. Volume 20, Number 2. Pages 66–68.

Proposes a system of universal military training involving young men between the ages of 17 and 21. All peacetime military service by graduate trainees would be on a voluntary basis; only in the event of a national emergency would the element of compulsion appear. "The great military advantage gained under such a system," Wadsworth believes, "will lie in the fact that whether as volunteers in time of peace or as selectees in time of war, every recruit will have had one year of training, an advantage we have never enjoyed in our history."

WOOD, LEONARD. *Plattsburg and Citizenship.* The Century. May 1917. Volume 94, Number 1. Pages 49–54.

Praises the voluntary Plattsburg training camp movement as "the forerunner of universal obligatory training and service." Predicts that the effect of the movement will be "preparedness without militarism, strength without aggression."

Pamphlets, Reprints, and Speeches

AMERICAN FRIENDS SERVICE COMMITTEE. *Universal Peacetime Conscription: A Question for Every Teacher to Consider.* 1944. Philadelphia. 10 pages.

This pamphlet, discussing conscription from the viewpoint of educators, urges teachers to take an active role in stimulating discussion of the question in the community. Educational groups and individual educators opposed to peacetime conscription are quoted.

AMERICAN LEGION. *Universal Military Training: Responsibility to Community, State and Nation.* Circa 1945. Indianapolis, Indiana. Illustrations. 32 pages.

Maintains that preparedness in a modern technocracy demands either the maintenance of a colossal professional and full-time armed force or a practical substitute. Thus the sole practical and sound alternative, in keeping with the nation's democratic institutions, is the peacetime military training of males 18 to 23 years of age to provide a continuing reservoir of trained manpower for defense and national security. It is believed that universal military training would give the youth of the nation improved health, develop latent qualities of leadership, build self-reliance, teach the value of teamwork, and instill the benefits of discipline. Universal military training is viewed as "insurance against future war" and as "a guarantee of America's ability in cooperation with other peaceloving peoples to preserve law and order in the family of nations."

AMERICAN UNION AGAINST MILITARISM. *New Jersey Says: "No!"* 1918. Reprint. Washington, D.C. 15 pages.

Report of the Commission on Military Training and Instruction in High Schools to the New Jersey Legislature, Session of 1917. This report is said to have contributed to the defeat of a proposal for compulsory military training in the secondary schools of New Jersey.

AMERICAN UNION AGAINST MILITARISM. *New York's Sober Second Thought: No Compulsory Military Drill for Growing Boys.* 1919. Washington, D.C. Illustrations. 15 pages.

Contains the 1919 Report of the New York State Reconstruction Commission on military training under the Welsh-Slater Acts of 1916, which prescribed military training for boys aged 16, 17, and 18. Provides a description of the law and arguments for and against. The commission recommends that legislation be introduced transferring the functions of the State Military Commission to the State Department of Education.

AMERICAN UNION AGAINST MILITARISM. *Universal Military Training.* Circa 1919. Reprint from The Arbitrator. Washington, D.C. 15 pages.

A literary debate between Charles T. Hallinan of the American Union Against Militarism and Henry L. West and Lloyd Taylor of the National Security League, respectively opposing and upholding universal military training.

CHAMBER OF COMMERCE OF THE UNITED STATES. *Referendum No. 15 on the Report of the Special Committee on National Defense.* 1916. Washington, D.C. 42 pages.

Contains the recommendation that "universal military training be adopted as a fundamental democratic principle of our military policy and be enforced by law to furnish adequate land, sea, and industrial forces in peace and war." A summary of arguments against the Special Committee's recommendations notes that any proposal to train the nine or ten million men who would constantly be eligible is impracticable. The appendix includes comments on the economic value of military training.

COMPTON, KARL T. *National Security: Supported by (I) Scientific Research, (II) Universal Military Training.* 1945. Technology Press, Massachusetts Institute of Technology. Cambridge, Massachusetts. 19 pages.

Contains the texts of two addresses by the president of the Massachusetts Institute of Technology. The second address, on national security and universal military training, was given before a gathering sponsored by the Women's National Committee for Universal Training of Young Men. Compton upholds a proposal to inaugurate universal military training after World War II as the means to assuring rapid mobilization of an effective armed force in time of national danger. He opposes exemptions, and considers that military training could have "a very wholesome influence" from the standpoints of discipline, character, and idealism.

CUSHING, RICHARD J. *The Third Choice: Americanism.* 1948. National
Council Against Conscription. Washington, D.C. 14 pages.

An address against universal military training by the Archbishop of
Boston, asserting that it is not necessary to make a choice between communism and militarism. Discusses the implications of universal training
with respect to morality, cost, and education.

DONOVAN, WILLIAM. *National Defense Demands Conscription.* 1940.
Station WGN. Chicago. 8 pages.

Text of a radio address on August 17, 1940, urging support for the
immediate passage of the Burke–Wadsworth selective training and service
bill then pending before Congress. This bill provided for compulsory
military training in time of peace and military service in time of war.

DRUM, HUGH A. *An Essential of Defense.* Vital Speeches of the Day.
August 1, 1940. Volume 6, Number 20. Pages 627–629.

Argues in favor of the current proposal for universal military service,
whereby men between 21 and 45 years of age would be subject to brief
periods of military training and service. Contends: "Aside from the question of obligation of national service, adequate trained defense forces to
meet the demands of modern war cannot be created by the haphazard
methods we have followed in the past."

ERSKINE, JOHN. *Universal Training for National Defense.* 1940. Civilian
Military Education Fund. Washington, D.C. Reprint from Review
of Reviews. October 1919. 15 pages.

The author, chairman of the Army Educational Committee of the
American Expeditionary Forces in 1918–1919, upholds universal military
training as an economic and practical educational plan that would serve
not only to prepare for the emergencies of war but also to relieve unemployment and further national unity in peacetime.

FELLOWSHIP OF RECONCILIATION. *Operation High School.* Circa 1951.
New York. 2 pages.

Charges that, with the cooperation of the Defense Department, American militarism is launching a campaign for the military indoctrination of
American youth through the use of "educational" films claiming to "help

boys prepare" for military service. Alleges that these films—produced under the general title "Are You Ready for Service?"—are being shown in the schools in anticipation of universal military training legislation that would draft 18-year-olds, and that the true purpose of the films is to advance the psychological adjustment of youth to permanent conscription.

HAVIGHURST, ROBERT, ARTHUR RUBIN, and ELBERT THOMAS. *Compulsory Peacetime Military Training: Can the United States Avoid It?* Round Table. September 16, 1945. Number 391. 17 pages.

A radio discussion of the proposed compulsory peacetime military training system in relation to the United Nations and efforts toward world peace.

HUTCHINS, ROBERT, JOHN McCLOY, and FLOYD REEVES. *Should We Have Universal Military Training in Peacetime?* Round Table. November 26, 1944. Number 349. 26 pages.

A radio discussion in which the participants agree that the proposal for universal military training in peacetime "must stand or fall by military necessity. If a very large army is a military necessity after the war, universal military training is the democratic way to get it."

IMPEY, E. ADAIR. *Military Training Considered as Part of General Education.* Circa 1916. National Peace Council. London. 8 pages.

Argues against military training in the schools on the basis that the purpose of training a soldier is to fit him for war, whereas that of school training should be general education. If military training in the schools does in fact improve one's mental and physical condition, then the schools should be provided with physical education teachers of adequate training to enable them to meet these general education requirements.

NATIONAL COUNCIL AGAINST CONSCRIPTION. *An Analysis of the Report of the President's Advisory Commission on Universal Training.* 1947. Washington, D.C. 28 pages.

A critical examination by 20 prominent individuals from diverse fields of the President's Advisory Commission on Universal Training's *Program for National Security* (see page 220, below). It is argued that the supposed benefits of universal military training are questionable, that the nation's talent would be claimed by the military, that universal military training would encourage the growth of militarism, that it would reduce neither the size nor the cost of the army, that the commission's program would militarize education and religion, and that it would be a forerunner to conscription of labor and women. Universal disarmament is seen as the only road to world peace and security. The appendix contains a discussion of the shortcomings of the Swiss military training system.

NATIONAL COUNCIL AGAINST CONSCRIPTION. *The Facts Behind the Report.* 1952. Washington, D.C. 40 pages.

An analysis of the report of the National Security Training Commission issued in 1951 under the title *Universal Military Training: Foundation of Enduring National Strength.* It is concluded that (1) nothing in the report offers any benefits to education; (2) a program of universal military training would establish the new principle that the state has a right to expect every American to obey orders in peace as well as in war; and (3) the commission's conclusion that approval of universal military training would be at once a recognition of "grave errors of our past and a partial reassurance that they will not recur" was based on the fallacious assertion that the United States was "unarmed" in the years following both World Wars.

NATIONAL COUNCIL AGAINST CONSCRIPTION. *Freedom's Future Is in Your Hands.* 1951. Washington, D.C. 14 pages.

Appeals for public support to influence the forthcoming congressional debates against the adoption of universal military training. Asserts that the proponents of universal military training are using the "emergency psychology" of the Korean crisis as a means to establish the principle of permanent peacetime conscription. Universal military training, it is argued, would neither reduce casualties in a future war nor strengthen democracy, but could increase international tension.

NATIONAL COUNCIL AGAINST CONSCRIPTION. *Gullible's Travels.* Circa 1947. Washington, D.C. 7 pages.

A satirical account of a voyage to Switzerland where universal military training guarantees peace. Suggests that by adopting such a course the United States could also secure a lasting peace.

NATIONAL COUNCIL AGAINST CONSCRIPTION. *Neither Peace nor Security.* Circa 1947. Washington, D.C. 6 pages.

Pamphlet issued by 26 U.S. historians to express their "concern about the current drive for universal military training."

NATIONAL COUNCIL AGAINST CONSCRIPTION. *U.M.T. and the Reserves.* Circa 1952. Washington, D.C. 15 pages.

Compilation of questions and answers on universal military training and the reserves, with testimony before the House Armed Services Committee. Concludes that universal military training is not essential to building an effective reserve system.

NATIONAL EDUCATION ASSOCIATION OF THE UNITED STATES and the AMERICAN ASSOCIATION OF SCHOOL ADMINISTRATORS. *Compulsory Peacetime Military Training.* 1945. Washington, D.C. 15 pages.

Contains the joint declaration of two major educational organizations following extensive studies. Concludes that "the incidental educational results claimed for compulsory military service would be of limited value and short duration, and that better and more lasting results can be secured more cheaply, effectively, and safely by other means that are readily available."

NATIONAL OPINION RESEARCH CENTER. *Compulsory Military Training in Peacetime?* 1944. Report No. 23. University of Denver. Denver, Colorado. 15 pages.

A collection of results of public polls taken shortly before and during World War II, reflecting dramatic changes in public attitudes toward compulsory military service and training. In 1938 only slightly over one-third of the population supported conscription; by June 1940 those approving had increased to nearly two-thirds.

NATIONAL PEACE CONFERENCE. *Pros and Cons of Universal Military Training.* 1946. New York. 11 pages.

Issued by the Commission on the World Community of the National Peace Conference, this pamphlet presents arguments for and against compulsory peacetime military training in regard to preparation for war, the advent of the atomic bomb, and international security.

NATIONAL POLICY COMMITTEE. *Universal Military Training.* 1944. National Policy Memoranda No. 35. Washington, D.C. 21 pages.

Proceedings of a meeting on the pros and cons of universal military training, with representatives from government, education, research, labor, industry, public relations, and the press.

NATIONAL POLICY COMMITTEE. *Universal Military Training.* 1946. National Policy Report No. 44. Washington, D.C. 21 pages.

Proceedings of a meeting convened to consider recent proposals for universal military training, in particular the War Department's "plan for Universal Military Training," released in October 1946. Representatives are from industry, labor, law, banking, the government, political office, education, the press, medicine, and the military.

ORTON, EDWARD, JR. *The Age for Universal Military Training.* Reprint from The Infantry Journal. April 1917. 4 pages.

In this educator's view, a plan making 18 the minimum age and 21 the maximum age for joining the armed forces would be best on physical, mental, and economic grounds. And a bill for universal military training would be more likely to succeed if, rather than insistence on the "theoretcal ideal" of one to two years, only a six-month program were proposed.

POST WAR WORLD COUNCIL. *Don't Let America Go Isolationist!* Circa 1945. New York. 2 pages.

Urges popular opposition to compulsory military training in peacetime, as provided in two proposals currently before Congress: House Resolution 515 (by Representative Andrew J. May) and Senate bill 188 (by Senator Chan Gurney). These provide for a year's compulsory military training for every male citizen and alien resident between the ages of 18 and 22 and subsequent reserve enrollment for six years.

REILLY, HENRY J. *Are Our Young Men to Have a Chance?* 1940. Civilian Military Education Fund. Washington, D.C. 24 pages.

Presents the case for universal military service, discussing historical precedents, the cost of national defense, and the advantages of universal training.

SMITH, FREDERICK C. *Compulsory Military Training—for What?* Vital Speeches of the Day. August 1, 1940. Volume 6, Number 20. Pages 629–631.

Suggests that those who advocate U.S. entrance into World War II "are largely the same group who advocate universal compulsory military service." Had the United States had a large standing army, "there is little doubt that the necessary incident, or excuse, would have been found for declaring war."

STIMSON, HENRY L. *The Basis for National Military Training.* National Security League. New York. Reprint from Scribner's Magazine. April 1917. 9 pages.

The former secretary of war urges that no "half-way measures" be taken to "lay the statutory foundations of a proper system of land-defense"; nor should "improvisation . . . take the form of patching up our discredited militia system." He recommends that universal obligatory military training be introduced without delay as a part of a permanent national system. The reprint also contains an appeal by Assistant Secretary of the Navy Franklin D. Roosevelt for military preparedness in general and for some form of universal military training in particular.

STUDENTS' ANTI-DRILL SOCIETY. *Compulsory Military Drill: A Great College Menace.* 1915. Seattle, Washington. 18 pages.

Urges students to organize against the compulsion feature of military drill in colleges.

VILLARD, OSWALD GARRISON. *Universal Military Training: Our Latest Cure-all.* Circa 1918. American Union Against Militarism. Washington, D.C. 8 pages.

A critical review of proposals for universal military service, by the chairman of the American Union Against Militarism and editor of the *New York Nation.*

Government Documents: Publications

U.S. ADVISORY COMMISSION ON UNIVERSAL TRAINING. *Program for National Security.* 1947. Government Printing Office. Washington, D.C. Tables. 453 pages.

The commission's report, dated May 29, 1947, contains the findings of the commission regarding the international, economic, educational, medical, and religious implications of universal training, and considers the possible types and risks of future war as well as the requirements of military strategy. It is recommended that universal military training be considered "an essential element in an integrated program of national security intended to safeguard the United States and to enable us to fulfill our responsibilities to the cause of world peace and the success of the United Nations." The appendix includes a summary of public opinion polls on universal military training and national security, a survey of foreign systems of military service, and a historical summary of universal military training in the United States.

U.S. CONGRESS. HOUSE. COMMITTEE ON ARMED SERVICES. *Universal Military Training.* 1952. Government Printing Office. Washington, D.C. 11 pages.

Compilation of 36 questions and answers with respect to House Resolution 5904 to provide for the administration and discipline of the National Security Training Corps.

U.S. CONGRESS. HOUSE. COMMITTEE ON ARMED SERVICES. *Universal Military Training and Service Act.* 1966. Government Printing Office. Washington, D.C. 55 pages.

Compilation of materials relating to the Universal Military Training and Service Act, prepared for the House Committee on Armed Services. Dated March 1, 1966. Includes a record of all statutory changes in the Universal Military Training and Service Act as amended to August 30, 1965, an analysis and explanation of the act, and a brief description of the Selective Service System and its administration.

U.S. CONGRESS. SENATE. COMMITTEE ON MILITARY AFFAIRS. *Universal*

Military Training. 1917. Government Printing Office. Washington, D.C. Tables. 120 pages.

Letter from the secretary of war submitting to the chairman of the Senate Committee on Military Affairs "certain papers and data relative to carrying into effect liability to universal military training in the United States." Includes four memorandums prepared for the Chief of Staff, a draft act on universal military training and service, a table showing the strength and organization of land forces, and cost tables.

U.S. LIBRARY OF CONGRESS. *Educational Aspects of Universal Military Training and Alternative Proposals.* 1952. Government Printing Office. Washington, D.C. Tables. 94 pages.

Report prepared by the Legislative Reference Service for the House Committee on Education and Labor. Provides a comprehensive digest and analysis of significant publications relating to the universal military training issue and points out, without making recommendations, the educational considerations and implications.

U.S. LIBRARY OF CONGRESS. *Universal Military Training.* 1947. Public Affairs Bulletin Number 54. Washington, D.C. Illustrations, tables. 90 pages.

Paper by defense analysts in the Legislative Reference Service, covering manpower needs and universal military training, arguments for and against universal military training, the problems of voluntary recruitment in 1947–1948, a survey of public opinion on universal military training in the atomic age, and the Army and Navy Reserve training programs.

U.S. LIBRARY OF CONGRESS. *Universal Military Training and Related Proposals.* 1946. Public.Affairs Bulletin Number 43. Washington, D.C. 103 pages.

Selected data on the nature and scope of universal military training. Summarizes legislative proposals since World War I, and presents arguments for and against universal military training from the viewpoints of national security, education, politics, and economics.

Government Documents: Congressional Hearings

1917. U.S. CONGRESS. HOUSE. COMMITTEE ON MILITARY AFFAIRS. *Universal Military Training.* Government Printing Office. Washington, D.C. 308 pages.

Statements by Leonard Wood before the House and Senate Committees on Military Affairs on a bill to provide for the military and naval training of the citizen forces of the United States.

1926. U.S. CONGRESS. HOUSE. COMMITTEE ON MILITARY AFFAIRS. *Abolishment of Compulsory Military Training at Schools and Colleges.* Government Printing Office. Washington, D.C. 276 pages.

Hearings between April 29 and June 15, 1926, before the House Committee on Military Affairs on House bill 8538 prohibiting any course of military training from being made compulsory for any student in any educational institution other than a military school, amending the acts of June 4, 1920, and June 3, 1916.

1945. U.S. CONGRESS. HOUSE. SELECT COMMITTEE ON POSTWAR MILITARY POLICY. *Universal Military Training.* 2 parts. Government Printing Office. Washington, D.C. Part 1: 614 pages. Part 2: 96 pages.

Hearings between June 4 and 19, 1945, on House Resolution 465 to establish a select committee on postwar military policy.

1946. U.S. CONGRESS. HOUSE. COMMITTEE ON MILITARY AFFAIRS. *Universal Military Training.* 2 parts. Government Printing Office. Washington, D.C. Part 1: 827 pages. Part 2: Circa 225 pages.

Hearings before the House Committee on Military Affairs on House Resolution 515 to provide military or naval training for all male citizens 18 years of age. Part 1 covers hearings between November 8 and December 19, 1945; Part 2, those between February 18 and 21, 1946.

1947. U.S. CONGRESS. HOUSE. COMMITTEE ON ARMED SERVICES. *Universal Military Training.* Government Printing Office. Washington, D.C. 208 pages.

Hearings between June 11 and July 11, 1947, before the House Committee on Armed Services on universal military training. Includes the testimony of Karl Compton, chairman of the President's Advisory Commission on Universal Training, which prepared the report entitled *Program for National Security* (see above, page 220).

1947. U.S. CONGRESS. HOUSE. COMMITTEE ON ARMED SERVICES. *Universal Military Training.* Government Printing Office. Washington, D.C. 102 pages.

Hearings between July 14 and 17, 1947, before Subcommittee No. 2, Education and Training, of the House Committee on Armed Services on House bill 4121 on universal military training.

1948. U.S. CONGRESS. SENATE. COMMITTEE ON ARMED SERVICES. *Universal Military Training.* Government Printing Office. Washington, D.C. 1112 pages.

Hearings between March 17 and April 3, 1948, before the Senate Committee on Armed Services on the question of establishing a universal military training program.

1949. U.S. CONGRESS. SENATE. COMMITTEE ON ARMED SERVICES. *Universal Military Training.* Government Printing Office. Washington, D.C. 33 pages.

Hearing on March 3, 1949, before the Senate Committee on Armed Services on Senate bill 66 requiring that for the national security of the nation, all qualified young men undergo a period of training.

1950. U.S. CONGRESS. SENATE. COMMITTEE ON ARMED SERVICES. *Universal Military Training.* Government Printing Office. Washington, D.C. 100 pages.

Hearings on August 22 and 23, 1950, before the Senate Committee on Armed Services on Senate bill 4062 to provide for the common defense by establishing a universal training program.

1951. U.S. CONGRESS. SENATE. COMMITTEE ON ARMED SERVICES. *Universal Military Training and Service Act of 1951.* Government Printing Office. Washington, D.C. 1243 pages.

Hearings between January 10 and February 2, 1951, before the Preparedness Subcommittee of the Senate Committee on Armed Services on Senate bill 1 to provide for the common defense and security of the United States and to permit the more effective utilization of its manpower resources by authorizing universal military service and training.

1951. U.S. CONGRESS. HOUSE. COMMITTEE ON ARMED SERVICES. *Universal Military Training.* Government Printing Office. Washington, D.C. 969 pages.

Hearings between January 23 and March 8, 1951, before the House Committee on Armed Services on House bill 1752 to provide for the common defense and security of the United States and to permit the more effective utilization of its manpower resources by authorizing universal military service and training.

1952. U.S. CONGRESS. HOUSE. COMMITTEE ON ARMED SERVICES. *Universal Military Training.* Government Printing Office. Washington, D.C. 857 pages.

Hearings between January 15 and 31, 1952, before the House Committee on Armed Services on House bill 5904 to provide for the administration and discipline of the National Security Training Corps.

1952. U.S. CONGRESS. SENATE. COMMITTEE ON ARMED SERVICES. *National Security Training Corps Act.* Government Printing Office. Washington, D.C. 582 pages.

Hearings between February 7 and 14, 1952, before the Senate Committee on Armed Services on Senate bill 2441 to provide for the administration and discipline of the National Security Training Corps.

1953. U.S. CONGRESS. SENATE. COMMITTEE ON ARMED SERVICES. *Doctors Draft Law Amendments.* Government Printing Office. Washington, D.C. 170 pages.

Hearings between May 18 and 21, 1953, before the Senate Committee on Armed Services on House bill 4495 (Senate bill 1531) to amend the Universal Military Training and Service Act to provide for special registration, classification, and induction of certain medical, dental, and allied specialist categories.

1954. U.S. CONGRESS. SENATE. COMMITTEE ON ARMED SERVICES. *Doctor Draft Act Amendments.* Government Printing Office. Washington, D.C. 166 pages.

Hearings between March 18 and April 8, 1954, before the Senate Committee on Armed Services on Senate bill 3096 to amend the Universal Military Training and Service Act in relation to the utilization in an enlisted grade or rank in the armed forces of physicians, dentists, or those in an allied specialist category.

1954. U.S. CONGRESS. HOUSE. COMMITTEE ON ARMED SERVICES. *Universal Military Training and Service Act.* Government Printing Office. Washington, D.C. 9 pages.

Hearing on June 2, 1954, before Subcommittee No. 2 of the House Committee on Armed Services on House bill 9007 to amend the Universal Military Training and Service Act so as to exempt certain aliens from liability to service in the armed forces of the United States.

1954. U.S. CONGRESS. HOUSE. COMMITTEE ON ARMED SERVICES. *Doctor Draft Act.* Government Printing Office. Washington, D.C. 3 pages.

Hearing on June 8, 1954, before the House Committee on Armed Services on Senate bill 3096 to amend the Universal Military Training and Service Act in regard to the authority of the armed services to retain and utilize in a professional capacity in an enlisted grade or rank any doctor inducted or ordered to active duty under Public Law 84, enacted in 1950. Includes testimony on the discriminatory class legislation aspect of the doctor draft law.

1955. U.S. CONGRESS. HOUSE. COMMITTEE ON ARMED SERVICES. *Universal Military Training and Service Act.* Government Printing Office. Washington, D.C. 187 pages.

Hearings between February 1 and 3, 1955, before the House Committee on Armed Services on House bill 3005 to amend the Universal Military Training and Service Act by extending the authority to induct certain individuals.

1955. U.S. CONGRESS. SENATE. COMMITTEE ON ARMED SERVICES. *Amendments to the Universal Military Training and Service Act.* Government Printing Office. Washington, D.C. 250 pages.

Hearings on June 9 and 10, 1955, before the Senate Committee on Armed Services on (1) House bill 3005 to amend the Universal Military Training and Service Act by extending the authority to induct certain individuals and to extend benefits under the Dependents Assistance Act to July 1, 1959; (2) House bill 6057 to extend the authority to require the special registration, classification, and induction of certain medical, dental, and allied specialist categories and to provide for the continuation of special pay for physicians, dentists, and veterinarians; and (3) Senate bill 1467 to amend the Universal Military Training and Service Act to provide for the deferment and exemption of certain persons employed as veterinarians by the Department of Agriculture.

1957. U.S. CONGRESS. HOUSE. COMMITTEE ON ARMED SERVICES. *Universal Military Training and Service Act.* Government Printing Office. Washington, D.C. 75 pages.

Hearings on May 7 and 8, 1957, before the House Committee on Armed Services on House bill 6548 to amend the Universal Military Training and Service Act in regard to persons in medical, dental, and allied specialist categories.

1957. U.S. CONGRESS. SENATE. COMMITTEE ON ARMED SERVICES. *Doctor Draft Substitute.* Government Printing Office. Washington, D.C. 51 pages.

Hearing on June 6, 1957, before the Senate Committee on Armed Services on House bill 6548 amending the Universal Military Training and Service Act in regard to persons in the medical, dental, and allied specialist categories.

1958. U.S. CONGRESS. SENATE. COMMITTEE ON ARMED SERVICES. *Reemployment Provisions of the Universal Military Training and Service Act.* Government Printing Office. Washington, D.C. 45 pages.

Hearing on June 12, 1958, before the Senate Committee on Armed Services on House bill 8522 to amend and clarify the reemployment provisions of the Universal Military Training and Service Act.

1959. U.S. CONGRESS. HOUSE. COMMITTEE ON ARMED SERVICES. *Universal Military Training and Service Act.* Government Printing Office. Washington, D.C. 189 pages.

Hearings between January 26 and 30, 1959, before the House Committee on Armed Services on House bill 2260 to extend until July 1, 1963, the induction provisions of the Universal Military Training and Service Act.

1963. U.S. CONGRESS. HOUSE. COMMITTEE ON ARMED SERVICES. *Universal Military Training and Service Act.* Government Printing Office. Washington, D.C. 158 pages.

Hearings between March 1 and 5, 1963, before the House Committee on Armed Services on House bill 2438 to extend for four years the induction provisions of the Universal Military Training and Service Act.

1963. U.S. CONGRESS. SENATE. COMMITTEE ON ARMED SERVICES. *Extension of the Draft and Related Authorities.* Government Printing Office. Washington, D.C. 128 pages.

Hearing on March 12, 1963, before a subcommittee of the Senate Committee on Armed Services on House bill 2438 (Senate bill 846) to extend the induction provisions of the Universal Military Training and Service Act.

1963. U.S. CONGRESS. SENATE. COMMITTEE ON ARMED SERVICES. *Providing a Special Enlistment Training Program.* Government Printing Office. Washington, D.C. 27 pages.

Hearing on July 11, 1963, before the Senate Committee on Armed Services on House bill 6996 to (1) repeal Section 262 of the Armed Forces Reserve Act, and (2) amend the Universal Military Training and Service Act to revise and consolidate authority for deferment and exemption from liability for induction for training and service for certain Reserve membership and participation, and to provide a special enlistment program.

1965. U.S. CONGRESS. HOUSE. COMMITTEE ON ARMED SERVICES. *Universal Military Training and Service Act.* Government Printing Office. Washington, D.C. 3 pages.

Hearing on August 6, 1965, before the House Committee on Armed Services on House bill 10306 to amend the Universal Military Training and Service Act. Considers legislation concerning the burning of draft cards.

1966. U.S. CONGRESS. HOUSE. COMMITTEE ON ARMED SERVICES. *Universal Military Training and Service Act.* Government Printing Office. Washington, D.C. 12 pages.

Hearing on February 23, 1966, before Subcommittee No. 3 of the House Committee on Armed Services on House bill 11509 to amend and clarify the reemployment provisions of the Universal Military Training and Service Act.

1966. U.S. CONGRESS. HOUSE. COMMITTEE ON ARMED SERVICES. *Universal Military Training and Service Act.* Government Printing Office. Washington, D.C. 7 pages.

Hearing on March 1, 1966, before the House Committee on Armed Services on House bill 11509 to amend and clarify the reemployment provisions of the Universal Military Training and Service Act.

1967. U.S. CONGRESS. SENATE. COMMITTEE ON ARMED SERVICES. *Amending and Extending the Draft Law and Related Authorities.* Government Printing Office. Washington, D.C. 657 pages.

Hearings between April 12 and 19, 1967, before the Senate Committee on Armed Services on Senate bill 1432 to amend the Universal Military Training and Service Act.

1967. U.S. CONGRESS. HOUSE. COMMITTEE ON ARMED SERVICES. *Universal Military Training and Service Act.* Government Printing Office. Washington, D.C. Figures, tables. 806 pages.

Hearings between May 2 and 11, 1967, before the House Committee on Armed Services, considering possible modifications to the Universal Military Training and Service Act.

1968. U.S. CONGRESS. HOUSE. COMMITTEE ON ARMED SERVICES. *Universal Military Training and Service Act.* Government Printing Office. Washington, D.C. 9 pages.

Hearing on March 20, 1968, before Subcommittee No. 3 of the House Committee on Armed Services on House bill 1093 to amend and clarify the reemployment provisions of the Universal Military Training and Service Act.

Chapter 7

National Guard and Reserves

A well-regulated militia being necessary to the security of a
free state, the right of the people to keep and bear arms
shall not be infringed.
                    —Constitution of the United States,
                              Amendment II, 1791

Books

BINKIN, MARTIN. *U.S. Reserve Forces: The Problem of the Weekend
Warrior.* 1974. The Brookings Institution. Washington, D.C. Figures,
tables. 63 pages.

An analysis "directed principally toward streamlining the reserve forces
by phasing out the less effective elements of the reserves and, where appro-
riate, by assigning to selected reserve units a greater responsibility for meeting current U.S. military commitments." In the author's view, "substantial
economies can be achieved in the costs of the reserves without appreciably
affecting their present military missions."

DERTHICK, MARTHA. *The National Guard in Politics.* 1965. Harvard
University Press. Cambridge, Massachusetts. Index. Notes: pages 181–
196. 202 pages.

As a basis for analyzing the concept of group power, this study looks at
the National Guard as a pressure group, from the standpoint of its foundation in the militia clause of the Constitution. Derthick traces the development of the National Guard from its beginning in the late 1870s, when it
was regarded as a collection of "scattered units of men held together by a
shared enthusiasm for military activity," to the Militia Act of 1903, militia
reform and the campaign for drill pay, the National Defense Act of 1916,

and the Selective Training and Service Act of 1940. She also examines the development of the National Guard Association in recent years into a sophisticated political organization and the challenge to the guard's autonomy by the expansion of federal authority into military affairs, notably the fact that draftees were able to fulfil their military obligation in the National Guard.

HILL, JIM DAN. *The Minute Man in Peace and War: A History of the National Guard.* 1964. Stackpole Co. Harrisburg, Pennsylvania. Index. Bibliographical note at end of each chapter. 585 pages.

Foreword by George Fielding Eliot. General Jim Dan Hill was chairman of the Army's General Staff Committee on National Guard and Reserve Policy during the Korean War and later served as a member of Defense Reserve Forces Policy Board. His book traces the National Guard from its colonial origins to its present organizational and manpower patterns.

HUNTINGTON, SAMUEL P. (editor). *Changing Patterns of Military Politics.* 1962. Free Press of Glencoe. New York. 272 pages.

Of particular interest is the study by Martha Derthick entitled "Militia Lobby in the Missile Age: The Politics of the National Guard" (pages 190–234). This is a brief political history of the National Guard, charting its growth and influence. The author expects that "the institutional interest of Congress in the Guard will diminish as the Guard's relative significance for U.S. military policy declines."

LEVANTROSSER, WILLIAM F. *Congress and the Citizen-Soldier.* 1967. Ohio State University Press. Columbus, Ohio. Index. Tables, figures. Bibliography: pages 231–250. 267 pages.

An analysis of six major aspects of national military reserve affairs: (1) retirement pay for reserve personnel based on inactive reserve training as well as active duty; (2) categories of readiness for reserve forces and obligations to serve in them; (3) promotion criteria for reserve officers; (4) retention of paid-drill strength in the army reserve; (5) officer recruitment on the college campus; and (6) realignment and reduction in strength of units in the army reserve components. Policies concerning the draft, compulsory military training, and volunteering are discussed as they pertain to the reserves.

LYONS, GENE M., and JOHN W. MASLAND. *Education and Military Leadership: A Study of the R.O.T.C.* 1959. Princeton University Press. Princeton, New Jersey. Index. Charts, tables. 283 pages.

Foreword by John Sloan Dickey. This analysis of the Reserve Officers' Training Corps programs is a study of the relationship of higher education to the national defense. It considers the nature of the officer requirements of the armed services, and the limitations on the relationship between the federal government and colleges and universities. The authors provide a brief history of the ROTC, consider current issues regarding it, and offer proposals for its future.

MILLIS, WALTER. *Individual Freedom and the Common Defense.* 1957. Fund for the Republic. New York. 80 pages.

A discussion of the ROTC, the Reserve Act of 1955, and their relation to universal military obligation. Millis finds that "the universal military obligation and the manpower system which has been built around it fails to meet the real requirements of national defense today, is inefficient in fulfilling the supposed requirements, and is increasingly unjust and discriminatory in its operation."

RIKER, WILLIAM H. *Soldiers of the States: The Role of the National Guard in American Democracy.* 1957. Public Affairs Press. Washington, D.C. Index. Charts. Bibliographic references: pages 118–125. 129 pages.

A history of public policy on the National Guard, dealing with its historical roots, constitutional setting, the degeneration of the militia in the periods 1792–1860 and 1877–1903, and the development of the National Guard. The final chapter discusses federalism and the militia.

Unpublished Manuscripts

CANTOR, LOUIS. *The Creation of the Modern National Guard: The Dick Militia Act of 1903.* 1963. Ph.D. dissertation. Duke University. Durham, North Carolina. 310 pages.

The purpose of this dissertation is twofold: (1) to analyze the shift in

1903 that converted the National Guard from a disorganized state militia into an effectively organized federal reserve force, and (2) to demonstrate more clearly why the guard has developed along certain lines since 1903.

WESTOVER, JOHN GLENDOWER. *The Evolution of the Missouri Militia 1840–1919*. 1948. Ph.D. dissertation. University of Missouri. Columbia, Missouri. 300 pages.

Traces the evolution of the present National Guardsman from the pioneer militiaman as the United States moved "away from preoccupation with such purely domestic problems as the settlement of the frontier and the Indian menace to an increasing consciousness of [its role] as a world power with world responsibilities." Concludes that it was the militia's use as a reserve force for federal action, rather than its use in state disorders and disasters, that "led to the most widespread acceptance and expansion of the militia system."

Articles

ANSELL, S. T. *Legal and Historical Aspects of the Militia*. Yale Law Journal. April 1917. Volume 26, Number 6. Pages 471–480.

Examines the militia and its relation, when called into federal service, to the U.S. Army. Ansell notes that the army is exclusively a federal institution and as such may be raised as Congress sees fit, by voluntary enlistment or compulsory draft. The militia, in contrast, under the Constitution is not a part of the "land forces" of the United States and is under only limited federal control. In regard to the National Guard created by the National Defense Act of 1916, therefore, the author poses the question whether the National Guard legally is still the militia of the several states subject only to the limited constitutional use of the federal government, or whether it is an army of the United States over which the power of Congress is unlimited.

BLUMENFELD, C. H. *The Case for ROTC*. Military Review. March 1963. Volume XLIII, Number 3. Pages 3–13.

Discusses the ROTC and the concept of military service obligation. Points out advantages to the individual and to the nation of ROTC training and calls upon students to respond by undertaking not merely "the obligation of academic development and preparation for civilian leadership," but the obligation of "preparation for military leadership as well."

BRAYTON, ABBOT A. *American Reserve Policies Since World War II.* Military Affairs. December 1972. Volume XXXVI, Number 4. Pages 139–144.

Notes that early American reserve policies were characterized by a reliance upon a traditional militia system, a true citizen-army that augmented the Regular Army upon mobilization. Suggesting that this system was "outpaced" by the development of modern warfare, the author predicts that future military policies will include greater emphasis on reserve forces and mobilization capabilities.

CANTOR, LOUIS. *Elihu Root and the National Guard: Friend or Foe?* Military Affairs. December 1969. Volume XXXIII, Number 3. Pages 361–373.

Examines the Dick Militia Act of 1903 and the respective roles played in its passage by Secretary of War Elihu Root on the one hand and the National Guard, represented by the Interstate National Guard Association, on the other.

COLBY, ELBRIDGE. *Elihu Root and the National Guard.* Military Affairs. Spring 1959. Volume XXIII, Number 1. Pages 28–34.

Examines the attitudes of Secretary of War Elihu Root toward the National Guard during the years following the Spanish–American War, especially in regard to the events leading to the Militia Act of 1903. Shows how Root was influenced by Emory Upton's critique of the militia in the latter's *Military Policy of the United States* (see page 46, above), and how Root's attempts to influence others were subsequently "responsible for much prejudice in the Regular Army against the militia of the States, responsible perhaps for the growth of the whole Continental Army idea in 1916 which would have relegated the National Guard to the status of state police." In this view, Root's support of the subsequently adopted Dick recommendations should be viewed more as acceptance of a policy advanced by others than as any initiative on his part to afford national recognition to the state militias.

GANS, DANIEL. *Active Army Support of Reserve Components.* Military Review. July 1974. Volume LIV, Number 7. Pages 78–89.

Discusses mobilization and deployment capabilities of the U.S. Army Reserve Components, suggesting ways in which readiness conditions can be improved.

GARLAND, ALBERT N. *ROTC: White Elephant.* Military Review. January 1971. Volume LI, Number 1. Pages 110–112.

Recommends abolition of the ROTC program. Contends that "the Army will never have any trouble getting all the officers it needs, and that those officers can be drawn from any walk of life and any level of society the Army chooses."

GRAY, GEORGE H. *What Are U.S. Reserve Forces Really For?* Military Review. June 1975. Volume LV, Number 6. Pages 82–90.

Reviews the purposes of reserve forces: (1) to provide a primary source for augmenting the Regular Army in any war or other emergency requiring a rapid and substantial expansion of the army; (2) to preserve a basic part of the U.S. system of government and of the nation's heritage—the tradition of not maintaining a large standing army; (3) to serve as the main link between the Regular Army and the citizenry; and (4) to act as a brake on ill-advised and unwise military ventures conceived by civilian authority.

IKEDA, MOSS M. *Reserve Strength in Face of the Zero Draft.* Military Review. May 1973. Volume LIII, Number 5. Pages 58–66.

Makes 16 recommendations to aid in formulating a plan of action to resolve the problem of maintaining adequate enlisted strength in the Army Reserve. These recommendations deal with the improvement of service conditions and educational and other benefits.

KETCHUM, OMAR B. *Military Training Through the National Guard.* The Annals of the American Academy of Political and Social Science. September 1945. Volume 241. Pages 138–143.

Presents the Veterans of Foreign Wars' view on preparedness and universal military training, and outlines that organization's plan "to employ the National Guard, Naval, and Marine Reserves in giving military training over a period of years to every young man." Such training would be compulsory and require a three-year enlistment, the expected result being that each youth would automatically become a member of either the National Guard, the Naval Reserve, or the Marine Reserve for a period of military training. The necessary expansion of the guard would be underwritten by the federal government. Ketchum suggests that "the idea of training men at home, in the company of intimate friends, should quiet many of the fears of those opponents of any type of compulsory military training."

LEE, JOHN. *The National Guard and National Security.* Military Review. January 1972. Volume LII, Number 1. Pages 9–16.

Recommends that state guard units be in proportion to population size. This would give the larger, urbanized states a well-trained military police capable of rapid mobilization in case of localized riots, and provide a combat-ready backup for the federal government.

LEVANTROSSER, WILLIAM F. *The Army Reserve Merger Proposal.* Military Affairs. Fall 1966. Volume XXX, Number 3. Pages 135–147.

Examines the proposal of the Department of Defense to merge the paid-drill units of the Army Reserve with those of the National Guard under the latter's control and to reduce the total numerical strength of the new combination. Considers the basic issues involved in the merger proposal as the basis for an appraisal of the role of the reserve forces in national defense strategy and of the "adequacy of the citizen-soldier concept."

LYONS, GENE M., and JOHN W. MASLAND. *The Origins of the ROTC.* Military Affairs. Spring 1959. Volume XXIII, Number 1. Pages 1–12.

Examines in particular the relationships of the ROTC to the concept of the early militia system and to the development of a federal reserve. Concludes that the ROTC, like other military manpower programs, must be geared to a modern mobilization policy by which military forces can be expanded rapidly through the incorporation of reserves.

MEYER, RICHARD M. *Is Your Army ROTC Legitimate?* Military Review. June 1975. Volume LV, Number 6. Pages 70–81.

Calls for efforts to make the ROTC "academically legitimate" on college and university campuses where ROTC courses do not have accreditation or where the program demands an academic overload. Proposes a revised academic program aimed at promoting the attractiveness of the ROTC and complementing recruiting and retention efforts.

MILITARY AFFAIRS. *The Reserves of the Armed Forces: A Historical Symposium.* Spring 1953. Volume XVII, Number 1. Pages 1–36.

The papers in the symposium consider a number of important aspects of military manpower procurement policy. The papers include: "Development of the Army Reserve Forces," by Arthur Roth; "Development of the Naval Reserve," by K. M. McManes; "The Air Force Reserve," by Robert L. Copsey; "The Marine Reserves in Action," by William W. Stickney; "History of the Reserves Since the Second World War," by I. M. McQuiston; and "The Idea of a Citizen Army," by Arthur A. Ekirch.

NEIMANIS, GEORGE J. *Defense Expenditures and the Combat Readiness of Reserve Forces: Some Quantitative Reflections.* Military Review. February 1975. Volume LV, Number 2. Pages 26–34.

Attempts to measure the combat readiness of the reserve forces by analyzing U.S. military budgets between 1921 and 1970. The hypothesis is that despite claims to the contrary the measurable combat readiness of organized reserves after World War II has not increased because relative expenditures on organized reserves have not increased. The findings, supporting the hypothesis, "cast some doubts on the belief that there has been a radical improvement in the peacetime combat readiness of organized Reserves."

RICH, BENNETT M., and PHILIP H. BURCH, JR. *The Changing Role of the National Guard.* American Political Science Review. September 3, 1956. Volume 50, Number 3. Pages 702–706.

Suggests that "without benefit of legislation or much public notice the domestic function of the [National] Guard has been subtly and radically transformed during the past decade. From an embodiment of force it has become largely an instrument of rescue and relief." Recommends a provision for the enlargement of the guard with a mutual federal-state understanding that in the event of guard mobilization for national purposes a small percentage of each state's total manpower and equipment be retained for local emergencies.

Scott, Joseph W. *ROTC Retreat.* Trans-action. September 1969. Volume 6, Number 10. Pages 47–52.

Examines the recent change in attitudes toward ROTC programs at universities and colleges. Foresees the removal of ROTC units from the campuses of high-quality schools unless additional legislation provides more autonomy to participating institutions.

Stotesbury, Louis W. *Compulsory Training Under State Auspices and the Place of State Militia in National Defense.* Proceedings of the Academy of Political Science. July 1916. Volume 6, Number 4. Pages 234–243.

Deals with "the failure of the Congress for more than a century to fully exercise its power over the militia." Claiming that "Congress does possess all adequate powers of organization and control," Stotesbury proposes that it remove the limitation upon the wartime use of the National Guard beyond U.S. territorial limits and adopt a military policy based upon compulsion.

Todd, Frederick P. *Our National Guard: An Introduction to Its History* (two parts). Military Affairs. (1) Summer 1941. Volume V, Number 2. Pages 73–86. (2) Fall 1941. Volume V, Number 2. Pages 152–170.

Examines the origins, composition, and activities of the National Guard: (1) the American volunteer from 1775 to 1783, (2) independent volunteer companies from 1783 to 1861, (3) the state regiments from 1865 to 1903, and (4) the process of federalization from 1903 to 1933, when the National Guard was established as a full-fledged reserve component of the U.S. Army.

Wood, Eric Fisher. *The New Army Act and the Militia.* The Century. October 1916. Volume 92, Number 6. Pages 801–812.

Criticizes the Army Reorganization Act of June 3, 1916, as "worse than nothing" and discusses the militia in regard to federal and state authorities to raise men.

Worsnop, Richard L. *Reserve Forces and the Draft.* Editorial Research Reports. January 20, 1965. Volume 1. Pages 41–60.

Considers the McNamara proposal to reorganize U.S. reserve forces, examines the evolution of the dual reserve–guard setup, and reviews the changing reserve needs and the draft.

WYCKOFF, THEODORE. *Required ROTC: The New Look.* Military Review. November 1964. Volume XLIV, Number 11. Pages 24–28.

Discusses the voluntary and required systems of ROTC at colleges and universities. The author regards required basic ROTC as "the cornerstone of success in producing acceptable numbers of good quality officers."

YOUNG, DAVID M. *ROTC: Required or Elective?* Military Review. February 1962. Volume XLII, Number 2. Pages 21–32.

Discusses the widespread compulsory feature of the ROTC program that requires students at some universities and colleges to take two years of military training. Calls for clarification and reform of the ROTC program.

YOUNG, THOMAS F. *Thinking the Unthinkable About Army ROTC.* Military Review. March 1974. Volume LIV, Number 3. Pages 75–84.

Report on a study of the Army ROTC program's relations with institutions of higher education. Includes recommendations for upgrading and improving the ROTC program.

Pamphlets, Reprints, and Speeches

BARNES, ROSWELL P. *Militarizing Our Youth: The Significance of the Reserve Officers' Training Corps in Our Schools and Colleges.* 1927. Committee on Militarism in Education. New York. 46 pages.

Introduction by John Dewey. Presents arguments against ROTC, with quotations from proponents and opponents of military training in schools and colleges. Charges that "the promotion, direct supervision, and ultimate control of this military training in public high schools by the military arm of the federal government is a new departure in American history" permitted under the National Defense Act of 1916, and that compulsory drill in colleges under the direct and final control of the War Department has also been promoted under this act.

Government Documents: Publications

U.S. CONGRESS. HOUSE. COMMITTEE ON ARMED SERVICES. *Armed Forces Reserve Act of 1951.* 1951. Government Printing Office. Washington, D.C. 10 pages.

Compilation of 50 questions and answers on House bill 5426 relating to the reserve components of the armed forces, as passed by the House on October 15, 1951.

U.S. CONGRESS. HOUSE. COMMITTEE ON ARMED SERVICES. *History of United States Military Policy on Reserve Forces 1775–1956.* Prepared by Eilene Galloway, Legislative Reference Service, Library of Congress. 1957. Government Printing Office. Washington, D.C. Bibliography: pages 494–498. 498 pages.

A historical outline recording the experience of the United States in raising armed forces during times of emergency. The evolution of the militia from early colonial days is traced through successive stages of federal-state relationships to the modern concept of the National Guard. Military manpower policies are described in the context of the eight principal wars in which the United States has been engaged, up to and including the Korean War. The historical pattern is shown as being one of expanding a small armed force to peak numbers and of training men after the conflict has started, with rapid demobilization following the cessation of hostilities. This pattern was unbroken until the 1953 cease-fire in Korea. Since that time deterrent forces have been stabilized at a higher level than ever before, necessitating trained reservists and reserve units that can be readily mobilized.

U.S. CONGRESS. HOUSE. COMMITTEE ON ARMED SERVICES. *Military Reserve Posture.* 1962. Government Printing Office. Washington, D.C. 40 pages.

Report of Subcommittee No. 3 of the House Committee on Armed Services. Dated August 17, 1962.

U.S. CONGRESS. HOUSE. COMMITTEE ON ARMED SERVICES. *Recall and Release of Reservists.* 1951. Government Printing Office. Washington. D.C. 10 pages.

First Interim Report of the Special Subcommittee on Civilian Components of the House Armed Services Committee, dealing with the expansion of the armed forces for the Korean War. Dated July 13, 1951.

U.S. CONGRESS. HOUSE. COMMITTEE ON ARMED SERVICES. *Reserve Forces Act of 1955.* 1956. Government Printing Office. Washington, D.C. 8 pages.

First Interim Report of Subcommittee No. 1 of the House Committee on Armed Services on Implementation of the Reserve Forces Act of 1955. reviewing progress under the act. Dated January 1956.

U.S. CONGRESS. HOUSE. COMMITTEE ON ARMED SERVICES. *Reserve Forces Act of 1955.* 1956. Government Printing Office. Washington. D.C. 14 pages.

Second Interim Report of Subcommittee No. 1 of the House Committee on Armed Services on implementation of the Reserve Forces Act of 1955 and review of the reserve program. Dated May 1956.

U.S. CONGRESS. HOUSE. COMMITTEE ON ARMED SERVICES. *Reserve Forces Legislation.* Prepared by Eilene Galloway, Library of Congress. 1955. Government Printing Office. Washington, D.C. 56 pages.

A legislative history of the Reserve Forces Act of 1955 prepared for the House Committee on Armed Services.

U.S. CONGRESS. SENATE. COMMITTEE ON ARMED SERVICES. *Investigation of the Preparedness Program.* 1966. Government Printing Office. Washington, D.C. 13 pages.

Report of the Preparedness Investigating Subcommittee of the Senate Committee on Armed Services on the personnel, training, equipment, and readiness status of Army Reserve components. The report, prepared under authority of Senate Resolution 212 (89th Congress), recommends against the proposed merger of the Army Reserve and the Army National Guard.

U.S. CONGRESS. SENATE. COMMITTEE ON ARMED SERVICES. *Status of Reserve and National Guard Forces of the Armed Services.* 1955. Government Printing Office. Washington, D.C. 12 pages.

Report of the Interim Subcommittee on Preparedness of the Senate Committee on Armed Services, under authority of Senate Resolution 185 (83rd Congress). Dated December 28, 1954.

U.S. DEPARTMENT OF THE ARMY. *Reserve Forces for National Security.* 1948. Government Printing Office. Washington, D.C. 211 pages.

Report prepared by the Committee on Civilian Components of the Department of the Army for the Secretary of Defense. Includes the committee's conclusions and recommendations, as well as reference material.

U.S. WAR DEPARTMENT. *Training for Citizenship and National Defense.* 1923. Government Printing Office. Washington, D.C. 36 pages.

Report of the Conference on Training for Citizenship and National Defense held at the War Department in November 1922. Representatives of public-school systems, universities, land-grant colleges, welfare organizations, the National Guard, and the Reserve Officers Association discuss implementation of the National Defense Act in regard to citizenship training, the ROTC, and military training camps.

Government Documents: Congressional Hearings

1930. U.S. CONGRESS. HOUSE. COMMITTEE ON MILITARY AFFAIRS. *Officers' Reserve Corps—National Guard.* Government Printing Office. Washington, D.C. 84 pages.

Hearings between April 14 and May 16, 1930, before the House Committee on Military Affairs on House bill 10478, considering proposed amendments to the National Defense Act in regard to the Officers' Reserve Corps and the National Guard.

1935. U.S. CONGRESS. HOUSE. COMMITTEE ON MILITARY AFFAIRS. *National Defense Act of June 3, 1916.* Government Printing Office. Washington, D.C. 37 pages.

Hearing on April 11, 1935, before the House Committee on Military Affairs on House bill 5720 in regard to enlistment, pay, and other conditions of service in the National Guard.

1936. U.S. CONGRESS. HOUSE. COMMITTEE ON MILITARY AFFAIRS. *To Promote National Defense by Organizing the Junior Air Reserve.* Government Printing Office. Washington, D.C. 65 pages.

Hearing on January 23, 1936, before the House Committee on Military Affairs on House bill 4336 to promote national defense by organizing the Junior Air Reserve.

1947. U.S. CONGRESS. HOUSE. COMMITTEE ON ARMED SERVICES. *Reserve Officers' Training Corps.* Government Printing Office. Washington, D.C. 20 pages.

Hearing on June 23, 1947, before Subcommittee No. 2, Education and Training, of the House Committee on Armed Services on House bill 3280 to provide for the effective operation and expansion of the ROTC.

1950. U.S. CONGRESS. HOUSE. COMMITTEE ON ARMED SERVICES. *Amendments to National Defense Act.* Government Printing Office. Washington, D.C. 15 pages.

Hearing on September 18, 1950, before the House Committee on Armed Services on Senate bill 4088 to amend Section 61 of the National Defense Act and to permit the states to organize military forces, other than as parts of their National Guard units, to serve while the National Guard is in active federal service.

1951. U.S. CONGRESS. HOUSE. COMMITTEE ON ARMED SERVICES. *Reserve Components.* Government Printing Office. Washington, D.C. 1160 pages.

Hearings between January 8 and August 22, 1951, before the House Committee on Armed Services on House bill 4860, investigating the operations and methods used in inducting members of the reserve components.

1952. U.S. CONGRESS. SENATE. COMMITTEE ON ARMED SERVICES. *Armed Forces Reserve Act.* Government Printing Office. Washington, D.C. 347 pages.

Hearings between May 26 and 29, 1952, before a subcommittee of the Senate Committee on Armed Services on House bill 5426 relating to the reserve components of the armed forces.

1953. U.S. CONGRESS. HOUSE. COMMITTEE ON ARMED SERVICES. *Reserve Officer Personnel Act.* Government Printing Office. Washington, D.C. 578 pages.

Hearings between May 27 and July 28, 1953, before the House Committee on Armed Services on House bill 1222 to provide for the promotion, precedence, constructive credit, distribution, retention, and elimination of officers of the reserve components of the armed forces.

1954. U.S. CONGRESS. HOUSE. COMMITTEE ON ARMED SERVICES. *ROTC Problems in Military Colleges.* Government Printing Office. Washington, D.C. 22 pages.

Hearing on January 18, 1954, before Subcommittee No. 3 of the House Committee on Armed Services, considering testimony relating to the ROTC and military manpower needs.

1954. U.S. CONGRESS. HOUSE. COMMITTEE ON ARMED SERVICES. *Air Force Reserve Program.* Government Printing Office. Washington, D.C. 55 pages.

Hearings between April 1 and 5, 1954, before Subcommittee No. 3 of the House Committee on Armed Services, considering testimony relating to the Reserve Program Review Board's report of 1953 (the Johnson Report).

1954. U.S. CONGRESS. SENATE. COMMITTEE ON ARMED SERVICES. *Reserve Officer Personnel Act of 1954.* Government Printing Office. Washington, D.C. 181 pages.

Hearing on April 22, 1954, before the Senate Committee on Armed Services on House bill 6573 to provide for the promotion, precedence, constructive credit, distribution, retention, and elimination of officers of the reserve components of the armed forces.

1955. U.S. CONGRESS. HOUSE. COMMITTEE ON ARMED SERVICES. *National Reserve Plan.* Government Printing Office. Washington, D.C. 1279 pages.

Hearings between February 8 and March 25, 1955, before Subcommittee No. 1 of the House Committee on Armed Services on House bill 2967 to provide for the strengthening of the reserve forces.

1955. U.S. CONGRESS. HOUSE. COMMITTEE ON ARMED SERVICES. *National Reserve Plan.* Government Printing Office. Washington, D.C. 63 pages.

Hearings between April 18 and 26, 1955, before the House Committee on Armed Services on House bill 5297, considering establishment of the National Reserve Plan.

1955. U.S. CONGRESS. HOUSE. COMMITTEE ON ARMED SERVICES. *Reserve Forces.* Government Printing Office. Washington, D.C. 82 pages.

Hearings between June 22 and 27, 1955, before Subcommittee No. 1 of the House Committee on Armed Services on House bills 6900 and 7000 to provide for the strengthening of the reserve forces.

1955. U.S. CONGRESS. SENATE. COMMITTEE ON ARMED SERVICES. *A National Reserve Plan.* Government Printing Office. Washington, D.C. 393 pages.

Hearings between July 7 and 11, 1955, before the Senate Committee on Armed Services on House bill 7000 to provide for the strengthening of the reserve forces.

1956. U.S. CONGRESS. HOUSE. COMMITTEE ON ARMED SERVICES. *Reserve Forces Act of 1955.* Government Printing Office. Washington, D.C. 115 pages.

Hearings on January 5 and 6, 1956, before the House Committee on Armed Services, reviewing progress under the Reserve Forces Act of 1955.

1956. U.S. CONGRESS. HOUSE. COMMITTEE ON ARMED SERVICES. *Review of Reserve Program.* Government Printing Office. Washington, D.C. 175 pages.

Hearings between May 2 and 4, 1956, before Subcommittee No. 1 of the House Committeee on Armed Services, reviewing the progress of the reserve program under the Reserve Forces Act of 1955.

1957. U.S. CONGRESS. HOUSE. COMMITTEE ON ARMED SERVICES. *Review of the Reserve Program.* Government Printing Office, Washington, D.C. 477 pages.

Hearings between February 4 and 21, 1957, before Subcommittee No. 1 of the House Committee on Armed Services on the implementation of the Reserve Forces Act of 1955.

1957. U.S. CONGRESS. HOUSE. COMMITTEE ON ARMED SERVICES. *Review of the Reserve Program.* Government Printing Office. Washington, D.C. 49 pages.

Hearing on May 13, 1957, before the House Committtee on Armed Services, reviewing progress under the Reserve Forces Act of 1955.

1959. U.S. CONGRESS. HOUSE. COMMITTEE ON ARMED SERVICES. *Armed Forces Reserve Act.* Government Printing Office. Washington, D.C. 56 pages.

Hearing on February 18, 1959, before Subcommittee No. 3 of the House Committee on Armed Services on House bill 3368 to extend the Special Enlistment Programs provided by Section 262 of the Armed Forces Reserve Act of 1952 as amended.

1959. U.S. CONGRESS. HOUSE. COMMITTEE ON ARMED SERVICES. *Amendments to Reserve Officers Personnel Act.* Government Printing Office. Washington, D.C. 491 pages.

Hearings between May 28 and July 9, 1959, before Subcommittee No. 3 of the House Committee on Armed Services on House bills 5083 and 7325 to amend Title 10 of the U.S. Code with respect to the procurement, promotion, and retention of reserve commissioned officers.

1960. U.S. CONGRESS. HOUSE. COMMITTEE ON ARMED SERVICES. *Review of the Reserve Program.* Government Printing Office. Washington, D.C. 343 pages.

Hearings between May 11 and 25, 1960, before Subcommittee No. 3 of the House Committee on Armed Services, reviewing the reserve forces, their objectives, and their degree of attainment of those objectives.

1960. U.S. CONGRESS. SENATE. COMMITTEE ON ARMED SERVICES. *Assistance to Civil Defense by Reserves.* Government Printing Office. Washington, D.C. 40 pages.

Hearing on June 1, 1960, before the Senate Committee on Armed Services on Senate Resolution 67 authorizing a study to determine whether the civil defense program may be furthered by assistance from the reserve components of the armed forces.

1960. U.S. CONGRESS. SENATE. COMMITTEE ON ARMED SERVICES. *Reserve Officer Incentive Act.* Government Printing Office. Washington, D.C. 47 pages.

Hearing on June 21, 1960, before the Senate Committee on Armed Services on House bill 5132 to amend Title 10 of the U.S. Code with respect to active duty agreements for reserve officers.

1961. U.S. CONGRESS. SENATE. COMMITTEE ON ARMED SERVICES. *Ready Reserves.* Government Printing Office. Washington, D.C. 63 pages.

Hearing on July 27, 1961, before the Senate Committee on Armed Services on Senate Joint Resolution 120 authorizing the President to order additional units of the Ready Reserves to active duty for 12 months.

1962. U.S. CONGRESS. HOUSE. COMMITTEE ON ARMED SERVICES. *Military Reserve Posture.* Government Printing Office. Washington, D.C. 1127 pages.

Hearings between April 16 and July 13, 1962, before Subcommittee No. 3 of the House Committee on Armed Services, reviewing mobilization policies to determine whether administrative or legislative changes are required.

1962. U.S. CONGRESS. SENATE. COMMITTEE ON ARMED SERVICES. *Ready Reserve.* Government Printing Office. Washington, D.C. 35 pages.

Hearing on September 10, 1962, before the Senate Committee on Armed Services on Senate Joint Resolution 224 authorizing the President to order units and members in the Ready Reserve to active duty for not more than 12 months.

1962. U.S. CONGRESS. HOUSE. COMMITTEE ON ARMED SERVICES. *Ready Reserve.* Government Printing Office. Washington, D.C. 45 pages.

Hearing on September 13, 1962, before the House Committee on Armed Services on House Joint Resolution 876 authorizing the President to order units and members in the Ready Reserve to active duty for not more than 12 months. Includes the testimony of Secretary of Defense Robert McNamara.

1963. U.S. CONGRESS. HOUSE. COMMITTEE ON ARMED SERVICES. *Reserve Officers' Training Corps Program.* Government Printing Office. Washington, D.C. 483 pages.

Hearings between March 6 and November 19, 1963, before Subcommittee No. 3 of the House Committee on Armed Services on (1) House bills 4427 and 4444 to amend Title 10, U.S. Code, to provide for the establishment and maintenance of a Junior ROTC program; (2) House bill 8130 to amend Title 10, U.S. Code, to provide for the establishment and maintenance of Junior and Senior ROTC programs; and (3) House bill 9124 to amend Title 10, U.S. Code, to vitalize the ROTC programs of the army, navy, and air force.

1964. U.S. CONGRESS. SENATE. COMMITTEE ON ARMED SERVICES. *ROTC Vitalization Act of 1964.* Government Printing Office. Washington, D.C. 71 pages.

Hearing on August 13, 1964, before the Senate Committee on Armed Services on House bill 9124 to amend Title 10 of the U.S. Code to vitalize the ROTC programs of the army, navy, and air force.

1965. U.S. CONGRESS. SENATE. COMMITTEE ON ARMED SERVICES. *Proposal to Realine the Army National Guard and the Army Reserve Forces.* 2 parts. Government Printing Office. Washington, D.C. Part 1: 342 pages. Part 2: 635 pages.

Hearings held before the Preparedness Investigating Subcommittee of the Senate Committee on Armed Services to consider a proposal to realine the Army National Guard and the Army Reserve Forces. Part 1 covers hearings between March 1 and 23, 1965; Part 2, those between March 25 and May 13, 1965.

1965. U.S. CONGRESS. HOUSE. COMMITTEE ON ARMED SERVICES. *Army Reserve Components.* Government Printing Office. Washington, D.C. 900 pages.

Hearings between March 25 and September 30, 1965, before Subcommittee No. 2 of the House Committee on Armed Services to consider the proposal to merge the Army Reserve and the Army National Guard.

1966. U.S. CONGRESS. SENATE. COMMITTEE ON ARMED SERVICES. *Personnel, Training, Equipment, and Readiness Status of Army Reserve Components.* Government Printing Office. Washington, D.C. 48 pages.

Hearing on March 23, 1966, before the Preparedness Investigating Subcommittee of the Senate Committee on Armed Services to consider the current readiness of army reserve components, plans for improving their readiness, and the proposal for merger of the Army Reserve and the Army National Guard as separate organizations within the Army Reserve Forces.

1966. U.S. CONGRESS. HOUSE. COMMITTEE ON ARMED SERVICES. *Reserve Components of the Armed Forces.* Government Printing Office. Washington, D.C. 162 pages.

Hearings between August 4 and 29, 1966, before Subcommittee No. 2 and the full House Committee on Armed Services, considering House bills 16435 and 17195 to amend Titles 10, 14, 32, and 37, U.S. Code, to strengthen the reserve components of the armed forces and to clarify the status of National Guard technicians.

1967. U.S. CONGRESS. HOUSE. COMMITTEE ON ARMED SERVICES. *Reserve Components.* Government Printing Office. Washington, D.C. 24 pages.

Hearing on February 8, 1967, before the House Committee on Armed Services on House bill 2 to amend Titles 10, 14, 32, and 37, U.S. Code, to strengthen the reserve components of the armed forces and to clarify the status of National Guard technicians.

1967. U.S. CONGRESS. SENATE. COMMITTEE ON ARMED SERVICES. *Reserve Components of the Armed Forces and National Guard Technicians.* Government Printing Office. Washington, D.C. 304 pages.

Hearings between June 26 and October 3, 1967, before the Senate Committee on Armed Services on House bill 2 to amend Titles 10, 14, 32, and 37, U.S. Code, to strengthen the reserve components of the armed forces and to clarify the status of National Guard technicians.

1968. U.S. CONGRESS. HOUSE. COMMITTEE ON ARMED SERVICES. *National Guard.* Government Printing Office. Washington, D.C. 15 pages.

Hearing on July 30, 1968, before Subcommittee No. 2 of the House Committee on Armed Services, considering Senate bill 3865 to clarify the status of National Guard technicians.

1968. U.S. CONGRESS. HOUSE. COMMITTEE ON ARMED SERVICES. *National Guard and Universal Military Training and Service Act.* Government Printing Office. Washington, D.C. 28 pages.

Hearings on July 31 and August 1, 1968, before the House Committee on Armed Services, considering (1) Senate bill 3865 to clarify the status of National Guard technicians, and (2) House bill 1093 to amend and clarify the reemployment provisions of the Universal Military Training and Service Act.

1972. U.S. CONGRESS. HOUSE. COMMITTEE ON ARMED SERVICES. *Reserve Officers' Training Corps.* Government Printing Office. Washington, D.C. 15 pages.

Hearing on January 27, 1972, before Subcommittee No. 2 of the House Committee on Armed Services, considering the Status Report on Junior and Senior ROTC programs.

CHAPTER 8

Universal National Service

> If now—and this is my idea—there were, instead of military conscription a conscription of the whole population to form for a certain number of years a part of the army enlisted against *Nature*, the injustices would tend to be evened out, and numerous other goods to the commonwealth would follow. . . . To coal and iron mines, to freight trains, to fishing fleets in December, to dishwashing, clothes-washing, and window-washing, to road-building and tunnel-making, to founderies and stoke-holes, and to the frames of skyscrapers, would our gilded youths be drafted off, according to their choice, to get the childness knocked out of them, and to come back into society with healthier sympathies and soberer. They would have paid their blood-tax.
>
> —William James, *The Moral Equivalent of War*, 1910

Books

BAILEY, L. H. *Universal Service.* 1919. Comstock Publishing Co. Ithaca, New York. 165 pages.

Calls for a program of compulsory national service in the United States. According to the proposed program, "What one is, that shall one give. Society will learn of every man and woman what these gifts may be. Some day it will be expected that every able person will report himself, at determined occasions, for definite service, without pay, in one or more of the following privileges, and other privileges, under orderly management and recognized public authority." The "privileges" include such activities as street-cleaning, construction of public halls, keeping oneself physically fit, visiting the sick, and relieving the poor. The individual has a "personal responsibility" to "be his own soldier," as necessary, in order to protect his possessions and his civil liberties.

BELLAMY, EDWARD. *Looking Backward 2000–1887*. 1888. Ticknor & Co. Boston. 470 pages.

In Bellamy's "utopia" the principle of universal compulsory military service is applied to all the citizens of the nation. The state is the sole "employer," and all citizens—by virtue of their being citizens—are compelled to become "employees" of the state. Where they work and what kind of job they hold is determined by those in positions of political power. Applying compulsion more rigorously than any modern Communist state, Bellamy sketches out a blueprint of what might be called the ultimate totalitarian state.

BULLARD, ARTHUR. *Mobilising America*. 1917. Macmillan Co. New York. 129 pages.

Chapter 5 considers the relative merits of voluntary and compulsory systems of military manpower recruiting. While "the fundamental laws of the nation have always recognized the obligation of all citizens to rally for national defence," full benefit could not be derived from a system of universal military service for at least a decade. Volunteering is seen as being more effective as an emergency measure and less disturbing to industry and national policy, provided only a relatively small army is needed. Should a large force prove necessary, universal service would be "the only democratic way to recruit it," and the author recommends contingency plans for the larger structure.

CITIZENS COMMITTEE FOR A NATIONAL WAR SERVICE ACT. *The Effort for a National Service Law in World War II 1942–1945*. 1947. Dedham, Massachusetts. 80 pages.

Report to the National Council of the Citizens Committee for a National War Service Act, by Committee Chairman Grenville Clark and Secretary Arthur L. Williston. Describes the committee's initiation of proposals for national service, involving military and industrial conscription, and the work of the committee as "the most important and constant force in keeping the subject before Congress and the public." It is concluded that "World War II was definitely and unnecessarily prolonged, at the cost of great human and material loss, primarily because of failure to achieve full mobilization of our man and woman power," which would have been possible "only under Selective Service combined with a National Service Law."

EBERLY, DONALD J. (editor). *National Service: A Report of a Conference.* 1968. Russell Sage Foundation. New York. Index. Bibliography: pages 564–596. 598 pages.

This volume comprises papers delivered at the 1967 National Service Conference in Washington, D.C. Several papers concern national service, the armed forces, and the draft, with pro and con viewpoints on compulsory military service. Included is a workshop discussion summary on national service and the military.

MARX, HERBERT L., JR. (editor). *Universal Conscription for Essential Service.* 1951. The Reference Shelf, Volume 23, Number 3. H. W. Wilson Co. New York. Bibliography: pages 168–178. 178 pages.

A pro and con discussion of universal military training and service and of universal conscription, both military and civilian, for essential service. Comprised of 37 excerpts from articles, speeches, and pamphlets by various authors.

UNGER, JAMES J., and WILLIAM M. REYNOLDS. *Second Thoughts on the Question of Manpower for National Security.* 1968. National Textbook Co. Skokie, Illinois. Bibliography: pages 135–138. 138 pages.

Developed for high-school debaters, this book deals with the issues involved in the question whether the United States should establish a system of universal compulsory service, both military and nonmilitary. The second section contains transcripts of two debates and two model affirmative cases exploring different aspects of the question.

WALCH, J. WESTON. *Complete Handbook on Compulsory National Service*, Volume 1: *The Discussion Handbook*; Volume 2: *The Debate Handbook*. 1968. J. Weston Walch. Portland, Maine. Volume 1: Index. Charts, tables. Bibliographies. 224 pages. Volume 2: Index. Charts. Bibliographies. 212 pages.

In Volume 1, Part I considers the type of military manpower policy needed for the security and social welfare of the United States and discusses the history of compulsory military service in the United States and abroad. Part II looks at the Selective Service System, examining proposals for its improvement and including an annotated bibliography. Part III deals with policy toward an individual's refusal to be inducted for military service, discusses the history of the conscientious-objector policy, and provides an annotated bibliography. The final chapter offers a "Who's Who" on compulsory national service. In Volume 2, Part I considers the resolution "that the United States should establish a system of compulsory service for all citizens," discussing the roots of national service and presenting a sample plan and an annotated bibliography. Part II treats the resolution "that the United States should establish a lottery system of national conscription," analyzing the lottery topic and providing a bibliography on the lottery plan. Part III deals with the resolution "that all military service for the United States today should be voluntary except in time of declared war," and presents a discussion and a bibliography on voluntary military service.

WALTON, GEORGE. *Let's End the Draft Mess.* 1967. David McKay Co. New York. Index. Graphs, charts, tables. 171 pages.

The author sees military conscription as necessary in the United States in the future but contends that the draft process must be modernized and "democratized" by the institution of "true universality." He recommends a compulsory universal service system under which "all able young men (and, very possibly, young women) would be required to give two years of service to the nation," either military or civilian.

WISE, JENNINGS C. *The Call of the Republic: A National Army and Universal Military Service.* 1917. E. P. Dutton & Co. New York. Bibliography: pages 139–141. 141 pages.

A case for universal military training and service, this book attempts to illuminate the "illogical retention by the American people of the mercenary system in the mistaken belief that universal compulsory service is an undemocratic institution" and to show that, historically, the reverse holds true and that universal compulsory military service accords with the system of citizen soldiery favored by the Bill of Rights. Because social and economic change eliminated the militia system and engendered a deterioration of civilians in military capacity, "government must do that which nature formerly did." The author urges adoption of "that system of defense which has been universally adopted as best, except by the

United States," by annual peacetime drafts under a new constitutional law.

Articles

BOURNE, RANDOLPH. *A Moral Equivalent for Universal Military Service.*
The New Republic. July 1, 1916. Volume VII, Number 87. Pages
217–219.

Suggests that the public-school system in the United States is "the one
universally national, compulsory service which we possess or are ever likely
to consent to" and that education is the only form of "conscription" to
which Americans would ever have given their consent. To introduce compulsory military service in the United States, therefore, would require
decades of Napoleonic political evangelism." Bourne charges that "military
service is a sham universality" inasmuch as "it omits the feminine half of
the nation's youth" while "of the masculine half it uses only the physically
best." Criticizing William James's "thought of turning his army of youth
into the drudgery of the world, where they might win in heroic toil and
self-sacrifice the moral rewards which war had formerly given," Bourne
advocates an educational "national service" that could include military
training, rather than a universal military service that "is neither universal
nor educational nor productive."

BRECKINRIDGE, HENRY B. *Universal Service as the Basis of National
Unity and National Defense.* Proceedings of the Academy of Political
Science. July 1916. Volume 6, Number 4. Pages 12–17.

Considers universal service as "the best foundation for national defense"
and "the most powerful agency for effecting the national unity." Asserts
that "universal military service is essential to the safety of America and the
integrity of its policies, that it is morally just, and that it impairs not one
iota the ideals of Democracy."

CULLINAN, TERRENCE. *National Service Programs Abroad.* Current History. August 1968. Volume 55, Number 324. Pages 97–102, 110–111.

Surveying national service programs in 91 countries, the author contends that national service "appears to be a rapidly growing phenomenon
internationally," with a 25 percent growth during 1967 alone. He notes:

"The success of the United States Peace Corps has seen inauguration of Peace Corps–style programs in other countries. Three—Italy, West Germany, and the Netherlands—now give exemption from military obligation to those who have successfully completed a tour of duty in their 'Peace Corps.' "

EBERLY, DONALD J. *National Needs and National Service.* Current History. August 1968. Volume 55, Number 324. Pages 65–71.

Advocates a program of national service embracing both military and nonmilitary service. Such a program, it is claimed, "would help to balance the equation between society's needs and resources."

FULLER, J. F. C. *Conscription Pros and Cons.* The Spectator. June 24, 1938. Volume 160, Number 5739. Pages 1138–1139.

Proposes three separate forms of national service: (1) for boys and girls, (2) for men, and (3) for women. Under these schemes individuals would be conscripted for military and other service according to peacetime or wartime needs.

GLICK, EDWARD BERNARD. *The Draft and Nonmilitary National Service.* Military Review. December 1969. Volume XLIX, Number 12. Pages 86–90.

Reviews currently proposed alternatives to the draft system in the United States. Suggests that "what is needed is the inclusion of military service within the larger framework of national service that includes nonmilitary and noncombat tasks at home and abroad. If this were coupled with a selection system that was both more equally applied and nationally useful, much would be done to lessen the draft's injustices and simultaneously meet contemporary social needs within our country."

HALL, EDWARD F. *National Service and the American Tradition.* Current History. August 1968. Volume 55, Number 324. Pages 72–77, 110.

Tracing the history of America's tradition of service, this writer says: "Just as the townspeople of the Massachusetts Colony found in 1647 that 'universal education of youth is essential to the well-being of the state,' so universal compulsory national service would be a further step in education for the good life of tomorrow's world."

HUDDLE, FRANK P. *Universal Service*. Editorial Research Reports. April 15, 1944. Volume 1, Number 15. Pages 265–281.

Discussing the issues relating to proposals for universal military service before Congress, the author analyzes the movement for peacetime conscription, looks at peacetime conscription in other nations, and touches on the military and nonmilitary ramifications of such a program. He opposes the program on the basis that "taken by itself, [it] is neither a guarantee against aggression nor an assurance of an efficient military force." He further argues that if the United States were successful in establishing a highly efficient military force, this might lead to unfriendly relations with other nations and to an imperialistic foreign policy.

JACKSON, JOHN P. *A Plea for Universal Service*. United States Naval Institute Proceedings. February 1917. Volume 43, Number 2. Pages 295–311.

Attempts to show that (1) the United States needs a large army or a trained force that can be formed at short notice into an army, (2) the present system is inadequate to the nation's needs, (3) universal service is the best way of acquiring a trained force, and (4) universal service, aside from military considerations, would be beneficial "to the individual and to the race."

JANOWITZ, MORRIS. *American Democracy and Military Service*. Transaction. March 1967. Volume 4, Number 4. Pages 5–11, 57–59.

Examines some of the social-class and demographic factors involved in the impact of the Selective Service System. Proposes an alternative form of "national service in which most young men of draft age serve the country either in the armed forces or in other national programs." This system is held to be "more compatible with the needs and goals of a political democracy."

JANOWITZ, MORRIS. *The Case for a National Service System*. The Public Interest. Fall 1966. Number 5. Pages 90–109.

Presents arguments in favor of a national service system in which young people would be required to serve the nation for a period of one or two years in governmental or nongovernmental programs. Such national service "would be based on the widest degree of voluntary choice; but to insure military needs, selective service would have priority and would rely on a lottery."

KNOEPPEL, C. E. *Compulsory Training and Industrial Preparedness.* Proceedings of the Academy of Political Science. July 1916. Volume 6, Number 4. Pages 40–49.

An appeal for national unity based on "standardization" as opposed to "individualism" to "prepare industrially as well as in a military sense to lead the world." Knoeppel takes the position that "compulsory service ceases to be compulsory when there is a willingness to serve. Our problem is, therefore, to determine how to induce this willingness."

MEAD, MARGARET. *The Case for Compulsory National Service.* Current History. August 1968. Volume 55, Number 324. Pages 84–85, 106–107.

Suggests that "a national service in which all . . . participated would make a tremendous contribution to citizen-knowledge of the country and citizen-participation in the benefits of our increasingly affluent but inequitable society."

SANDERS, MARION K. *The Case for a National Service Corps.* New York Times Magazine. August 7, 1966. Pages 16–17, 73–78, 80.

Considers a "National Service Corps" as an alternative to the existing Selective Service System. Discussed are possible forms such a corps might take, suggested areas of service, and whether the corps should be voluntary or compulsory. Similar institutions in other countries are examined. Specific recommendations are made, including the expansion of existing organizations such as the Peace Corps, Vista, the Teachers Corps, and the Job Corps.

TAX, SOL. *Society, the Individual and National Service.* Current History. August 1968. Volume 55, Number 324. Pages 78–83, 109.

Presents a voluntary National Service Model that "would include all people, of both sexes and all ages," and "integrate and personalize our society at any level—neighborhood, city, region, nation." The model suggests ways to assure that the system would change with the times and in response to individual needs and desires. Military service would be included in this system, "the soldier's points for 'service' supplementing his pay."

VELVEL, LAWRENCE R. *Economic Service Abroad and the Draft.* The Midwest Quarterly. January 1967. Volume VIII, Number 2. Pages 115–126.

Proposes that draft-liable men be permitted to "volunteer" for economic service abroad as a substitute for compulsory military service. It is reasoned that such service abroad would aid world economic prosperity and peace while alleviating the problem of a surplus of draft-liable men.

Pamphlets, Reprints, and Speeches

CITIZENS COMMITTEE FOR A NATIONAL WAR SERVICE ACT. [Unlisted material] (Hoover Institution Collection). 1943–1944. New York.

Collections of several letters and pamphlets issued by the committee in support of the Austin–Wadsworth national war service bill to "provide further for the successful prosecution of the war through a system of civilian selective war service with the aid of the Selective Service System" and for the "comprehensive, orderly, and effective mobilization of the manpower and womanpower of the Nation in support of the war effort."

EBERLY, DONALD J. (editor). *A Profile of National Service.* 1966. Overseas Educational Service. New York. Index. 60 pages.

Papers and findings of the National Service Conference convened in New York in May 1966. Includes a discussion of the relationship of military service obligations to the concept of national service.

NASMYTH, GEORGE. *Universal Military Service and Democracy.* Reprint from Journal of Race Development. October 1916. 14 pages.

A short treatise on the incompatibility of conscription and democracy. Contends that New York laws providing for military training in the high school and for universal military service for men between 18 and 21, together with the National Defense Act of July 1916, have established conscription as a legal principle "without adequate discussion and without complete understanding on the part of the people on the issues involved." The author proposes "an army of social service" in which "useful and productive work" in reforestation, irrigation, and highway construction, coupled with adequate compensation, would avert the need for conscription.

CHAPTER 9

Economics

> The first duty of the sovereign, that of protecting the society from the violence and invasion of other independent societies, can be performed only by means of a military force. But the expense both of preparing this military force in time of peace, and of employing it in time of war, is very different in the different states of society, in the different periods of improvement.
>
> —Adam Smith, *An Inquiry into the Nature and Causes of the Wealth of Nations,* 1776

Books

BECKER, GARY S. *Human Capital: A Theoretical and Empirical Analysis, with Special Reference to Education.* 1964. National Bureau of Economic Research. New York. Index. Tables. 187 pages.

This study is concerned with the economic effects of education and other investments in human capital that "improve skills, knowledge, or health, and thereby raise money or psychic incomes." Underlying the contemporary efforts to improve measures of physical capital and increase the knowledge of less tangible related entities are such factors as "the strong dependence of modern military technology on education and skills, the rapid growth in expenditures on education and health, the age-old quest for an understanding of the personal distribution of income, the recent growth in unemployment in the United States, the Leontief scarce-factor paradox, and several other important economic problems." The empirical analysis measures rates of return from college and high-school education, and discusses private money gains, social productivity gains, and trends over time.

BUCHANAN, JAMES M., and ROBERT D. TOLLISON (editors). *Theory of Public Choice: Political Applications of Economics.* 1972. University of Michigan Press. Ann Arbor, Michigan. 329 pages.

Of particular interest are Richard E. Wagner's "Conscription, Voluntary Service, and Democratic Fiscal Choice" (pages 136–152) and Robert D. Tollison's "The Political Economy of the Military Draft" (pages 302–314). Wagner examines the impact of fiscal institutions on the budgetary patterns that emerge through democratic processes of fiscal choice, contrasting conscription and voluntary service with respect to the choice of (1) size of the military budget, (2) output mix within the public budget, and (3) degree of militancy in military foreign policy. Tollison analyzes the military draft from the standpoint of the theoretical integration of tax and expenditure processes and the political origin of fiscal institutions, including development of a model that "explains in a very simplistic way the political origin and stability of a military draft in a democratic setting."

CANBY, STEVEN L., and B. P. KLOTZ. *The Budget Cost of a Volunteer Military.* 1970. The Rand Corporation. Santa Monica, California. Figures, tables. Bibliography: page 97. 97 pages.

Finds that the added cost to the 1970 federal budget of a volunteer military is between $2.1 and $2.5 billion. The largest cost increases are caused by higher retention rates, which in turn cause higher seniority and retirement costs that become manifest only in the long run. The authors' cost estimate, based on ten different factors, is considerably lower than several previous estimates made by others.

ENKE, STEPHEN (editor). *Defense Management.* 1967. Prentice-Hall. Englewood Cliffs, New Jersey. 385 pages.

Of particular interest is the study by Harry J. Gilman, "Military Manpower Utilization" (pages 246–266), which evaluates the impact of institutional or budgetary constraints on military manpower utilization. Gilman finds that "at least three factors are unique to the military establishment: (1) no other sector can acquire part of its manpower at below market clearing prices (the draft); (2) no other sector demands that its personnel enter almost exclusively at the bottom rung of a highly structured promotion ladder; and (3) no other sector, including the Soviet military establishment, has a compensation system that is as paternalistic and egalitarian as the U.S. military system."

Economics

FECHTER, ALAN E. *The Supply of First-Term Military Officers.* 1967. Institute for Defense Analysis. Arlington, Virginia. Figures, tables. 116 pages.

Prepared for the Office of the Assistant Secretary of Defense (Manpower). This study examines the effects of population trends, military conscription, and pay on the supply of newly commissioned officers and, based on these factors, estimates the additional budgetary costs that would be incurred by the Department of Defense in eliminating the draft as a source of officer procurement. Fechter reviews current trends and patterns of officer procurement; discusses the factors thought to be important determinants of officer supply—eligible population, the draft, and earnings opportunities for potential officers in military and nonmilitary careers; estimates the effect of population trends on the supply of newly commissioned officers; examines the effects of military conscription; investigates the effects on officer supply of military and nonmilitary earnings opportunities; and presents an illustrative example of how the findings may be used to estimate the cost of shifting to an all-volunteer officer force.

HITCH, CHARLES J., and ROLAND N. McKEAN. *The Economics of Defense in the Nuclear Age.* 1960. Harvard University Press. Cambridge, Massachusetts. Index. Figures, tables. Bibliography: pages 407–418. 422 pages.

With contributions by Stephen Enke, Alain Enthoven, Malcolm W. Hoag, C. B. McGuire, and Albert Wohstetter. An examination of the resources available for defense, efficiency in using defense resources, and special problems and applications. Chapter 17 discusses mobilization, civil defense, and recuperation, and finds that "the nation has been devoting several billion dollars a year to preparations for an outmoded kind of mobilization [as used in less limited wars such as World War II]. These preparations constitute insurance against the kind of war that is least likely to occur and in which the United States would have an advantage anyway." It is recommended that the nation prepare for rapid mobilization for limited wars, since experience in recent years suggests that prompt deployment of both regular forces-in-being and reserve forces will become increasingly vital to national security.

LEE, DWIGHT R., and ROBERT F. McNOWN. *Economics in Our Time:*

Concepts and Issues. 1975. Science Research Associates, Inc. Chicago. 213 pages.

In Chapter 10, "Markets and Mythology" the authors discuss the high cost of the military draft. They contend that an all-volunteer force is not more costly than a system with conscription: "Manpower costs are not less under the draft, they are simply shifted onto one particular group, namely the draftees."

NORTH, DOUGLASS C., and ROGER L. MILLER. *The Economics of Public Issues.* 1971. Harper & Row. New York. Index. 158 pages.

Includes a brief discussion (Chapter 11) on "The Economics of the Draft vs. an All-Volunteer Army."

SILBERNER, EDMUND. *The Problems of War in Nineteenth Century Economic Thought.* 1946. Princeton University Press. Princeton, New Jersey. Index. Bibliography: pages 299–324. 332 pages.

Translated by Alexander H. Krappe. Of particular interest is Chapter 10, which discusses the views of two 19th century political economists, Wilhelm Roscher and Karl Knies. The author notes that Knies, while favoring a system of compulsory military service and standing armies, "in his critical observations on the system of conscription . . . suggests that the State should fully compensate each soldier for the material loss he incurs by military service."

SMITH, ADAM. *An Inquiry into the Nature and Causes of the Wealth of Nations.* 2 volumes. 1776. Printed for W. Strahan and T. Cadell. London. 1097 pages.

In Book V, Chapter 2, Part I, entitled "Of the Expence of Defence" (pages 291–313), Smith discusses methods of providing for defense as society advances. Claiming that history shows the superiority of the standing army over a militia, he avers: "It is only by means of a standing army, therefore, that the civilization of any country can be perpetuated, or even preserved for any considerable time."

WEIDENBAUM, MURRAY L. *The Economics of Peacetime Defense.* 1974. Praeger Publishers. New York. Index. Figures, tables. Bibliography at end of each chapter. 193 pages.

In Chapter 7, "The Military as an Employer," the author considers the question of an all-volunteer military force. Noting that direct personnel costs of the uniformed and civilian employees of the Department of Defense "have come, in just the last few years, to dominate the military budget," Weidenbaum attributes this trend to the long-term trend of increased specialization and skill required, and to the more recent cost of shifting to a volunteer armed force—that is, the cost of making a military career more attractive. "While the 'grade creep' (higher average officer and enlisted grades) has accounted for close to 20 percent of the increase in the average cost of individual military personnel since 1968, the most substantial increases in military manpower costs during the last few years have resulted from the generous pay raises the Congress has voted, partly because of its desire to reduce the military's dependence on the draft." The movement to a volunteer armed force, in this view, only exacerbates the existing economic and financial pressures on the military budget. "We should expect, however," Weidenbaum acknowledges, "that the effectiveness of a voluntary, well-motivated military force will be considerably higher than at present, thus permitting some further reductions in the number of men under arms."

Unpublished Manuscripts

ARBOGAST, KATE AVERY. *The Procurement of Women for the Armed Forces: An Analysis of Occupational Choice.* 1974. Ph.D. dissertation. The George Washington University. Washington, D.C. Bibliography: pages 257–266. 266 pages.

Discusses the use of womanpower as a military resource and personnel alternative under a voluntary military system. The author develops a model for the female decision to enlist, stating that because women have a noncareer occupational alternative (housewifery), the investment approach to occupational choice is not an adequate one. She postulates that choices are made on the basis of utility maximization—the maximization of the net advantage of a given occupation—and examines the supply of and demand for enlisted military female personnel, focusing on the navy.

FISHER, ANTHONY CLINTON. *The Supply of Enlisted Volunteers for Military Service.* 1968. Ph.D. dissertation. Columbia University. New York. 81 pages.

The first part of this study builds a model for the supply of volunteers for military service. The supply of volunteers as a proportion of the population—i.e., the enlistment rate—is determined by the level of military earnings with respect to the distributions of civilian earnings and tastes for military service. An equation relating the enlistment rate to military and civilian earnings, to the unemployment rate, and to a measure of the effect of the draft is derived from the model. The second part of the study presents and discusses results of ordinary least-squares regression estimation of the parameters of the equation. The estimated relations between earnings and enlistments, on the one hand, and the draft and enlistments on the other, are used to calculate the money cost of ending the draft to the Department of Defense and the general taxpayer.

FITZGERALD, BRUCE DAVID. *Voluntarism, Conscription and the Likelihood of War.* 1974. Ph.D. dissertation. Duke University. Durham, North Carolina. Bibliography: pages 201–208. 210 pages.

Discusses the public-choice implications of alternative means of raising an army. Fitzgerald finds a direct relationship between levels of defense spending and the likelihood of war. Moreover, he concludes that, under conscription, higher levels of armed forces will be maintained and the probability of a declaration of war will thus be greater.

HAMER, THOMAS PHILIP. *The Labor Cost of an All-Volunteer Armed Force: A Comparative Analysis Based on Police Wages and Occupational Earnings.* 1975. Ph.D. dissertation. Claremont Graduate School. Claremont, California. Bibliography: pages 198–217. 217 pages.

Evaluates whether military compensation for the fiscal year 1974 is sufficient to maintain an adequate level of armed forces in a system of voluntary procurement. Discusses the conditions necessary for a volunteer army to be the optimal means of manpower procurement. Hamer uses the economic theory of occupational choice, comparing military to civilian pay and estimating the annual compensation needed to meet manpower goals. He concludes that enlistment under a voluntary system will fall short of 1974 goals and that enlistment bonuses rather than higher wages should be used to attract recruits.

KNAPP, CHARLES BOYNTON. *A Human Capital Approach to the Burden of the Military Draft.* 1972. Ph.D. dissertation. University of Wisconsin. Madison, Wisconsin. Bibliography: pages 117–118. 127 pages.

Seeks to estimate the size of the human capital burden produced by the present military draft and the size of that which would be produced under alternative manpower procurement schemes. A model representing conscription as a disinvestment in human capital is constructed. The model allows the representation of two measures of the draft's impact on human capital: (1) the change in present value due to induction or equivalently the human capital burden of the drafts, and (2) the internal rate of return to income foregone while in the service. Two hypotheses are tested concerning the impact of the draft on future incomes.

PISCIOTTOLI, LOUIS FRANCIS. *Allocational and Distributional Effects of Conscription.* 1972. Ph.D. dissertation. Duke University. Durham, North Carolina. Bibliography: pages 132–139. 139 pages.

Deals with the impact of military conscription on the efficiency of resource allocation and on the equitable division of tax burdens. It is hypothesized that military conscription is a tax with significant allocational and distributional effects. The author examines (1) the effect of conscription on the efficiency of resource allocation and (2) methods of evasion and avoidance of the conscription tax. Estimates are made of the extent of resource misallocation in the Civil War, in the two world wars, and in the year before the Vietnam buildup, the extent of output loss being found to vary according to deferment patterns and the difference between military and relevant civilian pay. Given the size and nature of the tax burdens and output loss thus discovered, the hypothesis that conscription was responsible for significant allocational and distributional effects cannot be rejected.

SHEPARD, JAMES. *A Multiple Linear Correlation Analysis of Certain Variables and Their Relationship to Military Reenlistment and Retention Rates.* 1965. Ph.D. dissertation. St. Louis University. St. Louis, Missouri. Bibliography: pages 192–194. 204 pages.

Attempts to identify, in order of reenlistment-rate responsiveness, the best criteria on which to base the military compensation system. Inductive statistics are used to support the hypothesis of a causal relationship between different economic variables and historical reenlistment rates. From the statistically derived conclusions, it is generalized that an individual's selection of a career is influenced by economic variables that may be grouped in a hierarchical order according to their roles.

TOLLISON, ROBERT D. *An Analysis of the Taxation and Collective Choice Aspects of the Military Draft.* 1969. Ph.D. dissertation. University of Virginia. Charlottesville, Virginia. Figures, tables. Bibliography: pages 145–149. 149 pages.

An investigation of the military draft in the United States, based on its being (1) a taxation device that effectively taxes draft-affected individuals by the amount of income they are forced to forego in the process, and (2) a transfer mechanism through which the taxpaying public is subsidized through lower budgetary outlays for military manpower. Empirical data lead to conclusions concerning the magnitude and character of the tax-subsidy effects of conscription, bureaucratic and voter behavior in support of the draft, and draft reform prospects.

WICKS, ELLIOT KUNDERT. *The Economics of Military Conscription and Its Alternatives.* 1971. Ph.D. dissertation. Syracuse University. Syracuse, New York. Figures, tables. Bibliography: pages 227–230. 230 pages.

Assesses alternative methods of procuring military manpower, examining the economic and, to a lesser extent, the social consequences and costs of each alternative. An economic analysis of military conscription as a form of taxation is followed by an estimate of the economic costs that a switch to an all-volunteer force would entail. The author then provides a detailed analysis of the two principal alternatives to military conscription—universal national service and an all-volunteer force—and considers the economic, military, and social arguments for and against each alternative.

WILBURN, ROBERT CHARLES. *The Supply of Military Manpower: The Impact of Income, the Draft and Other Factors on the Retention of Air Force Enlisted Men.* 1970. Ph.D. dissertation. Princeton University. Princeton, New Jersey. Bibliography: pages 158–162. 164 pages.

Seeks primarily to measure the impact of changes in military compensation and of civilian alternative income on the enlisted man's decision to pursue a military career. Because of the role of the draft in the initial enlistment decision, reenlistment is the first truly voluntary choice; and reenlistment is considered to be the point at which a career decision is made. The impact of the draft at enlistment on the ultimate career decision is also estimated. In addition, differences by race, mental ability, education, and service occupation are investigated.

Articles

ALTMAN, STUART H. *Earnings, Unemployment, and the Supply of Enlisted Volunteers.* The Journal of Human Resources. Winter 1969. Volume 4, Number 1. Pages 38–59.

Measures the likely impact on potential new enlistments of raising military pay by estimating the extent to which regional enlistments have varied in relation to relative military-to-civilian earnings. Concludes that volunteers could be attracted to active duty by raising military pay, but that the larger the proportion of the eligible population in military service, the more expensive it would become to recruit additional manpower.

ALTMAN, STUART H., and ROBERT J. BARRO. *Officer Supply—The Impact of Pay, the Draft, and the Vietnam War.* American Economic Review. September 1971. Volume 61, Number 4. Pages 649–664.

The authors develop a model to estimate a labor supply function of military officers. They consider: (1) the extent to which officer supply is positively related to military earnings, (2) whether a premium has to be paid to the average civilian to volunteer for the officer corps, and if so, how large a premium, (3) the effect of the Vietnam War on enlistments, and (4) the impact of the changed probability of being drafted on potential officer supply.

ALTMAN, STUART H., and ALAN E. FECHTER. *The Supply of Military Personnel in the Absence of a Draft.* American Economic Review. May 1967. Volume 57, Number 2. Pages 19–31.

This article reports on a Department of Defense review estimating the budgetary costs of shifting to an all-volunteer military manpower procurement system. It notes that "the higher budgetary costs of an all-volunteer force reflect, in part, the income transfer that will occur between inductees and involuntary recruits, who are now bearing some of these additional costs implicitly, and the taxpayer, who will be required to bear these costs explicitly when we achieve an all-volunteer force."

BAILEY, DUNCAN, and THOMAS F. CARGILL. *The Military Draft and Future Income.* Western Economic Journal. December 1969. Volume 7, Number 4. Pages 365–370.

The authors contend that an analysis of how the draft affects the time stream of income rather than income sacrificed at a particular time is required to properly determine the rate of tax implied by the draft system. Empirical data are employed to obtain a realistic measure of the implicit tax rate imposed by the military draft on the two most important education-income groups affected: high-school graduates and college students.

BERNEY, ROBERT E. *The Incidence of the Draft—Is It Progressive?* Western Economic Journal. September 1969. Volume 7, Number 3. Pages 244–247.

Seeks to show that under certain definitions of progressivity, the incidence of the draft is not distributed in a progressive manner. Progression refers to the increasing share of income absorbed by taxes, as income, or other measures of ability to pay, grow. Data analysis reveals that the draft is not progressive throughout all income brackets since the numbers being drafted in the high-income brackets are smaller than those in middle-income brackets. Similarly, if one approaches progressivity from an individualistic point of view but discounts the tax burden by the probability of being drafted, the burden is no longer found to be progressive in the upper-income ranges.

BORCHERDING, THOMAS E. *Bureaucracy and the Welfare Consequences of Conscription and Voluntarism.* Western Economic Journal. September 1972. Volume 10, Number 3. Pages 356–357.

The author cites his article "A Neglected Social Cost of a Voluntary Military" (see next entry), which argues that "instituting a voluntary military force would not, distributional consequences aside, necessarily improve resource allocation." He discusses William Niskanen's book *Bureaucracy and Representative Government*, which maintains that bureaus are not passive equivalents to competitive firms but embody substantial monopoly power that they exercise in their self-interest by being budget maximizers. Borcherding states the conditions necessary for voluntarism to become the socially preferred mechanism of military manpower procurement, and recommends further study in assessing the monopoly power of bureaus in order to develop more general theories about their behavior.

BORCHERDING, THOMAS E. *A Neglected Social Cost of a Voluntary Military*. American Economic Review. March 1971. Volume 61, Number 1. Pages 195–196.

An economic analysis attempting to demonstrate that a "potentially important welfare cost may arise under voluntarism from the monopsonistic behavior of the defense establishment as a purchaser of enlisted personnel."

BRADFORD, DAVID F. *A Model of the Enlistment Decision Under Draft Uncertainty*. Quarterly Journal of Economics. November 1965. Volume 82, Number 4. Pages 621–638.

Presents a mathematical model of the environment of "draft uncertainty" confronting an individual subject to possible induction, and derives rules for his optimal behavior under the assumption that his objective can be properly represented as the maximization of the expected value of a utility function. A model is developed relating to problems of choice under uncertainty, particularly problems of sequential decision in career choice.

BULLOCK, CHARLES J. *Adam Smith's Views upon National Defence*. The Military Historian and Economist. July 1916. Volume 1, Number 3. Pages 249–257.

Examining Adam Smith's *Wealth of Nations*, Bullock finds that Smith did not intend to oppose military training for the people at large, or any other means of combating such a "loathsome and offensive disease" as the decay of military virtue. Smith is said to have considered such training as good in itself, as a part of the citizen's ordinary education; if it was effective in preserving the martial spirit of the people, it would enable a state to get along with a smaller standing army than would otherwise be necessary. The idea that Smith combated "was that by a militia system, a standing army could be dispensed with." (See Smith, page 264, above.)

CLARK, ROLF H., and ROBERT A. COMERFORD. *Manpower Planning and Resource Allocation in Defense: Some Issues*. Naval War College Review. March–April 1975. Volume XXVII, Number 5. Pages 32–42.

Examines four aspects of manpower planning and resource allocations: (1) manpower costing, (2) supply-demand dynamics, (3) capital-labor trade-offs, and (4) discounting. Includes discussion of available quantitative techniques whose implementation could help prevent misallocations.

CLATANOFF, WILLIAM B., JR. *The Role of the Armed Forces.* Current History. July 1968. Volume 55, Number 323. Pages 13–17, 52.

The author discusses the alleged monetary waste involved in military conscription. He notes that the more intensively the armed forces train a recruit, the more valuable he becomes within the service. Since the trained man can command higher wages in the civilian sector, however, retention rates in the armed forces are lowest among the highly skilled and semi-professionals.

CORTRIGHT, DAVID. *Economic Conscription.* Society. May–June 1975. Volume 12, Number 4. Pages 43–47.

Suggests that the establishment of the all-volunteer armed force in the United States has brought about "economic conscription" because, "while the overt compulsion of conscription may be absent, economic impressment is not voluntary." Cortright examines "the workings of the recruitment system and its disturbing impact on society" in a climate of economic slump and high unemployment. Ultimately, he contends, "what is most disturbing about the all-volunteer force is the fact that because young people have so few opportunities in civilian life, they must turn to the military for jobs and training. . . . When preparation for war is the principal source of economic security and job training, our national life has become dangerously militarized." While no alternatives are offered, the author seems to object mainly to the fact that "the market has replaced government directive."

DAVIS, J. RONNIE, and NEIL A. PALOMBA. *On the Shifting of the Military Draft as a Progressive Tax-in-Kind.* Western Economic Journal. March 1968. Volume 6, Number 2. Pages 150–153.

The authors find that although the military draft tax rate structure is markedly progressive, its progressivity is seriously tempered by the fact that it is not a general tax. The lack of generality of the military tax-in-kind is attributed to opportunities to shift the burden of the draft, the two major modifications of behavior that allowed part or all of the military burden to be shifted being identified as college and parenthood.

EPPS, THOMAS W. *An Econometric Analysis of the Effectiveness of the U.S. Army's 1971 Paid Advertising Campaign.* Applied Economics. 1973. Number 5. Pages 261–269.

The findings of this study "suggest that non-prior-service, male enlistments in the summer following the Army's 1971 prime-time advertising campaign were indeed higher than indicated by seasonality and the behaviour of economic forces and other policy instruments alone." Assuming accuracy of the specification of the model tested, and validity of the variable used to account for the effects of advertising, "it is reasonable to conclude that the advertising campaign contributed around 11,000 or 12,000 of a total of 60,000 enlistments in June to September, 1971."

EVANS, ROBERT, JR. *The Military Draft as a Slave System: An Economic View.* Social Science Quarterly. December 1969. Volume 50, Number 3. Pages 535–543.

Examining the draft system in analogy to a forced labor or slave system, Evans presents the necessary conditions for slavery and some of its operational characteristics, illustrates the degree to which the military draft is consistent with a slave system, and discusses some of the implications of the analysis. "The parallels between the draft and all aspects of the slave systems may not be perfect. It is sufficient if they are exact enough for this approach to heighten our understanding of the military manpower situation."

FISHER, ANTHONY C. *The Cost of the Draft and the Cost of Ending the Draft.* American Economic Review. June 1969. Volume 59, Number 3. Pages 239–254.

Compares a price system—eliminating the service obligation and letting the military services compete in the labor market for volunteers—to a draft system. Finds that "given the projected values for enlistments, population, earnings and unemployment, the additional money cost to the Department of Defense of an all-volunteer force would not be more than five to seven and a half billion dollars annually." Moreover "a more economical use of resources by the military, and a reduction in their training costs, both implied in a volunteer system, would reduce the projected tax increase. Increased output and earnings in the civilian sector, also implied in a volunteer system, would benefit some young men directly (the increased earnings), and the general taxpayer indirectly, through tax revenues generated by the increased earnings."

FISHER, ANTHONY C. *The Cost of Ending the Draft: Reply.* American Economic Review. December 1970. Volume 60, Number 5. Pages 979–983.

A reply to Benjamin Klotz's "The Cost of Ending the Draft: Comment" (see below, page 275), regarding previous work done by Fisher on the cost of ending the draft and the economic models used to estimate this figure. Fisher indicates on what points he is in agreement and in disagreement with Klotz, discusses the economic models each uses, and contrasts the predictions these models make.

FISHER, FRANKLIN M., and ANTON S. MORTON. *Reenlistments in the U.S. Navy: A Cost Effectiveness Study.* American Economic Review. May 1967. Volume 57, Number 2. Pages 32–38.

A report on a study of the first-term reenlistment decision in connection with the navy's shortage of technically trained career enlisted men. The authors estimate the effects on the first-term reenlistment rate of a large number of possible incentives in six general classes: (1) active duty pay, (2) retirement pay, (3) educational benefits, (4) assignment, housing, and other policies, (5) other fringe benefits, and (6) promotion opportunities. The present incentive system is also analyzed. The authors find that "with existing later survival rates or pay scales, the Navy can accomplish a given mission more cheaply with a somewhat larger turnover of relatively inexperienced men than it can by encouraging those men to stay for an additional sixteen years."

HANSEN, W. LEE, and BURTON A. WEISBROD. *Economics of the Military Draft.* Quarterly Journal of Economics. August 1967. Volume 81, Number 3. Pages 395–421.

Investigates two consequences of the current military draft system: (1) distributive effects—the impact on the distribution of real output, resulting from the relatively low rate of pay to draft-affected men, and (2) allocative costs—the impact on the size of that output, resulting from the effects of the military personnel system on the efficiency with which a given level of resources is allocated among alternative uses.

HILDEBRAND, GEORGE. *Military Manpower Procurement: Discussion.* American Economic Review. May 1967. Volume LVII, Number 2. Pages 63–66.

Finds that "the present draft system is a coercive method for the procurement of real resources by the State." Not to couple selective service to payment of equivalent market wages is "to hold down the cost of the military payroll at the expense of those men in service whose transfer prices or equalizing differentials exceed their military earnings. . . . On equity grounds this tax ought to be borne by the civilian community."

KIKER, B. F., and JON BIRKELI. *Human Capital Losses Resulting from U.S. Casualties of the War in Vietnam.* Journal of Political Economy. September–October 1972. Volume 80, Number 5. Pages 1023–1030.

The authors first present a model for determining the value of human capital loss to society resulting directly from casualties in a war. They then apply U.S. casualty data from the war in Vietnam as of early 1970 to the model to obtain a range of estimates of the value of human capital loss.

KLOTZ, BENJAMIN P. *The Cost of Ending the Draft: Comment.* American Economic Review. December 1970. Volume 60, Number 5. Pages 970–978.

Discusses Anthony Fisher's article "The Cost of the Draft and the Cost of Ending the Draft" (see above, page 273), in which Fisher seeks to derive a supply curve of military volunteers from an economic theory. Contending that Fisher overestimates the cost of a volunteer military, Klotz develops his case for this view. He concludes that there is "a supply elasticity exceeding unity in the ranges necessary to stock a 2.65 million volunteer force in 1970," and that the cost of an all-volunteer military would be far below Fisher's projections.

MILLER, JAMES C., III, and ROBERT D. TOLLISON. *The Implicit Tax on Reluctant Military Recruits.* Social Science Quarterly. March 1971. Volume 51, Number 4. Pages 924–931.

After developing a model for the present value reduction in future earnings, the authors estimate the implicit tax from aggregate life-cycle income data and compare the results with estimates provided by others.

MILLER, JAMES C., III, ROBERT D. TOLLISON, and THOMAS D. WILLETT. *Marginal Criteria and Draft Deferment Policy.* Quarterly Review of Economics and Business. Summer 1968. Volume 8, Number 2. Pages 69–73.

This paper examines the inefficiency costs of a system of conscription that fails to take into account the marginal social benefit of potential conscriptees. It presents a model illustrating the trade-offs involved between alternative systems of deferment under conscription.

OI, WALTER Y. *Can We Afford the Draft?* Current History. July 1968. Volume 55, Number 323. Pages 34–39, 49.

Noting that "the budgetary cost of a professional army is nothing more than a reflection of the real cost of the draft," the author evaluates the "hidden costs" of the Selective Service and contrasts them with estimates of the cost of an all-volunteer army.

OI, WALTER Y. *The Economic Cost of the Draft.* American Economic Review. May 1967. Volume 57, Number 2. Pages 39–62.

Compares financial cost to the economy and the full economic cost of the draft for two hypothetical forces with the same active duty strength of 2.65 million men: one a purely voluntary force and the other a mixed force composed of conscripts and true and reluctant volunteers. Financial cost to the economy is defined as the value of civilian outputs that could have been produced by the labor resources that were allocated to the armed forces. The full economic cost of the draft, in contrast, acknowledges occupational preferences for military versus civilian employments. It is estimated that, with its lower personnel turnover, a voluntary force of the same size as a draft force could be sustained by recruiting only 27.5 percent of qualified males, while the budgetary payroll cost would have to be raised by $4 billion per year.

OI, WALTER Y. *The Real Costs of a Volunteer Military.* New Individualist Review. Spring 1967. Volume 4, Number 4. Pages 13–16.

A report on the costs of an all-volunteer force compared with those of the force that has evolved under the current draft law. Three separate financial costs are considered: (1) budgetary cost, (2) cost to the economy, and (3) cost to the individual military service participants. The author finds that a force strength of 2.65 million men could be achieved on a purely voluntary basis by 1970–1975 if the military pay budget were increased by approximately $4 billion.

PAULY, MARK V., and THOMAS D. WILLETT. *Two Concepts of Equity and Their Implications for Public Policy.* Social Science Quarterly. June 1972. Volume 53, Number 1. Pages 8–19.

Distinguishes two concepts of equity, "ex ante" and "ex post," in relation to military manpower procurement policy in the United States and to the problem of "determining equitably who will serve in the armed forces when not all are needed."

RENSHAW, EDWARD F. *The Economics of Conscription.* Southern Economic Journal. October 1960. Volume 27, Number 2. Pages 111–117.

Suggests that the tools of economic analysis provide a basis for clearing away some of the confusion that surrounds the increasingly controversial issue of the peacetime draft, and possibly also offer a basis for reconciling the views of individuals and groups who appear to be in opposition. Examines the welfare loss associated with random conscription expressed as a proportion of its tax value, and the substitution loss associated with conscription expressed as a proportion of the tax value of conscription.

SCHICKELE, RAINER, and GLENN EVERETT. *The Economic Implications of Universal Military Training.* The Annals of the American Academy of Political and Social Science. September 1945. Volume 241. Pages 102–112.

Attempts to describe the impact and evaluate the economic costs of the projected program of universal compulsory military training. Taken into account are such factors as the size of the armed forces, estimates of armament costs and indirect costs, and incidental benefits. "Whether or not these large additional costs are justified," the authors state, "depends upon what such a training program can add in concrete benefits to America's military potential that are not already obtained by the Nation's industrial capacity and its proposed regular armed forces."

WEINSTEIN, PAUL A. *Military Manpower Procurement: Discussion.* American Economic Review. May 1967. Volume LVII, Number 2. Pages 66–69.

Suggests that "the questions of the size and the burden of the draft's implicit tax are central to evaluating the resource implications of the current draft."

WILLETT, THOMAS D. *Another Cost of Conscription.* Western Economic Journal. December 1968. Volume 6, Number 5. Pages 425–426.

This note points out one of the possible costs of conscription that has not been considered in the literature: "This cost takes the form of additional distortions in individuals' lifetime allocation of expenditures caused by the combination of typically humped income streams and imperfect capital markets, which make it difficult for many individuals to transfer expected future purchasing power to the present."

WOOL, HAROLD. *Military Manpower Procurement: Discussion.* American Economic Review. May 1967. Volume LVII, Number 2. Pages 69–70.

"The very fact that a draft law has been necessary almost continuously since the end of World War II," says Wool, "is evidence that conventional labor market mechanisms under the existing levels of pay and incentives have been insufficient to attract a sufficient number of volunteers to military service." He believes, however, that "any single unqualified estimate of the 'cost of an all-volunteer force,' tempting though it may be, exceeds our capability at the present time."

Pamphlets, Reprints, and Speeches

AMACHER, RYAN C., and others. *The Economics of the Military Draft.* 1973. General Learning Press. Morristown, New Jersey. Bibliography: page 20. 20 pages.

This essay uses "basic economic analysis to gain insights into the draft and the related social questions raised by military manpower policy." The authors discuss the draft as a form of taxation and examine the equity aspects of the draft and the effects of alternative systems of military conscription on allocative efficiency. "In view of the inequities and inefficiencies arising from conscription," they conclude, "we find little justification for its continuance."

COOPER, RICHARD V. L. *The Social Cost of Maintaining a Military Labor Force.* 1975. The Rand Corporation. Santa Monica, California. Figures. Bibliography: pages 31–32. 32 pages plus errata.

An economic analysis of social costs under alternative manpower procurement policies. Shows that social welfare losses are possible both with and without the draft, although those associated with the draft are several times larger than those associated with a volunteer military.

ENTHOVEN, ALAIN C. *The Mathematics of Military Pay.* 1957. The Rand Corporation. Santa Monica, California. 30 pages.

Attempts to explain the mathematical theory of maximization of military effectiveness within the limitations of a fixed budget and to show that the theory has an appropriate application in the pay question.

ENTHOVEN, ALAIN C. *Supply and Demand and Military Pay.* 1957. The Rand Corporation. Santa Monica, California. 14 pages.

An analysis of the question of salary levels and differentials, from the viewpoint of the tax-paying citizens whose interests are best served by an economically or efficiently managed military establishment. Based on the criterion that salary scales should be chosen in such a way as to maximize the effectiveness of the military services, salary levels may be judged too high if more is being paid than is necessary for particular skills, and too low if not enough is being offered to attract men whose services are needed. Enthoven concludes that "when there are large differences in supply and demand in different categories, it is wasteful to pay the same salary scales across the board," as the present pay system forces the services to do.

JAQUETTE, DAVID J., and GARY R. NELSON. *The Implications of Manpower Supply and Productivity for the Pay and Composition of the Military Force: An Optimization Model.* July 1974. The Rand Corporation. Santa Monica, California. Tables, charts. Bibliography: pages 39–40. 40 pages.

In presenting a mathematical model of military manpower, the authors seek "to determine the optimal military wage rates and lengths of service under steady-state and long-run conditions" in order to ascertain the optimal distribution of the enlisted military force by years of service. The "optimal force" is defined as "that force which provides the greatest military capacity for a given budget cost." The relationship of compensation levels to enlistment and reenlistment rates is examined to determine the level that maximizes the size of the force subject to an annual budget constraint.

MCGAURR, DARCY. *Conscription and Australian Military Capability.* 1971. Canberra Papers on Strategy and Defence, Number 11. Australian National University Press. Canberra, Australia. Figures, tables. 32 pages.

Drawing heavily on the U.S. *Report of the President's Commission on an All-Volunteer Armed Force,* published in 1970 (see page 155, above), this paper deals with the cost and effectiveness of conscription as a factor in Australian military capability. It examines the supply of manpower (particularly volunteers) to the services generally. McGaurr concludes that "in terms of real or opportunity cost, conscription is the most expensive system of military manpower procurement. Under conscription, military managers allocate resources in response to a false price ratio of capital to labour and are therefore very likely to misallocate resources."

NELSON, GARY R. *An Economic Analysis of First-Term Reenlistments in the Army.* 1970. Institute for Defense Analysis. Arlington, Virginia. Figures, tables. 52 pages.

Presents a theoretical and statistical analysis of first-term reenlistments in the army. The statistical analysis provides estimates of the supply of first-term enlistments as a function of estimated earnings and the other factors. The data for the study come from the first reenlistment decision of army enlistees who entered military service in 1964. The observations consist of 300 groups of enlisted men classified by level of education, mental test score, race, and military occupational specialty. Army personnel tapes were used to estimate military pay. The Current Population Survey for 1967 and a Department of Defense survey of recent separations provided estimates of civilian earnings ability. The primary conclusions are: the reenlistment rate is strongly influenced by variations in both estimated military and estimated civilian earnings; the results indicate that a 10 percent change in the ratio of military to civilian pay may affect reenlistments by 20 to 30 percent. A very rough estimate indicates that a post-Vietnam, all-volunteer army may have 70 percent more reenlistments than the 1967 army. Reenlistment rates for whites are dramatically lower than that for black due, most likely, to difference in civilian earnings ability.

Government Documents: Publications

LIGHTMAN, ERNIE STANLEY. *The Economics of Military Manpower Supply in Canada.* 1972. National Technical Information Service, U.S.

Department of Commerce. Springfield, Virginia. Diagrams, tables. Bibliography: pages 219–224. 224 pages.

Also issued as a Ph.D. dissertation by the University of California, this study was sponsored by the Manpower Administration in the U.S. Department of Labor. It examines the supply curve of labor in a volunteer armed force, focusing on the role of economic considerations, as well as institutional, cultural, and other "taste" factors, as determinants of the net applicant rate among various cohorts of the population. The theory builds on Milton Friedman's discussion of the relative supply curve of labor to two occupations, and presents specific hypotheses that are tested for the case of Canada. Lightman basically concludes that each service functions within a unique context.

CHAPTER 10

Law and the Constitution

> I am of opinion that this Act of Congress [Conscription] is unconstitutional and void,—and confers no lawful authority on the persons appointed to execute it.
>
> —Chief Justice Roger B. Taney (1777–1864)

> It may not be doubted that the very conception of a just government and its duty to the citizen includes the reciprocal obligation of the citizen to render military service in case of need and the right to compel it.
>
> —Chief Justice Edward White (1845–1921)

Books

GRAHAM, JOHN REMINGTON. *A Constitutional History of the Military Draft.* 1971. Ross & Haines, Inc. Minneapolis, Minnesota. Bibliography: pages 136–140, 146. 147 pages.

A legal discussion dealing with first principles; the roots of the distinction between "armies" and "militia"; the Federal Convention in Philadelphia; the significance of the Second Amendment; proposals, declarations, and debates of the State Constitutional Ratification Conventions; the Knox militia plan; early statutes to "raise armies" and for "calling forth the militia"; the Framers and conscientious objection; draft proposals during the War of 1812; the draft in the North and South during the Civil War; and the constitutionality of direct federal conscription in the 20th century. The author concludes that the Supreme Court was "deeply wrong . . . in its essential premise that the Framers thought of conscription as a 'necessary and proper' means to 'raise armies,' " that the Military Service Act of 1967 is unconstitutional, and that no proposal as yet has accommodated "all practical realities connected with a military establishment."

MITCHELL, MEMORY F. *Legal Aspects of Conscription and Exemption in North Carolina 1861–1865.* 1965. University of North Carolina Press. Chapel Hill, North Carolina. Index. Bibliography: pages 92–95. 103 pages.

Based on case records of the North Carolina Supreme Court, this book examines the enactment of Confederate conscription and exemption laws as they were applied in the state, as well as contemporary judicial interpretation and legal opinions. It is noted that with the individual states' adherence to a doctrine of sovereignty, a draftee could obtain release from military authorities with relative ease, while there was little the Confederate government could do but protest. Additional legislation enacted by the Confederate Congress in 1864 to deal with this dilemma failed to significantly help the Confederate military effort.

RANDALL, JAMES G. *Constitutional Problems Under Lincoln.* 1926. D. Appleton & Co. New York. Index. Bibliography: pages 531–548. 580 pages.

Chapter 11, "Legal and Constitutional Bearings on Conscription," deals with American tradition and law regarding conscription in 1861, conscription by presidential regulation and through state authority in 1862, the conscription law of 1863, discretionary power of the President, military custody over drafted men, the use of the state militia for suppressing draft troubles, the conscientious objector, the liability of aliens under the draft, and the constitutionality of the Conscription Acts.

Unpublished Manuscripts

BALDINGER, MILTON I. *The Constitutionality and Operation of Certain Phases of the Selective Service System.* 1941. J.D. dissertation. Georgetown University. Washington, D.C. Table of authorities: pages 181–192. 192 pages.

This study discusses the historical background in raising men by conscription in the United States, analyzes the character and scope of the powers of Congress in raising an army by conscription, and considers the registration, classification, and deferment of men under the Selective Service System. Baldinger concludes that "it will not be a difficult task for the

Supreme Court of the United States to sustain conscription of men for training and service as provided in the Selective Training and Service Act of 1940, if a case comes to it." As to a permanent peacetime conscription, however, he doubts that its proponents would be successful in persuading Congress to adopt a system that is costly not only "in dollars and cents [but] also . . . in fields for which no measuring stick has as yet been evolved," such as delaying marriage, interrupting education, and cutting the birth rate.

MARKHAM, WALTER GRAY. *Draft Offenders in the Federal Courts: A Search for the Social Correlation of Justice.* 1972. Ph.D. dissertation. University of Pennsylvania. Philadelphia, Pennsylvania. 276 pages.

Attempts to measure the influences of environment on judicial behavior and to seek the social correlates of the distribution of justice. Five groups of indicators—legal-structural, demographic, draft administration, education, and economic-social—are analyzed, supporting the general theory that "the prevailing notion of justice, as it is measured by the punitive dispositions of judges in criminal cases, is shaped by the general level of culture."

Articles

BELL, ROBERT C. *Selective Service and the Courts.* American Bar Association Journal. March 1942. Volume 28. Pages 164–167.

Discusses legal decisions in regard to habeas corpus. States that the U.S. government historically has been "exceedingly generous" in its treatment of the manpower within its jurisdiction "when it is remembered that Congress, under the Constitution, has plenary and exclusive power 'to raise and support armies,' that this power is not limited to accepting voluntary enlistments but includes the power to exact and enforce military duty, and that Congress can determine how the army shall be raised, the period of service, the age at which the soldier shall be inducted, the compensation he may receive and the service to which he shall be assigned."

BERNSTEIN, J. L. *Conscription and the Constitution: The Amazing Case of Kneedler v. Lane.* American Bar Association Journal. August 1967. Volume 53. Pages 708–712.

Reviews the constitutional basis for military conscription as interpreted by the Pennsylvania Supreme Court in 1863. The court, "the only one in the country to consider at length the legality of the first military draft in the United States," ruled the draft unconstitutional in the *Kneedler* v. *Lane* case in November 1863. This decision was subsequently reversed.

BLACK, FORREST R. *The Selective Draft Cases—A Judicial Milepost on the Road to Absolutism.* Boston University Law Review. 1931. Volume 11. Pages 37–53.

A critical examination of the Supreme Court decision (245 U.S. 266) that upheld the use of conscription for foreign service. Attempts to show that "the Constitution is ambiguous as it relates to the respective powers of the Federal government and of the states over the militia" and "as it relates to the power of conscripting men for foreign service."

CAIN, A. W., JR. *Constitutionality of Draft Legislation.* Law Notes. September 1941. Volume 45, Number 3. Pages 15–17.

Contends that the power of Congress to raise and support armies was never questioned as long as it was exercised through its authority under the militia clause of the Constitution. In this view, any attempts to legally invalidate the Selective Draft Act, or individual provisions of the act, are not likely to succeed. First, the exemption of certain classes of persons from its provisions does not invalidate it as a denial of equal protection of the laws inasmuch as the provisions of the act are separable. Second, it is not a deprivation of property under the Fifth Amendment inasmuch as the individual has no property rights in his occupation for the purposes of the act.

CARTER, WILLIAM HARDING. *Universal Service in War and the Taxation to Support It.* Journal of the Military Service Institution. September–October 1917. Volume 61, Number 209. Pages 123–138.

Examines the constitutional provisions for raising taxes and providing for the common defense. Maintains that universal training for military service was conceptualized in the Constitution, and that the cost of such a system should be borne by universal taxation. The "most commendable" form of public revenue for this purpose, the author suggests, would be "a small income tax, without exception, addition or surtax, universally applied."

Law and the Constitution

COLUMBIA LAW REVIEW, HARVARD LAW REVIEW, and YALE LAW REVIEW,
EDITORS OF. *Mobilization for Defense: Notes.* Columbia Law Review.
December 1940. Volume 40, Number 8. Pages 1374–1429.

Part 1 of this joint article (pages 1374–1389) deals with the conscription of men for the armed forces, discussing the political and economic
implications of conscription under the Selective Service Act of 1917. The
authors find that "on the basis of past experience, the conscription law
appears adequately designed to fulfill the primary purpose of drafting men
with the minimum dislocation of political rights or national economy."
The legal framework established, however, "is capable of being used to
exert tremendous power over the political and economic freedom of
Americans." This situation demands "a constant balancing of the necessity
for the use of these powers against the probable consequences."

DELEHANT, JOHN W. *A Judicial Revisitation Finds Kneedler v. Lane Not
So "Amazing."* American Bar Association Journal. December 1967.
Volume 53. Pages 1132–1135.

Finds that the 1863 *Kneedler* v. *Lane* case, in which the Pennsylvania
Supreme Court found the draft unconstitutional, "is quite inadequate to
prompt—even more inadequate to support—a conclusion or a suspicion
that the present Universal Military Training and Service Act is unconstitutional."

DONAHUE, BERNARD, and MARSHALL SMELSER. *The Congressional Power
to Raise Armies: The Constitutional and Ratifying Conventions 1787–
1788.* Review of Politics. April 1971. Volume 33, Number 2. Pages
202–211.

Examines the points of contention between the federalists and the
advocates of states' rights in the controversy over what provisions for
raising an army should be included in the U.S. Constitution. Concludes
that "if the debate did nothing else, it would be important because it
showed that both the opponents and the defenders of the military power
of the Congress were in agreement on the principle of civil control of the
military affairs of the United States."

FITZHUGH, WILLIAM W., JR., and CHARLES C. HYDE. *The Drafting of
Neutral Aliens by the United States.* American Journal of International
Law. July 1942. Volume 36, Number 3. Pages 369–382.

The authors present evidence in support of the view that "no controversial issue of international law need be raised, and that no such issue need interfere with the legal and domestic right of the U.S. to request alien service." It is held that "the U.S. has in substance merely asserted that military service is the price to be paid by the neutral national for the acquisition of citizenship . . . [or] for the privilege of permanent residence within American territory. No rule of international law intimates that the exaction of that price is wrongful."

FREEMAN, HARROP. *Compulsory Universal Military Training in Peacetime.* American Bar Association Journal. May 1946. Volume 32. Pages 259–262, 314–315.

Argues against the constitutionality of compulsory universal military training in peacetime and in favor of its international abolition.

FREEMAN, HARROP A. *The Constitutionality of Peacetime Conscription.* Virginia Law Review. December 1944. Volume 31, Number 1. Pages 40–82.

Examines several judicial approaches to the issue of conscription, and presents a delimitation of federal power based on constitutional provisions and court decisions. Finding that peacetime conscription is unconstitutional, the author concludes that "either the Constitution will have to be amended or the military system will have to be formed in accordance with the present Constitution."

FRIEDMAN, LEON. *Conscription and the Constitution: The Original Understanding.* Michigan Law Review. May 1969. Volume 67, Number 7. Pages 1493–1552.

Attempts to show that the Military Service Act of 1967 is unconstitutional since it exceeds the powers granted to the federal government. Presents historical evidence to support the position that the framers of the Constitution did not intend to grant Congress the power to conscript.

GREEN, ROBIN M. *On the Unconstitutionality of Involuntary Military Service.* Case & Comment. January–February 1973. Volume 78, Number 1. Pages 14–21.

A brief historical review of court holdings on the constitutionality of the draft in the United States, essentially maintaining the view that the draft is unconstitutional, that the Supreme Court has evaded this issue in the past, and that it is important to face it directly in the fuure. The author takes the position that "national survival does not depend on the government's ability to draft young men."

HARVARD LAW REVIEW. *Mobilization for Defense: Conscription of Men Under the Burke-Wadsworth Act.* December 1970. Volume LIV. Pages 278–292.

A look at the legal problems of mobilizing a democracy, both militarily and industrially. Specifically, the article examines the Excess Profits Tax Act of 1940 in the context of military mobilization and its impact on the political and economic rights of the individual and on his present mode of life. Also discussed are possible future tendencies in the event of a swing toward or away from war, problems of expediting and coordinating procurement, expansion of productive facilities, and adjustments of the national economy to conscription.

HOLZER, HENRY MARK, and PHYLLIS HOLZER. *The Constitution and the Draft* (two parts). The Objectivist. (1) October 1967. Volume 6, Number 10. Pages 10–15. (2) November 1967. Volume 6, Number 11. Pages 9–14.

A critical review of the Supreme Court decision upholding the constitutionality of the draft. Relying on the Ninth Amendment ("The enumeration in the Constitution, of certain rights, shall not be construed to deny or disparage others retained by the people"), the authors conclude: "It is the right to life that conscription denies. It is the right to life—and, consequently, to liberty and property—that the Ninth Amendment protects. It is the Ninth Amendment that represents the most effective constitutional defense against conscription."

HUNTINGTON, SAMUEL P. *Civilian Control and the Constitution.* American Political Science Review. September 1956. Volume 50, Number 3. Pages 676–699.

This article attempts (1) to show how the meaning of civilian control of the military has changed over the years since the Constitution was written, (2) to describe the Framers' concept and show how it was embodied in the Constitution, and (3) to demonstrate how the provisions they thought would guarantee it impair its effectiveness today.

LAYTON, ROBERT, and RALPH I. FINE. *The Draft and Exhaustion of Administrative Remedies.* Georgetown Law Journal. December 1967. Volume 56. Pages 315–335.

A consideration of the statutory and constitutional problems that arise when an agency whose actions are "final" violates First Amendment rights —specifically the Military Selective Service Act of 1967, which restores judicial review of Selective Service classifications. The House Armed Services Committee was disturbed by the Court's review of classification actions of local draft boards before the registrant had exhausted his administrative remedies, contending that this practice could seriously affect the administrattion of the Selective Service System. The authors examine the validity of that belief by analyzing the doctrine of exhaustion of administrative remedies both in Selective Service cases and in other areas of administrative law. They also explore the implications of the Wolff decision and the effect of the Military Selective Service Act of 1967 on it, and suggest the role the courts should play in Selective Service administration.

MICKELWAIT, CLAUDE B. *Legal Basis for Conscription.* American Bar Association Journal. September 1940. Volume 26, Number 9. Pages 701–705.

Reviews antecedents for conscription in the United States and contends that "the validity of conscription when authorized by the Congress as a necessary and proper measure in the exercise of its enumerated powers has been sustained in numerous cases." Concludes that, just as the laws relating to conscription subject the citizen to liability for military service, this obligation adheres to the citizen "wherever he may be."

MONTGOMERY, W. RANDOLPH. *Compulsory Universal Military Training in Peacetime.* American Bar Association Journal. May 1946. Volume 32. Pages 262–266, 313.

Argues in favor of the constitutionality of compulsory universal military training in peacetime. Asserts that the conclusions reached by the Supreme Court have been sound as to the interpretation and application of the army and militia clauses of the Constitution, and that they are equally applicable in peacetime and in wartime.

O'NEIL, ROBERT M. *Review of Selective Service Reclassifications.* George Washington Law Review. March 1969. Volume 37, Number 3. Pages 536–563.

Considers the constitutional and legal implications of the punitive use of Selective Service reclassification as, for example, in the case of draft protestors. Reviews the respective legal positions of Congress, the district courts, and the local Selective Service boards.

PERRY, ROSARIO. *The Draft: A Taking Without Just Compensation.* Southern California Law Review. Winter 1972. Volume 45, Number 1. Pages 313–334.

Deals with the economic inequity associated with the draft: "When the Government conscripts men into the Armed Forces it has deprived them of their property for the time they are obligated to serve." Charging that the forced-induction policy's failure to pay just compensation is unconstitutional, the author offers a solution that would not be contingent upon congressional action, but could be inaugurated by the federal courts. It would require "that the draftee be reimbursed for property losses (reduction in labor value) through a just compensation award." Three main points are covered: (1) labor as a property right, (2) the draft as a taking of property, and (3) financial and political implications.

RITTER, JOHN. *New Draft Law: Its Failures and Future.* Case Western Reserve Law Review. January 1968. Volume 19, Number 2. Pages 292–326.

Describes the process of selective service under the Military Service Act of 1967, examining alleged inequities both within the Selective Service System and within the draft itself, and analyzing the legal basis for conscription under the Constitution. Finds that while past court decisions have upheld draft laws on the basis of necessity in the defense of the nation, the implementation of the 1967 law is suspect when draftees are used not for national defense "but for the support of vaguely worded foreign policy goals." To the extent that an alternative to the draft exists, the draft's premise of necessity becomes weaker still. And even if conscription can be justified on the basis of defending national or world freedom, it is "incongruous" that the federal government denies individual liberty in an effort to protect national freedom.

ROSENSOHN, SAMUEL J. *Legal Aspects of Federal Compulsory Service of State Militia.* Proceedings of the Academy of Political Science. July 1916. Volume 6, Number 4. Pages 244–256.

Examines the question whether there is any limitation in the Constitution on the power of Congress to require compulsory military service. Rosensohn points out that "the power of Congress to raise armies is general and plenary." He notes, however, that there is one important limitation on the power of the federal government to use the militia, namely that the militia may be mobilized only to repel invasion and not to attack another nation. While a constitutional amendment might be called for, the author suggests that the courts would hold "that in a defensive war the militia may be used offensively where such tactics are necessary to repel an invasion."

SCOTT, LAWRENCE, A. *A Case Against Conscription*. Persuasion. August 1966. Volume 3, Number 8. Pages 107–114.

Reviews a pending legal challenge to the constitutionality of the Universal Military Training and Service Act.

STRAMBERG, LOUIS C. *International Law and the Conscription of Aliens*. Albany Law Review. 1963. Volume 27. Pages 11–44.

Traces the history of alien conscription in an effort to determine the validity of the widely held belief that the conscription of aliens, if not a direct violation of an established rule of international law, is at least contrary to international custom and practice. Concludes that there never has been a rule of international law forbidding the imposition of military service on aliens and that "even if this were not so, any once-presumptive rule to the contrary no longer exists."

SWISHER, CARL BRENT. *The Supreme Court and Conscription*. Current History. June 1968. Volume 54, Number 322. Pages 351–357, 365–366.

Reviews the Supreme Court's decisions with regard to conscription, pointing out that in 1963 the Court declared that "the powers of Congress to require military service for the common defense are broad and far-reaching, for while the Constitution protects against invasions of individual rights, it is not a suicide pact."

TANEY, ROGER B. *Thoughts on the Conscription Law of the United States*. Tyler's Quarterly Historical and Genealogical Magazine. October 1936. Volume 18, Number 2. Pages 74–87.

Undated and previously unpublished manuscript in which Supreme Court Justice Taney discusses the constitutionality of the draft. He concludes that "this Act of Congress is unconstitutional and void—and confers no lawful authority on the persons appointed to execute it." It is reasoned that Congress acted without constitutional authority when it passed the Conscription Act delegating to the federal government the authority to draft men.

TATE, DAVID A. *Draft Evasion and the Problem of Extradition.* Albany Law Review. Winter 1968. Volume 32, Number 2. Pages 337–358.

Examines current law in regard to the question of extradition to the United States of draft evaders who have fled to Canada or to other countries. Considers the respective legal rights of the nation and of the individual citizen, and discusses prospects for legal change affecting extradition.

WIENER, FREDERICK B. *The Militia Clause of the Constitution.* Harvard Law Review. December 1940. Volume 54, Number 2. Pages 181–220.

Examines the legal aspects of the militia clause, contending that it is impossible to provide the "well-regulated Militia" conceived by the Founders within the limitations of the clause. It is considered significant that "when, after a century and a half, the Congress finally organized the militia under Washington's plan, it could not do so under the militia clause." The author gives particular attention to the demarcation between state and federal powers over the militia (National Guard).

Pamphlets, Reprints, and Speeches

AMERICAN UNION AGAINST MILITARISM. *Some Aspects of the Constitutional Questions Involved in the Draft Act of May 18, 1917.* Circa 1918. Washington, D.C. 36 pages.

Extracts from attorneys' briefs in cases then in preparation. It is contended that Congress "has not the constitutional power to raise an army by draft to send overseas to engage in offensive war in foreign lands" and that even if Congress has that power, "the Act of May 18, 1917 is nevertheless unconstitutional."

CHAPTER 11

Philosophy

> Of all the statist violations of individual's rights in a mixed economy, the military draft is the worst. It is an abrogation of rights. It negates man's fundamental right—the right to life—and establishes the fundamental principle of statism: that a man's life belongs to the state, and the state may claim it by compelling to sacrifice it in battle.
>
> —Ayn Rand, 1967

Books

JAMES, WILLIAM. *Memories and Studies.* 1911. Longmans, Green & Co. New York. 411 pages.

Includes the essay "The Moral Equivalent of War" (pages 267–296), in which James proposes, instead of merely military conscription, "a conscription of the whole youthful population to form for a certain number of years a part of the army enlisted against Nature." In this way, it is suggested, "the injustice would tend to be evened out, and numerous other goods to the commonwealth would follow." He concludes that "war must have its way" until a discipline "equivalent" to war is organized in "obligatory service to the state."

O'TOOLE, GEORGE BARRY. *War and Conscription at the Bar of Christian Morals.* 1941. Catholic Worker Press. New York. 90 pages.

A collection of articles by a philosophy professor and priest, written for *The Catholic Worker* between October 1939 and November 1940, "when involvement in war seemed imminent and the enactment of conscription a foregone conclusion." It seeks to enable Catholic conscripts to solve the moral question of conscription in light of Christian principles. The author advocates taking away from Congress its arrogated power to draft men and capital for foreign wars, although he suggests that conscription may be justified in the case of purely defensive war. He declares that Catholics have the right, though not the duty, to be conscientious objectors. Since the professed purpose of the proposed Conscription Act is for the legitimate defense of their country, "Catholics need fear no sin in submitting to conscription or even in accepting military service." The author concludes that while conscription should be fought at the polls, "the public good demands that for the present we bear patiently conscription and the evils which it brings."

PERRY, RALPH BARTON. *The Free Man and the Soldier: Essays on the Reconciliation of Liberty and Discipline.* 1916. Charles Scribner's Sons. New York. 237 pages.

A philosopher espouses compulsory military service and universal military training. Discusses such questions as conscription and democracy, and individualism and the collective interest.

WALZER, MICHAEL. *Obligations: Essays on Disobedience, War, and Citizenship.* 1970. Harvard University Press. Cambridge, Massachusetts. Index. 244 pages.

Part 2 comprises four philosophical essays on obligations and war: (1) "The Obligation to Die for the State," (2) "Political Alienation and Military Service," (3) "Conscientious Objection," and (4) "Prisoners of War." Conscription is said to be "morally appropriate only when it is used on behalf of, and is necessary to the safety of, society as a whole, for then the nature of the obligation and the identity of the obligated persons are both reasonably clear." The author finds, further, that "the myths of common citizenship and common obligation are very important to the modern state, and perhaps even generally useful to its inhabitants, but they are myths nonetheless and cannot be allowed to determine the actual commitments of actual men and women."

Unpublished Manuscripts

ACKLEY, CHARLES WALTON. *The Modern Military: An Ethical and Theological Critique.* 1968. Ph.D. dissertation. Claremont Graduate School. Claremont, California. 374 pages.

Examines ethically the increasing role of the military in American life from the standpoint of a Christian understanding of power, justice, freedom, and love. The core materials chosen to determine military attitudes include especially the Moral Leadership Training materials and service magazines of the past decade. Criteria for ethical evaluation are drawn from Tillich. Ackley finds that "the military as such is hardly the threat to our way of life but rather it is our own deep, well camouflaged disposition to violence and moral crusades."

SHUE, HENRY GREYSON. *Selective Objection and Conscription: A Search for a Principle.* 1970. Ph.D. dissertation. Princeton University. Princeton, New Jersey. 222 pages.

A philosophical analysis of whether selective objectors (persons who oppose participation in a particular war but who are not total pacifists) may be conscripted. Each of four principles—correctness, morality, commitment, and shared commitment—is evaluated by means of a hypothetical-consent argument "designed to show what an intelligently far-sighted person could accept." The major conclusion is that "in a group with a shared objective involving moral issues, dissent is so valuable as a means to knowledge about the objective, that dissent is to be encouraged by allowing an exemption from conscription for those whose dissent leads them to oppose a war."

STAFFORD, ROBERT H. *The Morality of Universal Military Conscription in Peacetime.* S.T.D. dissertation. 1952. The Catholic University of America. Washington, D.C. Bibliography: pages 172–181. 181 pages.

Stafford acknowledges, "A sane approach to the moral problem posed by conscription must steer the difficult course between the Scylla of militarism and the 'garrison state' and the Charybdis of absolute pacifism and national indolence." The object of his study is "to determine, in the light of Catholic moral principles and the directives found in the papal encyclicals and allocutions, the norms within which the state may exercise its right to demand military service of the citizen. It insists upon the fact that the citizen is obliged in conscience to render military service whenever his government is actually engaged in a just war, or is preparing to meet the certain and imminent danger of one. On the other hand, it declares that universal conscription in time of peace, when there exists no justifying military necessity is an unjust infringement upon individual and family rights, and is consequently morally unjustifiable."

CONSCRIPTION

Articles

DAWSON, DAVID J. *John Locke, the Draft, and the Divine Right of Kings.*
Persuasion. May 1968. Volume 5, Number 5. Pages 1–20.

Warns that further postponement of a legislative decision on conscription may lead the United States to become "a conscript state by default." Draws on Locke's views on the nature of rights to argue that "a free society is . . . the only moral" and "the most practical form of government," and that any form of compulsion is incompatible with a free society.

HUGO, JOHN J. *The Immorality of Conscription.* The Catholic Worker.
November 1944. Special supplement, Volume 11, Number 9. Pages 3–10.

"On the plane of ethics," the author contends, "conscription must be condemned as opposed to democratic principles, as an infringement upon individual rights, a violation of the family, and as contradicting the patriotic duty that citizens owe to the State itself." These and other ethical and moral aspects of compulsory military service are examined individually.

MEYER, FRANK S. *The Draft: Principles and Heresies.* National Review.
August 9, 1966. Volume XVIII, Number 32. Page 785.

Maintains that "the principle of universal military obligation is justly derived from the constitution of civil society," but that the free state has the right to enforce that obligation "only in circumstances of paramount necessity." Therefore "a free society can of necessity morally demand universal military service of its citizens; but when overriding necessity is not present, conscription is immoral—be the excuse ideology, convenience, or expense."

RAND, AYN. *The Wreckage of the Consensus (Part II).* The Objectivist.
May 1967. Volume 6, Number 5. Pages 1–8.

Concerned primarily with the moral aspects of conscription. The author considers that "the question of the draft is, perhaps, the most important single issue debated today. . . . Of all the statist violations of individual rights in a mixed economy, the military draft is the worst. It is an abrogation of rights." Moreover, she believes that the draft is not needed either for military purposes or for the protection of the country, asserting that there is a deeper motivation for the draft: "The statists are struggling not to relinquish the power it gave them and the unnamed principle (and precedent) it established—above all, not to relinquish the principle: that man's life belongs to the state."

SWOMLEY, JOHN M., JR. *Why the Draft Should Go.* The Nation. August 11, 1969. Volume CCIX, Number 4. Pages 108–110.

Arguments against abolishment of the draft are examined and rebutted, and a moral argument in favor of freedom is made. "In the final analysis," the author concludes, "the issue is freedom, rather than equality under compulsion."

WALZER, MICHAEL. *Democracy and the Conscript.* Dissent. January–February 1966. Volume XIII, Number 1. Pages 16–22.

A view of political justifications for the draft and the moral reasons for conscientious objection couched in the form of two questions: (1) "Is it just to require men to fight if neither their homeland nor the security of their nation is in actual danger?" and (2) "Ought I fight in a war which I believe to be unjust?"

CHAPTER 12

Conscientious Objection

A man without a stick will be bitten even by a sheep.
—Hindu proverb

Books

BROCK, PETER. *Twentieth-Century Pacifism.* 1970. Van Nostrand Reinhold Co. New York. Index. Bibliography: pages 165–169. 174 pages.

A survey of pacifism—a movement that combines "advocacy of personal nonparticipation in war of any kind or in violent revolution with an endeavor to find nonviolent means of resolving conflict." Brock discusses the relationship between pacifism, conscientious objection, and war resistance, contrasts pacifism in various parts of the world, and examines the wide spectrum of opinions on the subject of war as well as other political, religious, and moral issues within the pacifist community.

COATE, LOWELL HARRIS. *The Conscription of Conscience.* 1934. Stonehurst Press. Los Angeles. 127 pages.

Notes that, following the adoption of the U.S. Constitution, little was said or written on the subject of conscience until the conscientious objector appeared as a direct result of the new conscription law enacted during World War I. Even then, conscientious objection to bearing arms involved only a small minority, receiving its main support from certain religious sects and such groups as the Libertarians, Socialists, Industrial Workers of the World, Philosophic Anarchists, and Rationalists. The Supreme Court's "conscription of conscience" in its 1931 decision (*U.S.* v. *Macintosh*) that the refusal to bear arms should constitute grounds for denial of citizenship affected not only applicants for citizenship but also the millions of public employees required to take the oath to defend the Constitution. This, the author states, was the first time in the history of the United States that the oath to defend the Constitution was interpreted to mean the bearing of arms in its defense. Coate concludes by advocating resistance to war and to conscription through legal methods and, if necessary, through passive resistance.

CORNELL, JULIEN. *The Conscientious Objector and the Law.* 1943. John Day Co. New York. Index. 158 pages.

Foreword by Harry Emerson Fosdick. A review of regulations and practice in World War II relating to "a minority who place moral duties above duty to the State." Aspects considered include the test of conscientious objection in the draft law, the appeals system, and constitutional questions. A comparison is drawn with the British draft procedure.

GRAHAM, JOHN W. *Conscription and Conscience: A History 1916–1919.* 1922. George Allen & Unwin. London. Index. Bibliography: pages 381–382. 388 pages.

Preface by Clifford Allen. The author, a Quaker chaplain and university professor, describes the activities of conscientious objectors in Britain during World War I. The book deals largely with those whose resistance is based on religious conviction; the preface discusses social and political aspects. A summarized survey of the draft resistance movement in ten countries is provided in the appendix.

HASSLER, R. ALFRED. *Conscripts of Conscience: The Story of Sixteen Objectors to Conscription.* 1942. Fellowship of Reconciliation. New York. 71 pages.

Preface by John Nevin Sayre. Tells the story of 16 Americans between the ages of 45 and 65 who, on April 27, 1942, refused to register under the Selective Service and Training Act of 1940. It was on that date that the conscription law was extended to include the age-group of men from 45 to 65.

KELLOGG, WALTER G. *The Conscientious Objector.* 1919. Boni & Liveright. New York. 141 pages.

Introduction by Newton D. Baker. A member of the Board of Inquiry appointed to investigate the cases of conscientious objectors in World War I, the author examines briefly the historical background of conscientious objection and discusses the various ideologies represented by objectors in World War I. Kellogg notes that the plan adopted by the U.S. government did not differ in essential aspects from that adopted by Britain, certain of whose features were said to date from the Roman Empire. Appealing for legislation regarding the objector, he supports those individuals who are prepared to accept alternate, noncombatant service, but considers that the penalty for "absolutists"—those who refuse conscription for any kind of service—should be deportation or, at least, disenfranchisement.

NATIONAL SERVICE BOARD FOR RELIGIOUS OBJECTORS. *Congress Looks at the Conscientious Objector.* 1943. Washington, D.C. 96 pages.

Presents chronologically the complete text of all discussion held in committee and on the floor of the U.S. Senate and House on the subject of conscientious objection since the beginning of the Selective Training Service Act of 1940. The bulk of the study is devoted to question-and-answer testimony involving the legislators so as to reveal their peacetime and wartime attitudes toward the conscientious objector. Prepared statements of witnesses are presented in the appendix.

ROHR, JOHN A. *Prophets Without Honor: Public Policy and the Selective Conscientious Objector.* 1971. Abingdon Press. Nashville, Tennessee. Index. Select bibliography: pages 185–188. 191 pages.

Presents constitutional and policy arguments for and against selective conscientious objection to military conscription. The first section of the book takes up the constitutional question: Is there a constitutional right to selective conscientious objection? The second section considers possible congressional policy once the Supreme Court has decided the constitutional standing of the case for selective objectors.

SCHLISSEL, LILLIAN (compiler). *Conscience in America: A Documentary History of Conscientious Objection in America 1757–1967.* 1968. E. P. Dutton & Co. New York. 444 pages.

A collection of 55 documents reflecting the legislative and judicial history of conscientious objection, as well as the personal views of eminent spokesmen in many walks of life opposed to military conscription on religious, political, or moral grounds. Includes statements of such individuals as Daniel Webster, Henry David Thoreau, and Chief Justice Holmes.

SIBLEY, MULFORD Q., and PHILIP E. JACOB. *Conscription of Conscience: The American State and the Conscientious Objector 1940–1947.* 1952. Cornell University Press. Ithaca, New York. Index. Tables. Bibliography: pages 549–567. 580 pages.

This comprehensive study is divided into five parts that respectively discuss (1) conscience in the modern state, (2) conscription of the objector, (3) alternative civilian service, (4) objectors as law violators, and (5) prospects for legislative change.

TATUM, ARLO (editor). *Handbook for Conscientious Objectors.* 1968. Central Committee for Conscientious Objectors. Philadelphia. Index. Bibliography: pages 96–106. 110 pages.

A manual for the conscientious objector, informing him of his rights and obligations under the Selective Service System. Contains recommendations as to conduct and procedure in the various situations that could confront him, such as opting for noncooperation and possible criminal prosecution rather than accepting a noncombat role.

THOMAS, NORMAN. *The Conscientious Objector in America.* 1923. B. W. Huebsch. New York. Index. 299 pages.

Introduction by Robert M. La Follette. The story of conscientious objection in World War I, as told by a leading Socialist. Based largely on the files of the American Civil Liberties Union, the book describes the basis for conscientious objection, the various types of objectors, the social and political backgrounds of conscientious objection, the development of government policy, camp conditions, courts-martial, and prison sentences.

WRIGHT, EDWARD N. *Conscientious Objectors in the Civil War.* 1931. University of Pennsylvania Press. Philadelphia. Index. Bibliography: pages 248–262. 274 pages.

Discusses the attitudes of civil and military authorities toward conscientious objectors, as well as the attitudes of various objector groups in the North and the South toward the system of conscription. A comparison is drawn between conscientious objection in the Civil War and that in World War I.

ZAHN, GORDON C. *War, Conscience and Dissent.* 1967. Hawthorn Books. New York. Index. 317 pages.

A collection of previously published articles discussing the immorality of war from a Catholic pacifist position. The first part of the book focuses on the realities of modern war and its implications vis-à-vis traditional concepts of morally justifiable wars, with Zahn contending that modern war invalidates the traditional concepts. The second part takes up questions of conscience versus legitimate state power, discussing private conscience and conscientious objection in the United States, in Nazi Germany, and among Catholics. The third part, on the Church and dissent, considers the German Catholic press in Hitler's Germany, makes a case for Christian dissent, and comments on the Church as a source of dissent.

Unpublished Manuscripts

DAVIS, ROGER GUION. *Conscientious Cooperators: The Seventh-Day Adventists and Military Service 1860–1945.* 1970. Ph.D. dissertation. George Washington University. Washington, D.C. 259 pages.

Describes how, in 1862, Seventh-Day Adventists began to engage in a heated debate on the question of military service, which resulted in the adoption of a position approving noncombatant service for its members. When the United States entered World War I, the church renewed its official noncombatant position and created a war service commission to oversee problems associated with military service. While many churches adopted strong pacifistic stands after 1919, the Seventh-Day Adventists did not alter their tradition of noncombatancy, but made greater preparations for such service. The author concludes: "The church's cooperation and the government's willingness to compromise with sincere conscientious objections seems to indicate that opportunities exist for the expression of conscience and the fulfillment of civil duty within the state's structure."

Articles

ARNOLD, WALTER. *Selective Objection and the Public Interest.* The Christian Century. September 27, 1967. Volume LXXIV, Number 39. Pages 1218–1221.

Refutes specific conclusions of the Marshall Committee on Selective Service. The author argues in favor of selective conscientious objection, stating that a strong constitutional as well as moral, ethical, and political case can be made for his position. The *U.S.* v. *Seeger* case is discussed.

BEISER, EDWARD. *God and the Draft.* Commonweal. March 4, 1966. Volume LXXXIII. Number 21. Pages 631–633.

Discusses the atheists' rights as conscientious objectors. Notes the absence of provisions for conscientious objection in the Bill of Rights, recalling deletion of the clause "no person religiously scrupulous shall be compelled to bear arms" in the drafting of the Bill of Rights. Beiser considers crucial whether, by definition, the term "religious belief," as provided for in the Conscription Statute of 1917 and the Selective Service and Training Act of 1940, presupposes acknowledgment of a supreme being. If so, under the First Amendment, the freedom of religious rights of adherents of Buddhism, Taoism, Ethical Culture, and Secular Humanism is violated. Beiser concludes that the courts have avoided dealing with this issue and that, if they did so, the result would be a repeal of conscientious objection rather than extension of the option to atheists.

CARNAHAN, WILLIAM A. *Freedom of Conscience and Compulsory Military Service.* Buffalo Law Review. Winter 1964. Volume 13, Number 2. Pages 463–476.

Contends that neither Congress nor the courts have found an acceptable solution to the question of conscientious objectors. Takes the position that personal liberty and individual rights under the Constitution "must be placed in relation to the national good," and that "liberty of conscience is no exception."

KELMAN, HERBERT C. *War Criminals and War Resisters.* Society. May–June 1975. Volume 12, Number 4. Pages 18–22.

Examines some of the social effects of the Vietnam War for the United States, including the consequences of draft refusal and conscientious objection. Kelman maintains: "Our society has no better opportunity to express its commitment to the principle of individual responsibility than by granting universal and unconditional amnesty to all those who, as a result of their protest against the war in Indochina, find themselves in legal jeopardy or suffer continuing legal and economic disadvantages."

ROHR, JOHN A. *Just Wars and Selective Objectors.* Review of Politics. April 1971. Volume 33, Number 2. Pages 185–201.

A survey of the literature supporting the selective conscientious objector —that person whose scruples do not extend to all wars, but only to wars that fail to meet certain moral norms. Examines the arguments offered by selective objectors and points out the limitations of those arguments. Rohr concentrates on what he considers to be two major defects in the case for selective objection: "the tendency to dichotomize politics and morality" and "the tendency to structure the case for selective conscientious objection in terms of the conscience of the citizen without considering the public interest."

SHAFFER, HELEN B. *Resistance to Military Service.* Editorial Research Reports. March 20, 1968. Volume 1. Pages 201–220.

Reviews the resistance to the draft for the Vietnam War, Selective Service deferment policies, and some of the legal and constitutional issues in resistance to military service.

SHERK, J. HAROLD. *The Position of the Conscientious Objector.* Current History. July 1968. Volume 55, Number 323. Pages 18–22.

Reviews the legal and historical position of the conscientious objector. Considers "impressive" the American record in handling cases of conscientious objection to war and military service.

Pamphlets, Reprints, and Speeches

FELLOWSHIP OF RECONCILIATION. *Forty Years for Peace: A History of the Fellowship of Reconciliation.* 1954. New York. 16 pages.

Describes the activities of the Fellowship of Reconciliation since its founding in 1914. Notes the fellowship's efforts on behalf of conscientious objectors in World Wars I and II.

FELLOWSHIP OF RECONCILIATION. *Peace in Action: Position Taken by a Conscientious Objector Imprisoned for His Stand Against the War System.* Circa 1941. Minneapolis and St. Paul, Minnesota. 16 pages.

With comments by eminent persons in the peace movement. Statement to the U.S. District Court, District of Minnesota, by the Reverend Winslow Wilson, pleading guilty to the charge of refusing to register for the draft. Includes a supporting appeal by the Reverend James Irving Asher.

FELLOWSHIP OF RECONCILIATION and others. *Conscience Compels Them.* Circa 1942. New York. 7 pages.

Issued jointly by the Fellowship of Reconciliation, the American Friends Service Committee, the Brethren Service Committee, and the Mennonite Central Committee. Reports the status of the conscientious objector exempted from active military service in World War II, and describes the Civilian Public Service camps in which conscientious objectors may serve. The pamphlet appeals for financial contributions to the camp movement.

FELLOWSHIP OF RECONCILIATION and others. *Why We Refused to Register.* Circa 1941. New York. 12 pages.

States the cases of 16 nonregistrants to the Selective Service Act. Published jointly by the Fellowship of Reconciliation, Keep America Out of War Congress, National Council for Prevention of War, Youth Committee Against War, Young People's Socialist League, and War Resisters League.

FRENCH, PAUL COMLY. *Civilian Public Service.* 1942. National Service Board for Religious Objectors. Washington, D.C. 21 pages.

This essay by the executive secretary of the National Service Board for Religious Objectors sets forth the position of the organization on the Civilian Public Service programs for conscientious objectors exempted from military service in World War II. It is contended that "the Government, having recognized the right of individual conscience, has a moral obligation to provide work of national importance and to finance it."

NATIONAL SERVICE BOARD FOR RELIGIOUS OBJECTORS. *The Conscientious Objector Under the Selective Training and Service Act of 1940.* Revised edition. 1942. Washington, D.C. 20 pages.

A handbook for the conscientious objector to military service, setting forth the official status of the conscientious objector under the Selective Training and Service Act of 1940. Notes relevant executive orders and

Selective Service interpretations and regulations whereby the conscientious objector may render noncombatant or civilian public service.

NATIONAL SERVICE BOARD FOR RELIGIOUS OBJECTORS. *The Origins of Civilian Public Service.* Circa 1941. Washington, D.C. 27 pages.

A review of the negotiations during autumn 1940 between U.S. government officials and representatives of the churches most immediately affected by the drafting of conscientious objectors. Includes the texts of respective government and church statements in the negotiations on alternative service programs for conscientious objectors exempted from military service. The churches called for parallel programs: one under government control, with the government paying maintenance and wages to the men; the other under the control of private agencies that would pay maintenance but no wages for men who preferred to work with them and were acceptable to them. Following the rejection of this proposal by President Roosevelt, it was decided by the religious agencies that "a program under private administration would meet the wishes of the widest number of C.O.'s and should be attempted."

RIPON SOCIETY. *Selective Service: The Draft's Agony of Conscience.* 1968. Reprint from the Ripon Forum, October 1968. 5 pages.

Advocates the reform of military administrative procedures and the revision of standards to permit selective conscientious objection. States that such a program would serve at least "to make the draft, so long as it exists, more consistent with the ideals of a free society."

Government Documents: Publications

U.S. WAR DEPARTMENT. *Treatment of Conscientious Objectors in the Army.* 1919. Government Printing Office. Washington, D.C. 75 pages.

Statement concerning the treatment of drafted men professing conscientious objection to military service. Includes a brief historical review of conscientious objection to the draft and of legislation and policy concerning the history of conscientious objectors in the United States, as well as a compiled record of formal action taken by the War Department.

CHAPTER 13

Race

When the military phase of the Revolutionary War opened on April 19, 1775, blacks were among those who responded to the call to arms issued by Paul Revere and William Dawes. Blacks fought with the patriot forces at the Battle of Lexington and at Concord and were among the casualties in the battles.

—Jack D. Foner, *Blacks and the Military in American History*, 1974

Books

AYERS, JAMES T. *The Diary of James T. Ayers, Civil War Recruiter.* Edited by John Hope Franklin. 1947. Illinois State Historical Society. Springfield, Illinois. Index. Illustrations. 138 pages.

This diary of an Illinois preacher who served in Sherman's army describes a phase of the Civil War that has been largely overlooked by historians—the recruiting of Southern Negroes for the Union army. Loyalist slave-owners in the Southern states were compensated by Ayers, from funds whose source is not documented, for their consent to the enlistment of their slaves. A brief biography of Ayers is provided, along with a history of official policy toward Negro recruitment and a discussion of events surrounding Ayers's efforts at recruitment.

BARBEAU, ARTHUR E., and FLORETTE HENRI. *The Unknown Soldiers: Black American Troops in World War I.* 1974. Temple University Press. Philadelphia. Index. Illustrations. Bibliography: pages 249–269. 279 pages.

Foreword by Burghardt Turner. Based largely on military records and personal papers of participants, this study records the allegedly discriminatory policies and practices to which black American soldiers were subjected during World War I, from the prewar handling of the four black Regular Army units through the draft to postwar demobilization. It is contended that the established policies were designed to support and maintain racist social patterns rather than to produce an efficient military machine. Chapter 3 is of particular interest, dealing with blacks and the draft law. The appendix contains the text of the plan of the Operations Branch of the Army General Staff for the "Disposal of the Colored Drafted Men."

BROWN, WILLIAM WELLS. *The Negro in the American Rebellion: His Heroism and His Fidelity.* 1867. Lee & Shepard. Boston. 380 pages.

The author's purpose is to present an account of the Negro's part in suppressing the Slaveholders' Rebellion. Topics covered include the condition of blacks prior to the war, the Nat Turner insurrection, effects of the cotton-gin on slavery, the Dred Scott decision, John Brown's raid, the Emancipation Proclamation, the decision to let blacks fight in the army, the raising of black regiments in the North, and specific battles of the war.

CORNISH, DUDLEY T. *The Sable Arm: Negro Troops in the Union Army 1861–1865.* 1956. Longmans, Green & Co. New York. Index. Bibliography: pages 316–332. 337 pages.

A comprehensive treatment of the black soldier's role in the Civil War, heavily documented from official and contemporary sources. Describes the conditions that led to the extensive use of black troops in the war, and the methods of recruitment employed.

DALFIUME, RICHARD M. *Desegregation of the U.S. Armed Forces: Fighting on Two Fronts 1939–1953.* 1969. University of Missouri Press. Columbia, Missouri. Index. Bibliography: pages 227–241. 252 pages.

Analyzes changes in racial policy in the military services and the Negro's reaction to these changes from 1939 to 1953. Details events of the move from restriction and segregation of Negro soldiers to equal opportunity and integration. Dalfiume concludes that "by the end of 1954, segregation and discrimination were virtually eliminated from the internal organization of the military" but that there was still evidence of the problem "in areas where military life touched the surrounding off-post civilian communities."

DAVID, JAY, and ELAINE CRANE (editors). *The Black Soldier: From the American Revolution to Vietnam.* 1971. William Morrow & Co., Inc. New York. 248 pages.

A collection of excerpts and narratives depicting the role of the black man in American armies from the Revolutionary War to the Vietnam War. "The black soldier," it is stated, "has always carried on a two-front war. The first has been against America's common enemy and the second against the racism of his own country." The issues now are "acceptance as a human being and an American citizen and being granted the dignity and privileges those identities imply."

FONER, JACK D. *Blacks and the Military in American History: A New Perspective.* 1974. Praeger Publishers. New York. Index. Bibliographic essay: pages 263–272. 278 pages.

Foreword and conclusion by James P. Shenton. This study documents the role of blacks in the United States armed forces from the War for Independence to the Vietnam War, examining the shifts in official policy and popular attitudes.

GUTHRIE, JAMES M. *Campfires of the Afro-American; or, The Colored Man as a Patriot.* 1899. Afro-American Publishing Co. Philadelphia. Illustrations. 710 pages.

Lauds the patriotism of the black American as "soldier, sailor and hero in the cause of free America," as demonstrated in the colonial struggles, in the American Revolution, and in the War of 1812 and later conflicts, particularly the Civil War.

HIGGINSON, THOMAS WENTWORTH. *Army Life in a Black Regiment.* 1882. Lee & Shepard. New York. Index. 296 pages.

Written by the commander of the First South Carolina Volunteers, the first slave regiment mustered into the service of the United States late in the Civil War, this book gives a detailed account of events and conditions as well as soldier morale in the regiment. The author states that "till the blacks were armed, there was no guaranty of their freedom. It was their demeanor under arms that shamed the nation into recognizing them as men."

McConnell, Roland C. *Negro Troops of Antebellum Louisiana.* 1968. Louisiana State University Press. Baton Rouge, Louisiana. 143 pages.

A history of Louisiana's first Negro unit, which had its historical precedents in the companies initially organized under the French during the Indian rebellion of 1729. In 1814 this volunteer militia battalion was enrolled into federal service.

Quarles, Benjamin. *The Negro in the Civil War.* 1953. Little, Brown, & Co. Boston. Index. Bibliography: pages 349–360. 379 pages.

Discusses the Civil War role of both the Northern Negroes, who fought for abolition of slavery, and the Southern slaves—those who were impressed for noncombat duty in the army, those who came into the Union lines, and those who volunteered to serve in the army. Accounts of Negro heroism in specific battles are told in anecdotal detail.

Singletary, Otis A. *Negro Militia and Reconstruction.* 1957. University of Texas Press. Austin, Texas. Index. Bibliography: pages 153–166. 181 pages.

Examines the Negro militia movement that, in most Southern states, originated as the protective arm of the newly created Radical state administrations during the Reconstruction period. Of particular interest is Chapter 2, "Organizing and Arming the Militia," which suggests that while most Southern state militia laws enacted during this period provided for the conscription of men, recruiting was generally achieved through volunteering. Most of the volunteers for the enlisted ranks were Negroes, attracted to the ranks largely by the pay rates, which were normally equivalent to those in the U.S. Army and considerably higher than those prevailing for civilian jobs.

Stillman, Richard J., II. *Integration of the Negro in the U.S. Armed Forces.* 1968. Frederick A. Praeger. New York. Tables. Bibliographical essay: pages 157–167. 167 pages.

Considers the political influences affecting integration of the U.S. armed forces, and how these influences became translated into military policy on the use of the Negro in the service. In reviewing the historical context of Negro recruitment, Stillman notes: "When the military needed men, Negroes served. When it did not, Negroes were rejected." The gradual movement from segregation to integration is traced from 1940 to 1953.

WILLIAMS, GEORGE W. *A History of the Negro Troops in the War of the Rebellion 1861–1865.* 1888. Harper & Bros. New York. Index. 353 pages.

Drawing from official and unofficial works, the author summarizes the military services of Negro soldiers in ancient and modern times, then discusses the role of the Negro in the War of the Rebellion, describing his "trials and triumphs in a holy struggle for human liberty." Topics include military employment of Negroes, military status of Negro troops, Negro troops in specific battles, and Negroes as prisoners of war.

Unpublished Manuscripts

BERRY, MARY FRANCES. *The Negro Soldier Movement and the Adoption of National Conscription 1652–1865.* 1966. Ph.D. dissertation. University of Michigan. Ann Arbor, Michigan. Bibliography: pages 208–219. 219 pages.

Examines the development of government policy and legislation leading to the general acceptance and conscription of Negroes for military service. The development both of national policy and of attitudes and practices at the state level is explored. Attention is focused on the military use of Negroes in Massachusetts—considered, in many ways, a typical Northern state—with a discussion of the recruitment and service of the 54th Massachusetts Regiment, the first free Negro troops raised in the North.

HENDRICKS, GEORGE L. *Union Army Occupation of the Southern Seaboard 1861–1865.* 1954. Ph.D. dissertation. Columbia University. New York. Bibliography: pages 247–256. 256 pages.

Discusses the raising of Negro troops on the Southern seaboard during the Civil War. Notes that Negro troops were first raised in the Sea Islands, without clear authority, in 1862. This regiment, although it was never mustered in, "attracted much attention and helped prepare the country to accept Negro troops." A second Negro regiment, authorized by the

War Department, was raised by volunteering six months later and these troops "had good morale." In 1863 troops were drafted, in violation of promises made, and in 1864 Northern recruiting agents were admitted to the War Department to recruit Negroes who were credited to Northern communities, at which time "recruiting became cynical and oppressive."

Articles

APTHEKER, HERBERT. *Negro Casualties in the Civil War.* Journal of Negro History. 1947. Volume XXXII, Number 1. Pages 10–80.

Challenges the notion "that the American Negroes are the only people in the history of the world that ever became free without any effort of their own." Discussed are the available statistics on Negro casualties during the Civil War with emphasis on possible reasons for their inaccuracies. These statistics are taken as evidence of Negro participation in the conflict. In attempting to elucidate the role of the Negro soldiers, Aptheker examines the events and battles in which they figured, the conditions they faced, their training, and their leadership; and he cites their hardships as a source of casualties. He concludes that the stereotyped view of the Negro as a passive onlooker in the Civil War is inaccurate, and that "his active role resulted in his liberation and the preservation of the union."

EBONY. *An All-Volunteer Army?* December 1970. Volume XXVI, Number 2. Page 174.

This editorial reviews the effect that the abolition of the draft might have on the nation in regard to the recruitment of blacks. It points out that, "regardless of how many promises there will be to the contrary, black folk can rest assured that when the day of the all-volunteer Army returns, blacks will again meet discrimination, though it is doubtful if the military could ever return to full segregation."

FLETCHER, MARVIN E. *The Negro Volunteer in Reconstruction 1865–1866.* Military Affairs. Volume XXXII, Number 3. December 1968. Pages 124–131.

Reviews the role of the Negro volunteer in the postbellum South.

Ford, William Freithaler, and Robert Tollison. *Notes on the Color of the Volunteer Army.* Social Science Quarterly. December 1969. Volume 50, Number 3. Pages 544–547.

Examines the argument that a volunteer army in the United States would be manned primarily by economically disadvantaged minorities, especially Negroes. A preliminary analysis of the relevant theoretical issues and empirical data indicates that this assertion is implausible.

Janowitz, Morris, and Ronald V. Dellums. *Blacks in the Military: Are There Too Many?* Focus. June 1975. Volume 3, Number 8. Pages 1–8.

Discussing recruitment policy for an all-volunteer armed force, Janowitz suggests that the military should be "representative" of the larger society and that there should not be "black overconcentration" in the armed forces. Dellums counters that if, through the exercise of free choice, a disproportionate number of blacks seek the opportunity for military service, the rejection of these individuals on racial grounds would mean a perpetuation of racial discrimination in the society at large.

Janowitz, Morris, and Charles C. Moskos, Jr. *Racial Composition of the Volunteer Armed Forces.* Society. May–June 1975. Volume 12, Number 4. Pages 37–42.

The authors express serious concern over the fact that the representation of blacks in the armed forces of the United States is slightly higher than for the general population. They state, "Overrepresentation of blacks in the armed forces, while not yet an issue of national debate, can be defined as a problem from several perspectives. . . . Some professional military officers and civilian commentators view a large concentration of blacks as exacerbating race tensions and management problems within the services. A few are apprehensive about the internal reliability of such a force, while others—not only blacks—are distressed about the potential disproportion of black casualties in time of war." On the other hand, it is also noted that, "oddly enough, there has been a lack of public debate on a subject as controversial as the racial composition of the all-volunteer force. . . . Within the black community, public leaders and elected officials in general have also been indifferent to the issue."

LEE, ULYSSES. *The Draft and the Negro.* Current History. July 1968. Volume 55, Number 323. Pages 28–33, 47–48.

Tracing the history of the Negro in the U.S. armed forces, the author points out that "in a more nearly perfect democracy, there would be little reason to discuss Negroes and the draft." But despite massive alteration of the position of Negroes in American life, no one can argue "that Negroes do not constitute a special, still 'unfinished business' for the American democracy."

MABRA, FRED J. *Manpower Utilization.* Military Review. December 1966. Volume XLVI, Number 12. Pages 92–97.

Examines the history of the recruitment of Negroes for the U.S. armed forces. Noting the continuing difficulties in regard to public acceptance of Negroes in the military, the author calls for specific actions to address this problem.

McCONNELL, ROLAND C. *Concerning the Procurement of Negro Troops in the South During the Civil War.* Journal of Negro History. July 1950. Volume XXXV, Number 3. Pages 315–319.

Contains the text of an early statistical report of the U.S. Adjutant General's progress in procuring Negroes in the Southern states for military service in the Union army. The report is dated December 24, 1863.

MAN, ALBON P., JR. *Labor Competition and the New York Draft Riots of 1863.* Journal of Negro History. October 1951. Volume XXXVI, Number 4. Pages 375–405.

Contends that the New York draft riots of July 1863 "had their origin largely in a fear of black labor competition which possessed the city's Irish unskilled workers." Supporting this contention is the fact that in the first half of 1863 the longshoremen of New York "went on strike after strike for increased pay, only to see their places filled by colored men working for less money under police protection."

PASZET, LAWRENCE J. *Negroes and the Air Force 1939–1949.* Military Affairs. Spring 1967. Volume XXXI, Number 1. Pages 1–9.

Traces the development of recruiting policies and practices in the U.S. Air Force following passage of the Selective Service Act in 1940, which required all arms and services to enlist Negroes. Examines some of the problems encountered in implementing the "separate-but-equal" doctrine and the resolution of these problems by President Harry S. Truman's order that Negro personnel be reassigned to white units and that Negro organizations be inactivated.

REDDICK, L. D. *The Negro Policy of the United States Army 1775–1945.* Journal of Negro History. 1949. Volume XXXIV, Number 1. Pages 9–29.

Contends that throughout the history of army policy toward Negro soldiers, the substance of that policy has been racist and segregationist. The author follows the record from the War for Independence through World War II to see how well these generalizations hold true. He concludes with a call for the military to act in keeping with democratic principles, stating that citizens should share equally the obligations and privileges, the duties and honors of defending the land.

SHANNON, FRED A. *The Federal Government and the Negro Soldier 1861–1865.* Journal of Negro History. 1926. Volume XI, Number 4. Pages 563–583.

Discusses the impact of events on government policy toward Negroes with respect to slavery and military service during 1861–1865. The author maintains that "the Federal Administration during the Civil War had but very rudimentary notions concerning the rights which were proper to be afforded to Negro soldiers. Just as emancipation was not the outgrowth of any policy, but merely the result of military exigencies, so the employment of Negroes in the army was in a sense forced upon the administration and was accepted only with the greatest reluctance." Moreover, after being allowed into the army, the Negro was classified as inferior and further distinction was made at the time of muster between Negroes who were free and those who were slave—all this, the author states, "with the tacit consent of him whom we have been wont to call 'The Great Emancipator.'"

SINGLETARY, OTIS A. *The Negro Militia During Radical Reconstruction.* Military Affairs. Winter 1955. Volume XIX, Number 4. Pages 177–186.

Documents the failure of the militia established in the South during the Reconstruction period. Finds that the organization of this protective force, which, owing to peculiar local conditions, developed into a Negro militia, "caused so violent a reaction that it guaranteed the destruction of the very thing it was created to protect."

THOMPSON, CHARLES H. *Peacetime Compulsory Military Training and the Negro's Status in the Armed Forces.* Journal of Negro Education. April 1945. Volume XIV, Number 2. Pages 127–131.

A discussion of the national military training bill of 1945 that would provide for compulsory military training of males age 18 and older. The main provisions of the bill are quoted and contrasted with similar proposals pending in Congress. Results of polls taken at five Negro colleges are analyzed and the reactions to the proposed bills outlined. The author concludes with a call for an end to segregation and discrimination in the armed forces, stating that a strong country is precluded by treating one tenth of the population as second-class citizens in peacetime and expecting them to make first-class soldiers in war.

YOUNG, WARREN L. *Minority Group Participation in the U.S. and U.K. Armed Forces: An Overview.* Quarterly Journal. Winter 1973. Volume 4, Number 4. Pages 3–55.

Published by the Foundation for the Study of Plural Societies. Examines the variant structures that characterize the differences between the British and American systems of military organization and their effect on the nature and significance of minority group participation. Notes the struggle for equal pay for the Negro soldier during the Civil War and the eventual equalization of pay rates between the U.S. Colored Troops and the Regular Army, while, in the British army, " 'wage riots' and protests against discrimination by men of the West Indies Regiment, the British Indian Army and the East African forces . . . [show] the extent to which the discriminatory policies . . . were carried out and the resentment generated by them."

Pamphlets, Reprints, and Speeches

APTHEKER, HERBERT. *The Negro in the Civil War.* 1938. International Publishers. New York. Bibliography: pages 47–48. 48 pages.

Attempts to dispel myths about living conditions of Southern slaves prior to and during the Civil War. Aptheker challenges descriptions of that life as idyllic and of slaves as docile, passive, and nonmoralistic. Specific organizations and events in nonslave, border, and Confederate states are discussed in the context of the Negro's struggle for economic and personal liberty. Phenomena such as strikes, sabotage, aid to the slavocracy's enemies, struggles against enslavement, flight from slavery, outlaw communities, runaways, and information networks are described. Aptheker contends that the War of the Rebellion was part of a continuing struggle against oppression that was foiled by a "shameful betrayal by the industrial and financial bourgeoisie of the North" but that the struggle continues.

NATIONAL COUNCIL AGAINST CONSCRIPTION. *Conscription Is Too High a Price to Pay for Prejudice.* Circa 1949. Washington, D.C. 16 pages.

Argues that it is because of the 10 percent restriction on the recruitment of Negroes that a draft and universal military training appear to be the sole means for the armed services to reach their authorized strength.

Government Documents: Publications

U.S. DEPARTMENT OF THE ARMY. *The Employment of Negro Troops.* By Ulysses Lee. 1966. Office of the Chief of Military History, Department of the Army. Washington, D.C. Index. Illustrations, maps, tables. Bibliographical note: pages 707–708. 740 pages.

This volume is part of the Special Studies subseries of United States Army in World War II. The author describes Negro participation in military service during World War II, pointing up problems in the development and application of policy, as well as the clash of public and private views on the employment of Negroes as soldiers.

U.S. DEPARTMENT OF THE ARMY. *Utilization of Negroes in the Post War Army.* 1948. Government Printing Office. Washington, D.C. 10 pages.

Available on loan from the Army Library at the Pentagon, this is the text of the Gillem Board report, which surveyed the utilization of blacks in the army after World War II.

Chapter 14

England

Let not England forget her precedence of teaching nations how to live.

—Milton, *The Doctrine and Discipline of Divorce*, 1633

Books: History

BARNETT, CORRELLI. *Britain and Her Army 1509–1970: A Military, Political and Social Survey.* 1970. William Morrow & Co. New York. Index. Maps, plates. Bibliography: pages 501–505. 530 pages.

The course of British history is seen as having been shaped by war and by military institutions even though the British, bolstered by their geographical situation and naval supremacy, "have always been reluctant to accept that they needed" a permanent military institution. Instead of the continuous development of a national army, therefore, there has been a history of "recurrent need rending aside the anti-military illusions of the nation." The author describes how universal military service, "an English tradition and obligation," fell into disfavor with the advent of Napoleonic conscription, and how a vigorous campaign for its institution in the early 1900s failed. When, in 1914, the government once again decided against conscription, the "ancient English obligation to bear arms in national defence" was "utterly . . . eclipsed by the later belief that conscription was incompatible with British liberty." Finally, when National Service, which came about "so tardily in British history" following World War II, was abolished in 1960 the army and nation were seen once again to "drift apart."

BEELER, JOHN. *Warfare in England 1066–1189.* 1966. Cornell University Press. Ithaca, New York. Index. Maps. Bibliographic notes: pages 319–396. 493 pages.

Of particular interest are Chapters 10 and 11 on military service and military manpower, which discuss the conditions of service of knights and nonfeudal elements.

BEITH, JOHN HAY [Ian Hay, pseudonym]. *The British Infantryman: An Informal History.* Abridged edition. 1942. Penguin Books. Harmondsworth, England. 223 pages.

Traces briefly the various methods of army recruiting used in Britain, from the 17th century system of "mercenary" regiments to the national volunteer force of the 1930s. The army's difficulty in recruiting in peacetime is seen largely as being due to inadequate pay in comparison with civilian employment, poor conditions, and to long terms of overseas service without home leave. The author notes that long after the army has ceased to be the monarch's private property, Britons continue to be suspicious of all soldiers. He concludes that Britain has no need of a "vast conscript army" inasmuch as the nation has no land frontiers to defend, but advocates "some satisfactory mean" between universal service and the current voluntary system. Such a mean would improve on the inefficient and wasteful custom of conducting a frantic campaign of recruiting and intensive training in time of crisis, only to disband the force after the crisis and repeat the process when the next one arises.

BOYNTON, LINDSAY. *The Elizabethan Militia 1558–1638.* 1967. Routledge & Kegan Paul. London. Index. Illustrations. Bibliography: pages 300–315. 334 pages.

A study of the militia's history, examining how successfully or unsuccessfully the government was able to enforce such measures as it considered necessary for the defense of England. The failure of Elizabeth I and her successors to establish an efficient military system is attributed largely to the inability of the crown, and the refusal of the crown's subjects, to pay for a military establishment. The militia, however, succeeded in maintaining internal peace, even though its organization against invasion was never put to test. The nobility served as administrators and the gentry were liable to serve as officers, while the rest of the male lay population were subject not only to taxation for military purposes, but also to service in the ranks of the militia. The trained bands, the first important innovation in the militia, are followed from their development in 1573 to the period immediately preceding the Armada. The book concludes with the collapse of the militia that accompanied the collapse of government and authority as a whole during the 1630s.

CLODE, CHARLES M. *Military Forces of the Crown: Their Administration and Government.* 2 volumes. 1869. John Murray. London. Volume 1: 596 pages. Volume 2: 804 pages.

A collection of materials, based on public documents, related to the constitutional history of the British army from 1688 to 1869. The author states in the preface that he has "endeavored to trace the outline of those Constitutional Safeguards that were ... devised for the security of the Public Treasure, and for the freedom of the People against the possible adverse action in time of Peace of a Standing Army. It will be seen how vigilant the guardianship of Parliament has been over the people's money and liberties; how continually present to the Lords and Commons was the conviction that all Standing Armies are by nature aggressive; and how settled the purpose to prevent, under any circumstances, the exhibition of this aggressive spirit by the Army of England." The author concludes, in Volume 2: "No doubt, the Civil administration of the Army—like every other organization—may need revision; but, as the Army is a Political power which, of all others, it is the least prudent to trifle with, such reorganization—even if suggested by the Army—should surely—unless the time be indeed come for responsible Ministers to repudiate all responsibility—be the work of Statesmen; that the Constituencies may hold a substantial guarantee, in a measure so critical, that no encroachment will be allowed on the part of the Army, either on the Prerogatives of the Crown or on the Functions of Parliament."

COUSINS, GEOFFREY. *The Defenders: A History of the British Volunteer.* 1968. Frederick Muller. London. Index. Illustrations. Bibliography: pages 206–208. 224 pages.

Foreword by Tufton Beamish. Traces the history of the British volunteer through nearly 2,000 years to the present, showing that the fyrd of Anglo-Saxon times, the general levy of the Plantagenets, the trained bands of the first Elizabeth, the militia of the 16th and 17th centuries, and the yeomen and volunteers of the 18th and 19th, "were all representative of the idea of part-time service." This tradition has continued with the merger of the yeomanry and volunteers into the Territorial Force early in the 20th century, and with the force's recent transformation into the Territorial Army Volunteer Reserve. The appendix includes a list of statutes concerning volunteers and related subjects, and a chronology outlining the history of the volunteers.

DENNIS, PETER. *Decision by Default: Peacetime Conscription and British Defence 1919–39.* 1972. Routledge & Kegan Paul. London. Index. Bibliography: pages 227–233. 243 pages.

A detailed exposition of the circumstances surrounding the debate that began in 1935 and culminated in Britain's decision in April 1939 to institute temporarily the nation's first peacetime conscription. Drawing on government archives, interviews with public figures, and the private papers of military advisers and statesmen, the author traces the debate against the backdrop of international developments that eventually led the Chamberlain government to reverse its earliest promises not to introduce conscription in peacetime.

FIRTH, C. H. *Cromwell's Army: A History of the English Soldier During the Civil Wars, the Commonwealth and the Protectorate.* Revised edition. 1905. Methuen & Co. London. Index. 444 pages.

A study of Cromwell's military system and the character of the army he organized. Discusses the army prior to and after introduction of the New Model, which gradually absorbed other armies in the service of the Parliament. "Impressment for the army of the Commonwealth," Firth points out, "stopped in 1651, and it was not resumed under the Protectorate. From that date to 1660 the ranks of the army were filled by voluntary enlistment." A chapter on the pay of the army notes that despite the private soldier's modest pay, he was permitted to add to it by "lawful plunder." While plunder was sometimes used as a substitute for pay, generally it was "a mere supplement to it, the more important because the soldier's pay was generally in arrears."

FORTESCUE, JOHN WILLIAM. *The British Army 1783–1802.* 1905. Macmillan & Co. London. 148 pages.

Based on a lecture series, this book describes the pay system in force in the late-18th century British army, as well as recruitment problems and reforms. Discussing the costs and consequences of Pitt's military policies that left England unprepared for war in 1793, Fortescue states: "At the outbreak of hostilities there were practically no troops, and little prospect of obtaining any, so unpopular had Pitt rendered military service by starving the soldier."

FORTESCUE, JOHN WILLIAM. *The County Lieutenancies and the Army 1803–1814.* 1909. Macmillan & Co. London. Index. 328 pages.

A critical analysis of the various expedients tried by successive ministers from 1802 to 1814 to cope with the drain made on the British army by the war with France. Beginning with Addington's proposals for militia reform, it indicates the scope of the attempts made to reform the defensive force and to increase the Regular Army down to the time of Castlereagh. Several conclusions are drawn from these developments: England must resort to conscription in any large-scale war, but compulsion should not be applied for service outside Britain; substitution in any compulsory service system is expensive, demoralizing, and inefficient; basic arms training should be the responsibility of the individual citizen; and volunteers should expect pay only on active service.

FORTESCUE, JOHN WILLIAM. *The Empire and the Army.* 1928. Cassell & Co. London. Index. Maps. 338 pages.

Discusses recruiting methods in the British army, starting with the post-Restoration system, with regiments built up on the model of the old mercenary bands, and with the purchase-system and levy-money practices. Fortescue describes how Castlereagh in 1807 transformed the militia into a "recruiting depot" for the army and raised a new force of local militia by enforcing compulsory personal service; how the difficulties in gaining recruits for the West Indies resulted in the raising of Negro West India regiments, enlisting of foreigners, and relegation of "bad characters" to the West Indies in penal battalions; how the purchase-system was abolished in 1871 and pay and conditions gradually improved. The book concludes with Haldane's reorganization of the army in the early 1900s and his efforts to maintain an all-volunteer force, efforts which were successful until well into World War I when conscription was restored to.

FORTESCUE, JOHN WILLIAM. *A History of the British Army.* Volume 1. 2nd edition. 1910. Macmillan & Co. London. Index. Maps, plans. 608 pages.

Volume 1 of a 13-volume study of the political and military aspects of the British army's history to 1870. Traces the army from the time of the Norman Conquest to the early 1700s, when it was under Marlborough. For each period, the administration and practices prevailing are described in detail, against the backdrop of political and social developments, and comparisons are frequently drawn between the English system and that of other European nations, showing the various influences that were present.

HAYES, DENIS. *Conscription Conflict: The Conflict of Ideas in the Struggle For and Against Military Conscription in Britain Between 1901 and 1939.* 1949. Sheppard Press. London. Index. Bibliography: pages 384–395. 408 pages.

An attempt to render a complete historical account of the circumstances in which modern conscription twice came to Britain, with the reasons and principles advanced on each side. The author avoids analytical interpretation and discussion of the relative merits of opposing positions on the concept of military conscription.

HIGHAM, ROBIN. *Armed Forces in Peacetime: Britain 1918–1940, a Case Study.* 1962. Archon Books. Hamden, Connecticut. Index. Tables. Bibliographic references: pages 289–324. 332 pages.

Chapter 3, "Reorganization of the Army," deals with "the dilemmas of the British armed services from 1918 to the mid-1930s when rearmament became the first step in mobilization for the Second World War." Poor pay and poor conditions, it is noted, were responsible for low enlistment figures during much of this period. Chapter 4 discusses Depression-era pay cuts and a navy mutiny, while Chapter 6 deals with recruiting problems in a period of technological advance.

HOLLISTER, C. WARREN. *Anglo-Saxon Military Institutions on the Eve of the Norman Conquest.* 1962. Clarendon Press. Oxford, England. Index. Bibliography: pages 153–162. 170 pages.

A study of the organization of the late-Saxon military establishment, taking into consideration economic, social, and political influences. Individual chapters deal with mercenaries and war finance, the nation in arms, the select fyrd and the five-hide unit, and the late-Saxon navy. Hollister notes that "the pre-Conquest English army, like the later Anglo-Norman army, relied to a considerable extent on hired soldiers ['mercenaries']— men who served for wages as distinct from those whose basic military responsibility arose from personal or territorial obligations."

HOLLISTER, C. WARREN. *The Military Organization of Norman England.* 1965. Clarendon Press. Oxford, England. Index. Bibliography: pages 291–306. 319 pages.

A well-documented examination of Norman feudalism, with chapters on the knight's fee, the king's feudal army, castle service, mercenaries, scutage, and the post-Conquest fyrd. It is shown that a number of Anglo-Saxon military institutions persisted after the introduction into England of the Norman feudal system and remained a central feature of English military life.

HUTCHINSON, J. R. *The Press-Gang Afloat and Ashore.* 1914. E. P. Dutton & Co. New York. Index. Illustrations. 349 pages.

A history of the practice of impressment of men for the sea service of the British Crown, dealing especially with the period from the early 1700s until the practice was discontinued in 1833. Though orders were to press "no aged, diseased or infirm persons, nor boys," the press-gangs "raked in recruits with a lack of discrimination that [made the British fleet] the most gigantic collection of human freaks and derelicts under the sun." Reprieved and pardoned convicts were "bestowed in about equal proportions . . . upon the army and the navy," while "the insolent debtor was perhaps an even less desirable recruit than his cousin the emancipated convict." Hutchinson finds that "the demoralisation of the Navy through pressing, the excessive cost of pressing and the antagonising effects of pressing upon the nation at large contributed in no small degree to that final suppression of the press-gang which was in essence, if not in name, the beginning of Free Trade."

KNYVETT, HENRY. *The Defence of the Realme.* Revised edition. 1906. Clarendon Press. Oxford, England. 75 pages.

Introduction by Charles Hughes. Originally published in 1596, this is an Elizabethan soldier's treatise on the necessity of compulsory military training for all Englishmen. Knyvett suggests that if the manhood of England were properly organized, the country might be made safe against invasion. According to this scheme, England could, "without hiering any unproffitable and dangerous mercenary soldiers [levy British citizens in] sufficient number to encounter any Potentate in Europe and leave enowe behinde to supplie all other necessarie tournes." The levies would be divided into four categories: the first group, made up of those under 18, would be considered "not yett ripe enoughe" for military training; the second, aged from 18 to 50, would be trained and assigned according to "the stature of their bodies"; the third would be "horsemen"; while the fourth would comprise those above the age of 50, enrolled "under the title of Domisticalls for that theire age begineth to crave a dispensation from all martiall actions, and yett they maie for the benefitt of the Common wealth otherwise most necessarilie be used."

LAMBERT, RICHARD C. (compiler). *The Parliamentary History of Conscription in Great Britain.* 1917. George Allen & Unwin. London. Index. 367 pages.

A summary of the British parliamentary debates on conscription, 1914–1916, compiled from Hansard. Includes statements of Kitchener, Asquith, Balfour, Derby, and Lloyd George, as well as those parliamentarians active on both sides of the conscription issue. The work covers the various aspects of conscription such as compulsion, registration, recruiting, physical examination and reexamination, exemptions, appeals, conscientious objection, and cost, and includes a defense of the voluntary system. Among the measures debated are the Defence of the Realm Act, the Derby Report, and the military service bill.

OLIVER, FREDERICK SCOTT. *Ordeal by Battle.* 1916. Macmillan Co. New York. 437 pages.

Contending that World War I would not have been inevitable had Britain been militarily prepared, the author presents a case for the permanent establishment of compulsory military service based on the causes of war and the respective military systems, traditions, and experiences of Germany and Britain.

OMOND, J. S. *Parliament and the Army 1642–1904.* 1933. Cambridge University Press. Cambridge, England. Index. Bibliographic notes: pages 176–178. 187 pages.

Examines the growth of parliamentary control over the British army from the Restoration militia to the Cardwell and Haldane reforms in the late 19th and early 20th centuries. Omond outlines recruiting systems for each period, pointing up the gradual move away from a popular fear of a professional army and the abolition of such practices as purchase of promotion.

POWICKE, MICHAEL. *Military Obligation in Medieval England: A Study in Liberty and Duty.* 1962. Clarendon Press. Oxford, England. Index. 263 pages.

Provides an account of the development of military obligation in medieval England, relating the development of militia duty to general political and social history and analyzing the terms of military service. The survey is concerned primarily with the rights and duties of the subject rather than with the mechanics of the pay office or the technique of the soldier. The medieval trinity of king, nobles, and people is regarded as the key to the history of recruitment. The author sees the king's duty and right to declare war and to summon, lead, and direct armies as being balanced by his dependence on the nobility for mounted warriors and on the local communities for auxiliary and defense troops.

RAIKES, G. A. *The First Regiment of Militia.* 1876. Richard Bentley & Son. London. Illustrations. 334 pages.

In this history of the Yorkshire militia to 1875 its Anglo-Saxon origins are discussed, as well as such aspects as recruitment, pay, and conditions of service. The appendix includes a summary of statutes related to recruitment into the militia and from the militia into the Regular Army.

SANDERS, I. J. *Feudal Military Service in England: A Study of the Constitutional and Military Powers of the Barons in Medieval England.* 1956. Oxford University Press. London. Index. 173 pages.

Discusses fractional military service in Normandy and evidence of a similar system in England; the castle-guard as an alternative to service in the field; the fractional service summoned by the crown in the 12th and 13th centuries; evidence in the 13th century of the development of the new Servitium; factors influencing the size of the new quota; and the position of the baron in the feudal army. Obligation to the crown, recruitment, and conditions of service are also examined.

SCOULLER, R. E. *The Armies of Queen Anne.* 1966. Clarendon Press. Oxford, England. Index. Bibliography and reference key: pages 392–400. 420 pages.

Of particular interest in this study of the organization and administration of Queen Anne's armies are the chapters on recruiting and reinforcements, pay, and deserters. The appendix includes a breakdown of recruits for 1708–1709, and pay tables for the period.

CONSCRIPTION

Siddons, Joachim Heyward [J. H. Stocqueler, pseudonym]. *A Familiar History of the British Army, from the Restoration in 1660 to the Present Time, Including a Description of the Volunteer Movement, and the Progress of the Volunteer Organisation.* 1871. Edward Stanford. London. Index. 349 pages.

Includes discussions of military recruiting policy and practice in Britain during each period from the formation of a standing army under Charles II to the reforms of 1870, which reduced the required length of service and replaced the bounty by a bonus payable upon discharge.

Stephenson, Carl, and Frederick George Marcham (editors and translators). *Sources of English Constitutional History: A Selection of Documents from A.D. 600 to the Interregnum.* 2 volumes. Revised edition. 1972. Harper & Row. New York. Bibliographies. 953 pages.

Of particular interest is the section on the 1181 Assize of Arms, in which Henry II redefines the military obligations of all Englishmen. There are also several documents on the levy of men and taxes for military purposes, such as Edward III's restriction of military levies, and militia enactments of the 16th and 17th centuries.

Western, J. R. *The English Militia in the Eighteenth Century: The Story of a Political Issue 1660–1802.* 1965. Routledge & Kegan Paul. London. Index. Illustrations. 479 pages.

This study of the English militia begins with the Restoration militia acts and the measures of the Interregnum that were in force until 1757. The Civil War period of 1642–1652 had seen the first emergence of an English standing army, and the military and political implications of this for the militia are examined. The book describes militia agitations for reform, and the growth and modification of the militia up to 1802, when the consolidating militia act was passed. The 18th century militia is seen as representing two related military tendencies—the attempts "to create a reserve formation for home defense and to use an obligation of military service on the citizen as the basis for recruiting." Political factors made it impossible to introduce "true conscription" although, as the national danger increased, "parliament showed itself increasingly willing to move towards a real conscription." It is conjectured that had the national danger not abruptly ended in 1815, the militia and army together would have "gradually evolved into a conscript army of the modern type."

Books: General Works

AMERY, L. S. *The Problem of the Army.* 1903. Edward Arnold. London. Index. 319 pages.

An examination of current proposals for army reform, presenting the positions of such British statesmen as Brodrick, Hamilton, Roberts, Wolseley, and Wood. Considers that "the only true solution" to Britain's "military difficulties, both as regards the Home Army and the Imperial Army, is to be found in [military training] in the schools." Under such a scheme, secondary education would be extended for one year with the emphasis on military education so that the youth's "knowledge of the art of war . . . when perfected by one or two short periods of training in the national Militia [would] make sufficiently well-trained soldier for the purposes of home defence." The appendix includes the text of a memorandum written in August 1898 by General Kelly-Kenny, then Inspector-General of Recruiting, which was suppressed for several years. This memorandum is highly critical of the caliber of recruits, and asserts: "The pay must be largely increased, larger than ever yet proposed. . . . I go further: I say that so necessary is it to induce the right men to come into the ranks that it may be necessary to bid higher and higher till we get them."

BEGGS, S. T. *The Selection of the Recruit.* 1915. Bailliere, Tindall & Cox. London. Index. Tables. 108 pages.

Discusses recruiting procedures in the British army during World War I in regard to physical characteristics, focusing on the physical examination of the recruit and the causes of rejection for unfitness.

BOULTON, DAVID. *Objection Overruled.* 1967. Macgibbon & Kee. London. Index. Illustrations. 319 pages.

This study of conscientious objection in Britain in World War I examines the "political tradition" that produced conscientious objection to compulsory military service, and the various forms of resistance to it. Of particular interest are Chapters 3, 4, and 5, which deal respectively with the political development of the movement for conscription, the consolidation of opponents to the enactment of conscription and the tribunals organized to investigate and rule on individual cases of conscientious objection.

DONNINGTON, ROBERT, and BARBARA DONNINGTON. *The Citizen Faces War.* 1936. Victor Gollancz. London. 286 pages.

Introduction by Norman Angell. Examines from a pacifist viewpoint the record of conscientious objection in Britain during World War I. Describes the activities and interaction of such groups as the No-Conscription Fellowship, the Society of Friends, the Fellowship of Reconciliation, the National Council Against Conscription, and the Independent Labour Party—the last asserted to be the only political party that officially supported the conscientious objector. Accounts of tribunals and some contemporary press coverage are included.

FARRER, JAMES ANSON. *Invasion and Conscription: Some Letters from a Mere Civilian to a Famous General.* 1909. T. Fisher Unwin. London. 127 pages.

This collection of 22 letters addressed to Lord Roberts, head of the pro-conscription National Service League, assails one by one the arguments on which the league bases its advocacy of a compulsory system of military service in England. Farrer asserts that military service is not "every man's duty"; rather, that "historically, legally, and constitutionally, not service, but exemption from it, is the citizen's privilege." Until Parliament takes that privilege away from the citizen, "a vote for Parliament and immunity from the degradation of a military life are equally the rights of a free British citizen."

FULLER, J. F. C. *The Army in My Time.* 1935. Rich & Crown. London. Index. 246 pages.

In this narrative, the author discusses the Cardwell and Haldane reforms, and suggests that though each had some merit, increasing mechanization of the army and the decay in which it has been permitted to fall call for broad new reforms. Advocating measures that would permit the development of a smaller, more efficient professional army, Fuller would, for example, improve conditions of service so that the army could compete in the general labor market.

FULLER, J. F. C. *Towards Armageddon: The Defence Problem and Its Solution.* 1937. Lovat Dickson. London. Index. 244 pages.

In Chapter 6, on manpower, the author recommends that voluntary enlistment should continue in peacetime, but that in wartime "conscription should be applied to the entire nation in order morally to unite it and prevent the disgraceful profiteering of the last war [World War I]." He suggests that all citizens, irrespective of age or occupation, be divided into categories according to their trades or professions, and, on the outbreak of war, be placed on a common footing of pay and rationing. Included are a number of recommendations for stimulating voluntary enlistment in a peacetime professional army.

HALDANE, RICHARD B. *Army Reform and Other Addresses.* Circa 1907. T. Fisher Unwin. London. Index. 312 pages.

Part 1, "The Army," consists of three speeches delivered by the author in the British Parliament between March 1906 and February 1907. Haldane's proposed reforms include a smaller, more highly paid Regular Army. He discusses recruiting, terms of enlistment, the use and training of reserves, and the militia. Haldane is concerned largely with cost, and he is particularly opposed to short enlistments.

HALDANE, RICHARD B. *Before the War.* 1920. Cassell & Co., Ltd. London. Index. 208 pages.

A former war minister's postmortem on British policy toward Germany in the eight years preceding World War I. Chapter 4 is of particular interest, describing Britain's military manpower mobilization.

HAMILTON, IAN. *Compulsory Service: A Study of the Question in the Light of Experience.* 2nd edition. 1911. John Murray. London. 212 pages.

Introduction by Richard B. Haldane. Hamilton assesses military manpower needs in Britain and recommends establishing first- and second-line volunteer forces, with a latent draft law that could be invoked in time of war. His conclusions concerning various alternatives to the existing system are based on his experience as Adjutant-General. The appendices include related government documents as well as papers of the National Service League.

HAMILTON, IAN. *The Soul and Body of an Army.* 1921. Edward Arnold & Co. London. 303 pages.

A British army general's recommendations for improved military organization. Discusses British and foreign military systems with emphasis on the questions of discipline, training, and patriotism.

HAMLEY, EDWARD. *National Defence.* 1901. William Blackwood & Sons. London. 198 pages.

A compilation of articles and speeches dealing with Britain's military manpower needs. Considers the relative strengths of all British forces—Regulars, militia, and volunteers—and estimates that the volunteer force would constitute two-thirds of the army in case of invasion. Hamley terms a "delusion" the belief held by some in Britain that a conscript army is less costly than an all-volunteer system: "To point to the smaller expense of its pay and maintenance affords no index of the total burden [a conscript system] inflicts on the nation."

JAMES, DAVID. *Lord Roberts.* 1954. Hollis & Carter. London. Index. Illustrations, maps. 503 pages.

Foreword by L. S. Amery. Of particular interest is Chapter 14, "The Fight for National Service (1904–1913)," which describes Roberts's activities as head of the pro-conscription National Service League. Roberts espouses the position that if British parliamentarians can be brought to an acceptance of the concept of compulsory military service, then the nation at large would assent to the institution of such a system.

LIDDELL HART, B. H. *The Defence of Britain.* 1939. Random House. New York. Index. 444 pages.

Part 4, "The Reorganization of the Army," and Part 5, "Aspects of Army Reform," deal with the assessment and fulfilment of military manpower needs and distribution. Of particular interest are the author's recommendations for improved recruitment of four-year volunteers in the Territorial Army.

MACDONALD, J. RAMSEY. *National Defence: A Study in Militarism.* 1917. George Allen & Unwin. London. 132 pages.

Charges that Britain, in resorting to conscription in World War I, "set out upon the road to military victory through the ruin of civil liberty." Assailing the conscriptionists' "promise that a citizen force is a peace force," MacDonald warns trade unionists that the only result of national compulsion "will be that the citizen Army will teach obedience and military necessity to the people, and cripple their initiative and independence, and rob their political strength of authority as it did in the case of the German Social Democrats."

MAUDE, F. N. *Voluntary Versus Compulsory Service: An Essay.* 1897. Edward Stanford. London. 134 pages.

A consideration of whether voluntary or compulsory military manpower recruitment is best suited to England's needs. The author, a military officer and strategist, analyzes the cases of Germany and France as extreme examples of nations where compulsory military service was respectively an "unqualified boon" and "a heavy drain on national prosperity." England is seen as occupying a peculiar position between these two extremes. Maude suggests that the institution of compulsory service in England would result in higher rather than lower costs since, to be effective and just, it must be applied, if at all, universally. Arguing the military side of the question, he concludes that in the absence of any "special national advantage" to be derived from compulsory service, the military evidence is against compulsion; as long as the English army attracts an adequate number of suitable men for short service, it "can do all and more than has been achieved by any compulsory army whatever."

MAURICE, FREDERICK. *Haldane,* Volume 1: *1856–1915.* 1937. Faber & Faber. London. Index. 394 pages.

Describes Haldane's reform of the army during his tenure as Britain's secretary of war. In the pre-World War I discussions of military manpower policy, Haldane is said to have been "fully convinced" that compulsory service was "impracticable politically" and "by no means certain that it was advisable militarily." Haldane's conflict with conscriptionist Lord Roberts concerns the question whether Haldane's reorganized army is adequate to ward off possible invasion. The author notes France's efforts to persuade Britain to adopt a compulsory service system.

MEAKIN, A. M. B. *Enlistment or Conscription?* 1915. George Routledge & Sons. London. 129 pages.

An informal presentation of the case for conscription, describing the concept as a necessary and "voluntary act" that the British people will inevitably choose "in preference to bartering away our liberty in exchange for an obsolete idea." Meakin stresses the failure of government efforts to recruit sufficient men despite its "advertising wildly." He argues that there is a rapidly growing volume of opinion in favor of conscription and it therefore behooves the government to initiate a public debate on the question.

NO-CONSCRIPTION FELLOWSHIP. *The No-Conscription Fellowship: A Souvenir of Its Work During the Years 1914–1919.* Circa 1920. London. Illustrations. 95 pages.

Articles by National Committee members of the No-Conscription Fellowship describe the fellowship's anticonscription activities, its efforts on behalf of conscientious objectors, and its cooperation with other anti-conscription and pacifist groups such as the Quakers and the Socialists. Presents statistical data on civil and military actions against objectors, on grounds for objection, on objectors sentenced to death, and on the deaths of objectors after arrest. Included are the proceedings of the concluding convention of the fellowship in November 1919, when three committees were appointed to "watch the conscription situation, to link together pacifists, and to oppose military training in the schools."

NO-CONSCRIPTION FELLOWSHIP. *The Tribunal.* 1970. Klaus Reprint Co. New York. 730 pages.

Introduction by John G. Slater. This book contains every issue (numbers 1–182) of *The Tribunal,* the weekly published by the No-Cconscription Fellowship in London from March 8, 1916, to January 8, 1920. *The Tribunal* provides a record of its own history: how its offices were raided, its editors and publishers arrested and sentenced to prison terms, its printing equipment destroyed, as the British government sought to silence the paper. Information on the local tribunal hearings that ruled on applications for conscientious objector status and on the prisons to which many objectors were sentenced is interspersed with articles by Bertrand Russell, Clifford Allen, Fenner Brockway, and others, spelling out the arguments against conscription and war.

PASLEY, C. W. *Essay on the Military Policy and Institutions of the British Empire.* 1811. Edmund Lloyd. London. 531 pages.

England

An analysis and critique of the current state of British military preparedness, with recommendations for improvements in organization of the
Regular Army, militia, and volunteer forces. Comparisons are drawn
between contemporary British and French military policies and institutions.

RAE, JOHN. *Conscience and Politics: The British Government and the
Conscientious Objector to Military Service 1916–1919.* 1970. Oxford
University Press. London. Index. Illustrations, tables. Bibliography:
pages 259–270. 280 pages.

A historical study of the relations between the British government and
conscientious objectors in World War I. The author draws heavily on
official records and private papers of political leaders that become available only long after the war. Appendices include the records of tribunals
as well as tables outlining the nature of conscientious objection and the
wartime assignation of objectors.

RE-BARTLETT, LUCY. *Our Nascent Europe.* 1916. St. Catherine Press.
London. 61 pages.

Discusses the philosophical perspectives of conscription, the place of
women in solving future manpower and social needs, and England's
responsibility to the rest of Europe. The author appeals to Liberals still
opposing conscription after its introduction in Britain to recognize the
function of individual liberty as a component of national liberty, and urges
the adoption of a permanent system providing for universal military training and readiness.

ROBERTS, FREDERICK SLEIGH. *Fallacies and Facts: An Answer to "Compulsory Service."* 1911. John Murray. London. 247 pages.

In this critique of Ian Hamilton's book, *Compulsory Service* (see page
335, above). Roberts, head of the conscriptionist National Service League,
argues that there is in fact no precedent in British history for the anticonscriptionist thesis of the "free-born Briton" in opposition to "constraint
of any kind, especially compulsory military training."

ROBERTSON, JOHN M. [Roland, pseudonym]. *The Future of Militarism.*
1916. T. Fisher Unwin. London. 185 pages.

A personalized and frequently polemical critique of F. Scott Oliver's
Ordeal by Battle, which proposes the permanent establishment of conscription in Great Britain (see above, page 330).

SHEE, GEORGE F. *The Briton's First Duty: The Case for Conscription.*
1901. Grant Richards. London. Diagrams. 252 pages.

Discusses "the justice and necessity of compulsory service for home
defence" and "the advantages of universal military service," considering
also arguments against compulsory military service. Contends that "in
spite of every expedient of increased pay, lowered physical standard, larger
bounties, and the generous provision for the comfort, health and recreation
of the soldier, the difficulty in providing the men voted by Parliament
grows ever greater." In this view, the voluntary military system must be
considered to have failed to keep pace with national security needs, and
the institution of universal military service in Britain must be considered
a "necessity."

VOLUNTARY SERVICE COMMITTEE. *The Case for Voluntary Service.* Circa
1914. P. S. King & Son. London. Index. 200 pages.

Issued as a debate handbook in defense of the voluntary military-
recruiting system, this book explores military and strategical questions to
show that the voluntary system of recruiting is better suited than any other
to the peculiar needs of the British Empire, and that only voluntarism can
sustain the long-term enlistment needs at overseas posts. It attacks proposals of the National Service League and its chief spokesman, Lord
Roberts, for universal military service, contending that any purportedly
universal obligation would prove discriminatory in that it would not in
fact draft all, and would favor, for example, those found physically deficient for military but not nonmilitary activities.

WILKINSON, SPENSER. *Britain at Bay.* 2nd edition. 1910. Constable &
Co. London. 192 pages.

In this analysis of Britain's security needs, the author sees the nation
as "drifting unintentionally and half consciously into a war with the
German Empire." He reviews the Norfolk Commission report and the
respective positions of the voluntarists and conscriptionists, and calls for a
choice between the two systems "to be determined by the purpose in
hand." Wilkinson presents a scheme whereby annually 200,000 of "the
best manhood of the nation" would receive one year's compulsory military
training without pay. Each trained man would be bound to serve with the
army in a national war, and would have the option of enlisting for a term
of eight years in the British forces in India, Egypt, or the colonies. Wilkin-

son opposes as neither morally nor economically sound the concept of keeping a voluntary paid standing army "side by side with a national army raised upon the principle of universal duty."

WILLIAMS, BASIL. *Raising and Training the New Armies.* 1918. Constable & Co. London. 312 pages.

An examination of the manner in which large numbers of troops were raised in Britain during World War I. Part 1 describes recruiting problems and conscription, noting the "remarkable . . . ease and general acquiescence" with which Britons accepted conscription given their traditional "suspicion, not only of compulsory military service, but of a large standing army of any kind."

Unpublished Manuscripts

KENNEDY, THOMAS C. *The Hound of Conscience: A History of the No-Conscription Fellowship 1914–1919.* 1967. Ph.D. dissertation. University of South Carolina. Columbia, South Carolina. Bibliography: pages 455–470. 470 pages.

The first chapter considers the continuing debate on the issue of whether England has a tradition of voluntary or compulsory military service. The remainder of the study examines organized conscientious objection in England from the introduction of military conscription in World War I to the disbanding of the No-Conscription Fellowship after the war. It considers legal policies and practices instituted to deal with the conscientious objector, discusses the dissension that developed between alternativists (those prepared to perform noncombat service) and absolutists (those unwilling to perform any military-related service), and assesses any residual influence of the fellowship in regard to national policy.

MACKIE, WILLIAM ERNEST. *The Conscription Controversy and the End of Liberal Power in England 1905–1916.* 1966. Ph.D. dissertation. University of North Carolina. Chapel Hill, North Carolina. Bibliography: pages 299–307. 311 pages.

Describes the conscription controversy as the "most disruptive and virulent political problem in England during the first two years of the

First World War." Traces the roots of the debate from the 19th century, noting that the need for reorganization of the British army had become apparent in the South African (Boer) War. By May 1915 Lord Kitchener's efforts to obtain sufficient recruits were being questioned and the conscription controversy began in the press. Mackie concludes that the Liberal members of the coalition government were "predisposed to oppose conscription by the very difficulties which they had encountered in trying to make the Liberal creed work in the prewar years and that they held to 'voluntaryism' as a last bastion from which Liberalism could remake the postwar world."

NOYES, ARTHUR H. *The Military Obligation in Mediaeval England.* 1930. Ph.D. dissertation. Ohio State University. Columbus, Ohio. Index. Bibliography: pages 183–194. 200 pages.

Examines the history of the military obligation and the influence of military history upon constitutional development in England from the 13th to the 17th century. Includes a discussion of the nature and origin of the commission of array.

STEARNS, STEPHEN JEROLD. *The Caroline Military System 1625–1627: The Expeditions to Cadiz and Re.* 1967. Ph.D. dissertation. University of California. Berkeley, California. Bibliography: pages 407–418. 419 pages.

The Caroline expeditions undertaken by Charles I and the Duke of Buckingham against the Spanish and Austrian Hapsburgs are described as "utter failures." Contributing to the defeats was the fact that there was no standing army: "Men were selected for military service often on an arbitrary and corrupt basis with little attention paid to their fitness for service. It was thought more important to rid the country of its riffraff and prevent the loss of the economically useful." The troops were not regularly paid and they were badly fed, clothed, and armed; the poor supply system resulted in desertions, stealing, rioting, and mutinies. The expeditions were, as Stearns puts it, "the cause of the grievances embodied in the petition of right and began the process of dissolving the habits of automatic obedience and loyalty to the monarchy which was completed in 1642."

Articles

AMERY, L. S. *National Service.* National Review. December 1938. Volume CXI, Number 670. Pages 725–735.

Considers that, given reasonable conditions of pay and service, there should be no insuperable difficulty in maintaining British peacetime forces at strength. "But," Amery asserts, "when it comes to the numbers required for Home Defence on the modern scale, as well as for the creation of a reservoir of trained men and organized units to meet the need for the support and expansion of our exiguous Regular Army, it would be impossible, even at prohibitive cost, to secure them on those lines."

BARKER, J. ELLIS. *How America Became a Nation in Arms: Some Lessons for the Present Crisis.* The Nineteenth Century and After. September 1915. Volume LXXVIII, Number 463. Pages 507–540.

"Many Englishmen extol the voluntary system and oppose compulsory service because in their opinion compulsion, conscription, is undemocratic," writes Barker, and then points out: "Most of these are quite unaware that the greatest, the freest, and the most unruly democracy in the world gladly submitted to conscription half a century ago, and appear to forget that France and Switzerland recognise that the first duty of the citizen consists in defending his country. . . . The story of the Civil War . . . shows that the United States were saved by two factors, by one-man government and by conscription. . . . If the United States found conscription necessary to prevent the Southern States breaking away and forming a government of their own, how much more necessary is the abandonment of the voluntary system when not merely the integrity but the existence of Great Britain and of the Empire is at stake!"

BARNETT, CORRELLI. *The British Armed Forces in Transition.* The Royal United Service Institutional Journal. June 1970. Volume CXV, Number 658. Pages 13–21.

The author, a British military historian, is highly critical of Britain's current policy of maintaining a small, all-volunteer "Imperial" army to deal with "European" problems, and traces the historical causes of the situation. He disagrees with the belief that nuclear weapons obviate the need for substantial conventional forces, contending that present forces are too small to fulfil Britain's responsibilities in Europe, and that military strength can act as a deterrent to war only if it is capable of successfully waging war. Barnett expounds on the citizen's obligation to bear arms in defense of the state, advocating the adoption of some form of universal military training in order to maintain a large reserve force capable of rapid mobilization. Used as models are the systems of Sweden, Switzerland, and Israel.

BATTINE, CECIL. *Wanted: A Military Constitution.* The Nineteenth Century and After. April 1915. Volume LXXVII, Number 458. Pages 803–815.

Urges adoption of a military constitution in Britain, arguing: "It is absolutely necessary that the laws which regulate the existence of the British land forces should be crystalised and codified. Every subject of the King should know for certain in the future what demands can be made upon his personal service, and in return every one, whatever his grade, should be protected in the enjoyment of his rank and rights." Battine estimates that a million field troops, with at least a million trained reservists, will be needed, and contends that such numbers can be raised by conscription alone. A revision of the military laws could make conscription "possible and tolerable"; it could also "remove the abuses and anomalies which handicap the administration of our War Office."

BLAKE, HENRY A. *National Service: Compulsory Service as a Principle of the Constitution.* The Nineteenth Century and After. October 1915. Volume LXXVIII, Number 464. Pages 808–813.

Examines "the development of the principle of universal service" in British history, claiming that "the power of conscription has thus come down intact through all the centuries." In Blake's opinion, if the voluntary system provides the necessary men, "there will be no need to exercise the power of compulsion"; if it does not, "a demand for the power of compulsion for the duration of the war will be readily granted" by the public.

CALLWELL, CHARLES E. *The Official Case Against Compulsory Service.* Blackwood's Magazine. January 1911. Volume CLXXXIX, Number 1143. Pages 104–115.

A critique of Ian Hamilton's *Compulsory Service* (see page 335, above). Contends that the book deals with two divergent forms of obligatory military service—"conscription after the Continental pattern, and compulsory service, somewhat on the Swiss model"—but does not always clearly distinguish between them. Callwell favors "modified compulsory service, somewhat after the Swiss model," which, he believes, "would give [Britain] a home defence army of adequate strength and sufficiently well trained for practical purposes; and there is little reason to suppose that the adoption of such a system would hamper the provision of the military forces necessary for offensive operations."

COULTON, G. G. *Our Conscripts at Crecy.* The Nineteenth Century and After. February 1909. Volume LXV, Number 384. Pages 251–257.

Maintains that the system of compulsory military service "was an essentially English institution during the [14th] century which is singled out by historians of all schools as specially important for the formation of our national character."

COULTON, G. G. *The Volunteer Spirit.* The Nineteenth Century and After. January 1915. Volume LXXVII, Number 455. Pages 19–29.

Examines the alleged defects of a voluntary military system in England and declares: "If only we could pass all our able-bodied manhood through six months of serious drill for home defence, we could not only afford to make the fullest allowance for conscientious objections, but also leave all foreign service to the volunteer impulse."

CREGAN, T. A. *The Middle Way: A Reply to Colonel Maude and a Proposal.* The Nineteenth Century and After. February 1915. Volume LXXVII, Number 456. Pages 278–291.

Proposes a system of obligatory national service for home defense, with voluntary enlistment for service abroad. Cregan maintains that the voluntary system has been unable to meet the demands of the present war, and that his proposed system would relieve regular troops from duty for home defense, making them available for active service. He contends that Maude "has under-estimated the total available fighting strength of this country by nearly 1½ millions, a fact which, of course, vitiates the whole of his conclusions." Cregan states that while as an individualist he is on principle against compulsion, some form of compulsion has become necessary in the present crisis.

DEWAR, A. B. *An Individualist's Plea for Obligatory Service.* The Nineteenth Century and After. January 1915. Volume LXXVII, Number 455. Pages 13–18.

Argues that the present crisis in England dictates that political philosophies be set aside and an obligatory military service system introduced without delay in behalf of "our liberties and our Empire."

DEWAR, A. B. *An Individualist's Plea for Obligatory Service: A Postscript.* The Nineteenth Century and After. July 1915. Volume LXXVIII, Number 461. Pages 75–82.

A continuing discussion on the supposed advantages of a compulsory military service system in Britain. Suggests that there must be "limits to one's belief in the voluntary principle," and draws the analogy of the state trying to raise war taxes by the voluntary method.

DODD, NORMAN L. *Square Pegs in Square Holes: The Selection of Recruits in the British Army.* Military Review. January 1975. Volume LV, Number 1. Pages 58–64.

Describes recruiting efforts in the British army, emphasizing the need for accurate placement of the recruit. Concludes that the British recruiting system is working well "though, to some extent, all recruiting must depend upon the rates of pay offered, something not under the control of the selection centers."

DODD, NORMAN L. *Volunteer Recruiting.* Military Review. June 1973. Volume LIII, Number 6. Pages 77–84.

Examines the British army's efforts to solve its recruiting and retention problems. Notes that both of the two major political parties in Britain are opposed to any form of conscription, and that both have "accepted that decent conditions of service and realistic pay play an important part in the re-engagement rate." Dodd maintains that the volunteer British army offers competitive pay and good conditions, as well as "more idealistic and intangible" attractions such as education and travel. Given these circumstances he finds it ironic that public opinion polls in Britain have shown that the majority of people favor some form of compulsory military service.

ERICKSON, ARVEL B. *Abolition of Purchase in the British Army.* Military Affairs. Summer 1959. Volume XXIII, Number 2. Pages 65–76.

Describes the developments that led to the abolition, in 1872, of the system of the purchase of military commissions in Britain.

ERROLL [pseudonym]. *Mr. Haldane's Dream of a "National" Army.* The Nineteenth Century and After. April 1907. Volume LXI, Number 362. Pages 542–547.

Critique of British Secretary of State Haldane's plan for a "national" army involving short-term training and service on a voluntary basis. Erroll claims: "No army can be national unless all the manhood of the nation is represented in its ranks." To satisfy its military manpower needs, moreover, Britain "must either go into the highways and compel [suitable young men] to come in, or must pay them sufficiently well to secure their services voluntarily. It cannot be done on the cheap, and no object (except political) is served by pretending it can."

GEORGE, F. *Army Recruiting: A Solution from the Other End.* The Nineteenth Century and After. August 1936. Volume CXX, Number 714. Pages. 227–234.

Notes that service in the British army involves the risk, not only of death or dismemberment, "but also, more surely, unemployment and pauperisation." Suggests that the recruiting shortfall is tied to the soldier's employment prospects upon demobilization. The author believes that the state has "a legal obligation" to guarantee the soldier "a livelihood by honest toil" upon demobilization.

GERMAINS, VICTOR W. *The Case for Conscription.* National Review. October 1937. Volume CIX, Number 656. Pages 474–482.

Comparing French and British military needs, the author contends: "If conscription is necessary for the defence of France, it is equally necessary for the defence of Britain." He suggests that, "offered the grim choice between a conquered, Hitlerised Britain on the one hand, and accepting conscription on the other, [the present opponents of conscription] are not likely to show any great enthusiasm but are even less likely to venture any active opposition."

HALE, LONSDALE. *"Compulsory Service": A Minister's Manifesto.* The Nineteenth Century and After. February 1911. Volume LXIX, Number 408. Pages 225–235.

Critical review of *Compulsory Service* by Ian Hamilton (see page 335, above). Hale, who is "strongly in favor of Compulsory Service for Home Defence," takes issue with Hamilton's "denunciation of the effect of compulsory service on the German Army."

HALE, LONSDALE. *Forewarned but Not Forearmed: A Warning from 1870–71.* The Nineteenth Century and After. June 1909. Volume LXV, Number 388. Pages 936–945.

Drawing in analogy the fate in 1871 of an unprepared France at the hands of a prepared and belligerent Germany, the author urges that Britain immediately establish "a reliable Second Line Army on land for Home Defence." In his view the necessary numbers can be obtained only by conscription. He maintains that "if you adopt in Great Britain the principle of Compulsory Service for Home Defence, you have nothing to fear from all Europe."

HEARNSHAW, F. J. C. *Compulsory Military Service in England.* Quarterly Review. April 1916. Volume 225, Number 447. Pages 416–437.

Disagrees with those who claim that the principle of voluntary enlistment is a heritage of the English people: "Far from voluntarism being the immediate tradition of the English race, it is a mushroom innovation established (and that only tentatively and provisionally) under the eyes of our grandfathers. . . . Even if it could be shown, as it cannot, that voluntarism has an ancient and creditable tradition behind it, there would still be no possibility of laying a valid claim to it as a 'heritage.' "

HOLLISTER, C. WARREN. *The Annual Term of Military Service in Medieval England.* Medievalia et Humanistica. June 1960. Fasciculus XIII. Pages 40–47.

An investigation into the length of the military service obligation in post-Conquest England. Finds that all the contingents of the post-Conquest army, feudal and nonfeudal alike, fought as a body and served for the same term, and that it was not until nearly a century after the Conquest that the customary 40 days of Norman feudal service took root in England. "In this respect, at least, the military transformation which has long been associated with the Norman Conquest was far from revolutionary."

HOLLISTER, C. WARREN. *The Five-Hide Unit and the Old English Mili-*

tary Obligation. Speculum. January 1961. Volume XXXVI, Number 1. Pages 61–74.

Discusses the nature of the military-tenurial changes effected in England by the Normans, examining the relationship between the Anglo-Saxon territorial system of military recruitment and the network of feudal tenures subsequently introduced by the Normans.

HOLLISTER, C. WARREN. *The Significance of Scutage Rates in Eleventh- and Twelfth-Century England.* English Historical Review. October 1960. Volume LXXV, Number 294. Pages 577–588.

Discusses the interrelationship of fluctuations in knights' wages, scutage rates, and length of wartime service in 11th and 12th century England in the context of the impact of the Norman Conquest. Concludes that "all in all, the effect of the Norman Conquest upon English military institutions appears to have been considerably less drastic than many twentieth-century historians have supposed."

HOUGHTON, B. *Free Service or Conscription.* Contemporary Review. May 1915. Volume CVII. Pages 610–617.

Considers the military, political, and social impact on Germany of its compulsory military service system. From a military point of view, in the author's opinion, "conscription appears by no means necessary" in Britain, and he expresses the hope that Britain may "keep the peace without that peril to our national life and ideals which an enormous standing army inevitably entails."

HUIZINGA, J. H. *Democracy and Compulsory Service.* Fortnightly Review. May 1939. Volume CXLV. Pages 527–533.

Points out that the concepts of "democracy" and "compulsory military service" may have different interpretations according to national, cultural, and social norms and values. Thus, the question of compulsory military service might have different implications in England from those in other "democratic" countries.

HURD, ARCHIBALD. *Compulsory Service: The War Office Veto.* The Nineteenth Century and After. January 1911. Volume LXIX, Number 407. Pages 133–149.

Reviews Ian Hamilton's *Compulsory Service* (see page 335, above), and examines arguments for and against the introduction in Britain of conscription. "The problem of British defence," Hurd concludes, "is essentially a problem of sea defence and a problem of finance; and, while we do not need a great home defence army, it is equally certain that we cannot afford it."

HUTCHINSON, GRAHAM SETON. *The Army and Society.* The Nineteenth Century and After. September 1935. Volume CXVIII, Number 703. Pages 323–334.

Recommends that the British army be made part of a "national move‑ ment" that would embrace not only military service itself, but also arrangements for "guaranteed State service" after demobilization. Such a program, it is suggested, would address two national problems: (1) it would boost recruitment into the army, and (2) it would provide the "social regeneration" and "spiritual responsibility" necessary to "our derelict population."

KINLOCH-COOKE, CLEMENT. *National Service: The National Register and After.* The Nineteenth Century and After. October 1915. Volume LXXVIII, Number 464. Pages 792–807.

Discusses the new legislated National Registration Act in Britain and its possible impact on compulsion for military service. Views the act as a last effort by the government to persuade the necessary numbers of men to enlist: "If the Act fails to bring in a sufficient number of recruits, and recruits of the right kind and the right class, the only alternative is conscription." In this view, the act would greatly facilitate the introduction of conscription, because it would shorten the interval that would elapse between the decision to resort to compulsion and the actual application of the measure.

LATHBURY, D. C. *Right and Wrong Methods of Recruiting.* The Nineteenth Century and After. February 1915. Volume LXXVII, Number 456. Pages 292–302.

Opposes the introduction of compulsory military service, urging instead that a public campaign be launched to boost voluntary enlistments.

MASTER MARINER [pseudonym]. *Fallacies of the Doctrines of Compulsory*

Service. Contemporary Review. September 1909. Volume XCVI.
Pages 295–303.

In the author's opinion, compulsory service in Great Britain for defense
purposes "would be justifiable only to the very limited extent which might
become necessary to fill up gaps in the full establishment of the Territorial
Army if voluntary enlistment failed. That establishment is at present
nearly reached, but even if it were not the numbers required to make good
the shortage would at most be counted by thousands, and not by the super-
fluous and expensive millions which 'universal' service would provide."

MAUDE, F. N. *The Case for Volunteers.* The Nineteenth Century and
After. January 1915. Volume LXXVII, Number 455. Pages 1–12.

Suggests that, while the compulsory military system may be appropriate
for Germany, British traditions and values argue against its introduction
in England.

MAUDE, F. N. *Voluntary Versus Compulsory Service.* Contemporary
Review. July 1911. Volume C. Pages 31–43.

Considers that the shortcomings of a compulsory military service system,
such as economic dislocation, outweigh the potential advantages, to
Britain, of such a system.

MILLER, E. ARNOLD. *Some Arguments Used by English Pamphleteers,
1697–1700, Concerning a Standing Army.* Journal of Modern History.
December 1946. Volume XVIII, Number 4. Pages 306–313.

Examines the controversy that developed over William III's call for a
large standing army: "The king's attitude evoked opposition in parliament
and precipitated a flood of pamphlets decrying the dangers of a standing
army to the government and the nation. An equal number of replies
appeared in support of the king's stand."

QUARTERLY REVIEW. *Compulsory Service: Lord Roberts v. Lord Haldane.*
April 1911. Volume 214, Number 427. Pages 555–575.

Critical examination and comparison of three books: Ian Hamilton's
Compulsory Service, Earl Roberts's *Fallacies and Facts,* and Spenser
Wilkinson's *Britain at Bay* (see pages 335, 339, and 340, above).

ROBERTS, A. CARSON. *The National Service*. The Nineteenth Century and After. November 1915. Volume LXXVIII, Number 465. Pages 985–996.

Suggests that Britain "would gain far more than it could lose from a bold pronouncement that the time has come when the help of all must be claimed, and that the State can no longer admit the right to bargain in the nation's service." This position, the author claims, is "the proper complement to voluntary service in time of peace" and "the very antithesis of commitment to compulsory service in aftertime."

ROPP, THEODORE. *Conscription in Great Britain 1900–1914*. Military Affairs. Summer 1956. Volume XX, Number 2. Pages 71–76.

Contends that the failure of the movement for conscription in Britain prior to 1914 "shows that civil-military communications involve far more than the difficulties faced by military men in trying to persuade civilians to adopt new, unpopular policies, that the problem cannot be solved by catchwords about military wisdom and civilian shortsightedness." Ropp reviews developments in the pre-World War I period, pointing up this alleged failure in civil-military communications.

SIMPSON, H. B. *Compulsory Military Service in England: A Retrospect*. The Nineteenth Century and After. April 1915. Volume LXXVII, Number 458. Pages 816–829.

Examines the origins and the different levels of enforcement of the military service obligation in England under the Common Law of England, which "recognises on the part of every able-bodied adult male a liability to render military service, when required to do so in the defence of the realm."

WELLS, W. T. *National Service and a National Register*. Fortnightly Review. November 1938. Volume CXLIV. Pages 549–558.

"The case for military conscription," Wells asserts, "must clearly stand or fall on the question whether or not [Britain] will send a large expeditionary force to the Continent. . . . No responsible politician could possibly advocate military conscription, with the vast expense and appalling economic dislocation which it would cause, unless for some serious and definite military object."

WINTERTON, EARL. *The Army Recruiting Problem.* Fortnightly Review.
January 1937. Volume CXLI. Pages 41–49.

Examines the causes of the British army's failure to obtain sufficient
recruits. Winterton attributes this failure only marginally to "pacifiist
propaganda, and the opposition of certain sections of opinion" to the
armed forces. Low pay, he contends, is the principal deterrent to recruiting.

Pamphlets, Reprints, and Speeches

ALLEN, CLIFFORD. *Conscription and Conscience.* 1916. No-Conscription
Fellowship. London. 15 pages.

In this presidential address to the national convention of the No-
Conscription Fellowship in November 1915, Allen states the common
basis of the members' objection to military conscription: "We contend
that the individual conscience alone must decide whether a man will
sacrifice his own life, or inflict death upon other people, and that however far the State may impose its commands upon the will of the community, the right of private judgment in this particular must be left to
the individual, since human personality is a thing which must be held as
sacred."

ALLEN, CLIFFORD. *Why I Still Resist.* 1917. No-Conscription Fellowship.
London. 4 pages.

The text of this leaflet is the defense made by Allen, chairman of the
No-Conscription Fellowship, before his third court-martial for refusal to
obey military orders. He had already served two sentences of hard labor,
and after the completion of each term had been returned to his miltary
unit under arrest.

BARKER, J. ELLIS. *National Service and National Physique.* Circa 1909.
The National Service League. London. Reprint from the British Medical Journal. Tables. 16 pages.

On the basis of a study of various physical tests of military recruits in
England and elsewhere, the author asserts that "military service benefits
the national physique not only directly, but also indirectly, by improving
not only the bodies but also the habits and the mode of life of the recruits."

COULTON, G. G. *Workers and War.* 1914. Bowes & Bowes. Cambridge, England. 23 pages.

Scores the complacency of British policy-makers, as well as the alleged isolationism of the British labor movement, in the early stages of World War I. Argues that Britain must without delay implement a reliable national defense, no longer relying on its navy alone, and that the current voluntary system can no more secure efficient national defense than it has secured efficient national education. The worker must ask himself whether "real social progress" is possible without national defense and, in the absence of any "more efficient and truly democratic" system, should consider compulsory service—which, the author contends, is not synonymous with, but contrary to, militarism.

DUBERY, HARRY. *A Labour Case Against Conscription.* 1913. National Labour Press. London. 14 pages.

Foreword by J. Keir Hardie. This pamphlet presents the case of the Independent Labour Party in England, and appeals to workers to collectively assail the efforts of the National Service League to gain support for the institution of conscription. It outlines the league's increasing demands, from its initial advocacy of brief periods of universal military training for home defense to its eventual demands for compulsory military service, foreign as well as domestic.

DUFFY, G. GAVAN. *The Groundwork of Conscription: An Epitome of the Military Service Code in Great Britain, with the Disciplinary Measures, Civil & Military, for Its Enforcement.* 1918. Talbot Press. Dublin, Ireland. 31 pages.

Outlines the tenets of the English compulsory service system, and the position of the conscript with regard to civil and martial law.

FELDMAN, ELLIOT. *When the Empire Comes Home: Consequences of the Abolition of Military Conscription in Great Britain.* 1974. Discussion Paper No. 6. School of Advanced International Studies, The Johns Hopkins University. Bologna, Italy. Tables. Bibliographical notes: pages 35–45. 47 pages.

Contends that Britain's decision in 1957 to abolish National Service, while ostensibly enacted in the interests of economy and efficiency, in fact "was, for the Army's reduced capabilities, more costly." Instead of improving defense, moreover, it "left the imperial remnant defenseless." The decision to return to a volunteer army is seen as "fundamental to British political principles, signalling a return to 'normalcy' for British society," and as an "acknowledgement of Britain's reduced role in the world." Feldman concludes that the decision was primarily a politically motivated one and that the national decision-makers failed to examine its social consequences or to prepare for any but military contingencies.

GLASIER, J. BRUCE. *The Peril of Conscription*. 1915. Independent Labour Party. London. 23 pages.

An appeal to workers to combat conscriptionist propaganda. Argues that the voluntary system has not failed in Britain, and that it is "entirely due to the voluntary system that the rate of day, family allowances, and pensions in the British Army is six or more times higher than in any of the conscript armies abroad." National Service League and other conscriptionist proposals for universal military service and training are said to be aimed at "regaining for the ruling classes their political and industrial control of the workers."

HAGGARD, WILLIAM. *The Militia: Its Importance as a Constitutional Force*. 1857. Longman, Brown, Green, Longmans & Roberts. London. 41 pages.

Text of a lecture delivered to English troops in 1856. In this review of the history of the British militia Haggard covers: the time of the Saxon monarch Alfred, under whom every man owning property had his share of military duty; the days of Athelstan, who, because the militia had been permitted to decay, had raised the "Dane-geld" tax from the community to bribe the Danes not to invade; Henry II's assize of arms, by which all males were compelled to remain prepared to defend themselves and the realm; the commissions of array, which sent officers into every district to "set all the inhabitants in military order"; the time of Henry VIII, when lieutenants of counties were introduced to keep their counties in a state of military preparedness; James I's establishment of trained bands; and Charles II's constitution of the militia as it now exists. The author contends that a "better class" of soldier can be recruited if men are "chosen by ballot" rather than by voluntary enlistment and the bounty system.

HEARNSHAW, F. J. C. *The Ancient Defence of England: The Nation in Arms.* 1915. National Service League. London. 11 pages.

Presents the case for the universal obligation to serve in the military, based on historical precedents.

HUNTER, ERNEST E. *The Home Office Compounds: A Statement as to How Conscientious Objectors Are Penalized.* Circa 1918. No-Conscription Fellowship. London. 16 pages.

Describes the conditions of industrial servitude in the government-operated work camps for conscientious objectors in World War I.

INDEPENDENT LABOUR PARTY. *What's This National Service?* 1939. London. 8 pages.

Pamphlet issued by the Independent Labour Party shortly before World War II. It predicts that Britain will follow the same path in World War II that it followed in World War I in regard to military and industrial conscription, and that the government's current efforts to stimulate recruiting will soon give way to a national registration and, ultimately, to military and industrial conscription.

KIPLING, RUDYARD. *The New Army in Training.* 1915. Macmillan & Co., Ltd. London. 64 pages.

An account of the life and training of soldiers in the English army in India. Kipling details service conditions and drills and describes the morale of the soldiers. He draws a distinction between the character of those who serve and that of those who ignore their duty, and comments, "Pride of city, calling, class and creed impose standards and obligations which men hold above themselves at a pinch and steady them through long strain. One meets it in the New Army at every turn."

KNEESHAW, J. W. *Conscription and Motherhood.* Circa 1916. National Labour Press. Manchester, England. 11 pages.

Urges women, as voters and as mothers of draft-eligible men, to support repeal of conscription in England following the end of World War I. Includes the text of a poem entitled "The Death Sentence," whose publication in Australia is credited by Kneeshaw with the defeat of conscription in that country.

England

KNEESHAW, J. W. *Conscription Enters the Workshops.* 1917. National
Labour Press. Manchester, England. 14 pages.

This pamphlet, issued by a parliamentary candidate awaiting trial (and
subsequently convicted) for having in his possession a number of anti-
conscription leaflets, charges that the true purpose of the 1916 conscription
law was to reduce the strength of trade unionism and introduce industrial
conscription. Over the assurances of Prime Minister Asquith, Kneeshaw
points out, two of three pledges have been broken—that there would be
no industrial conscription, nor conscription of married men. The third—
that there would be no peacetime conscription after the war—was in
danger of being broken too, under the propaganda of universal service
advocates and in the interests of big business.

KNEESHAW, J. W. *Conscription or Trade Unionism!* Circa 1915. National
Labour Press. Manchester, England. 11 pages.

Campaign pamphlet urging trade unionists to oppose permanent peacetime conscription in England when World War I ends. Kneeshaw contends
that conscription was introduced in spite of the overwhelming opposition
of the trade-union movement only because it was alleged to be necessary
as a war measure, and that "in no other form could Conscription have
found its way into English law." In his view the question of permanent
conscription "will be a fight for Conscription or Trade Unionism."

KNEESHAW, J. W. *How Conscription Works!* 1917. National Labour
Press. Manchester, England. 12 pages.

An appeal for trade-union support against industrial conscription.
Argues that men whose skills were fully utilized in civilian life are being
wasted in lesser capacities in the army, and that men physically fit for the
civilian jobs they were filling but unfit for army life are being drafted.
Individual cases of alleged injustice or inefficiency are cited.

LABOUR PARTY. *To the Soldier, Serving and Discharged.* 1918. Labour
Party Leaflet No. 23. London. 2 pages.

Election leaflet of the Labour Party addressed to the soldier, telling him
what the Labour Party has done for him while he was in the field and
what the party will do for him when he is demobilized.

LABOUR PARTY. LABOUR RESEARCH DEPARTMENT. *National Service and the Workers.* 1939. London. 23 pages.

Attempts to answer four questions: (1) Who is behind national service? (2) Does it mean conscription? (3) Does it threaten the trade unions? (4) Does it hinder fascism—or help it? Examines the British government's current national service scheme for recruiting and registering volunteers for military and industrial jobs, pointing to the danger that this voluntary scheme might lead to military and industrial conscription.

LAMBERT, UVEDALE. *National Service: An Address.* 1915. Blechingley, England. 12 pages.

Text of an address given by Lambert at the Village Hall, Blechingley, England, on August 26, 1915. Appealing for support for national service, Lambert urges "putting at the service of the country of all the powers and capabilities in it; that each may cheerfully and willingly take whatever share he can take in the work for our great end." In this view, each man should be prepared to serve his country in whatever way is needed for the greater good. Lambert sees France, with its adherence to military conscription, as "the most democratic country in Europe."

LEE, ARTHUR. *The Need of Compulsory National Service.* 1915. National Service League. London. 16 pages.

A British army officer asserts that the voluntary system must be replaced immediately by compulsory national service if Britain is to win the war and maintain an adequate force thereafter. Under a voluntary system, says Lee, the army recruits "willing and gallant spirits" but not always the men most fitted for soldiering, while factories are "denuded" of the most skilled workers. Compulsion would assign each adult male to the task in which he can do "most good" for his country, and would make "short work of the shirker and habitual slacker." A "less wasteful" system of compensation would provide for a uniform rate of pay for all soldiers.

MALLESON, MILES. *The Out-and-Outer.* 1916. No-Conscription Fellowship. London. 12 pages.

A criticism of the British government's handling of the "out-and-outer," or "absolutist" draftee, whose refusal to perform alternative, nonmilitary service subjects him to imprisonment as a criminal.

England

No-Conscription Fellowship. *The Court-Martial Friend and Prison Guide.* Circa 1916. London. 8 pages.

A handbook of procedures with regard to conscientious objectors before, during, and after court-martial.

No-Conscription Fellowship. *Final Agenda for the National Convention of the No-Conscription Fellowship.* 1919. London. 30 pages.

Includes a National Committee Report covering the operations of the fellowship during the years 1916–1919.

No-Conscription Fellowship. *The No-Conscription Fellowship: A Record of Its Activities.* Circa 1916. London. 8 pages.

A brief description of the policies and operations of the fellowship in its first two years.

No-Conscription Fellowship. *Rex v. Bertrand Russell.* 1916. London. 23 pages.

Report of proceedings before the Lord Mayor, in which Russell is found guilty of prejudicing military recruiting and discipline by authoring and circulating a pamphlet encouraging conscientious objector noncompliance with the noncombatant service provision of the conscription law.

No-Conscription Fellowship. *Why I Am a Conscientious Objector.* 1916. London. 20 pages.

Text of the questionnaire to applicants for conscientious objector status in England in World War I, and the responses of seven prominent conscientious objectors reflecting differing schools of thought.

Ridley, F. A. *Why We Oppose Conscription . . . The Badge of the Slave.* 1946. Independent Labour Party. London. 15 pages.

An attack on the ruling Labour Party's proposal to introduce peacetime compulsory military service in Britain—assertedly the precursor to industrial conscription and the servile state. Maintains that, even though conceived as an instrument of democratic liberation, conscription inevitably evolves as an instrument of nationalist and imperialist aggression.

ROBERTS, FREDERICK SLEIGH. *A Nation in Arms.* 1912. World Friendship Society and British Branch of the Conciliation Internationale. N.p. [England]. 35 pages.

Contains the text of Roberts's speech of October 22, 1917, along with comments, protests, and replies. Roberts describes the alleged danger of a German invasion and calls for a military system of compulsory "national service" to replace the "modified and remodified . . . effete voluntary system" in the British armed forces. The responses to Roberts's speech protest that his remarks are inflammatory and a threat to peace in Europe.

SNOWDEN, PHILIP. *British Prussianism: The Scandal of the Tribunals.* 1916. Independent Labour Party. Manchester, England. 24 pages.

This pamphlet contains the texts of two speeches by the Independent Labour Party member of Parliament delivered in the House of Commons on March 22 and April 6, 1916. Snowden places before the House evidence that the Military Service Act "is not being administered in a fair and judicial manner, and that its provisions are being most flagrantly violated by those who have had imposed upon them the responsibility of its administration." Snowden's criticism is directed toward the local tribunals appointed to rule on individual applications for exemption from compulsory military service under the act. He contends that unfit men are being pressed into service by the tribunals, and that the treatment by the tribunals of conscientious objectors "has been nothing short of an outrage and a public scandal." And he calls for an impartial inquiry into the administration of the Military Service Act.

SNOWDEN, PHILIP. *The Military Service Acts: A Full and Clear Explanation of the Acts and the Regulations.* Revised edition. 1916. Independent Labour Party. Manchester, England. 16 pages.

This pamphlet, prepared by an Independent Labour Party member of Parliament, describes the Military Service Acts of 1916, which subject British males between 18 and 40 years of age to compulsory military service. The pamphlet explains the grounds for claiming exemption under the acts, and discusses various other rights of individuals opposed to compulsory military service.

England

SOCIALIST PARTY OF GREAT BRITAIN. *The Socialist and Conscription.* 1939. London. 6 pages.

Opposes current proposals for peacetime conscription in Britain: "Our opposition to conscription differs fundamentally from that of the Labour Party, the Communist Party and the Pacifists. To the Labour Party and the Communist Party conscription is merely a tactical question—one of policy that may be revised at any moment. To the Pacifist it is a humanitarian question. To us, however, it is one of the ugly fruits of a social system in which there is a class division between capitalist and worker, a fundamental opposition of interests and hence an opposing class point of view. The threatened war for which it is proposed to call upon conscripts, would be a capitalist war like all modern wars; and just as we are opposed to war on this ground so we are opposed to any form of compulsion being used to force workers to fight for interests that are not their own but their masters'."

SOCIETY OF FRIENDS. *Compulsory Military Training: A Plea Addressed to All Those Who Value Christian Liberty.* By E. J. Wilson. Circa 1918. The Friends Service Committee. London. 2 pages.

States that "of all preparations for war, Conscription, whether for military service in time of war or for military training in time of peace, is the greatest challenge to the Christian conception of society." The Society of Friends "regards all life as being essentially religious, and Conscription as being directly antagonistic to the spirit of religious freedom."

SPECIAL AD HOC COMMITTEE. *Anti-Conscription Manifesto.* 1926. Enfield, England. 1 page.

Released by a "Special Ad Hoc Committee" on August 29, 1926, this document calls for "some definite steps towards complete disarmament, and the demilitarising of the mind of civilised nations." The manifesto asks the League of Nations to propose the international abolition of compulsory military service "as a first step towards true disarmament." Included among some 70 prominent signatories are Albert Einstein and Bertrand Russell.

WORKERS' NATIONAL COMMITTEE (WAR EMERGENCY). *Compulsory Military Service and Industrial Conscription: What They Mean to the Workers.* Circa 1916. London. 15 pages.

Urges opposition to national service bills that would authorize the government to compel men to serve in the military. It is suggested that "what is being proposed by many of those who are demanding the National Service Law is that the compulsory enlistment should be for service in whatever capacity the Government may require." In this way, it is contended, military service could be made "the instrument for Industrial Conscription."

Government Documents: Publications

BEITH, JOHN HAY [Ian Hay, pseudonym]. *Arms and the Men.* 1950. H. M. Stationery Office. London. Index. 330 pages.

First of an eight-volume series of a popular military history of World War II, issued by the British government pending publication of the Official Histories. Relates the role played by the British army, with emphasis on the internal development of the army and the changes brought about in its composition, training, leadership, and administration by the introduction of total mechanized warfare.

GREAT BRITAIN. WAR OFFICE. *Group and Class Systems: Notes on Administration.* 1916. H.M. Stationery Office. London. Index. 140 pages.

This handbook updates *Notes on the Administration of the Group System* issued in 1915 (see next entry). The appendix includes the text of the Military Service Act and a question-and-answer section outlining the act.

GREAT BRITAIN. WAR OFFICE. *Notes on the Administration of the Group System.* 1915. H.M. Stationery Office. London. 71 pages.

A handbook for administration of recruiting in Great Britain during World War I. The appendix includes instructions to local tribunals authorized to rule on applications for exemption and on violations, as well as a series of questions and answers concerning the group system, under which an enlistee continues in his civilian employment until the group to which he belongs is called up for training. (See also preceding entry.)

England

GREAT BRITAIN. WAR OFFICE. *Regulations for Recruiting for the Regular Army and the Special Reserve.* 1914. H.M. Stationery Office. London. Index. 71 pages.

A reprint of the 1912 edition with amendments to August 31, 1914, this handbook for recruiting officials includes provisions and procedures. The appendix contains sample forms used in recruiting, and a schedule of physical qualifications for enlistment.

CHAPTER 15

Other Foreign Countries

> In order to fully protect the achievements of the workers'
> and peasants' revolution, the Russian Soviet Federated
> Socialist Republic declares it to be the duty of all the citizens
> of the Republic to protect their Socialist country and intro-
> duces conscription. The honorable right to defend the revo-
> lution by force of arms is bestowed only on the workers. Non-
> working elements have to carry out other military duties.
> —Constitution of the U.S.S.R., 1924

Books

CHALLENER, RICHARD D. *The French Theory of the Nation in Arms
1866–1939.* 1955. Columbia University Press. New York. Index. Bibliography: pages 278–296. 305 pages.

Discusses French thought on the nation in arms from the time when
Napoleon III initiated military reform after the Austro–Prussian War of
1866 to the year of the outbreak of World War II. Challener deals with
the various opinions and programs advanced by military writers and
political spokesmen but concentrates upon the development of theory,
attempting to show "how the idea of the nation in arms changed from an
essentially political concept centering upon endless arguments over divergent conscription policies to a body of doctrine which by 1939 imposed
upon France a consistent, detailed set of regulations for the total exploita-
tion of her human and economic resources in time of war."

CHAMBERS, ERNEST J. *The Canadian Militia: A History of the Origin
and Development of the Force.* 1907. L. M. Fresco. Montreal. Illustrations, tables. 115 pages.

Describes the Canadian militia of the French regime, the first British Canadian militia and volunteers, the militias of upper, lower, and united Canada, the maritime province militia, the first Dominion militia act and amending legislation, and the assumption by Canada of its own defense and the departure of the last British Regulars.

DAVIS, SHELBY CULLOM. *The French War Machine.* 1937. George Allen & Unwin. London. Index. 221 pages.

An examination of French military policy in the two decades from World War I to the mid-1930s, dealing with specific measures dictated by the changes in the international situation and with problems of manpower and organization. Includes chapters on France's attempt to induce a higher birth rate, the mobilization of youth, conscripts, the "regulars," the nation in arms, colored troops, and the colonial army.

DAWSON, R. MACGREGOR. *The Conscription Crisis of 1944.* 1961. University of Toronto Press. Toronto, Canada. Index. 136 pages.

The contents of this book were to have formed part of a biography by Dawson of Canadian Prime Minister W. L. Mackenzie King, but were published separately when Dawson died before the biography was completed. Based largely on parliamentary and other official records and on contemporary media coverage, the book traces the political and legislative background of the conscription crisis.

EVATT, H. V. *Australian Labour Leader: The Story of W. A. Holman and the Labour Movement.* 1945. Angus & Robertson. Sydney, Australia. Index. 597 pages.

Includes a lengthy discussion of the issue of conscription in Australia in World War I: the unorganized recruiting at the outset of war, the development of Australian political and public opinion toward conscription, and the government decision to submit the issue to referendum (both the first referendum in 1916 and a second one, held a year later, were defeated).

EX-TROOPER [pseudonym]. *The French Army from Within.* 1914. Hodder & Stoughton. London. 186 pages.

Describes service in the French army during the pre-World War I period. The author upholds the system of conscription in France and discusses the various conditions of service for the conscript.

FORWARD, ROY, and BOB REECE (editors). *Conscription in Australia.* 1968. University of Queensland Press. St. Lucia, Australia. Figures, tables. Bibliographical notes at end of each chapter. 284 pages.

Contains 15 individual essays on the history of conscription in Australia from 1911 to 1968. Covers such issues as conscription and civil rights, conscription in peace and war, national service training, military considerations, international law and the conscription of non-nationals, anticonscription activities, and political and religious attitudes toward conscription and conscientious objection.

GARDER, MICHEL. *A History of the Soviet Army.* 1966. Frederick A. Praeger, Publishers. New York. Index. Bibliography: pages 214–217. 226 pages.

Includes a treatment of recruitment and reenlistment policies and practices in the Soviet Union, discussing the Imperial Russian Army and, more fully, the Red Army and the present army.

GOLLAN, ROBIN. *Radical and Working Class Politics: A Study of Eastern Australia 1850–1910.* 1960. Cambridge University Press. London. Index. Bibliography: pages 215–221. 226 pages.

Chapter 11, "A National Party and a National Policy," describes the political developments that led to the Labour Party's early advocacy, in its party platform, of compulsory military service.

GOURE, LEON. *The Military Indoctrination of Soviet Youth.* 1973. National Strategy Information Center. New York. 75 pages.

Documents the extent and intensity of the Soviet Union's military programs, starting with obligatory military training in the schools. Compares preinduction training at Soviet educational institutions with the U.S. Reserve Officers' Training Corps (ROTC) program.

GRANDE, JULIAN. *A Citizens' Army: The Swiss System.* 1916. Robert M. MacBride & Co. New York. Illustrations. 148 pages.

Describes the Swiss universal service system, pointing out that "it is possible to have an army without militarism." The final chapter looks at the "possible application to the United States" of the Swiss military system.

HEATHCOTE, T. A. *The Indian Army: The Garrison of British Imperial India 1822–1922.* 1974. David & Charles. Vancouver, Canada. Index. Illustrations, maps, tables. Bibliography: pages 205–207. 215 pages.

Describing the small, well-trained army of the Raj as the shield between the British in India and the various factions that would "drive the accursed English into the sea," the author seeks to provide an accurate picture of that army: to show its soldiers as ordinary men with hopes, problems, and lives of their own and how they were organized, equipped, and commanded. Heathcote concentrates on the period when British power was at its height in India in his discussion of the Indian and European men and officers, the fighting arms, the supporting troops, the reserves, and operations.

HOWARD, MICHAEL. *Soldiers and Governments: Nine Studies in Civil-Military Relations.* 1959. Indiana University Press. Bloomington, Indiana. Index. Bibliographic footnotes. 192 pages.

In the context of the armed forces as political problem, the author analyzes nine case studies of issues and conflicts in the relationships between military organizations and civilian governments. France, Russia, Japan, and the United States are among the countries covered.

JAUNCEY, L. C. *The Story of Conscription in Australia.* 1968. Macmillan of Australia. Melbourne, Australia. Index. Illustrations. 365 pages.

Foreword by P. O'Farrell. First published in 1935 by George Allen & Unwin Ltd., London. Writing from an anticonscriptionist viewpoint, the author discusses moves toward conscription in Australia from the late 1800s to 1935, the British National Service League's attempts to establish compulsory military training in the colonies so as to make the British public "more receptive to the idea," the activities of socialist, religious, and other anticonscriptionist organizations, and the 1916 and 1917 referendums on conscription. The book is based largely on parliamentary and other official materials, newspapers, pamphlets, and handbills.

KUHN, PHILIP A. *Rebellion and Its Enemies in Late Imperial China: Militarization and Social Structure 1796–1864.* 1970. Harvard University Press. Cambridge, Massachusetts. Index. Figures. Bibliography: pages 227–239. 254 pages.

Traces the origins of the militia in China, demonstrating that local military units of a voluntary nature were part of the Chinese tradition. Examines the origin of the systems designed to halt rebellion during the years 1820 to 1860.

LIDDELL HART, B. H. (editor).*The Red Army.* 1968. Peter Smith. Gloucester, Massachusetts. Index. Illustrations, maps. 480 pages.

A collection of 59 short essays on the Red Army from 1918 to 1945 and on the Soviet army from 1946 to the present. Of particular interest are "The Birth of the Red Army," by Leonard Schapiro; "A General Assessment," by Louis B. Ely; "The Psychology of the Soviet Soldier," by David Kelly; "The Military-Political System," by A. Neissel and J. M. Mackintosh; and "The Soviet Soldiers' Conditions of Service," by J. M. Mackintosh. The volume was first published in 1956.

MARTEL, CHARLES. *Military Italy.* 1884. Macmillan & Co. London. 384 pages.

Examines the state of the Italian armed forces in 1884. Martel discusses various alternatives for recruiting, including universal conscription and short-term volunteering. He considers recent military reforms in Italy and elsewhere, and makes recommendations for modifications of the Italian recruiting system.

MASON, PHILIP. *A Matter of Honour.* 1974. Holt, Rinehart & Winston. New York. Index. Illustrations, maps. Notes and sources: pages 535–545. 580 pages.

In this account of the Indian army from its inception in the 18th century to the present day, the author sketches the changes in the relations of officers and men and in the social structure of the army. Recruiting policies and practices and their social effects during the various periods in the history of the army are discussed.

MASSEY, HECTOR J. (editor). *The Canadian Military: A Profile.* 1972. Copp Clark Publishing Co. Toronto, Canada. Tables. 290 pages.

A collection of nine essays of which the following are of particular interest: R. H. Roy, "The Canadian Military Tradition"; Richard Preston, "Military Influence on the Development of Canada"; Pierre Coulombe, "Social and Cultural Composition of the Canadian Armed

Forces"; and G. G. Simonds, "Commentary and Observations." The collection is said by the editor to indicate that "the emphasis on militia—on the amateur soldier who trains in his spare time—has been one of the hall-marks of the Canadian military system, and the full-time professional is a comparative newcomer."

MOTLEY, JOHN LOTHROP. *The Rise of the Dutch Republic.* 1898. Harper & Bros. New York. Index. Illustrations. 943 pages.

Condensed, with an introduction, notes, and a "Historical Sketch of the Dutch People from 1584 to 1897," by William Elliott Griffis. Griffis's chapter on "The Model Army" describes the army created in the 1590s by John of Barneveldt and Maurice of Nassau: "It was not until Maurice had created a new science of war, and Barneveldt had made the statecraft of Holland equal to its necessities, that the Dutch secured a standing army of patriots who were able, without quailing, to look the Spaniard in the face." Griffis favorably compares this model army—notably its efficient administration and tactical prowess—with the English, Spanish, and other armies.

NORMAN, E. HERBERT. *Soldier and Peasant in Japan: The Origins of Conscription.* 1943. Institute of Pacific Relations. New York. Illustrations. 76 pages.

A short examination of the historical circumstances that led the ruling class of Japan, only a few years after the establishment of the Meiji regime (1868), to introduce general conscription into a country that had just emerged from being a rigid feudal society. Some examples of the characteristics of the peasant armies before the Meiji Restoration of 1868 are given, followed by an account of how the experience gained in this fashion was utilized by the military leaders of the new regime. The real motivation for the adoption of conscription is interpreted as a combination of fear of the West and, perhaps most importantly, the fear of the growing anti-feudal and democratic revolution that was developing in Japan.

OGAWA, GOTARO. *Conscription System in Japan.* 1921. Oxford University Press. New York. Index. Tables. 245 pages.

Following a historical survey of Japanese conscription from the Meiji Restoration to 1920, this book discusses the economic effects of conscription on the population, development of towns, employment, labor, productivity, consumption, and social conditions. Ogawa concludes that "the system of conscription robs our productive world of its most valuable laboring power" and that the lower classes bear the greatest burden of the system.

PANKHURST, RICHARD. *An Introduction to the History of the Ethiopian Army.* 1967. 101st Training Centre, Imperial Ethiopian Air Force. Addis Ababa, Ethiopia. Illustrations. Bibliography at end of each chapter. 183 pages.

Traces the development of the Ethiopian armed forces in ancient and medieval times and in the 19th and early 20th centuries. Notes the speed with which the Ethiopians took to modern weapons, although "the absence of any system of payment for the troops was . . . a grave defect, for it obliged the men to live on the countryside and hence on the people at large and many were the injustices and disputes arising from this fact. Reforming rulers of former times, such as the Emperor Tewodros, were of course profoundly aware of the need for military reorganization and reform."

PRASAD, DAVI, and TONI SMYTHE (editors). *Conscription.* 1968. War Resisters' International. London. 166 pages.

A survey of compulsory military service and resistance to it in 101 countries. Issued primarily for conscientious objectors as a supplement to information on military service regulations and legislation previously published by the War Resisters' International in its quarterly, *War Resistance.* The appendix includes a country-by-country analysis of military service regulations, showing to whom conscription laws apply, whether there is provision for conscientious objection, the call-up age, and other pertinent information.

ROBSON, L. L. *The First A.I.F.: A Study of Its Recruitment 1914–1918.* 1970. Melbourne University Press. Carlton, Australia. Index. Illustrations. Bibliography: pages 217–220. 227 pages.

A study of the cause, course, and effects of the recruitment of the Australian Imperial Force in World War I. Covers the inability of the Australian government and its agencies to induce enough men to enlist voluntarily, the ill-fated conscription proposals, and the implications of the total recruiting effort for government, society, and the individual.

ROGERS, H. C. B. *Napoleon's Army.* 1974. Hippocrene Books, Inc. New York. Index. Illustrations, maps, tables. 192 pages.

Describes Napoleon's army as it existed during the quarter of a century between the battles of Valmy and Waterloo. A brief historical background of the various campaigns is followed by descriptions of the calvary, infantry, artillery, engineering and signals, administration, medical facilities, and Imperial Headquarters.

ROLBANT, SAMUEL. *The Israeli Soldier: Profile of an Army.* 1970. Thomas Yoseloff. South Brunswick, New Jersey. Index. 353 pages.

Chapter 2, "The Structure of the Army," discusses the universal draft, the reserve system, the system of mobilization, age and promotion, military gradation, and training. Chapter 3, "The Sociology of the Army," considers social diversity and moral cohesion, military leadership, problems of authority, the educational process, and religion. Chapter 4, "The Mind of the Army," explores the problem of militarism and the place of the army in the national consciousness.

SCHIFF, ZEER. *A History of the Israeli Army 1870–1974.* 1974. Straight Arrow Books. San Francisco. Index. Illustrations, maps, charts. 338 pages.

Translation and introduction by Raphael Rothstein. This work looks at the development of the Israeli army as an instrument of defense and social integration within the context of the Zionist movement, the birth of Israel, and Israeli culture. The army's battles, the doctrines of its leaders, and its place in Israeli life are described. Unique aspects of the Israeli Defense Forces discussed include the women's army, the relaxed discipline and easygoing esprit, the tradition of officers leading in battle, and the remarkable military successes.

SHANAHAN, WILLIAM OSWALD. *Prussian Military Reforms 1786–1813.* 1945. Columbia University Press. New York. Index. Bibliography: pages 241–253. 270 pages.

An examination of military reform efforts in Prussia in the period between the death of Frederick the Great and the War of Liberation.

Describes the Kruemper system, in effect from 1807 to 1813 following the defeat of Scharnhorst's conscription proposals, as "not an innovation but an expedient made necessary by the lack of a universal conscription law." The conscripted Landwehr of 1813 is seen as "the real basis of Prussia's renewed military strength." The author contends that it was shown in 1807 and again in 1919 that "if a nation retains the services of the professional officers and non-commissioned officers, a formidable mass army can be built with incredible speed by filling the ranks with hastily trained conscripts."

SHARMA, GAUTAM. *Indian Army Through the Ages.* 1966. Allied Publishers Private Ltd. Bombay, India. Index. Bibliography: pages 299–305. 311 pages.

Examines the evolution of the military system in India, from the armies of ancient times to the modern army of today. Discusses recruitment, pay, and conditions of service in each of the periods investigated.

STACEY, C. P. *The Military Problems of Canada: A Survey of Defence Policies and Strategic Conditions Past and Present.* 1940. Ryerson Press. Toronto, Canada. Index. 184 pages.

Outlines the history of Canadian defense policy, with emphasis on the pre-World War I period. Discusses Canada's early military obligations to Britain, which included a system of universal militia service; the Military Service Act of 1917, which introduced conscription after "a bitter parliamentary battle"; and the 1940 National Resources Mobilization Act, which provided for compulsory national registration, training, and emergency mobilization.

STANLEY, GEORGE F. G. *Canada's Soldiers: The Military History of an Unmilitary People.* Revised edition. 1960. Macmillan Co. Toronto, Canada. Index. Illustrations. Bibliography: pages 423–430. 449 pages.

This book traces Canada's military system from the local forces of the 17th century, to the beginning, in 1855, of the volunteer system as "the fundamental feature of Canadian defense policy," to the brief restoration of compulsory service in 1917 "in the stress of war and against strong political opposition," and finally to the reorganization of the army after both World War I and World War II.

TURNER, IAN. *Industrial Labour and Politics: The Dynamics of the Labour Movement in Eastern Australia 1900–1921.* 1965. Australian National University. Canberra, Australia. Index. Bibliography: pages 255–264. 272 pages.

Chapter 4 describes the conscription crisis in Australia during World War I, noting the respective positions of the labor unions and political parties involved, and analyzing the effects of the 1916 conscription referendum defeat.

WEINGARTNER, JAMES. *Hitler's Guard: The Story of the Leibstandarte SS Adolf Hitler 1933–1945.* 1974. Southern Illinois University Press. Carbondale, Illinois. Index. Bibliography: pages 180–184. 194 pages.

Challenges the notion that Hitler's Third Reich was a monolithic unity —a monistic political entity. The author claims, instead, that Hitler's Germany was an agglomeration of quasi-independent and often competing power centers presided over by individuals personally loyal to their superiors in a lord-vassal relationship, that the authority wielded by the vassal was legitimized by Hitler, but that the practical result was a fragmented power system. Emphasized are the political and military roles of the Leibstandarte in World War II as well as specific battles and their significance.

WILKINSON, SPENSER. *The French Army Before Napoleon.* 1916. The Clarendon Press. Oxford, England. 151 pages.

A collection of lectures delivered at the University of Oxford. Of particular interest are Chapters 5, 6, and 7—"Reforms," "The Officers and the Nation," and "Regulars, Volunteers, Conscripts." Wilkinson describes the rise of the new French army from 1791 to 1794, showing how a heterogenous army composed of royal guards, line regiments, militia, and volunteers (including many foreigners governed by the military laws and customs of their own countries, and corrupted by the practices of bounty, exemptions, and privilege) emerged as an amalgamated new army whose unity and homogeneity made it well qualified to defeat other European armies, "all of which clung to the ideas, methods, and institutions inherited from a dead past."

Unpublished Manuscripts

BAUER, THEODORE WILLIAM. *The Introduction of Conscription in Germany During the Napoleonic Period.* 1935. Ph.D. dissertation. University of Wisconsin. Madison, Wisconsin. Bibliography: pages i–xiv. 581 pages.

Analyzes the recruitment laws issued by the German states during the Napoleonic period, and examines other laws that compelled German subjects to become members of military organizations other than the active army, notably militias and national guards.

MOODY, WALTON SMITH. *The Introduction of Military Conscription in Napoleonic Europe 1798–1812.* 1971. Ph.D. dissertation. Duke University. Durham, North Carolina. Bibliography: pages 427–436. 464 pages.

Examines the Jourdan Law of 1798, which established in France the principle of universal liability of male citizens to military service. An institutionalization of ideas and practices of the Revolution, this law seemed designed to create a nation in arms. Yet, in the years which followed, Napoleon introduced conscription under the law to many areas where the people were not French and were not susceptible to the same appeal to nationalism. Moody concludes that, "overall, conscription throughout Europe established precedents on which states could draw in the future. It did not in itself do more than pave the way for the nation in arms of the nineteenth century."

SMUCK, THOMAS EDWARD. *Conscription in France 1870–1914: A Study in Parliamentary Action.* 1952. Ph.D. dissertation. University of California. Berkeley, California. Bibliography: pages 348–355. 359 pages.

The objectives of this study in parliamentary action are threefold: First, to investigate the conscription laws in France from the close of the

Franco-Prussian War to the beginning of the World War in 1914; second, to observe the effects of these laws on the development of the internal politics of the Third Republic and the effects of the politics of the period on the adoption of military laws; and third, to examine the positions of the various political groups in regard to compulsory military service.

TURLEY, WILLIAM S. *Army, Party and Society in the Democratic Republic of Vietnam: Civil-Military Relations in a Mass-Mobilization System.* 1972. Ph.D. dissertation. University of Washington. Seattle, Washington. Bibliography: pages 262–270. 284 pages.

This work contains two major sections. Section I describes the Lao Dong Party's model of civil-military relations and discusses the origins and basic concepts of the party's military doctrine. Section II traces the history of civil-military relations from the founding of the first "Platoon of National Salvation" in 1941 through the phases of reconstruction in 1954–1965, military modernization beginning in 1957, and the resumption of the Indochina War in the 1960s.

Articles

COFFEY, KENNETH J. *The Australian All-Volunteer Force* (two parts). Military Review. (1) April 1975. Volume LV, Number 4. Pages 34–41. (2) May 1975. Volume LV, Number 5. Pages 78–83.

Discusses the abandonment of the draft in Australia in 1972 and the transition from a conscript to an all-volunteer armed force. Traces the political and legislative developments that led to the decision to replace the draft, and draws lessons for the United States from the Australian experience.

COX, HAROLD. *The Swiss Army and England's Needs.* The Nineteenth Century and After. October 1907. Volume LXII, Number 368. Pages 524–537.

Assesses the Swiss military system of compulsory military training and its possible application to British military needs. Cox opposes the introduction of any compulsory military training program in England, countering arguments presented by the National Service League and other proponents of compulsion.

DENNERY, ETIENNE. *Democracy and the French Army.* Military Affairs. Winter 1941. Volume V, Number 4. Pages 233–240.

Examines the practice of conscription in France, showing its alleged traditional association with the idea of democracy.

FRANCE. MINISTRY OF DEFENSE. *Universal Military Service in France.* Military Review. January 1973. Volume LIII, Number 1. Pages 51–61.

A digest of the white paper on national defense. Chapter 3 discusses universal military service in France. It is pointed out that conscription in France has been "adapted to contemporary needs," and that "maintaining conscription is still the basic assurance we have of the effectiveness of deterrence since it expresses both the resolution and the capability of the country with regard to defense."

GILLIE, D. R. *The Frenchman's Military Service.* Fortnightly Review. June 1939. Volume CXLV. Pages 681–687.

Discusses the nature of compulsory military service in France, noting: "Above all, universal service has taken the army right out of politics. . . . [Compulsory] military service has provided the [French] Republic with a standard of civic solidarity and non-partisan discipline, without which the regime might well have foundered."

HAZARD, JOHN N. *National Security and the Soviet Union.* The Annals of the American Academy of Political and Social Science. September 1945. Volume 241. Pages 151–159.

Describes the compulsory military service law of the Soviet Union, and shows how, in its extended form, "the tradition of compulsory military training has served as the foundation for the Red Army and Navy." Predicts the retention of a strong army and navy as a guarantee of collective security, but notes that "conscription does not, however, lose sight of the state outside the armed forces, and a liberal policy of deferments to complete education in essential fields may be expected to emerge."

HEYMONT, IRVING. *The Israeli Career Officer Corps.* Military Review. October 1968. Volume XLVIII, Number 10. Pages 13–19.

Describes the military obligation in Israel under the universal conscription system, and the selection process for officer training. Suggests that "the transfer value of Israeli experience to another country is dependent, to a great degree, on compatibility with the over-all national, political, and social structure."

HEYMOUNT, IRVING, and MELVIN H. ROSEN. *Five Foreign Army Reserve Systems.* Military Review. March 1973. Volume LIII, Number 3. Pages 83–93.

Examines the army reserve systems of the Federal Republic of Germany, Israel, Switzerland, the United Kingdom, and the Soviet Union to determine similarities and differences and their probable causes. Concludes that "any economic and politically viable reserve system for a given nation is basically unique in its entirety and reflects the characteristics of that particular nation."

JOHNSTON, E. N. *The Australian System of Universal Training for Purposes of Military Defense.* Proceedings of the Academy of Political Science. July 1916. Volume 6, Number 4. Pages 113–133.

Describes the Defense Act of 1903–1912 under which universal military training was obligatory for all able-bodied males from 12 to 26 years of age.

MESNARD, ANDRÉ. *National Security and France.* The Annals of the American Academy of Political and Social Science. September 1945. Volume 241. Pages 160–166.

Because of France's "geographical fatality in the path of invasion," conscription in that nation "is not considered as a means of indoctrinating the youth of the nation with nationalistic or imperialistic ideas, but as one of the elements in a system of defense." The general tolerance of conscription as part of the system of national defense is attributed largely to its revolutionary origins and is associated among the great majority of Frenchmen with the notion of equality and the triumph of individual and popular liberties. The French attitude toward conscription is discussed against the background of international security.

MONTFORT, M. H. *A Look at the Swiss Army.* Military Review. February 1973. Volume LIII, Number 2. Pages 45–52.

A digest from the September 1972 issue of *Revue Militaire Suisse.* This article was prepared to help Swiss army officers and government officials explain the unique Swiss military system to others. Montfort notes that the Swiss militia system of universal military service "has grown up through the centuries," and that it "would no doubt be impossible to transplant it to a different culture or nation."

PARET, PETER. *Nationalism and the Sense of Military Obligation.* Military Affairs. February 1970. Volume XXXIV, Number 1. Pages 2–6.

Outlines some of the connections that exist between the development of nationalism in France and Germany and the attitudes held by governments and societies toward the question of military obligation.

RANEY, WILLIAM F. *Recruiting and Crimping in Canada for the Northern Forces 1861–1865.* Mississippi Valley Historical Review. June 1923. Volume 10, Number 1. Pages 21–23.

Describes the illegal recruiting of Canadians for the Union army in the Civil War. Bounties and other inducements persuaded substantial numbers of Canadians to enlist, notwithstanding the fact that the British had adopted a policy of neutrality in the conflict and had prohibited Canadians from enlisting in foreign armies.

STACEY, C. P. *John A. Macdonald on Raising Troops in Canada for Imperial Service 1885.* The Canadian Historical Review. March 1957. Volume 38, Number 1. Pages 37–40.

Deals with the recruitment of Canadians for overseas service in the British armed forces.

WARD, ALAN J. *Lloyd George and the 1918 Irish Conscription Crisis.* The Historical Journal. March 1974. Volume 17, Number 1. Pages 107–129.

A critical examination of the British prime minister's policy in his attempts to implement conscription in Ireland in 1918 following its introduction in the rest of Britain two years earlier.

WILLMS, A. M. *Conscription 1917: A Brief for the Defence.* The Canadian Historical Review. December 1956. Volume 37, Number 4. Pages 338–351.

Discusses the effect of conscription on Canadian politics and the election of 1917, and whether the military service bill introduced by the government was intended as a political expedient.

WRIGHT, GORDON. *Public Opinion and Conscription in France 1866–70.* The Journal of Modern History. March 1942. Volume 14, Number 1. Pages 26–45.

Describes how "Napoleon fell between two stools when he tried to reconcile full preparedness with public opinion." Had his original project of 1866 been ruthlessly forced upon the country, France might have met Prussia on even terms in 1870. The emperor, however, aware that such a policy might bring revolution, let the project be watered down repeatedly in the search for a compromise between military and political necessity. As finally adopted, the law added little except the *garde nationale* to the old system, and even this innovation was allowed to lapse for fear of its effect on the public.

Pamphlets, Reprints, and Speeches

AUSTRALIAN FREEDOM LEAGUE. *An Appeal to the Workers.* 1913. Melbourne, Australia. 4 pages.

An appeal to "all who love liberty and civil freedom to rally to its support in its fight against Conscription." Calls for the abolition of the Compulsory Clauses of the Commonwealth Defence Act requiring 14-year-old boys in Australia to register for compulsory military training.

AUSTRALIAN FREEDOM LEAGUE. *Child Conscription: Our Country's Shame.* By John F. Hills. Circa 1912. Sydney, Australia. 16 pages.

Written in support of the Australian Freedom League's agitation for the abolition of the Compulsory Clauses of the Commonwealth Defence Act requiring 14-year-old boys in Australia to register for compulsory military training. Notes that "twenty thousand lads (i.e., about 50 per cent of those who reach their fourteenth birthday in 1912) failed to register by the prescribed date in spite of the severe penalties advertised; many thousands are still unregistered, although prosecutions have been frequent, and the threats of punishment increasing in intensity."

AUSTRALIAN FREEDOM LEAGUE. *Compulsory Military Training: An Analysis and an Exposure.* Circa 1914. Melbourne, Australia. 16 pages.

Contains the text of the Manifesto to Members of the Conference of the Political Labour Council of Victoria. The manifesto analyzes the question of compulsory training for defense in Australia and counters arguments of proponents of such a system.

AUSTRALIAN FREEDOM LEAGUE. *The Myth of the "Citizen Soldier."* Circa 1913. Melbourne, Australia. 2 pages.

Contends that "the deadly nature" of the Commonwealth Defence Act for compulsory military training is "concealed under such cant phrases as 'Citizen Army,' 'A Nation in Arms,' and 'Democratic Service.'" The Australian Freedom League poses the question of proponents of conscription: "In what way are the citizen and other rights of the Australian adult trainee any better protected than those of, say, the German Conscript?"

AUSTRALIAN FREEDOM LEAGUE. *The Women's Appeal to the Public.* Circa 1913. Melbourne, Australia. 2 pages.

An appeal by the Women's Branch of the Victorian Council of the Australian Freedom League. Contends that "compulsion (besides being extremely distasteful to numberless youths, and their parents also) seriously menaces the home influence and training, and is a very grave infringement of our Commonwealth Constitution, and a still more grave infringement of that Unwritten Law of the sacredness of every human conscience—a liberty very dearly bought by our forefathers, and highly prized by the British peoples."

AUSTRALIAN FREEDOM LEAGUE. [Unlisted material] (Hoover Institution Collection). 1913–1914. Melbourne, Australia.

This collection contains pamphlets issued by the Australian Freedom League in 1913 and 1914 in opposition to the Compulsory Clauses of the Commonwealth Defence Act requiring 14-year-old boys in Australia to register for compulsory military training.

AUSTRALIAN LABOUR PARTY. [Unlisted material] (Hoover Institution Collection). 1918–1920. Australia.

This collection includes 15 pamphlets issued in opposition to conscription by various branches of the Australian Labour Party. Each pamphlet addresses a different aspect of conscription, as indicated by such titles as *Has the Voluntary System Failed?*, *The Official Figures Say NO*, *The Blood Vote*, *Will Married Men Be Conscripted?*, *Conscription and Agriculture*, and *The Lottery of Death*.

AUSTRALIAN PEACE ALLIANCE. *The Tragic Fate of the Conscientious Objectors: A Disgrace to British Civilisation*. By Henry Stead. Circa 1918. N.p. [Australia]. 16 pages.

Appeals for support for the conscientious objector in Australia. Cites British statistics on conscientious objectors in World War I as of November 1918: 6,051 men had resisted the Military Service Acts, and 5,479 men had been court-martialled. Of the latter, 4,114 had been court-martialled once, 605 twice, 507 three times, 230 four times, 20 five times, and 3 six times. Of the total number of conscientious objectors 1,504 were still in prison; 34 had died since arrest; 32 had become mentally affected; and 3,398 were performing alternative service under the Home Office Scheme.

CORDER, HERBERT. *Compulsory Military Service in Australia and New Zealand*. Circa 1913. N.p. 2 pages.

This pamphlet, distributed at prisons and military barracks in Australia and New Zealand, protests the compulsory military training system established in those countries in 1911 under which Australian and New Zealand males 12 to 25 years old and 14 to 21 years old, respectively, were compelled to drill. Corder notes that those who bear the burden of the conscript law do not have the right to vote for its repeal.

CORDER, HERBERT, and JOHN W. BARRY. *"Colonial Defence Acts of 1909."* 1913. Australia & New Zealand Freedom Leagues. Sunderland, England, and Melbourne, Australia. 7 pages.

A collection of seven reprints of protests and other documents pertaining to the administration of the Colonial Defence Acts of 1909 under which Australian and New Zealand males 12 to 25 years old and 14 to 21 years old, respectively, were compelled to drill. Describes resistance and prosecutions.

CORDIAN, ANDREW. *The Shadow of Prussianism.* Circa 1947. National
  Council Against Conscription. Washington, D.C. 7 pages.

The author, a former German Junker, recalls "how compulsory military
service destroyed democracy in Germany" and urges that the "fate of the
German democratic movement at the hands of a military caste" should
serve as a warning to the American people not to adopt peacetime conscription.

CRUICKSHANK, ROBERT W. *Aspects of Conscription.* Circa 1918. No
  Conscription Council. Sydney, Australia. 8 pages.

A strong statement by a representative of the Australian Labour Party
against establishment of conscription in Australia for the purpose of providing manpower to Allied forces during World War I. The author argues
that conscription as proposed is unnecessary, citing examples of Australia's
loyalty and support of the "Mother Country"—e.g., the voluntary enlistment of 300,000 soldiers at a cost of £100,000,000 per year. He further
argues that conscription of significant numbers of Australian men would
severely damage the economy without appreciably shortening the war.

DEXTER, GRANT. *The Conscription Debates of 1917 and 1944.* Circa
  1945. Winnipeg Free Press. Winnipeg, Canada. 10 pages.

Four short articles explore differences in anticonscriptionist attitudes in
the 1917 and 1944 Canadian parliamentary debates on conscription. The
articles are titled "Historic Attitudes," "Constitutional Aspects," "Quebec
Liberal Viewpoint," and " 'Colonial' Nationalists."

FAESCH, REMY. *The Swiss Army System.* 1916. G. E. Stechert & Co.
  New York. Illustrations. 24 pages.

Attempts to show how the state of military preparedness in Switzerland
"is partly the result of that military spirit of the Swiss population." According to Faesch, the military duties of the Swiss citizen and the communities
are "far greater than those demanded by the authorities of any other
nation," and the physical and military preparation of the Swiss youth is
"an essential part of the Swiss military system." He concludes that "general
conscription in Switzerland is unanimously considered to be a blessing for
the population," and that "general conscription and service . . . is the best
education for citizenship . . . [and] the most thorough training for life."

FRIENDS' PEACE COMMITTEE. *A Blot on the Empire: Conscription in New Zealand.* Circa 1913. London. 16 pages.

An assessment of New Zealand's compulsory military service, instituted in 1909. Compulsory military training of boys begins at age 14 (amended from age 12 in 1912), continues until 18 when the cadet is drafted and liable for active service until, at age 25, he is transferred to the reserve, remaining liable in time of emergency until age 30. The pamphlet describes the anticonscription movement in New Zealand and the support of Labour and Socialist organizations. It notes that as of January 1913 there had been 1,577 prosecutions for draft violation, with 1,058 convictions, 68 imprisonments, and an estimated 600 additional cases withdrawn. Contemporary press reports on the draft and resistance to it are quoted.

HOLLAND, HENRY EDMUND. *Boy Conscription and Camp Morality: The Menace of Sir James Allen's Policy.* Circa 1919. N.p. [New Zealand]. 9 pages.

In this election campaign pamphlet a New Zealand Labour Party member of Parliament argues against a proposal to conscript 18-year-old boys. He contends that immorality not only pervades military camp life but in instances has been condoned by the respective authorities (e.g., he cites an 1886 British military order to cantonments in India assertedly establishing government-controlled brothels for the troops).

MACKENZIE KING, W. L. *National Selective Service.* 1942. Director of Public Information. Ottawa, Canada. 8 pages.

Speech by the Canadian prime minister in the House of Commons on March 24, 1942, announcing that "the government's policy of national selective service will be extended, as generally and rapidly as may be necessary to effect the orderly and efficient employment of the men and women of Canada for the varied purposes of war."

SKEFFINGTON, F. SHEEHY. *Speech from the Dock.* 1917. Skeffington Memorial Committee. New York. 15 pages.

Text of Skeffington's defense speech in the Dublin, Ireland, police court in June 1915 at his trial under the Defence of the Realm Act for urging passive resistance to conscription. Skeffington was sentenced to six months' hard labor and six additional months in default of bail. The pamphlet includes a letter by George Bernard Shaw concerning the Skeffington case.

VALERA, EAMONN DE. *Ireland's Case Against Conscription.* 1918. Maunsel & Co. Dublin. 46 pages.

In this plea for international support addressed to President Woodrow Wilson, de Valera repudiates England's claim to the right to conscript the Irish. He maintains that only a parliament freely elected by, and directly answerable to, the people of Ireland has the right to conscript Irish men.

Chapter 16

Miscellanea

The human understanding is of its nature prone to suppose
the existence of more order and regularity in the world than
it finds.
—Francis Bacon, *Novum Organum*, I, 1620

Books

BUSWELL, LESLIE. *Ambulance No. 10: Personal Letters from the Front.*
1916. Houghton Mifflin Co. Boston. 155 pages.

A compilation of letters written from the French war front in World
War I by an American volunteer ambulance driver. Provides a record of
life in the service, describing the activities of the volunteer and the conditions that he encountered.

DURHAM, KNOWLTON. *Billions for Veterans: An Analysis of Bonus Problems—Yesterday, Today and Tomorrow.* 1932. Brewer, Warren &
Putnam. New York. 120 pages.

Presents arguments against the controversial proposal for bonus pay-
ments to World War I veterans during the Depression. Appealing to
patriotic self-sacrifice, the author declares that "to pay the bonus now
would be to gamble with the welfare of the nation."

FRIEDMAN, LEON. *The Wise Minority: An Argument for Draft Resistance
and Civil Disobedience.* 1971. Dial Press. New York. Index. Notes:
pages 195–215. 228 pages.

Investigates the circumstances under which defiance of the law can be
viewed as legitimate. Friedman examines instances of popular resistance
to certain laws in U.S. history, from the Whiskey Rebellion to the Vietnam

War. He contends that the contemporary concern among many Americans with peaceful reforms "has resulted in a curious amnesia regarding our violent history. The public reacts to our contemporary disobeyers—draft resisters and student rebels—as if they were dangerous violators not only of the law but also of our entire political tradition. In fact, they are following some of our finest torchbearers." The appendix includes statistics on draft resistance in the United States.

GINZBERG, ELI (editor). *The Nation's Children:* Volume 2: *Development and Education.* 1960. Published for Golden Anniversary White House Conference on Children and Youth. Columbia University Press. New York. Bibliography: pages 239–242. 242 pages.

Includes a study by Harold Wool entitled "The Armed Services as a Training Institution" (pages 158–185). Wool reviews the military skill structure, major skill trends, changes in the number and characteristics of personnel entering service, the nature and scope of military training programs, and some of the implications of this training for youth in relation to civilian work careers. He finds that "military skill training has made a direct and important contribution to the occupational skills of a significant minority of the youth who have returned to civilian life" and has been "a major source of trained personnel in selected industries and occupations closely allied with military technology." In the case of many other youth, training in military skills is believed to have contributed more generally to their total knowledge and capabilities, "but has not found a direct and closely identifiable application in their civilian employment."

HELMER, JOHN. *Bringing the War Home: The American Soldier in Vietnam and After.* 1974. Free Press. New York. Index. Tables, figures. 346 pages.

Written by a sociologist, this book is a study of the social institutions of war, of the groups men form in military service when exposed to the risks and adventures of combat. Using extensive data, Helmer focuses on the soldier of the Vietnam War, exploring what forces motivated performance and what primary groups instigated compliance and noncompliance with military command. The general objective is to examine the process by which extreme deprivation and pain generate the social and sociopsychological conditions of rebellion. Postulating that the realities of the Vietnam War were conducive to a high degree of objective alienation, the author delves into the relationship between objective and subjective alienation, measured in levels of AWOL, desertion, and open defiance. Helmer views the war as a crisis of long-term alienation of the working class, which pushed members of that class into rebellion against the army. He concludes that this has resulted in a broader attack on governing institutions of society in general.

HUZAR, ELIAS. *The Purse and the Sword: Control of the Army by Congress Through Military Appropriations 1933–1950.* 1950. Cornell University Press. Ithaca, New York. Index. 417 pages.

Case study of the appropriations process in Congress with special reference to the military establishment. The author concludes that, considering the growth of the military institution, the government's legislators and top administrators must exercise their authority over the armed forces more effectively if the constitutional principles that Congress should control the public purse and that civilians should control the military establishment are to be matters of practice and not merely of precept.

JANOWITZ, MORRIS. *Sociology and the Military Establishment.* 1959. Russell Sage Foundation. New York. Bibliography: pages 109–112. 112 pages.

Focusing on the internal social organization of military establishments—the hierarchy, authority, assimilation of military roles, primary groups, and techniques of organizational control—the author seeks to (1) evaluate the published and unpublished material on the subject, (2) outline and analyze the main organizational trends at work transforming the military establishment, and (3) interpret problems of applying a sociological perspective to the military establishment.

KEMBLE, C. ROBERT. *The Image of the Army Officer in America: Background for Current Views.* 1973. Contributions in Military History, No. 5. Greenwood Press. Westport, Connecticut. Bibliography: pages 243–268. 289 pages.

Notes that the American army officer has never enjoyed a single identifiable national external image. Moreover, while recognizing the necessity of a standing military force, the American people tend to distrust the motives of a large, strong standing army because of the potential political power in such a group. Thus, says Kemble, the myth of the citizen-soldier evolved.

MARTIN, H. B. *Conscript 2989: Experiences of a Drafted Man.* 1918. Dodd, Mead & Co. New York. Illustrations. 124 pages.

A whimsical narrative of a draftee's experiences in the U.S. Army during World War I. The book is offered to mothers and fathers "who spend hours wondering about the welfare of their son" with "the assurance that life in the big cantonment contains a full measure of real happiness, and that all hardships are mitigated by a sense of humor which develops even in the worst of pessimists."

MOSKOS, CHARLES C., JR. *The American Enlisted Man: The Rank and File in Today's Military.* 1970. Russell Sage Foundation. New York. Index. Tables. Bibliography: pages 249–261. 274 pages.

A sociological study of the rank and file in the U.S. armed services, covering the period from immediately prior to World War II to the present, and dealing with such questions as culture, race relations, and the behavior of combat soldiers. The author spent extended periods with army units in his field research; his findings suggest a need for improved relationships between the civilian and military structures of society.

PETERSEN, PETER. *Against the Tide: An Argument in Favor of the American Soldier.* 1974. Arlington House Publishers. New Rochelle, New York. Index. Illustrations, tables, graphs, charts. Bibliography: pages 275–284. 287 pages.

Argues in favor of the American soldier in Vietnam through a realistic description of certain self-reported beliefs (as opposed to aptitudes, training, or knowledge) that influence his success or failure. Specific areas examined are the individual's basic beliefs, activity preferences, personal values, and behavior styles. Basing his conclusions on the results of 6,727 questionnaires administered to 4,008 individuals, the author states that (1) the American soldier in the Vietnam War is described unfairly in much of the contemporary literature; (2) the effects of combat on the beliefs of infantrymen returning to civilian life are not detrimental to society; and (3) differences between subgroups in the army are significant but not negative. Petersen recommends that efforts be made to dispel misconceptions about the American soldier and that knowledge about what does influence behavior should be used positively in training.

SCHARDT, ARLIE, WILLIAM A. RUSHER, and MARK O. HATFIELD. *Amnesty? The Unsettled Question of Vietnam: Now! Never! If....*

1973. Sun River Press. Croton-on-Hudson, New York. Bibliographic references. 148 pages.

Consists of statements by three authors on amnesty: Should it be granted? how? why or why not? Schardt argues that the circumstances surrounding U.S. involvement in Vietnam require forgiveness of those who acted on conscience. Rusher contends that those who violate the law of the land must bear the consequences of that act and thus amnesty should not be granted. Hatfield, after outlining the basis of his opposition to the Vietnam War and his views on conscience versus state authority, suggests various amnesty terms for different types of war resisters—those in jail for refusal to serve, draft evaders, deserters, and conscientious objectors.

Stevens, Franklin. *If This Be Treason.* 1970. Peter H. Wyden, Inc. New York. 243 pages.

Includes a series of interviews with draft evaders and draft resisters and points up some of the motives for draft evasion and the means by which it is accomplished.

Stouffer, Samuel A., and others. *The American Soldier: Adjustment During Army Life.* 1914. Studies in Social Psychology in World War II, Volume I. Princeton University Press. Princeton, New Jersey. Charts, tables. 599 pages.

The series of which this is the first volume was prepared under the auspices of the Social Science Research Council. Based on War Department data, the series provides a record of the attitudes of the American soldier in World War II and of the techniques developed to study these attitudes. Volume I is of particular interest, examining personal adjustment in the army, social mobility, job assignment and job satisfaction, attitudes toward leadership and social control, and orientation of soldiers toward the war.

Unpublished Manuscripts

Berger, Martin Edgar. *War, Armies, and Revolution: Friedrich Engels' Military Thought.* 1969. Ph.D. dissertation. University of Pittsburgh. Pittsburgh, Pennsylvania. Bibliography: pages 358–372. 372 pages.

Demonstrates that Engels had little regard for the nonprofessional militia-systems popular among contemporary liberals, but that his respect for the long-service professional army was tempered by realization that such forces could not match the Prussian-style mass army in numbers. He propounded militia-schemes, with military training for youth and diminishing terms of service, as a sort of disarmament, which would equip all Europe with armies unsuited for sudden attacks—thus insuring peace and the uninterrupted development of Socialism. Engels believed that military necessity would force the governments to establish truly universal service; and the inevitability of the universal-service army determined his approach to revolutionary tactics in the 1880s and 1890s. His theory of the disappearing army allowed him to reconcile his faith in the eventual necessity of revolution with his conviction that any insurrection against an intact army would be disastrous.

McELIN, ALICE. *The National Security League: Its Work and Policy.* 1921. M.A. thesis. Stanford University. Stanford, California. Bibliography: pages 158–161. 161 pages.

Presents the history of the National Security League, as well as a critical survey of its policy, from its foundation in 1914 to the end of World War I. Describes the organization of the National Security League, its program of "patriotism through education," its efforts to influence national policy in favor of the adoption of universal military training, its participation in political campaigns, and the investigation of its activities by the House of Representatives. The author concludes that real as the league's patriotic services were, "its evils were so flagrant as to make its total force reactionary."

Articles

GOODMAN, JEFFREY. *How to Be Patriotic and Live with Yourself.* The Atlantic Monthly. February 1966. Volume 217, Number 2. Pages 61–62.

Considers the draft as a social issue. The author professes to see "no viable solution to the war/conscription problem other than rejecting the use of armed force as a means of prosecuting national policies and then dismantling the military establishment." For the near future, however, he

Miscellanea

believes that "the question is whether there is any structure which can satisfy both military needs and the social-moral issues implicit in the raising of armies."

LEIGH, DUANE E., and ROBERT E. BERNEY. *The Distribution of Hostile Casualties on Draft-Eligible Males with Differing Socioeconomic Characteristics.* Social Science Quarterly. March 1971. Volume 51, Number 4. Pages 932–940.

Analyzes the distribution of U.S. hostile casualties in Southeast Asia in order to discern to what extent, if any, the burden of combat action is disproportionately borne by socioeconomic groups characterized by low civilian income-earning opportunities. The empirical evidence suggests that hostile casualties tended to be disproportionately concentrated among those draftees and reluctant volunteers with relatively low civilian-income potentials. The authors conclude that "regardless of how the tax is measured, consideration of the effect of hostile casualties requires that the tax structure be judged less progressive or more regressive than previously estimated."

MARTIN, DONALD L. *The Economics of Jury Conscription.* Journal of Political Economy. July–August 1972. Volume 80, Number 4. Pages 680–702.

Notes that, unlike military conscription, the procurement of jurors by conscription has been widely accepted throughout the history of the Western world. This article estimates and analyzes the social costs, the wealth redistribution, and the resource allocative consequences of this judiciary institution. As an alternative, the implications of a volunteer system of juror procurement are discussed.

PEMBERTON, JOHN DE J., JR. *The War Protester.* Current History. July 1968. Volume 55, Number 323. Pages 23–27, 48.

Discusses the rights of, and alternatives open to, war protesters, contending that "the right of freedom of expression . . . is so important in a democracy that it may override an unimportant regulation so long as the violation of that regulation does not injure someone else."

SARKESIAN, SAM C. *Vietnam and the Professional Military.* Orbis. Spring 1974. Volume XVIII, Number 1. Pages 252–265.

Looks at the impact of certain characteristics of the Vietnam War on the professional military and on the relationship of the military to society. The author discusses the U.S. Army's internal reassessment and the resulting redefinition of professional roles, and analyzes the debate on whether the Vietnam experience was an aberration or a sign of the future. He concludes that "new rules of the game" fostering adaptability and dynamism are needed and that the issue is far from resolved because "the institution has a built-in socialization process which favors orthodoxy, and the danger is that the institution will capture [modernist] officers before they can capture the institution."

STREET, AUGUSTA J. *Hasty Marriage and the Draft.* Journal of Social Hygiene. May 1941. Volume 27, Number 5. Pages 228–231.

Offers evidence of an increase in the number of marriages prior to passage of the draft bill on October 16, 1940. Suggests, however, that the young man who married to evade the draft was not necessarily successful in his attempt at evasion.

SUCHMAN, EDWARD, ROBIN M. WILLIAMS, JR., and ROSE K. GOLDSEN. *Student Reaction to Impending Military Service.* American Sociological Review. June 1953. Volume 18, Number 3. Pages 293–304.

Reports on a survey of how students feel about being drafted and what factors play an important part in determining these attitudes.

UYEKI, EUGENE S. *Draftee Behavior in the Cold-War Army.* Social Problems. Fall 1960. Volume 8, Number 2. Pages 151–158.

Attempts to conceptualize a sociological perspective useful for viewing draftee behavior in the cold-war army.

Pamphlets, Reprints, and Speeches

FRIENDS COMMITTEE ON NATIONAL LEGISLATION. *How Did Those Who Represent You in Congress Vote on Conscription 1940–46?* 1946. Washington, D.C. 6 pages.

Tabulation of key House and Senate roll calls on various conscription measures.

NATIONAL COUNCIL AGAINST CONSCRIPTION. *Questions for Congressmen.* Circa 1955. Washington, D.C.

A series of eight leaflets with suggested questions on conscription to ask when writing to a congressman or other legislator.

POST WAR WORLD COUNCIL. *How to Make a Worker into a Strike-Breaker.* Circa 1945. New York. 3 pages.

Urges opposition to two bills pending in Congress: the Gurney-Wadsworth bill (House Resolution 1806), providing for the induction into the army or navy for training for one year of every male citizen and alien resident when he reaches the age of 18; and the May bill (House Resolution 3947), providing for induction at age 17, or immediately upon high school graduation—whichever occurs first—and subsequent reserve service for a period of eight years. It is contended that passage of the bills could mean that union members could be forced to become strike-breakers through the government's ordering strikers into the reserve and then sending them back, in uniform, to their jobs.

POST WAR WORLD COUNCIL. *The Post War World Council: Its Record, Its Program in the War for the Peace.* 1945. New York. 2 pages.

Describes the activities of the Post War World Council, including its establishment of the National Council Against Peacetime Conscription Now, under the chairmanship of Alonzo Myers. Notes that the Post War World Council opposed labor conscription during World War II, and that it has "led in coordinating opposition to peacetime military conscription under any name."

YOUNG PEOPLE'S SOCIALIST LEAGUE. *Against Conscription! Youth Rejects Wall Street's Goosestep Plan.* 1940. New York. 14 pages.

This pamphlet, issued by the youth section of the Workers Party (Fourth International), argues against the proposed conscription law, maintaining that it is intended as a preparation, not for a war against fascism, but rather for a war in the interests of "capitalist profits."

Government Documents: Publications—Military Compensation

U.S. CONGRESS. HOUSE. COMMITTEE ON ARMED SERVICES. *Pay and Allowances for the Uniformed Services.* 1975. Government Printing Office. Washington, D.C. 123 pages.

Report on pay and allowances of the uniformed services pursuant to Title 37, U.S. Code, as amended through March 1, 1975, and supplementary material.

U.S. CONGRESS. HOUSE. COMMITTEE ON MILITARY AFFAIRS. *Pay Readjustment Act.* 1926. Government Printing Office. Washington, D.C. 64 pages.

Text of the Pay Readjustment Act of June 10, 1922, with amendments, readjusting the pay received by the commissioned and enlisted personnel of the armed services.

U.S. CONGRESS. HOUSE. COMMITTEE ON MILITARY AFFAIRS. *The National Defense Act.* 1935. Government Printing Office. Washington, D.C. Index. Tables. 189 pages.

Contains the texts of (1) the National Defense Act approved June 3, 1916, as amended to August 26, 1935, with related acts, decisions, and opinions; (2) the Pay Readjustment Act approved June 10, 1922, as amended to August 26, 1935, with related acts, decisions, and opinions, and (3) Army and Navy Pay Tables, September 1935.

U.S. CONGRESS. SENATE. COMMITTEE ON ARMED SERVICES. *Differential Pays for the Armed Services of the United States.* 1953. Government Printing Office. Washington, D.C. 182 pages.

Report of the Strauss Commission on Incentive–Hazardous Duty and Special Pays prepared for the Senate Committee on Armed Services.

U.S. DEPARTMENT OF THE ARMY. *Career Compensation for the Uniformed Services.* 2 volumes. 1948. Government Printing Office. Washington, D.C. Volume 1: 66 pages. Volume 2: 245 pages.

Volume 1 presents a report and recommendations on career compensation for the uniformed services prepared for the secretary of defense by the Advisory Commission on Service Pay. Volume 2 comprises an appendix containing material supporting the findings and recommendations of the commission.

Government Documents: Publications—Other

U.S. CONGRESS. SENATE. COMMITTEE ON ARMED SERVICES. *Department of Defense Organization.* 1953. Government Printing Office. Washington, D.C. 25 pages.

Report of the Rockefeller Commission, which studied the organization of the Department of Defense. Includes recommendations.

U.S. CONGRESS. SENATE. COMMITTEE ON RETIREMENT POLICY FOR FEDERAL PERSONNEL. *Retirement Policy for Federal Personnel.* 5 parts. 1954. Government Printing Office. Washington, D.C. Illustrations. 1155 pages.

Report of the Kaplan Committee on retirement policy. Of particular interest is Part 2, which deals with retirement systems for the uniformed services.

U.S. DEPARTMENT OF DEFENSE. *Report of Working Group on Human Behavior Under Conditions of Military Service.* 1951. By Sidney Adams and others. Department of Defense. Washington, D.C. 426 pages.

Joint study conducted by the Research and Development Board and the Personnel Policy Board. Considers behavioral aspects of mobilization, selection and classification, transition from civilian to military life, training, combat effectiveness, and separation. Recommendations emphasize the need for "close teamwork between the executive military branches of the armed services and all branches of social science research." It is also suggested that "serious consideration be given to the possibility that physical and intelligence standards are too high and too inflexible at present in relation to military requirements and available manpower."

U.S. DEPARTMENT OF HEALTH, EDUCATION AND WELFARE. *Achievement, Mobility, and the Draft: Their Impact on the Earnings of Men.* 1973. By Phillips Cutright. Department of Health, Education and Welfare. Washington, D.C. Graphs, tables. 228 pages.

Employing Social Security Administration data, this study isolates the influence of such variables as geographic mobility, regional location, academic achievement, years of education, race, and military service on the level of earnings and changes in the earnings over time of a group of men born between 1927 and 1934. The study suggests that men subject to a high risk of low earnings do not display an earnings benefit from military service, and concludes that it is unlikely that nonmilitary programs of shorter duration, with goals limited to improving the personal habits or outlook of high-risk men, will have a positive impact on the postprogram earnings of recruits.

U.S. DEPARTMENT OF THE ARMY. *Attitudes of New Recruits in the Army.* 1948. Department of the Army. Washington, D.C. Figures, tables. 43 pages.

Study prepared for the Military Personnel Procurement Service, Adjutant General's Office, U.S. Army, on attitudes of new recruits in the army. Surveys attitudes toward the army as a career, reasons for enlisting, and attitudes concerning pay and promotion.

U.S. DEPARTMENT OF THE ARMY. *The Eddy Board Report of the Department of the Army Board on Educational Systems for Officers.* 1949. Government Printing Office. Washington, D.C. 90 pages.

Available on loan from the Army Library at the Pentagon, this is the report of the Eddy Board, which examined the training and education of army officers.

U.S. DEPARTMENT OF THE ARMY. *Infantrymen's Reactions to the Career Guidance Plan.* 1948. Department of the Army. Washington, D.C. Figures, tables. 32 pages.

Study prepared for the director of Personnel and Administration, General Staff, U.S. Army, on infantrymen's reactions to the Career Guidance Plan. Surveys attitudes toward reenlistment in the army.

Miscellanea

U.S. DEPARTMENT OF THE ARMY. *Officers' Attitudes Toward Their Careers.* 1949. Department of the Army. Washington, D.C. Tables. 91 pages.

Survey of officers' attitudes toward their careers in the army and air force from the point of view of officer retention.

U.S. DEPARTMENT OF THE ARMY. *Results of the Examination of Youths for Military Service 1968.* 1969. Department of the Army. Washington, D.C. Charts, tables. 107 pages.

Report of the Surgeon General's Office relating to both draftees and volunteers. Consists primarily of statistical data on preinduction and induction examination results, disqualifications for mental and physical reasons, and geographic and ethnic differentials. A brief discussion of the 1968 findings is included.

U.S. PUBLIC HEALTH SERVICE. *Summary of Physical Findings on Men Drafted in the World War.* By Rollo H. Britten and George St. J. Perrott. 1941. Public Health Reports, Volume 56, Number 2. Government Printing Office. Washington, D.C. Graphs, tables. 22 pages.

A survey of men drafted in World War I after May 1, 1918. Of these, 31.2 percent were classified as "not available for general military service," from which it is concluded that about 1.2 million men would have to be examined to meet the Selective Service quota of 0.8 million expected by July 1, 1941, and that the remainder would be rejected or placed in the "limited service group" on physical grounds. A breakdown is given of the physical defects of those rejected, as well as an estimated distribution by state—ranging from a high of 58.5 for Rhode Island to a low of 18.4 percent for Wyoming.

U.S. SPECIAL COMMITTEE. *Report to the President on Veterans' Medical Services.* 1950. Government Printing Office. Washington, D.C. Charts. 65 pages.

This report of the Rusk Committee includes an examination of the Veterans' Administration's medical standards and its paraplegic program, and calls for the coordination of federal health services.

U.S. SURGEON GENERAL. *Physical Examination of the First Million Draft Recruits: Methods and Results.* 1919. Bulletin No. 11. Government Printing Office. Washington, D.C. Index. Figures, plates, tables. 521 pages.

Report of the Surgeon General on various aspects of the World War I draft, including selection, classification, examining boards, and advisory boards. Notes that of the first 2,510,000 registrants examined, 29.1 percent were rejected on physical grounds.

U.S. WAR DEPARTMENT. *A Complete Digest of Laws in Relation to Bounty.* 1872. W. H. & O. H. Morrison. Washington, D.C. Index. 200 pages.

Prepared by the Auditor, War Department, this volume contains the texts of bounty-related documents from 1838 to 1872. Includes congressional enactments, presidential proclamations, War Department orders, Treasury Department circulars, and Supreme Court decisions.

WOMBLE, J. R., JR. *Ad Hoc Committee on the Future of Military Service as a Career That Will Attract and Retain Capable Career Personnel.* Army Information Digest. February 1954. Volume 9, Number 2. Pages 24–36.

The Ad Hoc Committee's report (Womble Report on Service Careers) examines the ability of the military services to provide solid career opportunities for capable career personnel.

Government Documents:
Congressional Hearings—Military Compensation

1946. U.S. CONGRESS. HOUSE. COMMITTEE ON MILITARY AFFAIRS. *Pay Increase for Personnel of the Armed Forces.* Government Printing Office. Washington, D.C. 79 pages.

Hearings on April 1 and 8, 1946, before the House Committee on Military Affairs on House bill 5625 to amend the Pay Readjustment Act of 1942 to provide an increase of 20 percent.

Miscellanea

1949. U.S. Congress. House. Committee on Armed Services. *Career Compensation for the Uniformed Forces.* Government Printing Office. Washington, D.C. 873 pages.

Hearings between February 21 and May 5, 1949, before a subcommittee of the House Committee on Armed Services on House bill 255 to provide pay, allowances, retirement, and survivor benefits for members of the army, navy, air force, Marine Corps, Coast Guard, Coast and Geodetic Survey, Public Health Service, the reserve components thereof, the National Guard, and the Air National Guard.

1952. U.S. Congress. Senate. Committee on Armed Services. *Military Pay Raise.* Government Printing Office. Washington, D.C. 130 pages.

Hearings between January 28 and 30, 1952, before the Senate Committee on Armed Services on House bill 5715 to amend Sections 201(2), 301(e), 302(f), 302(g), 508, 527, and 528 of Public Law 351 (81st Congress), as amended.

1952. U.S. Congress. Senate. Committee on Armed Services. *Incentive Pay and Overseas Allowances.* Government Printing Office, Washington, D.C. 162 pages.

Hearings on April 16 and 17, 1952, before the Task Force of the Preparedness Subcommittee of the Senate Committee on Armed Services, considering incentive pay and overseas allowances.

1954. U.S. Congress. Senate. Committee on Armed Services. *Reenlistment Bonuses.* Government Printing Office. Washington, D.C. 19 pages.

Hearing on June 10, 1954, before the Senate Committee on Armed Services on Senate bill 3539 to amend Title II of the Career Compensation Act of 1949 and to provide for the computation of reenlistment bonuses for members of the uniformed services.

1954. U.S. Congress. House. Committee on Armed Services. *Career Compensation Act.* Government Printing Office, Washington, D.C. 29 pages.

Hearing on July 8, 1954, before the House Committee on Armed Services on Senate bill 3939 to amend the Career Compensation Act to provide for reenlistment bonuses.

1955. U.S. CONGRESS. HOUSE. COMMITTEE ON ARMED SERVICES. *Career Incentive Act of 1955.* Government Printing Office. Washington, D.C. 829 pages.

Hearings between February 7 and March 4, 1955, before Subcommittee No. 2 of the House Committee on Armed Services on House bill 2607 to provide incentives for members of the uniformed services by increasing certain pays and allowances.

1955. U.S. CONGRESS. SENATE. COMMITTEE ON ARMED SERVICES. *Career Incentive Act of 1955.* Government Printing Office. Washington, D.C. 229 pages.

Hearings on March 17 and 18, 1955, before the Senate Committee on Armed Services on House bill 4720 to provide incentives for members of the uniformed services by increasing certain pays and allowances.

1957. U.S. CONGRESS. SENATE. COMMITTEE ON ARMED SERVICES. *Military Pay.* Part 1. Government Printing Office. Washington, D.C. 111 pages.

Hearing on August 21, 1957, before a subcommittee of the Senate Committee on Armed Services on Senate bill 2014 to consider changing the method of computing basic pay for members of the uniformed services and to provide term retention contracts for reserve officers.

1958. U.S. CONGRESS. HOUSE. COMMITTEE ON ARMED SERVICES. *Method of Computing Basic Pay.* Government Printing Office. Washington, D.C. 514 pages.

Hearings between February 18 and March 7, 1958, before Subcommittee No. 2 of the House Committee on Armed Services on House bill 9979 to change the method of computing basic pay for members of the uniformed services.

1958. U.S. CONGRESS. SENATE. COMMITTEE ON ARMED SERVICES. *Military Pay.* Part 2. Government Printing Office. Washington, D.C. 885 pages.

Hearings between February 25 and April 17, 1958, before a subcommittee of the Senate Committee on Armed Services on Senate bills 2014 and 3081 and House bill 11470 to consider changing the method of computing basic pay for members of the uniformed services and to provide term retention contracts for reserve officers.

1963. U.S. CONGRESS. HOUSE. COMMITTEE ON ARMED SERVICES. *Pay Increase.* Government Printing Office. Washington, D.C. 373 pages.

Hearings between February 26 and March 7, 1963, before Subcommittee No. 1 of the House Committee on Armed Services on House bill 3006 to amend Title 37, U.S. Code, to increase the rates of basic pay for members of the uniformed services.

1963. U.S. CONGRESS. SENATE. COMMITTEE ON ARMED SERVICES. *Military Pay Increase.* Government Printing Office. Washington, D.C. 299 pages.

Hearings between July 16 and 18, 1963, before a subcommittee of the Senate Committee on Armed Services on House bill 5555 to amend Title 37, U.S. Code, to increase the rates of basic pay for members of the uniformed services.

1964. U.S. CONGRESS. HOUSE. COMMITTEE ON ARMED SERVICES. *Pay Increase.* Government Printing Office. Washington, D.C. 36 pages.

Hearing on July 22, 1964, before Subcommitete No. 1 of the House Committee on Armed Services, considering Senate bill 3001 to amend Title 37, U.S. Code, to increase the rates of basic pay for members of the uniformed services.

1965. U.S. CONGRESS. HOUSE. COMMITTEE ON ARMED SERVICES. *Pay Increase.* Government Printing Office. Washington, D.C. 415 pages.

Hearings between June 7 and 15, 1965, before the House Committee on Armed Services on House bills 5725 and 8714 to amend Title 37, U.S. Code, to increase the rates of basic pay for members of the uniformed services.

1965. U.S. Congress. Senate. Committee on Armed Services. *Military Pay Increase*. Government Printing Office. Washington, D.C. 161 pages.

Hearing on July 29, 1965, before the Senate Committee on Armed Services on House bill 9075 and Senate bills 1095 and 2230 to amend Title 37, U.S. Code, to increase the rate of basic pay for members of the uniformed services.

1967. U.S. Congress. House. Committee on Armed Services. *Pay Increase*. Government Printing Office. Washington, D.C. 82 pages.

Hearings on September 19 and October 17, 1967, before the House Committee on Armed Services on House bills 8197, 9069, and 13510 to increase basic pay and to adjust retired and retainer pay for members and former members of the uniformed services.

1972. U.S. Congress. House. Committee on Armed Services. *Special Pay*. Government Printing Office. Washington, D.C. 153 pages.

Hearings between September 25 and 27, 1972, before Subcommittee No. 2 of the House Committee on Armed Services on (1) House bill 16603 to amend Title 37, U.S. Code, to provide special pay to certain nuclear-trained and qualified enlisted members of the naval service who agree to reenlist, and (2) House bill 14545 to amend Chapter 5, Title 37, U.S. Code, to revise the special pay structure relating to members of the uniformed services.

Government Documents: Congressional Hearings—Other

1919. U.S. Congress. House. 'Special Committee. *National Security League*. 2 volumes, 31 parts. Government Printing Office. Washington, D.C. Parts 1–13: 1089 pages. Parts 14–31: 995 pages.

Hearings before the House Special Committee on House Resolutions 469 and 476 to investigate and make report as to the officers, membership, financial support, expenditures, general character, activities, and purposes of the National Security League, a corporation of New York, and of any associated organizations. Parts 1–13 cover ·hearings between December

19, 1918, and January 21, 1919; Parts 14–31, those between January 22 and February 20, 1919.

1947. U.S. CONGRESS. HOUSE. COMMITTEE ON ARMED SERVICES. *Army, Navy, and Marine Corps Officers.* Government Printing Office. Washington, D.C. 458 pages.

Hearings between April 1 and May 22, 1947, before Subcommittee No. 1, Personnel, of the House Committee on Armed Services on (1) House bill 2536 to provide for the procurement, promotion, and elimination of Regular Army officers, and (2) House bill 2537 to regulate the distribution, promotion, and retirement of officers of the navy and Marine Corps and to provide for the advancement of enlisted personnel to the commissioned grades.

1947. U.S. CONGRESS. HOUSE. COMMITTEE ON ARMED SERVICES. *Additional Inducements to Physicians and Surgeons.* Government Printing Office. Washington, D.C. 100 pages.

Hearings between June 2 and 6, 1947, before Subcommittee No. 10, Pay and Administration, of the House Committee on Armed Services on (1) House bill 3254 to provide additional inducements to physicians and surgeons to make a career of the United States Naval Service, and (2) House bill 3174 to provide for the procurement of physicians and surgeons in the medical department of the army.

1950. U.S. CONGRESS. HOUSE. COMMITTEE ON ARMED SERVICES. *Enlistment of Aliens in the Regular Army.* Government Printing Office. Washington, D.C. 21 pages.

Hearing on January 24, 1950, before the House Committee on Armed Services on Senate bill 2269 to provide for the enlistment of aliens in the Regular Army.

1958. U.S. CONGRESS. HOUSE. COMMITTTEE ON ARMED SERVICES. *Investigation of National Defense Establishment.* Government Printing Office. Washington, D.C. 167 pages.

Hearings between March 14 and 31, 1958, before Special Subcommittee No. 6 of the House Committee on Armed Services on the Study of Procurement and Utilization of Scientists, Engineers, and Technical Skills, under authority of House Resolution 67.

1959. U.S. CONGRESS. SENATE. COMMITTEE ON ARMED SERVICES. *Improved Opportunity for Promotion and Retention for Certain Naval Officers.* Government Printing Office. Washington, D.C. 69 pages.

Hearing on June 22, 1959, before a subcommittee of the Senate Committee on Armed Services on House bill 4413 to provide improved opportunity for certain officers in the naval service.

1962. U.S. CONGRESS. SENATE. COMMITTEE ON ARMED SERVICES. *Amendment to Oath of Enlistment.* Government Printing Office. Washington, D.C. 37 pages.

Hearing on August 8, 1962, before a subcommittee of the Senate Committee on Armed Services on House bill 218 requiring individuals enlisted into the armed forces to take an oath to defend the U.S. Constitution.

1971. U.S. CONGRESS. HOUSE. COMMITTEE ON ARMED SERVICES. *Uniformed Services University for the Health Sciences.* Government Printing Office. Washington, D.C. 266 pages.

Hearings between September 21 and 23, 1971, before the House Committee on Armed Services on House bill 2 to establish a uniformed services university for the health sciences.

1974. U.S. CONGRESS. HOUSE. COMMITTEE ON THE JUDICIARY. *Amnesty.* Government Printing Office. Washington, D.C. 904 pages.

Hearings between March 8 and 13, 1974, before the Subcommittee on Courts, Civil Liberties, and the Administration of Justice of the House Committee on the Judiciary on House bills 236, 674, 2167, 3100, 5195, 10979, 10980, 13001, and House Concurrent Resolutions 144 and 385 relating to legislative aspects of the question of amnesty for those who refused to be inducted into military service during the Vietnam War.

CHAPTER 17

Bibliographies

There are more books upon books than upon all other subjects.
—Montaigne, *Essays*, 1568

BURT, RICHARD, and GEOFFREY KEMP (editors). *Congressional Hearings on American Defense Policy 1947–1971: An Annotated Bibliography.* 1974. University Press of Kansas. Lawrence, Kansas. 377 pages.

Focuses primarily on hearings by the House and Senate Armed Services Committee and the House and Senate Defense Appropriations subcommittees. The rationale for this selection is that "these four committees must legally authorize and appropriate funds for defense, and it is in the arena of the defense budget process that the most crucial decisions on procurement and long-term planning are made." Individual entries on congressional hearings list major witnesses and briefly describe the thrust of their testimony.

BYARS, GAYLE (compiler). *Volunteer Force, Zero Draft, and Selective Service: Selected References.* 1971. Special Bibliography Number 195 and Supplement. Air University Library. Maxwell Air Force Base, Alabama. 11 pages. Supplement: 10 pages.

Lists a total of 257 references on military manpower procurement. Includes books, government documents, and articles.

COUNCIL FOR A VOLUNTEER MILITARY. *Bibliography of Selected Books & Articles.* 1968. Chicago. 2 pages.

Contains 20 entries—books, symposia, reports, and articles—related to proposals for an all-volunteer armed force in the United States.

DANIEL, STEVEN F. *A Volunteer Military for the United States: An Annotated Bibliography.* 1972. American Institutes for Research. Kensington, Maryland. 43 pages.

Contains 115 items, including material on the broad topics of the draft, manpower requirements, costs, and effect on American institutions. The work is divided into three categories: Recent Historical Background, Economic and Operational Factors For and Against, and Philosophical Factors For and Against. A summary essay is included.

DOTY, HI (compiler). *Bibliography of Conscientious Objection to War: A Selected List of 173 Titles.* 1954. Central Committee for Conscientious Objectors. Philadelphia. 24 pages.

Lists books, pamphlets, articles, and periodicals on various aspects of conscientious objection. The background and development of the conscientious objector are covered, along with conscientious objection before, during, and since World War II.

INDIANA LAW JOURNAL. *Bibliography of Selective Service.* April 1942. Volume 17, Number 4. Pages 362–373.

Includes about 100 legal and nonlegal books, articles, and essays related to the question of selective service. Subject headings are: The Army, Conscientious Objectors, Conscription and National Defense, Criminals and Conscription, Education and Conscription, History of Selective Service, Judicial Review of the Selective Service Administration, Military Law, and Deferments.

LAMKIN, DAVID (compiler). *The "Amnesty" Issue and Conscientious Objection: A Selected Bibliography.* 1973. Center for the Study of Armament and Disarmament, California State University. Los Angeles. 42 pages.

Introduction by Charles Chatfield. Lamkin briefly discusses the history and ramifications of conscription, the grounds for conscientious objection, and the issue of amnesty. The approximately 400 references cover books, articles, government documents, legal works, Ph.D. dissertations, and films.

MATTHEWS, M. ALICE (compiler). *Conscription of Men, Material Resources and Wealth in Time of War.* Carnegie Endowment for International Peace. Washington, D.C. 15 pages.

Includes approximately 30 references to books, articles, and pamphlets pertaining to compulsory military service.

MILLETT, ALLAN R., and B. FRANKLIN COOLING (compilers). *Doctoral Dissertations in Military Affairs: A Bibliography.* 1972. Kansas State University Library. Manhattan, Kansas. 153 pages.

Lists approximately 2,900 Ph.D. dissertations. Divided into three sections: (1) world military affairs—e.g., medieval warfare, Latin America, Russia; (2) U.S. military affairs, including defense, air power, and wars; and (3) studies on war and the military, covering such topics as arms control, the ethics of war, and theories of war.

MILLETT, ALLAN R., and B. FRANKLIN COOLING (compilers). *Doctoral Dissertations in Military Affairs (Supplements 1 and 2).* Military Affairs. Supplement 1: April 1973. Volume XXXVII, Number 2. Pages 62–66. Supplement 2: February 1974. Volume XXXVIII, Number 1. Pages 12–16.

Supplement 1 lists approximately 270 Ph.D. dissertations; Supplement 2, approximately 200. In each of the supplements, section 1 covers studies on world military affairs with the focus on specific countries, section 2 deals with military affairs in the United States, and section 3 lists studies on war and the military.

REHM, THOMAS A. *Readings on Selective Service* (two parts). Current History. (1) July 1968. Volume 55, Number 323. Pages 40–41. (2) August 1968. Volume 55, Number 324. Pages 103–104.

Part 1 has 49 entries, comprising books, studies, and congressional reports. Part 2 has 36 entries, composed of Selective Service and military documents.

SIMON, AARON H. *Draft Law: A Selective Bibliography.* Law Library Journal. August 1971. Volume 64, Number 3. Pages 329–337.

Contains about 50 annotated entries pertaining to recent literature of a procedural or ideological nature.

SLONAKER, JOHN. *The Volunteer Army.* 1972. Special Bibliography 5. U.S. Army Military History Research Collection. Carlisle Barracks, Pennsylvania. 98 pages.

A bibliography of books and articles on topics pertinent to the volunteer army concept, based on the holdings of the U.S. Army Military History Research Collection at Carlisle Barracks, Pennsylvania. The contents are divided by country. The U.S. section is subdivided under 14 headings, such as: recent discussion on the Modern Volunteer Army; the draft, universal military training, and conscientious objectors; recruitment, reenlistment, and promotion; and manpower mobilization, utilization, and demobilization in times of crisis.

U.S. DEPARTMENT OF DEFENSE. *The College Graduate & National Security: Utilization of Manpower by the U.S. Armed Services.* Compiled by Harry Moskowitz and Jack Roberts. 1968. Department of Defense. Washington, D.C. Index. 74 pages.

An annotated selective bibliography issued following the general elimination of deferments for graduate study promulgated by the director of Selective Service on February 16, 1968. Contains 330 entries on various aspects of questions related to utilization of college graduates in the military services. The work is organized by title within major and subordinate subject groups.

U.S. DEPARTMENT OF DEFENSE. CENTRAL ALL-VOLUNTEER TASK FORCE. *Bibliography of Manpower Research.* 1972. Department of Defense. Washington, D.C. 44 pages.

Prepared in the Office of the Assistant Secretary of Defense (Manpower and Reserve Affairs), this is an organized listing of military manpower personnel research reports and studies. It includes reports and studies completed since January 1, 1968, or currently ongoing. Entries are divided into eight major categories: manpower requirements, manpower supply, manpower procurement and selection, classification and assignment, personnel management and utilization, training and education, veterans, and all-volunteer force in general.

U.S. DEPARTMENT OF THE ARMY. *Military Manpower Policy: A Bibliographic Survey.* 1965. Department of the Army. Washington, D.C. Index. 142 pages.

Contains brief abstracts of about 700 books, documents, and periodical articles. Prepared in connection with the 1965 Military Manpower Policy Study carried out by the Department of Defense in collaboration with other federal agencies. The work is divided into eight sections: (1) National Security, Manpower, and the U.S. Armed Services, (2) Manpower for the U.S. Armed Services, (3) Reserve Components, Selective Service System, (4) Compulsory Military Service: Pro and Con, (5) Military Manpower in Foreign Countries: Examples of Problems, Practices, and Perspectives, (6) Congressional Hearings and Legislation, (7) Special Reports Bearing on the Manpower Problem, and (8) Bibliographic and Reference Sources.

U.S. LIBRARY OF CONGRESS. *Compulsory Military Training: A Selected List of References and Supplement.* Compiled by Ann Duncan Brown. 1940. Division of Bibliography, Library of Congress. Washington, D.C. Index. 38 pages.

Lists bibliographies and general works. Topics include conscientious objection, war resisters, military training in schools, military systems of other countries, and democracy and compulsory service.

U.S. LIBRARY OF CONGRESS. *How Can the United States Best Maintain Manpower for an Effective Defense System? A Collection of Excerpts and a Bibliography Relating to the National High School Debate Topic 1968–1969.* 1968. Government Printing Office. Washington, D.C. Selected bibliography: pages 129–132. 132 pages.

Compiled by the Legislative Reference Service pursuant to Public Law 88-246, Senate bill 2311, to provide for the preparation and printing of compilations of materials relating to annual national high-school and college debate topics. The excerpts and bibliography are divided into three parts relating to three debate propositions: (1) that the United States should establish a lottery system of military conscription; (2) that all military service for the United States should be voluntary except in time of declared war; and (3) that the United States should establish a system of compulsory service for all citizens.

U.S. LIBRARY OF CONGRESS. *A List of Bibliographies on Questions Relating to National Defense, and Supplement.* Compiled by Grace Hadley Fuller. 1942. Division of Bibliography, Library of Congress. Washington, D.C. 59 pages.

Lists bibliographies and works containing bibliographies dealing with national defense. Topics include the cost of war, the Monroe Doctrine, relations with Latin America, police services during war, and the relation- U.S. government documents is included.

U.S. LIBRARY OF CONGRESS. *List of References on Conscientious Objectors.* 1917. Library of Congress. Washington, D.C. 2 pages.

Prepared in the Division of Bibliography, this short bibliography contains 20 references to articles and government papers on conscientious objection in Great Britain and the United States.

U.S. LIBRARY OF CONGRESS. *Maintaining Manpower for an Effective Defense System: An Introductory Bibliography on the High School Debate Subject 1968–1969.* Compiled by Elizabeth Anne Hodges. 1968. Library of Congress. Washington, D.C. 6 pages.

Prepared by the Legislative Reference Service, this bibliography contains 60 selected references on the general background of manpower for defense and on proposals for: (1) a lottery system of military conscription, (2) a system of compulsory national service for all citizens, and (3) a voluntary system, except in the event of a declared war. A section on U.S. government documents is included.

U.S. LIBRARY OF CONGRESS. *Military Forces: An Annotated Bibliography of Selected Statistical References.* Compiled by Nathaniel A. Gregory. 1972. Library of Congress. Washington, D.C. 13 pages.

Prepared by the Foreign Affairs Division of the Congressional Research Service. Identifies sources of unclassified information on the size and strength of armed forces around the world. The publications cited are divided into three sections: (1) documents published annually and yearbooks, (2) monographs published irregularly, and (3) periodical references.

U.S. LIBRARY OF CONGRESS. *Revision of the Selective Service System: A Bibliography.* 1967. Library of Congress. Washington, D.C. 4 pages.

Has approximately 70 entries, including congressional documents and periodicals.

Bibliographies

U.S. LIBRARY OF CONGRESS. *Selected List of Recent References on American National Defense.* Compiled by Grace Hadley Fuller. 1939. Division of Bibliography, Library of Congress. Washington, D.C. 40 pages.

Lists bibliographies and general works. Topics include air power in defense, military preparedness, armament and disarmament, and the effects of a national defense program on certain industries.

U.S. LIBRARY OF CONGRESS. *Universal Military Training: A Selected and Annotated List of References.* Compiled by Frances Cheney. 1945. Library of Congress. Washington, D.C. Index. 138 pages.

Prepared in the General Reference and Bibliography Division, this bibliography is comprised primarily of federal documents, books, and articles that appeared from January 1942 to March 1945. Included are some pamphlets issued by groups either actively supporting legislation or opposed to universal military training at any time. The 317 entries are organized as follows: Bibliographies, General Historical Background, Foreign Systems of Compulsory Military Training, United States Army and Navy Proposals, Alternate Proposals, National Security, Legal, Social Welfare, Political and Economic Aspects of Universal Military Training and Legislation.

U.S. LIBRARY OF CONGRESS. *Universal Military Training: A Selected and Annotated List of References; Supplement.* Compiled by Janice B. Harrington. 1945. Library of Congress. Washington, D.C. 118 pages.

Prepared in the General Reference and Bibliography Division, this is a list of works on universal military training published between March and September 1945. It attempts to include the views, pro and con, of as many individuals and organizations as possible. Specific topics include proposals for universal military training, its domestic and international aspects, and the question whether there should be legislation now or later.

Index of Titles

Titles are divided into five sections: (1) books, (2) unpublished manuscripts, (3) articles, (4) pamphlets, reprints, and speeches, and (5) government documents. An "n" following a page number indicates that the title appears in the annotation rather than in the bibliographic data of an entry.

Books

Index of Titles

Index of Titles

Unpublished Manuscripts

Index of Titles

Articles

Index of Titles

Index of Titles

Pamphlets, Reprints, and Speeches

Government Documents

Index of Titles

Index of Authors

An "n" following a page number indicates that the author's name appears in the annotation rather than in the bibliographic data of an entry.

Abshire, David M., 63
Ackley, Charles Walton, 296
Adams, Sidney, 397
Adcock, Frank E., 49
Aldridge, Frederick Stokes, 25
Alexander, J. Arthur, 34
Alger, John, 34
Allen, Clifford, 302n, 338n, 353
Allen, H. C., 1
Allen, Richard V., 63
Altman, Stuart H., 269
Aly, Bower, 193
Amacher, Ryan C., 278
Ambrose, Stephen E., 1, 35, 63
American Association of School Administrators, 217
American Bar Association, Committee on War Work, 181
American Friends Service Committee, 50, 64, 97, 98, 212, 308n
American Legion, 212
American Union Against Militarism, 212, 213, 293
Amery, L. S., 333, 336n, 343
Anderson, J. K., 50
Anderson, James K. 70n
Anderson, Paul Russell, 193, 200
Andreski, Stanislav, 50
Andrews, Charles McLean, 2
Angell, Norman, 89, 334n
Ansell, S. T., 232
Aptheker, Herbert, 316, 320
Arbogast, Kate Avery, 132, 265
Arnold, Walter, 305
Asbury, Herbert, 2
Asher, James Irving, 308n
Asquith, Herbert Henry, 330n
Association of the United States Army, 149
Australian Freedom League, 380, 381

Australian Labour Party, 382
Australian Peace Alliance, 382
Axtell, George C., Jr., 200
Ayers, James T., 311

Bachman, Jerald G., 125
Bacon, Corinne, 2
Bacon, Eugene H., 3
Bacon, Robert, 21
Bailey, Douglas L., 130
Bailey, Duncan, 270
Bailey, L. H., 251
Baker, Newton D., 9n, 35, 302n
Baldinger, Milton I., 284
Baldwin, Hanson W., 64, 89, 90
Bales, William A., 3
Balfour, Arthur James, 84n, 330n
Bancroft, William A., 200
Barbeau, Arthur E., 311
Barber, James Alden, Jr., 63, 64n
Barker, J. Ellis, 343, 353
Barnes, David M., 3
Barnes, Peter, 119, 132
Barnes, Roswell P., 238
Barnett, Corelli, 90, 323, 343
Barro, Robert J., 269
Barron's, 133
Barry, John W., 382
Bateman, C. W., 74n
Battine, Cecil, 344
Bauer, Theodore William, 375
Bauer, William E., 45
Baynes, J. C. M., 119
Beamish, Tufton, 325n
Beaumont, Roger, 50, 64
Beck, James M., 71n
Becker, Gary S., 261 .
Beeler, John, 59, 323
Beggs, S. T., 333

– 441 –

Index of Authors

Hershey, Lewis B., 39, 68n, 84n, 171, 176, 183n, 195n
Hess, Karl, 129
Hesseltine, William B., 45
Hewitt, H. J., 54
Heymont, Irving, 378
Higginson, Thomas Wentworth, 39, 313
Higham, Robin, 328
Hildebrand, George, 274
Hill, C. P., 1
Hill, Jim Dan, 230
Hills, John F., 380
Hitch, Charles J., 263
Hoag, Malcolm W., 263n
Hodges, Elizabeth Anne, 412
Hoefling, John A., 140
Holborn, Hajo, 207
Holbrook, James R., 140
Holland, Henry Edmund, 384
Hollister, C. Warren, 328, 348, 349
Holmes, Oliver Wendell, 303n
Holzer, Henry Mark, 289
Holzer, Phyllis, 289
Horton, Mildred McAfee, 171
Houghton, B., 349
Howard, Michael, 368
Howe, Lucien, 72
Howes, Raymond F., 195
Huddle, Frank P., 257
Hughes, Charles, 329n
Hugo, John J., 298
Huidekoper, Frederic Louis, 12, 18n, 80, 102
Huizinga, J. H., 349
Hull, William I., 12
Human Resources Research Organization, 123, 124
Hunter, Ernest E., 356
Huntington, Samuel, 18n, 72, 230, 289
Hurd, Archibald, 349
Huston, James A., 171
Hutchins, Robert, 215
Hutchinson, Graham Seton, 350
Hutchinson, J. R., 329
Huzar, Elias, 40, 172, 389
Hyde, Charles C., 287

Ikeda, Moss M., 234
Impey, E. Adair, 215
Independent Labour Party, 356
Indiana Law Journal, 408
Indianapolis Star, 71n

International Juridical Association Bulletin, 172

Jackson, John P., 257
Jacob, Philip E., 304
Jacobs, Clyde E., 162
Jacobs, James Ripley, 13
Jacobs, Randall, 207
James, David, 336
James, William, 295
Janowitz, Morris, 64n, 73, 75n, 84n, 130n, 141, 151, 257, 317, 389
Jaquette, David J., 279
Jauncey, L. C., 368
Jaurès, Jean, 73
Jeffrey, Timothy B., 141
Jessop, W. N., 73
Johannsen, Robert W., 74
Johnsen, Julia E., 74, 195
Johnson, Keith R., 94
Johnson, Lyndon B., 161n
Johnston, E. N., 81n, 378
Johnston, Jerome, 125
Johnston, John D., 154
Jomini, Baron de, 74
Jordan, Amos A., Jr., 75n
Jordan, David Starr, 75
Judge, John P., Jr.

Katenbrink, Irving G., Jr., 76n
Keast, William R., 111
Keep America Out of War Congress, 308n
Keesling, F. V., 187n
Kellogg, Walter G., 302
Kelly, David, 369n
Kelly, E. Lowell, 172
Kelly-Kenny, T., 333n
Kelman, Herbert C., 306
Kemble, C. Robert, 389
Kemp, Geoffrey, 407
Kennedy, Edward M., 84n, 129n, 172
Kennedy, Thomas C., 341
Ketchum, Omar B., 234
Kiker, B. F., 275
Kim, K. H., 125
Kimmons, Neil C., 40
King, Edward L., 126
Kinloch-Cooke, Clement, 350
Kipling, Rudyard, 356
Kirk, Grayson, 75

The typeface selected for this book is Baskerville, a facsimile of a Roman letter first used in England, about 1760, by John Baskerville, the greatest type founder and printer of his era. His types, most of which are based on the letters of Caslon, are of exceptional beauty, the italic forms in particular being superior to any created up to that time.

DESIGN AND TYPOGRAPHY BY TED LIGDA, REDWOOD CITY, CALIFORNIA